From a ....
Dormitory Window

A Boy's Life & Love at Boarding School

......a diary narrative

By

Ian McCart

'The Vale of Wenning I Resolved to tread'
(Thomas Wilson of Bentham 1781)

Published by New Generation Publishing in 2022

Copyright © Ian McCart 2022

First Edition

The author asserts the moral right under the Copyright, Designs and Patents Act 1988 to be identified as the author of this work.

All Rights reserved. No part of this publication may be reproduced, stored in a retrieval system or transmitted, in any form or by any means without the prior consent of the author, nor be otherwise circulated in any form of binding or cover other than that which it is published and without a similar condition being imposed on the subsequent purchaser.

Paperback ISBN: 978-1-80369-332-3
Hardback ISBN: 978-1-80369-333-0
Ebook ISBN: 978-1-80369-334-7

www.newgeneration-publishing.com

New Generation Publishing

Front cover design and section designs by Alexander Roberts.
'Spotting book' on page 1 kindly loaned by Peter Robinson

**Adolescence can never be re-lived,
But it can be nostalgically recalled.**

Author's note

The complete story of Bentham Grammar School has been well documented in two separate publications:
The History of Bentham Grammar School 1726–1976
J. S. Warbrick, R. E. Huddleston & J. R. Wilson (published 1976)
Bentham Grammar School: The Final Years 1976–2002
W. Stockdale (published 2019)

This publication is not a history, nor does it provide a critical assessment of the school's achievements. Instead, it portrays a 'snapshot' of life in the boarding house during a brief period within time. Perhaps most importantly though, it provides it from the viewpoint of a pupil. The two publications above have been almost exclusively written by former teachers at the school. They do, therefore, by necessity reflect the school's standpoint and its vision of day-to-day school life.

In that context, it should be accepted that there will, almost inevitably, be a divergence of views between, for instance, an experienced adult whose occupation has been in teaching and an 'ignorant' adolescent (ignorant of life, that is) who thinks he knows it all. It might be said that a teacher's view could well be presented through "rose-tinted spectacles" whereas that of a pupil will be "warts and all". The reality for both is most probably somewhere between those two extremes, but each will be at the opposite side of an invisible dividing line. Evelyn Waugh, it was, who summed up the differing views of schooldays with a three-act play ('The Tragedy of Youth') with the respective titles as follows: (i) 'School, as maiden aunts think it is'; (ii) 'School, as modern authors think it is'; (iii) 'School, as we all know it is'. This diary narrative is, quite obviously, most closely aligned to the last of Waugh's three suppositions. [An aside: were maiden aunts that gullible in the 1920s? Perhaps.]

Within this diary narrative, there is no intended malice toward the teaching staff. If, at times, it appears irreverent, that is because young male adolescents can often be so, particularly whilst at school. A piece of advice offered by a fellow pupil, though, was brief and to the point: "TELL IT AS IT WAS!" With the passage of time, the author would like to think that if those teachers (most of whom have now, sadly, passed away) were to have read this manuscript, they would perhaps have smiled to themselves as to how they were viewed and how they have been subsequently portrayed herein.

Some of the quotations and facts within this manuscript are not always totally accurate – it turns out that a young adolescent didn't know it all – even though he thought he did! For the purposes of the story, they have been left as quoted in a schoolboy diary. Where excerpts from letters are quoted, the punctuation within them has not been corrected/amended – they have been left as originally written, albeit that they are, in places, grammatically incorrect. Finally, the views expressed in this diary by an adolescent are not necessarily the views now held by the author as an adult.

Sadly, Bentham Grammar School closed in 2002, the victim of changing political and economic circumstances. Perhaps its closure is a dismal reflection of the fact that education has been, for as long as any of us can remember, a victim of a continuing, and a mostly politically motivated, football kick about.

Acknowledgements

Mention should be made of several individuals who have helped during the preparation of this book.

Three people, in particular, deserve special thanks and the author is indebted to them. John Hebblethwaite, an ex-pupil, has not only provided a good number of photographs from the era from his own collection (which are duly acknowledged individually), but has also given freely a good deal of his time (with corresponding effort!) with suggestions for improving presentation and format. His unfailing knack of highlighting anomalies and possible confusion within the storyline has also been invaluable.

My thanks should also be tendered to Clive Chase, who, with no previous connection to Bentham Grammar School, was able (and more than willing) to look objectively at the script, thereby suggesting several topical and useful ideas, particularly around the structure of chapters and the timeframe of the storyline. He also gave appropriate and prudent advice regarding grammar, reining in (quite rightly) the author's regular, and sometimes frustrating, habit of forgetting to bring sentences to a timely conclusion!

Matthew Barnes heroically took on the painstaking process of a thorough read, making many logical and sensible suggestions (which have been implemented, almost without exception), whilst also introducing the author to the stylish use of, where appropriate, an 'en dash' within the text! Any errors remaining rest entirely with the author!

The author's twin sister, Sheila, and elder brother (Keith) have also kindly given appropriate confirmation regarding events whilst the family was 'growing up' abroad. They have both helped in the clarification of various episodes with which the author was rather uncertain about. Just as important, perhaps, these discussions enabled us, as siblings, to relive the experience of travelling 'half-way around the world' whilst at a tender age.

Appropriate thanks are also extended (in no particular order) to ex-pupils Steve Lister and Peter Robinson and to ex-teacher Jack Warbrick, all who gave or supplied information. Finally, the photographs (where acknowledged) from the Frith collection are 'Copyright, The Francis Frith Collection'. All photographs not individually acknowledged are from the author's collection.

To Clive, thanks should also be tendered for the various topical sketches linked to the story.

Bentham Grammar School and the neighbouring church: an aerial view circa 1969. The sports field and railway line are opposite the church and the River Wenning skirts the eastern and southern boundary.

*A Summer Garden Fete with crowds around the
main drive and adjacent lawn.
School Crest and Motto: 'I Shall Arise'.
(Digital version supplied by Diane Clements - née Lumb)*

CONTENTS

(1) Looking back to 1966

I:	Where River, Road and Railway converge	3
II:	Does nostalgia only remember the good bits?	16
III:	For what we are about to receive	34
IV:	Who is talking?	46
V:	Keep still, McCart!	58
VI:	Let us pray	64
VII:	But I am left-handed, sir	77
VIII:	You will all be spotting trains	88

(2) Michaelmas Term 1972

IX:	A new academic year	97
X:	A room with a view	108
XI:	I thought you were fairly grown up	127
XII:	The finest of the Yorkshire mountains	142
XIII:	Inside, a battle now rages	150
XIV:	What if she says no?	161
XV:	I suppose I am a real country girl	167
XVI:	In it, can I plant myself?	178
XVII:	Perhaps we can enrol in dancing lessons	182
XVIII:	Narrow channels of water, glinting in the winter sun	195

(3) Lent Term 1973

XIX:	Ring on, ring on, you morning bell	203
XX:	Do not open this note until later tonight	217
XXI:	I hope he is behaving himself, Mrs. Russell	225
XXII:	That Kingdom by the Sea	234
XXIII:	She will call a spade a bloody spade	252
XXIV:	Where's the bloody defence?	263
XXV:	Bald men are the best for sex	275
XXVI:	I am getting to know more and more about you	286

(4) Hilary Term 1973

XXVII:	We get on so very well together	299
XXVIII:	You are still both very young	314
XXIX:	Return to that Kingdom by the Sea	328
XXX:	The song thrush has stopped showing off	344
XXXI:	You may start	347
XXXII:	Mucca, the First XI goalkeeper, writing poems!	352
XXXIII:	Beauty is truth, truth beauty	358
XXXIV:	Looking to the Future	367
XXXV:	He has been a most reliable Head of House	374
XXXVI:	Sincere gratitude to Arnold School	383

INTRODUCTION

DURING the autumn of 1971, ensconced in a cosy (some might have termed it as cramped!) and private dormitory room, a luxury afforded to all 6th form boarding pupils studying for 'A' Levels, the following rhyming couplet was written as the start of a long poem. A poem that was, on reflection, perhaps rather too long. It was ostensibly addressed to a twin sister and written to extol the virtues of the surrounding countryside,

'The pleasures of youth are many-fold,
But cruel fate leaves a hundred score untold...'

The verse then continued, as if to clarify that those pleasures were not in the past but were current – that is, at the time the poem was written, in the "here and now",

'So, they that have not been here, to my country home...'

That country home was, in fact, Low Bentham, a rather anonymous village, then in the West Riding of Yorkshire, now part of North Yorkshire following the wholesale local government re-organisation of 1974. More specifically, the country home referred to in that poem included not only the village, and the rural countryside surrounding it, but also Bentham Grammar School. The school was situated on the western fringe of the village, all but straddling the county border with Lancashire. The very fact that the boarding school was considered 'home' (rather than home being where parents were living at that time, in Germany) speaks volumes for how an adolescent mind was then thinking.

In fact, two main issues had been implementing themselves concurrently into an adolescent psyche at that time. Not at all by design but, nevertheless, they complimented each other perfectly. The pastoral countryside at the western edge of Yorkshire certainly, but also, the commencement of a two-year study of English Literature, with a syllabus that extolled the poetry of several early nineteenth-century 'Romantic' poets. Included among them was John Keats, an incurable sentimentalist indeed, who wrote from the heart. His early poetry included stories written specifically in rhyming couplets.

For example, from *Poems* published in 1817,

'I stood tip-toe upon a little hill,
The air was cooling, and so very still....'

And so, that rather crude attempt made at writing poetry, in the style of Keats, at the beginning of two years of 'A' Level study, in a sense a letter written to a twin sister, but written in verse, was a catalyst. It set in train the formation of a diary to note down those events that an adolescent 6th form student thought fate would otherwise, most certainly, *'leave untold'*.

Schooldays. A scrappy diary had, then, been faithfully kept (but not always kept religiously up to date) during those final two years at boarding school. A diary often scribbled in quickly and untidily at the end of a school day. (The excuse of being left-handed always justifying the appalling scrawl.) Invariably the scribbling was 'last thing'. A random collection of thoughts written late at night (very late) after prefect duty in the boarding house had been completed and after 'A' Level studies with the associated homework had been accomplished, the two being inextricably linked. A private study/dormitory, an absolute boon for 6th form students, was the ideal conduit for jotting down idle thoughts. A diary, sometimes verbose, at other times almost silent. Full of apprehension, criticism, hope, crudity, laughter, fretting, and frequently questioning – that is – not only questioning the learning process but also questioning the knuckling down to discipline – being told what to do! In that context, it was so easy to blithely postulate on one's own ideas and thoughts and to scribble them down in a diary and assume them to be correct. In fact, to be certain that they were correct! What folly! Ah well, the ignorance of youth.

However, deep down in the psyche at boarding school there was a lack of confidence and shyness, always fighting for ascendancy and generally being successful. And because of that, perhaps most important of all, the diary played the part of listener. (Along with *Teddy*, always sitting silently, and smugly, on his master's bed, watching!) A diary that acted as a secure refuge for what was an ongoing frustration with school officialdom and petty rules. Perhaps more importantly, during that final year of study, it was also a conduit for an outpouring of passion towards a young lady in the academic year below. Incredibly, inexplicably perhaps, it turned out that the young lady had also fallen in love with the keeper of the diary, an inwardly insecure and unconfident Upper 6th-form boarder. The outward appearance might have suggested confidence and authority, particularly to the juniors in the boarding house, but a book should not, of course, be judged by its cover. When, one November evening in 1972, there was a knock on the front door of a family home and a hesitant young man requested to speak with the daughter at the house, the young lady residing there rather hoped and indeed, half expected, that it might well be that rather shy Upper 6th-form lad. It was! Nevertheless, she could not have imagined the anguish and torment that had raged within before the decision was made to "go for broke" and to actually call at the house. The fear of rejection had been paramount and overcoming it was, quite simply, nerve-racking.

Memory can sometimes be slippery, sometimes confused and at other times, plainly incorrect. All in varying degrees and in a variety of ways. It can often let you down. Ask a sibling what they might recall about a specific childhood memory or event, and they might well provide a widely differing slant on a story compared to one's own recollection. Odd? Perhaps, but hardly unusual as the memory may only recall or pick out a part of the story with the rest being… perhaps… assumed, albeit in good faith. In addition, stories or events told to children by family or relatives and subsequently repeated by a child in good faith could quite often benefit from having an accompanying "Government Health Warning"! Having always believed (from being told as a child) that a father, born and brought up in Morecambe, was in the same class at school as Eric Morecambe (actually, Eric Bartholomew), it was only many years later that it was realised that this could not possibly have been the case with the three- year age difference between the two of them. Unless, of course, one or other of the two of them was incredibly brainy or, alternatively, slow at learning. Neither, in fact, was the case. At the same school and in the same town, yes, but not in the same class. Was the story inaccurate when it was originally told or was it misheard or even misunderstood?

So, whilst compiling the summary that follows of life within a boarding school in the 1960s and early 1970s and at the same time being acutely conscious of how the memory can fail, recourse to a diary of events has been pivotal in keeping faith with the urge for accuracy. That ramshackle diary kept during the final two years at boarding school has assisted in ensuring the tales related in this book are as faithful as possible. Where parts of a whole story, or even some stories in their entirety, were missing from the diary, then the school publications (in particular, the annual school *Crescent* magazine) have filled in gaps, as have the many letters written and received during that time, particularly those to and from a girlfriend. In addition, the individual recollections from other pupils in the period in question (1966–1973) have been immensely helpful. In particular Stephen Lister, still resident in Bentham and still as potty about steam engines as he was back in the 1960s, as indeed is the author. Even the school reports have played their part in recalling the story as they did not always just say "could do better" or "satisfactory"! The earlier years have, in the absence of a diary, also been independently vetted and discussed with a twin sister, also a veteran of those early boarding school days, in order that individual memories can concur. This has ensured that any anomalies, minor as they might have appeared, have been ironed out or corrected as far as possible.

This book then is presented for reading in the format of a diary from the beginning of the school year in September 1972 until walking out of the school grounds for the last time in July 1973. It is not, however, just a record of one school year. It also looks back at, and incorporates within, memories of growing up linked to the commencement of boarding school life in 1966, whilst just shy of teenage years. Returning to boarding school one Sunday afternoon in September 1972 to begin a second year of 'A' Level study and being, quite predictably, far too early, the author spent several hours "loitering" by the adjacent railway line. It provided ample opportunity to think back to the autumn of 1966, to the commencement of boarding school life. This book presents that sequence of events. The first eight chapters in Part 1, therefore, set the scene and look back. Part 2, commencing with chapter nine, then starts to take the reader through that final year of study.

Benefiting from hindsight is something the modern world loves to indulge in. Regarding this diary narrative, the temptation to comment on, or to qualify, or even refine the thought process from that time has been resisted. In that context, comments from the diary have been left in their 'raw' form with any urge to sanitise them to fit into twenty-first-century thinking necessarily resisted. To some, occasional comments in this narrative may fit quite readily into the "male chauvinist pig" category. Well, it was the early 1970s and the growing up was wholly within a male adolescent dormitory complex. The girls in the senior school were a constant topic of conversation, inevitably! There was always an on-going and semi-serious discussion as to whether, to paraphrase W. H. Auden, *'Jill would go down on her back'* although, even if she would be prepared to, it was most unlikely that a *'Jack'* (from within the boarding house) would follow her down! In reality, the mere thought of going down with her was sufficient! Talk was, of course, cheap. It was a group of adolescents thinking about sex but seeking nothing more. More than anything else though, that was how life was. Whether it was right or wrong is a discussion for quite a different type of publication. Suffice to say, a retrospective judgement is perhaps easy to make but hardly relevant if the person making that judgement did not grow up in that era or within such a restricted environment.

Here then is the story of those boarding school years. This is no *Tom Brown's School Days*, nor is it a re-run of *'Greyfriars School and Billy Bunter'*. Neither does it have a modern day 'Mr. Chips' – although, with some of the longer serving male teachers at the school during the period in question, that analogy is one that could almost have been made! As an Independent Grammar School (divorced from the state system) it did, however, seem to provide what one ex-pupil has described as (with tongue only slightly in cheek), "a honey pot for eccentrics". Some might say that that is only to be expected. Within those eccentrics were variously included within the male group – again in the words of that ex-pupil, "a teacher that needed certifying, one who was unhinged, one who should have been in charge of Auschwitz, one who loved living underground (actually a potholing fanatic), one who should have had shares in a Mars bar factory and one who might have been better modelling for 'Moss Bros.'". Rather strangely, the eccentric vein appeared to run specifically through the male teaching staff. Whilst on the female side there was certainly sufficient interest shown in them by the male pupils – one had legs that "went into next week" and one "a pair of bosoms the like of which would have been the envy of any number of Hollywood actresses" – there was no obvious eccentricity within the female teaching group. At least, that was the view firmly held by an adolescent male whilst doodling in a personal diary. Indeed, it was a view held by many other pupils. Why such obvious eccentricity should manifest itself in one sex and not the other is perhaps something for a psychiatrist to ponder on!

This diary is, though, more than anything else, a story of growing up away from home and coping as best one could. Yes, it was easier to cope once at the senior end of the school. There were, however, still problems, it was just that they were different problems to those that had been faced as a junior. So, the schooldays described within were never completely carefree, as perhaps school days should be, albeit that they most probably never are for the vast majority of pupils! Nevertheless, they ended in the knowledge that the future just might, despite all the worry and misgivings – and there were plenty – turn out to be what might be termed in a children's book as "a fairy tale". In that context, the self-confessed "country girl" who received that caller, a nervous 6th form boarder, on a dark November night with perfect equanimity, and who had already (secretly) taken a shine to him, was indeed a princess. But it was no "fairy tale"! It was true. This book, in its diary format, is the story of how it all came about and is dedicated to the memory of that princess.

FROM A DORMITORY WINDOW

A BOY'S LIFE & LOVE AT BOARDING SCHOOL

Ian McCart

LOOKING BACK TO 1966

CHAPTER I

WHERE RIVER, ROAD AND RAILWAY CONVERGE

"Will here do?" sounded the laconic voice of the Pennine bus driver as he looked briefly in his mirror to see a passenger struggling up the aisle, manhandling what was obviously a large, heavy and battered suitcase in one hand and a briefcase, also somewhat battle-scarred, in the other. Whilst it wasn't quite all one's worldly belongings in a well-worn and widely travelled suitcase, it certainly felt as though it might well have been, with red welts on the inside of the left-hand bearing testimony to the weight of the contents. The suitcase had already been carried across from Lancaster Castle railway station to the city bus station and whilst, fortuitously, the route is predominantly a downhill journey, nevertheless, the red welts provided a visual reminder (if one was indeed needed) of the weight burden a left hand had accepted somewhat begrudgingly.

Quite clearly, the bus driver was not particularly wanting, nor indeed requiring, a response to his question. He automatically brought the bus smoothly to a halt, the braking process being accompanied by a gentle whine of the brakes, a whine that had been annoyingly persistent throughout the journey every time they had been used. At the same time, he pushed firmly on a prominent red button on the dashboard and in doing so, immediately activated the door. It obediently, but rather tardily and half-heartedly, opened for its alighting passenger. Obviously, "here" was going to have to do! In actual fact, "here" is indeed convenient. It will save walking a longer distance with this bulky and unwieldy luggage, which would otherwise have been necessary, had the bus driver decided to continue to the official bus stop. In practical terms, the location of the various bus stops would seem to be of little or no consequence to drivers with the Pennine Bus Company. Almost all of them are, without exception, seemingly well versed in picking up and dropping off their clientele at the most convenient point for their passengers, bus stop or no bus stop. After all, out here in the 'sticks' with a bus route traversing the rolling hills at the western edge of the Pennines, the exact location of a bus stop is only significant, it seems, if there are prospective passengers waiting to board. From the time the company commenced operations in the 1920s and in the absence at that time of any formal bus stops, the Pennine bus drivers would happily pick up and drop off passengers at any appropriate spot. It is a tradition that has been continued right through to the present day. A driver will regularly make an 'ad hoc' assessment of where best to drop off a passenger who is well known to them. A convenient arrangement most definitely, particularly in inclement weather.

"Back to Bentham Grammar, is it?" suggested the elderly driver whilst making an almost involuntary and automatic adjustment to his well-worn Pennine bus company cap, proudly displaying the firm's name on the cap badge. Both driver and regulation cap have most likely been together for many years. Indeed, both look as though they have perhaps given upwards of a lifetime of loyal service. The question the driver asked wasn't really a question at all. It was confidently delivered more as a statement of fact. Indeed, the bus driver is absolutely correct. Without doubt, this well-worn suitcase and a rather ramshackle looking briefcase, both in the care of what some might consider to be a rather scruffy looking adolescent, had given the game away. It is indeed a return to boarding school on this blustery and changeable Sunday afternoon in early September. Back for another school year, although before a conversation could really begin, the bus door was already closing but this time, rather strangely, far more rapidly than when it had opened. The orange and black liveried Leyland Leopard, now looking slightly old-fashioned, ancient even, in comparison with the design of the more modern and the more comfortable Plaxton Supreme, which the company also operates, was then on its way. In its wake, a faint but distinctive and familiar smell of diesel exhaust as it turned the sharp bend by the public house and headed east towards its eventual destination of Skipton.

As the bus moved off, the handful of remaining passengers stared almost blankly out of their respective windows, the view for them being impaired somewhat by the remnants of a brief, but intense, shower of rain from earlier in the journey, which had left the windows stained with the wet. And after getting off the bus, as if on cue, a sudden welcome burst of warm early afternoon sunshine. Combined with the earlier rain, it causes the tarmac to steam slightly and makes the hedgerows glisten, giving the impression that they have yet to shake off a morning dew. The damp country road gives off that rather pleasing intoxicating aroma of tar, whilst the soil supporting the hedgerows provides the familiar welcoming smell of the earth, often noticeable when soil soaks up the rain after a prolonged period of dry weather. It is almost as though the countryside is saying "welcome back, Ian". Yes, welcome back to Low Bentham and, perhaps more pertinently, welcome back to boarding school. A return to boarding school and boarding school life. September 1972, the start of a new school year.

Where road, river and railway converge: Low Bentham.
(Copyright: The Frith Collection)

So, it is here, opposite this now familiar seventeenth century Punch Bowl Hotel, where road, river and railway converge, that the bus driver has deposited his fare, the only passenger to alight. Only a single ticket, as there is to be no return passage on this day. The Punch Bowl Hotel, whilst almost aching for a fresh coat of white masonry paint, is strangely welcoming, nonetheless. Its familiar, slightly tattered outward appearance somehow suits the building's 300-year-old credentials.

This, then, is on the outskirts of Low Bentham, a small rural village at the western extremity of the valley of the River Wenning, in the West Riding of Yorkshire. A map of the 'Yorkshire Dales' will show Low Bentham, surely, as the most westerly village in the West Riding, before Lancashire takes the surrounding countryside westwards towards the Irish sea, a distance of sixteen miles or thereabouts. This then is Yorkshire country. Taken as a whole, the Yorkshire Ridings so very nearly stretch from the waters of the North Sea, through to the opposite west coast and the Irish Sea. The White Rose is in ascendancy!

Low Bentham village boasts an ancient pedigree and was sufficiently important in the eleventh century to warrant a mention in the Domesday Book of 1086. More recently, the village has perhaps been better known in the nineteenth and twentieth centuries for producing quality silk, a legacy of the Industrial Revolution. Now, in the second half of the twentieth century, the village is quietly looking after itself with no great "hurrah". However, it is still doggedly expressing its independence by possessing a small cluster of village shops which are, as with any small rural village, invariably the centre and lifeblood of local affairs.

These shops include the 'Nip In', primarily a sweet shop where the proprietor, a rather stern-looking Mrs Russell, holds court. She will be checking up on the local village gossip whenever possible, whilst chatting with the mothers in the shop. At the same time, with typical shopkeeper's dexterity, she will be filling a sweet bag with what was once 1/- (one shilling) worth of sweets for the children. Pre-decimalisation, the contents would invariably include four 'Black Jacks' for 1d, four 'Fruit Salads' also costing 1d, two 'Flying Saucers' (1d each), a 'Sherbet Fountain' including a liquorice stick to dip into the sherbet, along with the almost obligatory 'Gobstopper' and various other "goodies" that 1/- could buy in a world long before 'E' numbers were dreamed up! Now, following decimalisation (and no complicated adding up to be done in the head) a bag of sweets is costing, perhaps, 10 (new) pence of a child's pocket money. Maybe not quite as romantic, but still filled with 'Black Jacks' and the like even if, perhaps, the bag never seems quite as full as in the past. Is that, though, a view one's imagination has formed assisted by the ever-powerful tool of nostalgia, causing a blurring of reality?

A rather old-fashioned post office also serves the village. This consists of a simple single cramped room, perhaps created out of part of the front of what was once a residential house. The room incorporates a counter and a grossly undersized customer area, not equipped to handle more than a couple of people at any one time. On pension day, one might imagine, there will be an inevitable queue on the pavement outside. It will most certainly be a good-mannered queue, most likely providing a useful opportunity to exchange local gossip! On the old wooden counter, worn with continual use and with scratches from countless years of money changing hands, the daily papers will be on sale. They are perhaps the only concession to selling non-post office goods and services apart from, that is, during the Christmas period. For the festivities, jigsaws and the popular children's annuals such as *The Dandy, Bunty* and *The Beano* will always take centre stage in the large glass window front. For the rest of the year, the display will feature rather faded adverts for the services available from the post office: Premium Savings Bonds, National Savings Certificates and the like.

A few yards from the post office and looking far more imposing and important, a Victorian designed, albeit early Edwardian built, village hall offering a venue for a multitude of meetings and evening entertainment. It sports a rather ornate roof. A billboard at the entrance ensures that adequate notice of forthcoming events is provided and advertised for the benefit of those not always "in tune" or up to date with what is happening in their village. The forthcoming village WI meetings will almost certainly be advertised on the billboard as a matter of course. Surely those stalwarts (or is "ladies of a certain age" a more appropriate description?) will not be needing a suitable reminder – will they?

A view looking out from Low Bentham eastwards, showing the village hall on the immediate right, then the post office.
Ellergill Cottages are on the immediate left (see chapter XV).
(Copyright: The Frith collection.)

In a central position within the village, the old faithful 'Co-op' store once stood in between the parting of the roads, rural roads heading to High Bentham and Burton-in-Lonsdale respectively. The 'Co-op' in Low Bentham had once mirrored so many others in villages across the rural West Riding of Yorkshire, being at one time a fixture and almost a necessity. With the store having only recently closed down, 'The Dairy', a 'grocers', situated just at the commencement of the Burton-in-Lonsdale Road, provides daily necessities. With the retirement of its most recent proprietor, Mary Frankland, 'The Dairy' has been purchased by Harry Walmsley and his wife who, hailing from the North-East, are what one might term retirement age themselves! It often seems as though running the shop is merely a sideline for this unassuming couple, almost as if it provides a pleasant, rather peaceful hobby so that they may keep themselves active in their retirement. Mr Walmsley somehow lacks the drive and perhaps the guile to be a successful village shopkeeper. However, there is a safety net in the skeletal form of his wife, seemingly more attuned to ordering stock and other such matters whilst staying alert to the varying customer needs.

Further up the road to Burton-in-Lonsdale, there is another general-stores, known locally merely as 'Woodys' (the proprietor being Mr Wood). With the Burton Road being steep and twisting, those living up the hill will invariably use this shop, rather than walking down to the bottom of the village. In fact, both general stores have their own loyal clientele and there would have to be a specific reason as to why villagers would suddenly decide to transfer their custom from one of the outlets to the other. Directly opposite 'The Dairy', is the 'Sun Dial' public house dispensing its 'Yates & Jackson' beer, brewed locally in Lancaster. Most definitely a public house in the traditional sense, with bar meals supplementing liquid sales. The tenants of the pub, Vernon and Renie Haslam, do, by all accounts, provide a welcoming sight to their reliable bunch of regulars on cold winter evenings and will invariably have a roaring coal fire "in situ". Also present in the village, various tradesmen, plumbers, electricians, builders, et al., some advertising and selling their services via small shop outlets, such as H. & R. Pridmore (radio and TV engineers), whilst others, such as G. E. Harrison & Son (coal merchants) are mobile, operating out of the old station yard, close to the post office.

Regrettably, the silk mill, Ford Ayrton & Co. Ltd., is no longer producing quality spun silk and fabrics. The late 1960s witnessed the final throes of its working life, an ever-increasing amount of cheaper overseas imports having a terminal effect on its order book and associated profitability. The company commenced operations in 1877, when the Industrial Revolution was in full swing, and its premises were situated a few hundred yards up the Mill Road, adjacent to the Wenning. Sadly, inevitably perhaps, Ford Ayrton and its archetypal Victorian mill just failed to reach and celebrate a centenary of trading. Where previously, and indeed until quite recently, there has been the familiar and industrious clash of looms, now all is silent and the building deserted. One thing leads to another. It is difficult not to see a direct correlation between the closure of Ayrton Mill and the village Co-op, one closure followed quickly by the other.

This, then, is Low Bentham village, on the western fringe of the Yorkshire Dales. Its stone buildings perhaps slightly austere and rugged in appearance but exuding a workmanlike air of Yorkshire grit in a similar vein to what one might assume was indicative of Victorian England. However, unlike the industrial suburbs and landscapes within the mind's eye associated with the Victorian legacy, the village nestles seamlessly within, and is surrounded by, a truly rural backdrop of rolling countryside. The Pennine Hills rise up on the horizon directly to the east and the fells of the Forest of Bowland lie immediately to the south. Of course, and in the words of Bob Dylan (you either love him or hate him – and the latter view predominates within the senior echelons of the boarding house!), *'the times they are a-changin'*. Now, in the early autumn of 1972, whilst almost self-sufficient in looking after its resident's basic needs, Low Bentham village has gradually and inexorably over a period of time been eclipsed both in size, services and employment opportunities by the neighbouring village of High Bentham, a mile-and-a-half to the east and a brisk twenty-five minute or so walk up the B6480, the main Lancaster-Skipton Road.

Across from the road junction by the Punch Bowl Hotel, a small five-arch viaduct, its piers displaying the original stonework from nineteenth century building, but its decking having been replaced by more mundane and purely functional twentieth century steel. This small viaduct enables the railway to traverse the River Wenning. The railway then disappears into a short cutting before reappearing and running alongside school playing fields. Passengers on this 'Little North Western' railway (so named to distinguish it from its far larger neighbour, the 'London and North Western Railway', which now forms the main West Coast route from London Euston to Carlisle and ultimately, Glasgow) will be making their journey across the north country between Skipton and Lancaster or Morecambe. Not an important main line route then, but a line which has survived the railway closures of the 1960s.

Whilst not a branch line in the strict sense, the section between Settle Junction, to the east, and Carnforth, on the West Coast main line, most definitely possesses that rather unique branch line feel. In the Ealing comedies of the 1950s, strange things happened on branch lines! Well in this corner of the West Riding, local legend tells the story of two Low Bentham lads, in their early teens, who a few years ago "liberated" (some would say highjacked…) a rail trolley from Low Bentham sidings, taking a ride on it westbound, running 'wrong line', on the falling gradient. Desperate attempts had then been made to bring the trolley to a halt when the sound of a diesel horn was heard a mile or so to the west. In the end, the two lads jumped off, hauled the trolley into the long grass beside the railway line and what you might term "legged it" across the fields, to then witness a few minutes later a diesel-hauled 'freightliner' train pass by! It had, apparently, been on a Sunday when, ordinarily, the lads would not have anticipated any freight trains using the line. They had been, of course, quite familiar with the times of the regular passenger trains.

With the nearest station to Low Bentham being a walk of just under two miles (a railway station for Low Bentham village having only been built, by design, as a temporary affair and having closed as long ago as 1853), it is the Pennine Bus Company that provides the obvious travel alternative. It has become a popular carrier over the years, operating out of its West Riding base at Gargrave, near Skipton. It has justifiably become synonymous for a friendly and efficient service and is eminently preferable to the Ribble bus company, based in Preston, Lancashire, with whom the local bus services are shared. A driver with the Preston-based company would not contemplate stopping on an 'ad hoc' basis to allow passengers to alight. Instead, the driver would undoubtedly have turned the sharp corner at the Punch Bowl Hotel and stopped at the authorised bus stop a hundred yards or so further along the road, just before the road performs an 'S' bend, which would be the envy of any motor racing circuit, to follow a course under the adjacent railway, over the river and into Low Bentham village itself.

Heading westwards then, away from the Punch Bowl Hotel, the road, running parallel with the railway, also makes its way across the river courtesy of a narrow hump-back bridge, conspicuously lacking the facility of a pedestrian pavement. A public footpath sign on the bridge signifies a regularly used walking route which leaves the bridge and heads northwards, alongside the riverbank before passing under the railway viaduct and ultimately cutting across the rolling fields to the higher north end of Low Bentham village. A walk of some fifty yards over this river bridge, however, will enable a grandstand view to be enjoyed of a large and rather stately original late nineteenth-century-built building. It is set back at the far end of a main drive, standing proudly next to an ancient church. It could easily be mistaken for a country house, having a similar architectural style. The building, built from local sandstone quarried from the nearby wood, exudes an opulent style and is visually enhanced by numerous mature trees standing alongside the entrance driveway – Wellingtonia, Beech and a Yew tree amongst others. One might surmise that these were planted concurrently with the building of the property. To the right of the main drive, an area of grass perfectly manicured with a well-maintained dry-stone wall and an established hedgerow at its west side, providing a border with the adjoining church.

Bentham Grammar School. The main school building designed by Norman Shaw, originally as the Rectory for the neighbouring church. (Copyright: The Frith Collection.)

At the top of the drive, the visually impressive main building, built in 1884 to a Tudor design by the famous Scottish architect Norman Shaw, he who designed the building in London which eventually became part of New Scotland Yard. The property was originally the vicarage for the neighbouring Anglican church, St. John the Baptist. It had clearly been built with an obvious grandeur to signify just how important the incumbent rector's position was in late nineteenth-century society. How times change! No longer is the incumbent of St. John the Baptist occupying such an opulent 'pile'. The rector is now housed in a rather anonymous (but no doubt more practical) detached house in the corner of the adjacent school playing fields.

This new position for the rectory does, however, enable its incumbent to keep a close eye and interest on the activities within the playing fields. Football and hockey played throughout the autumn and winter terms and cricket during the summer term. Two grass tennis courts are also directly adjacent to the vicarage garden. As to whether the positioning of the rectory on the playing fields has been advantageous with regard to looking after the spiritual welfare of the schoolchildren is a question which should not be asked. Why not? Just perhaps, it cannot be satisfactorily answered in the affirmative. Within the fabric of the school there seems to be (and perhaps there always has been) a deep chasm between the Christian teaching of the rector and the rather secular outlook of the senior pupils at the school. A chasm difficult to bridge, despite the continual efforts of the headmaster and teachers to foster a close and meaningful relationship between two patently unnatural allies!

But now, the sign at the entrance to the grounds of this Norman Shaw building makes plain and confirms its current use:

Bentham Grammar School: Founded 1726

Underneath the year and the school crest, a single word in Latin – *'Surgam'* – in translation meaning simply, *I shall arise.* (Although some of the more cynical within the school suggest it should mean, *'I might rise',* depending on the mood of any particular scholar!) No, not an ugly and entirely functional 1960s designed school built here. This is a school building that the board of governors can surely be proud to be part of. This is no monster comprehensive school with upwards of, for instance, 1,000 pupils, meaning that individual pupils would be unlikely to receive one to one support. This fully independent Grammar School has a roll call of, perhaps, 350, maybe slightly more, but certainly under 400. Over a period of just under two hundred and fifty years, no doubt many pupils will have risen on the back of industrious learning at the school. Perhaps some others will, unfortunately, have failed to rise to the occasion. The willingness to learn in one's formative years is not always clear cut. Whilst a school can 'lead a horse to water', so to speak, forcing it to drink will always depend on how wily and encouraging the teachers might be. Not only that but, perhaps more importantly, it also depends on how co-operative any individual pupil wishes to be. Learning and adolescence do not always make ideal bedfellows.

'Surgam'. Above that simple single Latin word, the school crest, a crescent incorporated within a diamond shaped lozenge, with wavy lines running horizontally across the crest, perhaps indicative of not only the adjacent river, the Wenning, but also of its tributary, the Eskew Beck. This brings its water off the high fells to the south, through the wood across from the school and into the Wenning opposite the school's south facing aspect. The river, fully surrounding the school on the east and the south perimeters, has undoubtedly proved an everyday distraction to the vagaries of an often mundane and no doubt at times difficult school life for some pupils over the past twenty-five years. It continues to do so. For it was in 1947 that this rather grand property had been disposed of by the Church Commissioners and purchased by the school. Part of this deal required the building of a new vicarage, eventually being completed, after considerable deliberation between church and school, in 1960 on its current site in the corner of the school playing fields.

These school playing fields, situated across from the school, directly opposite the church, and separated from both by the B6480 road. They occupy a generous tract of land astride the railway line, although only the area adjoining the road between road and railway is actively used. On this changeable afternoon and in readiness for the beginning of the new term tomorrow, the goalposts are already 'in situ' for a new season of football. Beyond the main football pitch, at the far end of the playing fields, the hockey goals are also in position. They will provide a suitable invitation to those 5th-and 6th-year girls, wearing their flimsy tops, sporty bras and short skirts, who have an enthusiasm for games. There is, indeed, an irresistible urge and a fascination in watching the girls in the senior years enthusiastically playing hockey and displaying, intentionally or otherwise, their attractive, shapely thighs. Shades of St. Trinian's perhaps. Something to look forward to when not practising and playing for the school First XI football team. This, not only a personal view but also one that is most definitely held by a majority of the male adolescents within the boarding house who have graduated to the 6th form. It invariably provides splendid entertainment watching the 5th-and 6th form girls play hockey. It will almost certainly at some stage during a match involve them jumping about wildly whilst attempting to avoid being hit by a fast-moving hockey ball. (And when they jump about with abandon, their breasts generally follow suit – providing they are sufficiently well endowed that is!) The occasional brief screams always, of course, a testament to how successful or otherwise their theatricals have proved to be. Girls' hockey: a violent sport perhaps – but something to look forward to certainly. (And indeed, one suspects that the young ladies themselves rather enjoy being watched by their 6th-form male colleagues, bare flesh and all!)

    The grand entrance and main driveway up to this 'Norman Shaw' building is, it perhaps hardly needs stating, strictly out of bounds to the residents of the boarding house and indeed, also to the day pupils. A small shingle surfaced path which runs parallel to the main entrance is the way in and out for boarders and day pupils. Using the main drive to gain entry and to exit the school will invariably lead to a suitable punishment unless prior agreement has been obtained. The only time the main entrance is permitted for use is at the beginning and ending of a school term and then, the driveway and entrance to the school building becomes a veritable hive of activity. Only then are the boarders given permission to use the main entrance, courtesy of their parents' vehicles in order that suitcases, tuck boxes and other boarding school paraphernalia can be loaded or unloaded. The scene on the front drive then becomes one of organised chaos. Parents, pupils and teachers all intermingled, everyone talking, no one listening, coming in and out of doorways, in and out of cars! Organised chaos indeed.

    Towards the top end of the more commonly used shingle path, which parallels the main driveway, are the school kitchens and then, at the very end of the path, a rather grand and imposing Assembly Hall. Built more recently as an 'add on' to the main building and with its main entrance facing west (an entrance that is rarely, if ever, used by the pupils who use a side entrance to gain entry), it looks out towards the original rectory property entrance. It has been designed and constructed in sympathy with the main building regarding its style and with the use of building materials, primarily stone. An Assembly Hall that is used for the daily morning assembly of course, but also providing a suitable venue for a multitude of other purposes. Indoor sports, school plays, for 'O' and 'A' Level examinations, visiting speakers, Speech Day and even for the boarding pupils to lounge about in doing nothing in particular, other than chatting perhaps, during periods of free time at the weekend.

Completing the view of the school from the head of the entrance driveway and to the east of the main school buildings and running parallel with the B6480 road until the river is reached, is a long single-storey, flat-roofed, modern building, slightly monotonous by design but entirely functional. Built within the last decade, the building houses a series of specialist classrooms, with a concentration on the sciences, all the classrooms possessing a generous helping of windows. All these windows look out onto a small gravel area used by the teachers' cars and the school buses and beyond that, to the main road where it crosses the river and to the railway.

With the bus journey over and having walked over the river bridge there, like a loyal servant, the school stands silent and patiently waiting on this Sunday afternoon. Waiting, not only for this boarding pupil but also for the rest of the boarding house, as it has done since the Church Commissioners sold it to Bentham Grammar School. The school had moved down to this site from *Moon's Acre*, a much smaller building between High and Low Bentham and which, by the mid-twentieth century was hardly fit for purpose as a functioning school with an ever-increasing pupil count. However, following the move to the old vicarage, *Moon's Acre* has remained part of the school, being successfully converted for use as the boarding house, specifically for the girl boarders up to the age of fifteen years and being renamed *Collingwood House*. Thereafter, the girls transfer to the boarding facilities at *Ford House,* also situated by the side of the road between High and Low Bentham, but slightly nearer to the school. Here they will stay up to their 'A' Level examinations and the completion of their boarding school life. By virtue of these two properties being situated some distance from the main school buildings, the girls are conveniently kept at arm's length (that is, a safe distance!) from the boys' boarding facilities within the main school building, with regard to sleeping arrangements. As might be anticipated, this is a situation constantly and predictably lamented upon by the male 6th-form boarding pupils.

It is now early afternoon, and quite plainly too early for the boarding house residents to return. All is still quiet on the front drive and at the school entrance. Clearly the resident housemaster and his family have not yet arrived back to re-open the boarding house for returning students. A suitcase and briefcase are, therefore, duly deposited by the large and imposing main entrance door and to kill time, a walk along the footpath by the river and towards the railway will provide an opportunity to consider the months ahead. This is invariably a muddy and messy footpath, being overhung by mature trees which, apart from the longest days of the year in early summer, prevent the sun from fully penetrating through the foliage to dry the path out. Only in high summer or during prolonged periods of sunny weather will it eventually become sandy and easier to walk along. The recent heavy shower earlier in the day has left it only suitable for traversing with the assistance of walking boots. Ordinary black regulation school shoes are hardly suitable and, as a consequence, are soon caked with mud. Not only that, but merely staying vertical proves to be a challenge. Only at a sedate pace and with great care, as if one is constipated, is progress possible. A liberal sprinkling of wet and squashed and long-abandoned cigarette butts at the start of the footpath perhaps provides a hint of the regular sessions of clandestine smoking that occur along this path during school time, almost certainly during the lunch break. Within 50 yards, the footpath follows a route under the railway viaduct, then making its way sharply upwards via some steps to an adjoining field and on towards Low Bentham village. Before the viaduct, however, a dirt path branches off westwards with this 'unauthorised' route making its way up by the side of the viaduct to a position standing inside the railway cutting.

Walking a short distance along the cutting, a view is obtained of trains approaching from the west, with the railway line being dead straight and clearly visible for a couple of miles as it makes its way up a ruling gradient of 1 in 126 from the village of Wennington, situated in neighbouring Lancashire. With the county border so very close, Low Bentham remains very protective of its Yorkshire roots. As is so often the case, county or regional borders follow the course of a river, which effectively and easily provides a suitable divider. By these school premises, the county border separating the West Riding from Lancashire follows the River Wenning. The north bank incorporates the school within the West Riding, whilst the south bank belongs in Lancashire. Less than a mile to the west, however, and for reasons perhaps now long forgotten, the county border abruptly parts company with the river and veers north midway between the two villages, leaving each village quite rightly proud of its respective county heritage. The school is, therefore, quite definitely in Yorkshire – but only just!

CHAPTER II

DOES NOSTALGIA ONLY REMEMBER THE GOOD BITS?

Now, standing alone and looking to the west alongside the railway after having arrived on that early bus – a situation entirely predictable when possessing a desperate urge not to be last minute and having an irrational fear of being late – there is ample time to reminisce and recall, with a hint of nostalgia perhaps, those formative years at this independent Church of England grammar school. Does nostalgia only remember the good bits? Someone suggested that nostalgia is an alternative form of depression. Surely not. This desire to look back (but not in anger, as John Osborne might have done!), albeit to a recent past, is a yearning that is, for some reason, really quite impossible to resist. Is it perhaps due to a childhood which has involved living in seven different places, more often than not scattered across the globe, during a time span of seventeen years? Within that period of continual upheaval, boarding school has certainly provided continuity. More importantly, it has provided friendship.

The memories of a school life away from home, incorporating both the excitement and the dread, are made up of a myriad of small events, sometimes insignificant at the time but memorable thereafter for a variety of reasons. For the laughter, the various causes of embarrassment, the sorrow, the regimentation and perhaps most important of all, for the camaraderie within a boarding house environment. After all, friends were and indeed still are, also growing up whilst spending their youth away from a family home.

This is a good moment to reminisce. It will most likely be an hour or two before the return to school of Mr Russell, the resident Housemaster, and his family. To begin with and with some considerable skill, ably assisted by the grass embankment adjoining the railway, the accumulated mud from a once clean pair of school shoes is wiped sufficiently clean to be presentable again. The urge to have clean and presentable shoes, even when away from the presence of others, is ever present. Of course, the walk back may well mean the exercise will need to be repeated when it can be seen that the school has re-opened for boarders to return. So be it. For the moment, though, from here – at the top of this railway embankment – there, across the school playing fields, stands the school and the neighbouring St. John the Baptist Church. The church clock chimes for the half hour. The regular chime and indeed the attendant church bells are, and most probably always will be, a poignant reminder of the time six years ago when life at Bentham Grammar School commenced.

Really? Can it be that it is now six years since that momentous Sunday evening in early September 1966 when, in the fading light of early autumn, a kindly and generous Auntie Olive drove her Rover 2000 through the imposing entrance gates of this school to be met immediately by a veritable host of people and cars, with the by now familiar trappings of a returning boarding house ensemble evident? In the lengthening shadows of that early evening however, the sight was a totally new and slightly alarming concept to a fresh-faced twelve-year-old who had been sent to boarding school from foreign climes to continue the educational process. Education. It was something which could not be offered in Iran, where parents were then living, once one had progressed through the junior school stage.

It need not have been Bentham Grammar School. Indeed, it should not have been. Application had initially been made for boarding provision at Arnold School, Blackpool. At that Lancashire resort, an innocent twelve-year-old imagined, educational progress might well have been enjoyed in conjunction with a neighbouring sandy beach and fairground roller coaster rides! This was the town where there had been the excitement of seeing the rather grand display of illuminations all along the seafront when in Lancashire during the autumn months whilst parents were visiting relations, generally on the return from an overseas posting. Blackpool would certainly be fun. That was the thought process. Something indeed to look forward to. It would easily make up for the prospect of leaving home at such a young age. Cue, the hugely disappointing reply that had made its way back to the British Embassy in Tehran. They were unable to accept any new boarders. They were full! "It will have to be the second choice at Bentham. They do have vacancies" advised a hardly sympathetic parent, adding enthusiastically, "and you will be very close to relatives in the Lancaster and Morecambe area." But it was Arnold School that had been the first choice and the expectation had been that Blackpool would indeed be the venue for educational progress that by necessity was going to have to be within the UK. In any case, where on earth was Bentham?

So it was that it had to be the second-choice school which, somewhat reluctantly, was accepted. In due course, the various booklets, pamphlets and official paperwork from the school arrived, containing a host of instructions. A great deal of information indeed, but there was still no real indication as to exactly where Bentham was. The official booklet, whilst showing this now familiar grand 'Norman Shaw' frontage and proudly stating the Patron to be the Lord Archbishop of York, gave no clue either. Exactly where was it? All that joining paperwork, but no indication as to where the school was situated. The GB atlas had to be recovered from the bottom of a bedroom drawer! The location found, yes – a tiny dot on the 'North of England' page – but it hardly registered.

The official and rather stuffy paperwork (at least in the view of a twelve-year-old) was pored over, oh so many times during that August of 1966, within the safe confines of a large grace-and-favour house encompassed within the British Embassy. On every occasion that the prospectus and those joining instructions were looked at, it inevitably rankled that entry to Arnold School had not been possible. For better or worse and despite regular protestations, Bentham Grammar School it was going to have to be. It could not be changed. It had to be accepted and so it was – but, for a good number of days, there was a long face readily on show. Nothing could alter what had been decided and, eventually, the long face got quite fed up with being a long face!

As a child, school holidays always seem to pass by so very quickly, even the long summer break. As August 1966 advanced inexorably towards September, the enjoyment of those dry and extremely hot, lazy days of an Iranian summer were coming to an end. Is it forever sunny and summertime within one's childhood memory? It may seem to be the case, with memories of constant sunshine at sandy beaches. In this case, though, indeed it has been the case. Having left a birthplace on the North Lancashire coast behind at a very tender age, only two years or thereabouts had subsequently been spent in the UK prior to the commencement of boarding school life – and the countries lived in abroad, they were hot. Hot all the time, sometimes too hot! As that summer holiday in a hot and very dry Tehran progressed, the days undoubtedly passed more quickly. Well, they do, don't they?

Within the space of a few weeks, the rather curious, albeit familiar wailing emanating from the mosques surrounding the Embassy, essentially a call to the faithful to attend prayers, would be replaced by the constant fifteen-minute chiming from a rather attractive and ancient St. John the Baptist Church. This meant that one knew instantly whether it was quarter past the hour (one chime) or half past the hour (two chimes) etc. and on the hour, the bells would indicate the time by four chimes and after a short pause, they would then ring out the hourly time. All very predictable but, nevertheless, it provided a much-needed continuity of sorts. A change of country, a change of climate, a change of friends, always difficult to deal with as a child, and perhaps most of all, a complete change of routine. For a twelve-year-old child, who was a little shy by nature and who found it somewhat difficult to 'get on' with strangers (albeit of a similar age), the changes were both formidable and challenging.

Ostensibly, the presence of a twin sister, also commencing a boarding school life at the school, would greatly help with the settling-in process. The "twins", a mother thought, would have each other for company. That, at least, was the rather naive view of a mother who was, in fact, also somewhat distraught at the prospect of losing the last two of her children still living at home. In fact, with the girls' and boys' boarding houses a couple of miles apart and with the streaming of pupils having placed brother and sister in separate 'streams' (and therefore in separate classes with different form teachers – form 3A and form 3Alpha), there was not a great deal of mutual contact, intentional or otherwise. In any case, the thought process, once into teenage years, had decided it would look soppy and, more importantly, be rather soppy (well, surely, in the view of school friends at least) to be regularly meeting with a sister. Whatever, the strict segregation of the sexes at that time within the school parameters meant that meetings would be necessarily brief. Brother and sister, therefore, went their own particular way within the confines of day-to-day school life. In effect, two independent lives operated in parallel, but each in quite a different universe. In short, the twin brother's universe was with trains and trainspotting, whilst a twin sister's universe was heavily involved in trying to attract the interest of the male of the species! (Not as easy as it sounds with the school's segregation policy, but it did not stop a sister trying.)

Looking back now, a full six years on, the separation was, perhaps, more of a help than a hindrance in a growing up process that boarding school life, by its very nature, necessitated. Mutual contact between the two youngest twin siblings was generally, therefore, brief – involving, for instance, the exchange of letters received from home (oh, those light blue 'air mail/par avion' envelopes – how welcome they were in the early days!), or perhaps a request from one or the other to borrow some money if the weekly pocket money had been spent.

So, with the summer of 1966, a great many things were about to come to an end. Those lethargic days during the long summer holiday spent lounging around the embassy swimming pool and playing 'dares' with one's swimming costume and towel with a host of young friends, just shy of teenage years, were drawing to a close. They were never to be repeated. Who dares to take off their swimming costume and then come out to the pool surrounds with just a towel on? Let's do it and, more importantly, hold up the bathing costume as proof! The boys did it. So did the girls, proudly holding up their respective one-piece costumes! Did they really have nothing on underneath their towel? Would anyone be prepared to prove it? None of the girls ever proved it – neither did the boys – although the thought and the sight of the girls standing there, adjacent to the swimming pool, wearing nothing but a towel was, perhaps, sufficient excitement for young teenagers. At that stage in life and with both sexes, the Rubicon was not yet ready to be crossed. Across on the other side of the embassy wall by the swimming pool stood the seemingly dilapidated high-rise flats of a typical Iranian city suburban street. Were their occupants watching, one wonders, in bewilderment at the antics of the British Embassy children, whose cosseted lives were safely ensconced within the walls of a westernized culture?

The swimming pool, British Embassy, Tehran...
'a cosseted life within the walls of a westernized culture'.

Away from the confines of the swimming pool, other pastimes were also ending. No more building small dams on the irrigation channel that circuited the green open space in the centre of the embassy, fronting the Ambassador's residence. The channel enabled the variety of plants and trees to obtain vital moisture in the arid summer climate of northern Iran. Then, after having made a small dam that would hold back an impressive volume of water, one would carve into the surrounding mud several grooves to create little streams filling with water from the self-made dam. Eventually a breach would be carefully made in the dam to allow the water to push its way through and refill the channel. A pointless exercise perhaps, but to a twelve-year-old child, endlessly fascinating. One day, during that hot Iranian summer, whilst playing alongside that irrigation channel, a seemingly important visitor arrived at one of the grand, posh houses within the Embassy grounds – Agatha Christie. Excitement indeed – but in 1966, a twelve-year-old had not yet started to read her murder mysteries, rather taking the shine off the event. In any case, the lady who stepped gingerly out of a chauffeured car was, well, just an old, rather overweight, ugly woman. Not in any way exciting. Memorable only now, some years after the event, by virtue of having read a large proportion of her novels.

Within the environs of that irrigation channel and all around the green vegetation, a vast array of butterflies of varying shapes and sizes and all of them displaying a myriad of colours and patterns. Perhaps the keenest interest being with the large, brightly decorated *Swallowtail* butterfly with its protruding opposite long 'tails', with the butterfly always seemingly quite oblivious to the immediate presence of youngsters. Motionless on a leaf, they seemed to make it quite easy to be picked up – youngsters not quite appreciating the fragility of their large wings. The butterflies were also of interest to some of the adults working within the embassy and one keen lepidopterist, having accumulated what might have been assumed to be an impressive collection, subsequently organised for them to be returned to the UK. Not, however, by traditional means using an Iranian postal system that was justifiably considered unreliable. Instead, via the suitcase of twelve-year-old travelling back to boarding school after a holiday. What trust! They were, as requested, put into the postal system once back in the UK via a kindly aunt. Nothing more was heard and, as 'no news is good news' they must have reached their destination safely. Not only that but, perhaps more importantly bearing in mind the cargo, intact.

In addition, there was to be no more walking around the embassy grounds with a father who, carrying an air gun, would every now and then take careful aim and shoot at the crows inhabiting the higher reaches of the trees. Occasionally, he would allow his son to take an active part. Fortuitously for the birds, a combination of being left-handed and having one 'lazy' and, therefore, hardly functional eye meant that, almost certainly, any crows that were aimed at survived to see another day! Should there have been some excitement involved from the comfort of holding a gun in the hands whilst looking skywards where unfortunate birds (or in this case, fortunate birds) sat only half hidden in the foliage waiting to be killed? A father seemed to derive some enthusiasm and enjoyment from the pastime. His youngest son would have much preferred to have been in the embassy home reading boyhood adventure stories, *Treasure Island*, *Kidnapped* or *Moby Dick*, in preference to an afternoon shooting at birds. It was hardly a suitable bonding exercise. In any case, this occasional 'sport' (of sorts) came to an ignoble ending in the fullness of time. A bird, badly wounded from one of father's not so precise aiming attempts, managed to fly away but eventually succumbed to the wound and dropped unannounced into the middle of a garden party being held in the private back garden of the Ambassador's residence. It caused some considerable consternation and, understandably, a moratorium thereafter on what was a rather pointless and needless activity.

Memories also of those days out walking in the neighbouring Elburz mountains, standing proudly in view to the north of Tehran with their peaks covered in snow virtually all year round. Tehran itself nestles at something like an elevation of just under 4,000 feet, the mountains a good deal higher. With the capital of Iran at that height, parents were always keen to stress to a young son that the air is thinner. Not too much playing, they would suggest, as the body would need a period of acclimatization – to a young lad in a foreign country, the only priority was playing out with friends within the embassy compound – never mind acclimatization!

There at the summit of the Elburz Mountain range, Mount Damavand – an extinct volcano – at an altitude of 18,000 feet and never devoid of snow at its summit. Standing proud on the horizon and well above the rest of the mountain range, its rather pleasing conical shape, an upside-down ice cream cone perhaps, was instantly recognisable. These mountain walks, with parents and a twin-sister, would be on well used paths and what enjoyment there was in finding, far away from humanity, a small ramshackle refreshment hut, seemingly in the middle of nowhere, where one's thirst would be quenched with a bottle of ice-cold *Fanta, 7up* or *Pepsi Cola*! The bottles of 'pop' were kept refreshingly cold by being immersed in a vast ice container and choosing a drink would always be accompanied by the familiar background sound of a generator faithfully doing its job. And those bottle tops had to be kept and added to what was already an impressive collection back at the embassy home. Even at such an early age, the 'collecting' gene was fully developed although subsequently, bottle tops were superseded by collecting stamps and then by collecting engine numbers! How does one explain it away?

Sometimes, instead of a day out walking, a drive would be taken through the Elburz Mountain range on incredibly narrow roads, negotiating numerous hairpin bends before reaching, and marveling at, the vast inland blue waters of the Caspian Sea. This was where, a father had enthused, that horrible black stuff (in the view of a young teenager, at least) was obtained, from the depths of the sea, albeit that he called it caviar. That small circular black stuff looked for all the world like the droppings of some unfortunate creature. It was served up on occasions when there were visitors to the British Embassy who were staying at a parent's house – the plush surrounds of that house made no difference to the taste of that weird black stuff. If, indeed, it is an acquired taste, then a youngest son never attained the taste for it – yuk – and it remains conspicuously absent from the boarding house fare. Far too posh obviously for boarding house rabble!

In addition, that area surrounding the Caspian Sea, explained a patient father, had, in ancient times been the kingdom of Armenia but was now divided between Iran, Russia and Turkey, much to the chagrin of educated locals. They, quite naturally perhaps, wished to see their self-proclaimed kingdom restored. A father has always been fascinated and interested in the local customs and in the history of the foreign lands visited. However, was a young impressionable son interested? Not really. There was more interest back at the embassy home looking through *Our Island History*, a book detailing, among other great events, the heroic exploits of Admiral Lord Nelson at the Battle of Trafalgar. He was a true boyhood hero. Notwithstanding that one's formative years, they were spent living across the globe, it was always (and indeed still is) British history that merited the interest and, as a teenager, absorbed any time that was spent reading.

Back in Tehran, there was also the excitement of being allowed to cross over the main road fronting the embassy to buy the locally made 'Barbari' bread, on sale at small roadside ovens, the bread being a lovely thick fresh flatbread. Pieces could be pulled off by hand and then eaten straightaway, whilst still hot and on its own. There was no need for butter etc. It might almost have represented a meal in itself and for the locals, it most probably was. And running back across to the embassy entrance, with the freshly baked bread, there, standing sentinel at the entrance gate, was the Lion and the Unicorn, proudly proclaiming the heritage of those within.

Accompanied visits would also be made to the local bazaars, within the confines of central Tehran. In these bazaars, the invasion of sound from seemingly frenetic, albeit quite ordinary, business transactions permanently in progress at the numerous stalls would, together with the smells from the limitless variety of herbs and essences on offer, accost the senses. If it is indeed the case that smells rekindle the memory, then those Iranian bazaars have succeeded handsomely. And then, if it wasn't the incredible variety of local foodstuffs on offer (pomegranates, pistachio nuts and apricots in abundance – but pomegranates – far too awkward getting the fruit out with a small pin!) within a typically confined and congested bazaar, then it always seemed as though every other second or third shop would be selling Persian carpets. The carpets, always predominantly red with a multitude of different patterns were, according to parents, far too expensive. Were they genuine or were they fake? The well-established Middle Eastern bartering system might have ensured a mutually agreeable price. (Assuming they were genuine; how could one tell?) A father has never been slow on the uptake with regard to a heady session of bartering on price – a skill he acquired and honed during years of living abroad in countries where haggling on an agreed price is not only anticipated but is actually expected as an integral part of the purchase. However, a fully furnished grace-and-favour house within the embassy meant that such a purchase would have been unnecessary and would most certainly have been considered by parents, both of Lancastrian descent, as a frivolous indulgence. It was not something either of them, conditioned by necessary wartime frugality, would contemplate. It is always better, they would espouse, to save money rather than to spend it. Really?

Nevertheless, they made just the one memorable exception to their seemingly rigid fiscal rules and a local purchase was indeed made. It was genuine, they had enthused, rather than being a good fake. The nature of the item meant it had to be genuine. It was a 'one-off'. Not a carpet, but a large oil painting of a young attractive Persian lady wearing tribal headgear. Not mass-produced but an original, painted in oils by a local artist. The fact that one would be extremely unlikely to see a local woman dressed as such within the bustling marketplace of that frenzied city seemed quite academic. Then again, as a mother has since pointedly remarked, "your dad has always had an eye for the ladies!" Mr Yartanian – Iranian artist in Tehran – did you, one wonders, make a killing with the sale of your Persian lady to a "tourist" on a three-year secondment to the British Embassy? Typical Iranian art? Perhaps. Typical Islamic art? Hardly.

The size of the painting meant that it needed a large wall (and indeed a large room) for proper appreciation and in that rather grand embassy home, there was certainly no shortage of suitable rooms. It was eventually hung in the incredibly spacious main living room, a room which was rather akin to a banqueting hall without the long rectangular table. It was a room that was rarely, if ever, used. It was far too grandiose for a family that then numbered four (shortly to be reduced to two), with two elder brothers having already left home before the 1965 posting to Tehran. Whilst the painting gained an element of interest initially in that oversized room, it was soon taken for granted and after a period of time, hardly noticed. The occasional embassy visitors from the UK (who were provided with sleeping accommodation in the house by virtue of the numerous surplus bedrooms available) would pay brief homage to it, perhaps feeling obliged to do so. The painting did, therefore, provide a suitable talking point for the visitors and their hosts. Useful enough, of course, if they had little else in common. (And was one of those visitors quite serious when casually announcing that the young tribal lady was obviously a virgin? This surprising fact he apparently gleaned from the absence of any number of rings in her right ear! Really? Was he joking?)

Visitors. Why, though, did they invariably feel obliged to try and persuade a teenage boy to eat and write with a right hand when using the left hand comes quite naturally? They seemed to take it on as their duty to prevent the left hand being used automatically. They would happily spend mealtimes and evening leisure time during their stay of several days, although sometimes it would be upwards of a week, persuading, cajoling or politely requesting the use of the right hand. All to no avail and a waste of time and effort. Is there something inherently wrong with being left-handed? Of course not. The visitors did, however, have their uses as on departure, they invariably presented a young lad and his twin sister with a present, more often than not in the form of ready cash. An Iranian ten rial note perhaps, sometimes more! To a young lad and his sister, the sometime tiresome visitors were then very welcome, and the monetary gift gratefully received. In fact, it was somewhat disappointing if a visitor left without providing "the twins" with a gift of some sort. And the painting? It eventually got moved onto the wall of the small 'ante-room' adjoining the large living room, which was used as a lounge. Even on display at this new location, it was, after a time, hardly noticed. The painting itself has faithfully followed its owners' regular overseas postings and currently resides in a house at the British Forces Camp at Rheindahlen, Germany. A traditionally dressed young Persian lady, hanging in a German house, lived in by a couple from Lancashire. Ah, well…

It was often a relief to return from the various shopping trips within that buzzing and crowded capital city to then enjoy the comparative quiet of an embassy compound. Only the regular call to prayers from adjacent mosques provided a reminder of such a different way of life being enacted outside those high and imposing embassy walls. From those tall, thin minarets – intricate, ornate, always turquoise blue in colour and pointing skywards high above the seemingly decrepit city buildings – would emanate what a father termed "the call of the Muezzin". Morning, noon and night (and perhaps more often than that) the wailing would begin. And so, worship at least three times a day was expected in that foreign land, whilst here, at the very edge of the West Riding, a weekly foray to the church standing opposite is perhaps considered rather too frequent.

It was quite easy to stand at a window on the top landing of that rather posh, stately embassy home and to look down over a hotchpotch of city buildings that appeared broken-down and haphazard in design. To look down and wonder. Even for a young child, it produced a strange inner feeling – perhaps undeserved – of safety and, yes, superiority. Was it something gleaned from listening to parents? The strange thing is, they often talk about their dislike for what they term 'the landed gentry' (or the "upper crust") but it almost felt as though the family was a part of that apparently despised group whilst living in Tehran.

The rather grand entrance in the grace-and-favour Embassy residence in Tehran. At the far end, a cloakroom and immediately to the right of it, a doorway to the basement, providing a sanctuary and a chemistry set.

At the rear of the large and rambling residence, which was at that time home, a fully enclosed, albeit modest, back garden surrounded by huge high walls that protected privacy. To a young lad, the garden was quite definitely in the exotic category, with a mature and flourishing fig tree and with vines climbing wildly over supporting decking and producing bunches of large white grapes. It was a garden that almost presented the image of a miniature jungle – greenery everywhere, seemingly running riot and taking over the small open spaces.

Within those walls and amid the foliage of rambling creepers and climbing plants lived "George", the resident tortoise, reputedly upwards of 100 years old! He belonged, not to the residents of the house, but to the house itself. The residents, merely his custodians, looking after him and keeping him regularly supplied with lettuce and tomatoes, strawberries and other such delicacies. He might ordinarily have been considered a slouch, but once he spotted food being put out by the kitchen door, he reverted to top gear and would walk surprisingly quickly. He was also adept at eating fast, munching away with what always appeared to be a mouth totally devoid of any teeth! Goodness knows why he felt the need to eat so rapidly as there was nothing to challenge his supremacy within the confines of that garden. He was indeed a character, marching around the garden surrounds, king of his little enclosed empire. Leading a rather lonely life of course (but a long one nonetheless) and eating any grapes which had fallen to the ground and even sampling overripe figs which had obeyed gravity once overripe and had also landed in the garden. Indeed, the ripe figs which remained fixed to their branches could be picked, and were picked, with relative ease from an open bedroom window. It hardly needs saying that the boarding house fare here at school, unsurprisingly, has offered nothing quite as glamorous or peculiar as large tree-ripened figs, which were casually eaten at all times of the day within the sun-parched surrounds of an Iranian summer.

Rather strangely, it was often the small, almost insignificant, episodes of daily life in a foreign country which were sorely missed once boarding school life commenced. They had helped to cement together the experience of family life outside the UK, where every effort was made to preserve and continue the British way of life within the embassy confines.

Memories of a father gamely attempting to find the BBC World Service on a huge, immovable, ancient-looking radio and regularly being defeated by interference from a hundred other radio stations all vying for the same or a similar frequency! He would quite often refuse to admit defeat despite the deafening tones from the many local (and not so local) stations broadcasting. In consequence, he would often be left in splendid isolation, with an ear fixed firmly against the radio, whilst the family melted away to find other interests. Just occasionally, he would triumph, and one would hear that familiar tone and message, "This is the BBC World Service", always spoken in a rather posh, detached voice.

Perhaps the only exception to leaving a father on his own, straining to hear those familiar sounds from the BBC overseas programme, would have been in July 1966 at the start of the summer holidays (and before any serious thought had been given to a forthcoming boarding house existence), when the highs and lows of the football World Cup were enjoyed. Clearly, the highs triumphed over the lows, with England being crowned world champions. Rather strangely though, the heroic exploits of an unknown football team from North Korea (and a father's *Times Atlas* clarified exactly where that country was) sparked just as much interest as the home team's progress did. This could be explained, perhaps, by a natural affection for the underdog. With North Korea leading 3-0 in the quarter final against Portugal (one of the favourites), that was indeed excitement, albeit that, sadly, they eventually lost 3-5. The enjoyment of that match and indeed the England matches were all, of course, within the obvious limitations of listening to a frequency being regularly interrupted and drowned out by a multitude of other radio channels.

Within these memories of life ensconced in a country justifiably boasting an ancient civilization (Percy Bysshe Shelley would have certainly termed Iran as an 'antique land' – as per, *'I met a traveller from an antique land'*, from his poem 'Ozymandias'), as a young teenager, no thought was ever given to the inequalities of everyday life actively on show and in progress right across Tehran outside those embassy walls. Watching one day, for instance, the ruler of Iran – the Shah – passing by the front of the embassy compound in procession with his entourage, displaying the obvious trappings of substantial wealth, with gold carriages etc., there was no comparison made at the time by a young teenager between that opulent sight and the frequent street beggars regularly witnessed when out and about in the capital city with parents. It would indeed provide a suitable discussion point within the framework of the 'A' Level Sociology course now being tackled (rather reluctantly), were it not for the fact that the sociological issues subject to debate within the syllabus at school are exclusively UK based. Nevertheless, the comparisons between sumptuous wealth and poverty do exist in this country. (With the reasons, causes and possible solutions to poverty featuring large in the 'A' Level syllabus and being, regrettably, the cause of some considerable consternation between teacher and pupil!) Where they do exist, it is surely not to such an exaggerated extent as witnessed daily in the Iranian capital at that time.

A weekly shopping trip to the nearby American equivalent of a UK forces NAAFI store would always involve a browse through the vast array of comics on sale. The interest was invariably with the likes of *Superman, Spiderman* and *Batman*, but it would always be *Superman* (alias Clark Kent), along with his news reporter girlfriend Lois Lane, who triumphed regarding a purchase. The other two magazines were generally read at leisure within the store whilst waiting for parents to complete their seemingly laborious circuit of the American shopping mall. One thing for sure was that Clark Kent and his entourage were certainly not in circulation at boarding school in 1966 or in the years following and nor, indeed, was *MAD* magazine, an American production with an almost ribald turn of humour, poking fun at anything and everything and designed specifically for teenagers.

Once back in the family home from the weekly shopping trip, it was always mandatory to volunteer to help with unpacking the shopping. Certainly not on the basis of being helpful but more specifically, to find the large tin of dried milk which would most definitely have been an obligatory purchase. With fresh milk not being available, large tins of milk powder were purchased, the powder to be mixed with water and then refrigerated. Oh, what a treat to be able to scoop out a spoonful of dried milk directly from the tin and eat it as it was. It was dry, it got stuck all around the mouth and in teeth. But it did taste nice. It was generally possible to scoop up a couple of mouthfuls before rather annoyed parents saw what was happening and called a halt to it!

At other times, when privacy was sought, it was readily available down in the house basement in the company of a chemistry set. It was a birthday present to a keen twelve-year-old wanting to experiment, where all sorts of different powders and liquids could be mixed and investigated, thereby producing all kinds of weird concoctions. Whilst the birthday chemistry set was enthusiastically received, for her birthday, a twin sister was given a gold signet ring. Iranian gold no less, made locally by a goldsmith in Tehran and annotated in a stylish pattern with her initials (SMc) engraved on the face. A chemistry set or a signet ring – who got the better of the birthday hand-outs? With the passage of six years, it matters not. It did at the time with inevitable sibling rivalry. Suffice to say that six years on, the chemistry set is now a fond memory, whilst a sister still wears her signet ring and indeed, may well do so for the rest of her days!

Unlike chemistry lessons here at boarding school, where all experiments involving teenagers are necessarily closely monitored, there in the privacy of a basement was freedom. Freedom to try any combination and mixture of substances with no requirement to have knowledge of the seemingly complicated chemical symbols. At boarding school in 1966, for whatever reason, the symbols needed to be learned by heart – the chemical equivalent, so to speak, of mathematics tables. It was always a puzzle (and indeed it still is) as to exactly when and why the knowledge of the various chemical symbols would be needed in everyday life. Similar questions were raised at that time in the mind of a teenager regarding the various mathematical symbols and equations within algebra. Such questions and queries were perhaps understandable – inevitable even – coming from someone always destined to study the Arts, rather than the seemingly complicated Sciences. (Are they really complicated?)

There was never anything but, perhaps, a few raised eyebrows from parents to the regular requests that were made for further supplies of chemical powders or indeed for more test tubes whilst living in the Embassy. The list of chemistry requirements would invariably be handed to a mother with the list headed up, 'Mum'. The list would in turn be handed over to the house servant (an Iranian local). Whilst mum and her son were somewhat perplexed when the chemistry requirements were subsequently delivered with the inclusion of a small '*Mum*' underarm anti-perspirant, perhaps, with hindsight, it was an understandable *'faux-pas'* for the Iranian servant to make!

Chemistry experiments in that basement were certainly more exciting (and invariably unpredictable) than the rather pedestrian procedures that were carried out in the school chemistry laboratory. There, one would be testing, for instance, as to whether a substance possessed an acid or alkaline base, with a simple piece of litmus paper providing the answer. There was, however, understandably an inquest into how the basement ceiling in that embassy property became sprayed one day with what was obviously a volatile mixture. The reality was that it had made its own way out of a flimsy test tube with such speed that it was impossible to hold it back! It was most definitely a concoction that was not included in the suggested book of experiments provided with that splendid chemistry set. All part and parcel of the haphazard learning process down in a basement away from the prying eyes of parents, enjoying the privacy, with the company only of a rudimentary Bunsen burner.

A Bunsen burner, in fact, not dissimilar to the one in use at boarding school and whilst it was always exciting to be messing about in a basement with a multitude of different powders and liquids, there was never quite the same interest within a regimented chemistry laboratory. At school, one was under the strict supervision of the chemistry teacher Mr Lethbridge, who had a rather odd habit of calling all the teenage lads, "sunshine". If one was seen to be lagging behind, therefore, in a particular experiment or in a theory test, it would be quite common to be berated with a sharp "come on, sunshine, the others are leaving you behind." (There are times, of course, when one does not mind being left behind!) In addition, there was always a rather unpleasant, pungent smell contained within the school chemistry laboratory, immediately noticeable when walking into the room. It was a strange sickly odour, not dissimilar to rotten eggs caused, no doubt, by continual experiments during the daily school timetable within a chemistry laboratory of wooden construction. That rather strange smell would follow him all around the school, as he invariably wore his white overalls, which were impregnated with the queer pong, throughout the school premises and not just in the chemistry classroom. Perhaps the only time he wasn't to be seen in his white chemistry coat would be on the stage at morning assembly. Then, the wearing of an obligatory black gown trumped chemistry overalls! His smelly overalls were also discarded when taking groups of boarders on weekend fell walking trips, around and across the nearby hills.

So, the ending of the summer holidays in 1966 brought all the experiences of growing up in a foreign land and being cocooned from the bustle of everyday life by an enclosed and private British Embassy to a conclusion. It had been an almost carefree life of semi-privilege, where even the schooling had not involved a full day's study. School only until lunchtime at a British Council school, which collected together an intriguing mix of non-Iranian nationalities within that capital city, all happily co-existing. It was to be replaced by a boarding school with a regimented way of life, a formal structure and as for freedom, there was none. Certainly, no freedom as a junior in the boarding house though it became obvious shortly after starting boarding school life that there did appear to be some 'unauthorised' privileges. However, these were only available once one was in the 6th form and resident in the boarding house! These privileges came in the form of "fagging" and were enjoyed by 6th-form prefects in the boarding house at the expense of the juniors. An occupant in one of the several junior dormitories became a reluctant fag – cleaning football boots or cleaning school shoes, sorting out and cleaning 'wet suits' that had been used for potholing in the nearby fells, being sent to the tuck shop and other similar menial tasks. Refusing to take on 'voluntary' duties such as these for and on behalf of the boarding prefects would without doubt result in life becoming extremely difficult. It was regularly made quite plain that it was advisable to "toe the line". If one did not, suddenly that anticipated free time one was expecting on a Saturday or on Sunday afternoon had mysteriously been cancelled. Instead, one would be allocated some onerous tasks in and around the school premises. It was easier, therefore, and it made for a quieter life within the boarding house, to acquiesce and obediently deal with any jobs that the prefects wanted doing, however frustrating and unfair.

Sometimes, particularly at the beginning of a new term or immediately following a half-term break, it was almost compulsory to hand over to the boarding house prefects some of the contents of a tuck box – a tuck box which had invariably been well filled by a generous aunt during the holiday break. In some ways, this was most probably just as well bearing in mind the short "shelf life" that some of the cakes and packets of biscuits would enjoy having once been opened and then shut up in a tuck box! It was generally only a matter of a week, or perhaps two weeks at the most, before the food started to become stale and it would then, by necessity, be thrown away. That is always assuming, of course, that it had not already been 'gifted' to one or other of the prefects under the threat of some onerous punishment.

The fagging system and voluntary donation of grub from a tuck box was, it seemed, an accepted way of life within the framework of the boarding house. There appeared to be an unwritten rule that the juniors should not complain. What would happen if they did? Did the housemaster, the resident matron or the teachers not appreciate the presence of a fagging system? Surely, they must have done. Did they condone it with tacit approval? Difficult questions with no satisfactory answers. In the intervening six years, the system has come to be seen, understandably, as somewhat outdated and has been largely eradicated. Timing is everything. Fagging for the 6th-form boarding prefects has had its day, even if one does hear the occasional lament within the senior boarding house with comments such as, "it never did me any harm!"

The complete 'Clothes and Equipment List' which had formed part of the joining instructions and was specifically for a boy boarding pupil had been somewhat disconcerting. It gave notice that growing up was, for the foreseeable future, going to be away from the safety and comfort of home. The list was nothing if not extensive. It was akin to taking everything out of one's own bedroom (and bathroom) at home and setting it up at school – all the paraphernalia of bedding, towels of various sizes, games kit (for summer – a cricket bat and winter – football boots) and all the various incidentals associated with living. Sponge bag, toothbrush, nailbrush, toothpaste, hairbrush, clothes-brush, etc. The main thrust of the listing covered the school uniform – school cap, blazer, scarf, ties, etc., with a helpful note advising where these could all be purchased. Scott-Richmond, outfitters domiciled in Lancaster, could provide everything needed. Alternatively, one could be measured for size at the school shop, located within the confines of the Grammar School. Rather ominously, the list confirmed that general or 'non-uniform' clothing could be brought to the boarding house, but that... 'all non-uniform clothing must pass scrutiny before being permitted'! In the event, for a twelve-year-old lad, there was to be no 'non-uniform' clothing worn at school at that time. Parents had decided themselves that the regulation trousers and shirts, that formed an integral part of the uniform, could be faithfully worn both during school hours and at all other times within the boarding house. Wartime frugality again? Funny how small things can rankle.

The option of visiting the school outfitting shop was the one a kind and patient auntie opted for, possibly to enable her to become familiar with the journey as, of course, it enabled the school to be visited. Not that the initial visit was seemingly that beneficial for Auntie Olive. She all but drove down a private farm entrance in Wennington (where the road takes a sharp right turn) on the journey back to the Grammar School, with her two nervous 'new-starters' in tow, at the start of that autumn term in 1966. Measurements had been taken, sizes determined and when an auntie drove out of the school gates following that initial visit, it was not only with a nephew and a niece but also, for the benefit of her nephew, with a school cap, school scarf, two school ties, a school blazer, four grey shirts, trousers both long and short and knee socks. The colour scheme was a rather attractive dark blue, perhaps navy blue, with a gold rim and the blazer, cap and scarf displaying the school crest. All that was then needed was for name tapes to be studiously stitched into all items of clothing and bedding. That was something a very patient (and skilful) aunt and her eldest daughter accomplished in the short time that elapsed between obtaining the school uniform and the start of term.

Everything was then ready for the start of a new school year. It was boarding school and a life, thereafter, away from the safety and comfort of the family home.

Is there an answer to that question then? Does nostalgia only remember the good bits? Has it been answered? It is with you, the reader, to determine.

CHAPTER III

FOR WHAT WE ARE ABOUT TO RECEIVE

The scene, then, on that early evening in September 1966 had been nothing short of bewildering. The school front driveway was awash with suitcases, large travel trunks, tuck boxes, sports equipment, kit bags, briefcases, satchels and just about anything else needed for a life where learning and leisure were to be incorporated within the same venue. Everything was new and everyone was, it seemed, on the move. It was a world away from anything previously experienced. Where there had been the privacy of home, now there was to be none at all. Where there were kindly parental requests to an impressionable near teenage son, now there were shouted commands. Not only that, but there were a great many people doing the shouting! Where there had been laughter and talking at home, now there was silence. (Well, laughter and talking at home certainly, except at the dinner table, when there was a strict *no talking* rule in force whilst food was being consumed. This inevitably and frequently led to sudden and uncontrolled bursts of laughter between siblings, borne out of no particular cause other than everyone having to remain silent. Such meaningless laughter incurred the ire and wrath of one or both parents, which only made the laughing worse. Eventually, one or other of the siblings would be sent down from the table, generally blaming it all on one of those still sat up at the table who would be desperately trying to eat their meal whilst suppressing laughter!) Silence, then, the order of the day. And the night. Silence in class. Silence whilst eating meals. (No change there then from home life!) Silence whilst doing prep in the school dining room on tables designed for eating. Ten on a table for meals, only four on a table by design for prep. This, of course, made it most difficult to copy what one's school friend was busy writing (and what he was writing was most probably wrong in any case).

Oh, dear! The dining arrangements from that era. A boarding house prefect and a 6th former took pride of place at the head of the individual dining tables and there would then be at least one boarder from each school year on the same table. This meant that those in the third year (the most junior members of the main boarding house, as the younger boarders in the first and second school year enjoyed their own living and dining arrangements at Bridge House, a school building situated in Low Bentham village) would be sat at the far end of the table. Ordinarily, there would be no problem with this type of arrangement, except that the food for the whole table was handed over by the catering staff to the prefect at the head of each individual table. Officially, the prefect then had the job of dishing out the food to each person, thereby ensuring it was distributed fairly. It didn't quite work like that (surprise, surprise)! What would happen instead is that they would help themselves and then pass on what remained on the serving dish down the table, each person taking their own share until the platter of food reached the lowly 3rd form. This might, on occasions, work satisfactorily, but many was the time when the greedy blighters more senior to the 3rd form – generally from the 5th and 6th forms – would take more than their fair share, leaving, well, not much for those junior members at the far end of the table. It was most definitely a rigorous 'pecking order' and the juniors received the scraps. As a system, therefore, it left many a junior still hungry and it seemed that it was an arrangement that had to be accepted stoically. There was an unspoken understanding that in the course of time, one would gradually move up the table (and have more to eat).

For the juniors, it made it even more crucial to make appropriate haste at morning lunch break to the entrance into the dining room in order to obtain the daily quota third-pint bottle of free milk on offer. Not only that, but it was always worth hanging around by the crates of milk bottles until the end of break time when, on hearing the bell for lessons, any bottles of milk unclaimed could then be consumed. A third-pint bottle of milk could be guzzled pretty rapidly when it needed to be! Juniors may have regularly missed out on adequate food rations, but frequently made up for it in their quota of milk. A cafeteria system that has subsequently been introduced for mealtimes, in conjunction with the new dining room, now ensures all receive an adequate share. And extra helpings are available if required. What! Those in the junior boarding houses now get plenty to eat, do they? Yes. If only that had been the case in 1966.

Of course, one distinct advantage of the meals at boarding school was that one did not have to eat – indeed would not be forced to eat – anything that one did not like. (Which, quite frankly, was just as well with some of the atrocious steamed puddings!) How different from life at home whilst growing up. The first law of McCart mealtimes was that everything on the plate/dish (whatever) had to be eaten up, irrespective. Not only that, but there was no getting down from the table until it had been eaten up. This invariably resulted in a war of attrition between parents and a twin sibling. An empty plate, save for a helping of peas reposing in splendid isolation (the rest of the meal having been consumed) on a dinner plate was a regular occurrence. A sister would be sat refusing point blank to eat them, with parents preventing her from leaving the table until they had been eaten. The battle would be a long and despairing one (for both parties), but the peas? They never did get eaten. A clash of willpowers. A twin sister invariably triumphed!

Most recently, in tandem with the new cafeteria system, the old wooden benches in the dining room, which at times during meals enabled a considerable amount of pushing and shoving to go on (boisterous behaviour in general, but occasionally becoming more serious) and considered to be an integral part of eating meals, have been replaced by hard plastic chairs. Sitting uncomfortably on those old wooden benches, mealtime would always start in a controlled manner and following the handing over of the first course to the prefects at the head of the table, the housemaster would then say Grace. The boarding pupils would lower their heads, whilst secretly looking at each other, pulling faces or smirking. Grace was as predictable as it was short. "For what we are about to receive, may the Lord make us truly thankful", announced the housemaster, although in time-honoured fashion, the second part of the thanks to the Lord was almost always changed, with juniors whispering quietly their alternative version, "the pigs have just refused"! (Sometimes, indeed, it was a sentiment that was not that far-fetched...) It was only after Grace as the prefects took their share (and more) from the serving dish, that the pushing and shoving started, before being halted by an angry bark from whichever boarding-house master was on duty. The frequent disruption, then, that used to be regularly experienced by the juniors whilst eating their meals is these days no more. To coin a phrase, "they [that is, the juniors] have never had it so good!"

The start of boarding house life had initially been in a dormitory housing eight young teenagers. This was in the 'Cottage' – not actually part of the main school building, but a separate small property which fronted the gravel drive used by day and boarding pupils when walking around to the various classrooms, the path also being used for entering and exiting the school on foot. The 'Cottage' had in a previous life (before the rectory had been purchased by the school) been the tied home for the gardener and the housekeeper, assumed to be a man and his wife, employed by the rector. In its school use, the building housed three dormitories, the largest one of which was upstairs, having been a hay loft which had been attached to the property. This had been converted to living quarters after the school took ownership of the whole rectory site. This dormitory, looking after the sleeping arrangements for eight youngsters as it did, stood adjacent to a couple of steps which went down to the bathroom and wash basins and to a smaller side dormitory which slept three boarders. To the right of the bathroom, steps descended to the ground floor, housing the school sick-bay, another small dormitory looking after a further three boarders and the office and private sleeping arrangements for the resident Housekeeper, cum-matron, cum-head of the school kitchens.

Of the eight young teenagers sharing that top main dormitory, only another one had been sent to the school by parents living and working abroad – although in this case, not from Asia but from Botswana in Southern Africa. This proved to be a distinct advantage because it meant that at the end of term, travelling down on the train to London Euston *en-route* to Heathrow airport (for a flight to Iran) would not only be with a twin sister, but also with the company of a school friend who would be flying out to Africa. Whilst the school would organise travel to Lancaster railway station and would have 'Universal Aunts' waiting to meet the train at Euston, the actual train journey was unaccompanied. It proved quite a challenging experience for twelve- or thirteen-year-olds, albeit that one was not travelling entirely alone.

The 'Cottage': the main dormitory was above the blue door, the two smaller dormitories in the adjoining building to the left. This was the scene of occasional, and generally unsuccessful, 'Colditz'-style escapes!
(Photograph: Courtesy BGS Archive)

*[**An aside:** 'Universal Aunts'. An interesting concept. A more appropriate name or description might have been a consort. Almost without exception the 'Universal Aunt' would be an elderly lady whose job it was to ensure safe onward passage to Heathrow Airport. Depending on flight times, sometimes an overnight stop would be necessary at her house, with accompanied travel to the airport the following morning. Those overnight stays always proved quite bewildering, more often than*

not providing a bedroom window looking across a London landscape of terraced housing. But the housing was never-ending. It stretched to the horizon and beyond! Quite alien to what a young teenager had been accustomed to whilst growing up. Particularly so with regard to living abroad, where the housing provided was, by comparison, rather stately and grand. A strange environment indeed. Sufficiently so to ensure that a young teenager withdrew pretty effectively into his shell whilst staying in an unfamiliar house, in what he considered to be a strange and bewildering city and being looked after by an old lady!

Travel by plane – by necessity, yes – as Iran, and its capital city, was not assessable by ship and, of course, plane travel, it was quick. 'Universal Aunts' – essential then. But, to a teenage lad, the flight in a BOAC VC-10 hardly compared with that of a sea journey – the accepted way of travelling to and from a father's foreign postings in earlier years. There was always an indescribable excitement when arriving at a foreign port on board a P & O ship – particularly in the dark. Looking out of the cabin porthole at a multitude of on-shore lights, small boats on seemingly endless missions across the harbour, people milling about all along the quayside and the mystery of the land looming up in the near distance – it was a thrill, always invoking a flush of excitement. Then, once on deck in the morning light, the smells, intriguing more so than exciting – the sea-salt smell of the air, the work-a-day whiff of an industrious dockside, the smell from the ship's restaurant filtering out of the various vents along the superstructure. Mixed in with all that, the mud-like colour of the dockside water. To a child, that combination of sight, sound and smell initiated undiluted excitement. Indeed, to a youngster, sea-travel itself was thrilling – being able to walk on deck listening to the constant sound of the sea – never-ending, with a distant blue horizon – or standing at the stern, watching a bubbling cauldron of water, churned white and stretching away endlessly until, finally, out of sight – whilst the ship steamed ever onwards.]

Of the others in that main 'Cottage' dormitory, the environs of Burnley and Nelson in Lancashire was the home turf for several young lads. (Who all, predictably, supported the claret and blue of Burnley F.C.) Kevin Green was, perhaps, an odd one out – boarding at the school, albeit that his parents lived in nearby Morecambe. It never occurred to young teenagers to query or understand as to why a boarding facility was actually necessary when his parents lived only 15 miles or so away. Ordinarily, it might have been considered rather odd or unusual but to youngsters, that was how it was. Within a couple of years, it was to take on a more poignant meaning.

The dual role, specifically within the 'Cottage', of matron and housekeeper was the responsibility of Miss Cecile Turner and it was a role which she always appeared to guard jealously. It was regularly made very plain, both verbally and visibly, to others on the payroll that she would not take any criticism levelled at her running of the 'Cottage' very gracefully. She might, one imagined, explode without warning. She was certainly vocal in her defence of the routines within her domain. Generally, however, the young boarders under her care were largely ambivalent towards her efforts in protecting the independence of 'Cottage'. Young teenagers, instead, preferring to reside in one of the upstairs dormitories, suitably out of the way of her downstairs office.

She was a small, rather rotund lady with, it seemed to young teenagers, a matching tiny spherical face, which always seemed to be permanently flushed. Her hair was wiry and tending towards ginger. It was not particularly attractive. In contrast, though, to the rest of her tiny frame, she had a pair of extremely large bosoms (is "enormous" the most appropriate adjective? No, perhaps "massive" is) which, at times, she appeared to have difficulty in supporting. The solution? She would regularly place one arm – bent slightly – across her stomach, thereby providing a handy ledge for her bosoms. Her huge bosoms meant that they would inevitably figure in a nickname. Within the boarding house, at the very least, she was referred to, as a matter of course in normal day to day speech, via a rather uncomplimentary moniker – that of "Titty" or "Titty Turner"! It was quite clear to all in the 'Cottage' that her hobby (and perhaps her only other interest in life away from the various school responsibilities) was golf, as she was invariably to be seen sitting downstairs at her office desk in the early evening, carefully cutting out from the newspaper small visual golfing tips given daily by Gary Player. These were then stuck into a large golfing scrapbook, presumably to be studied at leisure when she was 'off duty'. Did they improve her golfing handicap? Who knows! It was not something that concerned or particularly interested young teenagers, except that it seemed to be a rather odd pastime (that is, sticking bits of paper into a scrapbook) for a grown-up person to be involved with!

With the young teenagers in the 'Cottage' being conscious of her title ("Miss", it was thought, being an indication of her lack of involvement with males), a plan was hatched one evening by scurrilous youngsters in the top dormitory. It involved one of them going downstairs to consult with her in her capacity as matron about what were imaginary white spots on the inside of his 'willy'! It would obviously involve pulling back the foreskin of the 'willy' so that matron could have a good look! Oliver Way was a very willing volunteer and had eagerly stepped forward without pressure or duress. It was the sort of practical joke that he revelled in. Oliver and his twin brother Charles [Charles and Oliver – shades of the civil war perhaps and they were, indeed, continually arguing with each other. There seemed to be little evidence of brotherly love on visual show within day-to-day life in the boarding house], domiciled in the same upstairs dormitory, were never afraid to step forward and to take part in all kinds of pranks against other boarders and indeed, against the teachers – that is when they were not fighting each other. Whilst Oliver disappeared down the stairs, the other residents of the dormitory waited upstairs with baited-breath and indeed, with some element of excitement anticipating his return. It caused a good deal of hilarity until finding out, rather disappointingly, on his return from the consultation, that Titty had taken it in her stride and provided him with some ointment for his 'privates'! Had she, the other boarders in that main top room wondered, enjoyed looking at the inside of his 'willy'? Surely, the highlight of her day, or so it was thought.

Escapades there were plenty – some involving Titty, some not. It might be thought unlikely that young teenagers would get involved in daring night-time escape plans, rather in the style of prisoners escaping from Colditz, but they did. Some had the urge to return home by whatever means and for some, home was not that far away. In true comic book style and steeped in public school tradition, bed sheets were tied securely together, dropped out of the dormitory window in the 'Cottage' and a teenager would shin down! The first part of the plan executed perfectly. The miscreants were invariably apprehended before escaping the school grounds (although, incredibly, an odd one made it home) and were, not always unwillingly, returned to base. But the excitement and success had surely been in the planning and in implementing the escape. Reaching the ground (unscathed) was a real achievement. The 'hero' would be returned forthwith to the dormitory, having achieved a God-like status amongst those welcoming him back!

Escaping the school grounds was not confined to the male boarders! The girls at *Collingwood House* also made attempts to escape from time to time – although not by such 'gung-ho' methods as bedsheets tied together! They used much more sensible methods – climbing out of a downstairs window or using the front door! Escaping from boarding school – clearly a young teenager's province! The senior end of the boarding house would realise, of course, how futile it was…

It was Charles Way who, rather creatively and with some considerable skill, converted his school *Songs of Praise* hymn book into a rather splendid cigarette case. For Charles, the weekly woodwork lessons proved particularly helpful. He neatly chiseled out the pages to form a rectangular cavity – the ideal size for holding his *forbidden* fags. A perfectly disguised cigarette case. He then rather proudly (perhaps rather too proudly), kept his converted hymnbook in the top pocket of his school shirt. The rector would, no doubt, have been quite pleased at seeing such devotion. He was eventually found out. Hardly surprising when, to his boarding colleagues, there was no one less likely to be displaying such devotion to the hymns being sung in school assembly and in church. Whilst his stunt resulted in inevitable retribution (in the form of a small cylindrical stick against the backside), there was apparently some amusement among the teachers, including Mr Webb, the Headmaster, for such skill and, well, enterprise.

*[**An aside:** Cigarettes in the boys boarding house – if the current rumours are to be believed, Zambian Weed (?) circulates within the chaos that is Ford House!]*

This top dormitory, the larger of the two upstairs, was now a new surrogate home lacking, however, the privacy and the perceived safety of a parental home. The only privacy available was either a bedside cabinet for personal belongings or a locked tuck box in a room on the ground floor. It was to be home, however, for only a couple of terms. The large west-facing window (presumably what had been the end opening of the barn in its previous life) looked across to that area of grass in front of the main school building, rectangular shaped and kept in pristine condition. It had previously been used as a bowling green by local people when the property was in the ownership of the church, being situated on the far side – or the west side – of the main school drive. This is where the annual school fetes are held at the end of each academic year and the green has always been kept in such good condition with the assistance of a large 'drive-on' petrol lawn mower which was, at that time, when not in use by Mr Heal, the janitor, kept in a lean-to building, directly below the dormitory window.

Next to the lawn mower, the familiar and seemingly battered van belonging to Mr Green, the physics teacher and part-time Housemaster, would invariably be parked up. A rumour that circulated within the boarding house at that time suggested that he would buy a vehicle, use it continuously without maintenance until it was "knackered" and beyond economic repair – at which point, he would abandon it at some remote location and would then begin the search for a replacement vehicle. Such a reputation is difficult to shake off! The rumour, however, fitted in nicely with the use to which his vehicles were put – generally taking the more mature boarders on walking trips to the Lake District or the Pennine fells which invariably involved using roads or tracks more suited to a Land Rover or farm tractor and suchlike. For the older boarders, he was an ideal candidate for a relief housemaster, also teaching canoeing on the adjacent river as well as skiing and potholing on and in the nearby Pennine hills. All these pursuits overseen by Mr Green, sadly, came to an end in the spring of 1969 when, whilst potholing, the rope ladder he was on broke due to a design failure. He fell and paralysed the lower part of his body. So suddenly, those battered vans, they were no more. He returned briefly in a wheelchair to continue teaching physics but, sadly, continuing health issues determined that he could not continue. Mr Green was greatly missed in the boarding house and so, indeed, were his battered vans, which were always the subject of good-natured schoolboy quips and humour. Indeed, to his credit, he took the frequent youthful wisecracks in good spirit and with good grace, always being quite happy to engage and respond in kind, to the cheeky and scurrilous schoolboy banter.

Adjoining the school green on its west side, St. John the Baptist Church. The church, with its well-proportioned fourteenth-century tower filling the view from the dormitory window, soon became a singular part of the morning "getting up" routine, with its regular fifteen-minute chiming sounding out the time, thereby giving notice of the approach of the morning call – and breakfast! From the large dormitory window, that familiar square tower reached up to the sky, as it still does, above the surrounding foliage of mature fir trees and at each corner at the top of the tower an individual finial reached even further skywards. From a distance, they almost look like asparagus ready for picking, except that these finials are well organized, with a consistent height and design at each corner. Surrounding the top of the church tower, small castellated turrets which presented to a young teenager's mind the hint of a castle – or at least the design of a castle – but which is now assumed to be typical of the architectural style from the period when the tower was built. Almost hidden by the trees at the near east end of the church, was the huge stained-glass window within which is incorporated the chancel and, at the pinnacle of this part of the church building, a small religious cross, almost insignificant when viewed from that dormitory window. The interior of this small church was to become so very familiar with the compulsory weekly visit on Sunday morning accepted, albeit stoically, as a normal part of boarding-school life.

This, then, was the view from the dormitory window in those early months at boarding school. The church, inevitably, became a familiar morning view seen regularly through eyes filled with tears, figuratively speaking, whilst in the presence of others in the dormitory who did not appear to be, or seem to be, homesick. However, at night-time, with lights out, the tears, then they were for real. Were the others in that dormitory ever homesick? If they were, it was never obvious. Perhaps they also cried silently into the pillow once lights were turned out and the dormitory was bedded down for another night. Then, only the quarter-hour chime from the church across the school green was to be heard intruding on the silence once young teenagers had finally exhausted their whispering and laughing and, as one, had fallen asleep.

No sooner had this view from the dormitory window become a familiar one when it was time to move. The beginning of a new term after Easter 1967 heralded a transfer down the two steps from the main dormitory and into a side dormitory, housing just the three beds. A little more privacy, perhaps, but not quite so comfortable in cold weather, with merely a small wall mounted electric heater to provide warmth – nowhere near as effective as night storage heaters.

FROM A DORMITORY WINDOW

A view from that dormitory looking west – yes – but far more importantly, a window facing directly north. This provided a view to the main road passing the front of the school and, more importantly, on the far side of the road, a view to the railway. The train-spotting hobby at that time within the boarding house was an inevitable consequence of having the railway running parallel with the school playing fields. If you were not in the train-spotting group within the boarding house, then you would have few close friends. That new dormitory was tailor made for train spotters. After 'lights out' in this dormitory and particularly once dark, there was always the anticipation and excitement in hearing steam-hauled trains barking their way eastwards up the gradient from Wennington, be it a night-time mail train from Heysham or a heavy freight service, the steam locomotives making steady but sure progress, heading towards the various conurbations in Yorkshire's West Riding. The progress of an approaching steam locomotive could be plotted from the comfort and warmth of bed by following the steady even beat until the cutting behind the rector's house deadened the noise of the locomotive slightly. That was the signal to immediately jump out of bed, to rush across to the window and to watch the spectacle as the train crossed over the River Wenning on the viaduct and made its way into Low Bentham. Its progress could quite easily be followed with the advantage of height, gained from being on the first floor of the 'Cottage'. It was generally dark, of course, but not until late at night as this was the summer term. Once dark, however, the red glow from a locomotive's fire would often light up the immediate surrounds and with the engine working hard, sparks were regularly seen being thrown into the night air from the locomotive's chimney. Spectacular? Indeed, it was! For teenagers, it was an enthralling spectacle of sight and sound, albeit that it was accepted that it was never possible to get the engine number. It did not matter. What mattered was being part of it and watching the night-time action.

What really mattered, though, was that steam traction on the working railway was very shortly coming to an end and even at such a young age, there was an understanding that the enforced retirement of steam was indeed going to be the end of an era. It was a subject talked about continuously between the train spotters. Hardly a week would go by without news (more often than not from one or other of the day boys who were more in tune with obtaining information) of a particular area that had become devoid of steam traction or else, information on a particular locomotive or locomotive class that had been withdrawn. It became commonplace to learn such updates from Peter Robinson, ("Robbo"), an acknowledged expert within the school on all things that moved on the railway. "The last few Jubs (Jubilee class) have been withdrawn!", he would announce dramatically to his audience in the playground. "But one came past the school only last week", would be the almost typical reply at that time. Steam engines were seen one day and could quite easily have been withdrawn by the following day, such was the rate at which steam traction was being dispensed with.

When lying in bed awake, therefore, it was nigh impossible to ignore the sound of steam working hard, always heard quite faintly at first and almost rising to a crescendo as the locomotive made its way alongside the school playing fields. And then quite frequently after the locomotive had pulled its train away eastwards from Low Bentham towards High Bentham and beyond, the voice of Titty would be heard from the foot of the stairs.

"Can you lads get back into bed please? If I have to come up the stairs, I don't want to find anybody out of bed." It did not help, of course, having the dormitory directly above her private living accommodation!

At other times, after 'lights out', a regulation 12-inch wooden school ruler (religiously etched with one's name on one side or the other to prevent unauthorised pinching) was a necessary addition to larking about on the bed. The innocent youngster who had commenced boarding school the previous autumn was soon learning a thing or two from his compatriots, who were clearly more 'worldly-wise', and at night-time, this alternative 'education' involved a torch and a ruler. In turn, each of the three dormitory residents would stand devoid of pyjama bottoms on the bed and, after encouraging one's 'willy' to harden, a ruler was used to take an appropriate measurement – a torch highlighting the process for the benefit of the two spectators! Embarrassing, even with only two close friends being aware of how many 'inches' one was endowed with! Quite impossible, however, to have declined to take part – at least, not without losing face.

Poor Titty! The fact that the dormitory was above her private room was specifically the reason after 'lights out' for setting in motion regular sessions of jumping up and down on respective beds merely for the fun of it. It was done in the certain knowledge that, after a time lapse of five minutes or thereabouts, there would come that same familiar irate request, "Can you lads get back into bed please" and, bounding back under the individual bed sheets as one, the response would always be in unison, "We are in bed, Miss Turner". She would not have been fooled, of course, but generously gave the young charges under her care the benefit of the doubt. Well, most of the time!

CHAPTER IV

WHO IS TALKING?

After a single term in that small dormitory, there was an escape from Titty Turner. Ultimately, it gave impetus to the proverb, 'better the devil you know'. The new school year starting in September 1967 involved leaving the 'Cottage' behind with a transfer being made to boarding facilities in the main school building. It was almost like being a new boy again. The 'Cottage' had provided a certain degree of autonomy from the main boarding house. Most certainly it had in the evening, once prep in the dining room had been successfully (or otherwise) completed, with a privacy from the rest of the boarding house being provided by the separate building. Now, instead of being looked after and being under the charge and responsibility of Titty, authority transferred to not only the boarding house master, Mr Jackson and his understudy Mr Fife, but also to a dozen or more prefects. They religiously patrolled the dormitories and surrounding areas, always on the lookout for, and hoping to find, misbehaving juniors and metering out appropriate punishments. It wasn't, however, the end of involvement with Titty, who continued her reign within the school kitchens and the dining room. This ensured that breakfast continued to provide the usual lumpy porridge, whilst the evening meal would invariably include, at some time during the week, gooey semolina infested with horrible large bits stuck together, or steamed ginger pudding accompanied by thick knobbly custard. Yuk! (Although there were some boarders who thought both were great. Most despised such 'delicious' fare.) It was also a return to a dormitory with seven others, all of whom had progressed from the 'Cottage'. Amongst the seven were Charles Way and twin brother Oliver. They continued their almost daily sparring and fighting predominantly – but not exclusively – within the confines of the dormitory.

No regular chiming now to be heard from the nearby church tower, which had faithfully given guidance on the passage of time. And in the main building – for the Boarders' ablutions – a large, rather austere, unwelcoming and antique looking communal bathroom, housing several sinks and three baths. With no effective rota for the use of the baths, it was a case of "first there, first served". Even that did not always hold true and unless one had physically climbed into the bath, with the water generally still running, a more senior lad might muscle his way to the front. Not only that, but for still shy young teenagers, there was no joy in being on general display in the bath whilst others busied themselves with the trials of getting up, or in the evening, getting washed etc. for bed. Even when one had successfully "bagged" a bath and clambered in, it was never a leisurely experience. Invariably, a senior boarder from the fifth or sixth year would soon be queuing impatiently with various reprisals being threatened if one did not vacate the bath pretty smartly. Even worse, the matron in the boarding house and, indeed, the resident housemaster would regularly do their morning or evening 'rounds', walking into the open plan bathroom whilst one might be in the bath!

Unlike the juniors, the 6th form boarders and prefects did not seem to have any objection to this intrusion on their privacy. It goes without saying that they did, of course, in general terms have more to show off and were proud to display it! With a progression to the 6th form, the use of the bathroom is not now fraught with embarrassment. Indeed, it can be most entertaining if the current matron – the lively and high-spirited Mrs Russell – is doing her rounds! No problem these days showing off one's manhood to matron although, as she frequently reminds the senior boarders, as an ex-nurse, she has (in her words), "seen it all before." For the rather lovely Mrs Russell then, and specifically regarding the male torso, there is "nothing new under the sun". Nevertheless, she must, surely, gain some mild pleasure or interest walking into a bathroom filled with numerous semi-naked and fully naked young men busy with their ablutions. She must have a look – yes? Even a sneaky one! Does she compare, one wonders, the inevitable wide variety on show?

It was shortly after the transfer across to a dormitory in the main schoolhouse that Kevin Green, a close friend from the commencement of boarding house life in the 'Cottage', died tragically during the night. Kevin was a short, stocky, jovial lad from Morecambe, and he quickly became a close confidant – what young teenagers might term a 'best friend'. He suffered badly from asthma. He was regularly to be seen with inhaler in hand, taking deep gulps in between his coughing fits, in a fight to gain sufficient breath. With a keen sense of fun, he would regularly find things to laugh at. Inevitably, continuous laughing would then bring on an uncontrollable coughing fit. This would have the effect of pushing out his cheeks alarmingly, making his face quite red. It was always quite worrying to his dormitory colleagues as it was most difficult to assess quite how serious it was. However, such was the frequency of his continual coughing fits that it eventually became the norm to accept and, indeed, almost ignore them.

Night times in the dormitory would regularly be disrupted by Kevin and his continual coughing. Some slept through it, others would be woken up by it but there were no complaints. It was generally accepted that he was unable to help it. He would quite often open the dormitory window and sit by it, coughing freely until the fresh night air provided him with some temporary relief. It was easy to feel sympathy for him, seeing him struggle for breath, particularly as there was nothing to be done to help. Then one fateful night, Kevin had gone to the toilet, and he was never to return. The toilet room was long and narrow, but the window within it 'to the outside' was very high up, virtually at the ceiling. That night, Kevin was obviously needing some fresh air whilst no doubt having a coughing fit in the toilet. Having climbed up to the window, sadly, he must have lost his balance and fallen down onto the toilet floor. There – all alone – with no-one to help, his short life had ended. Life can be cruel and quite often brutal. For poor Kevin Green, it was indeed cruel. Even now, some three years later and when using the very same toilet, it is difficult not to look up at the window and think of Kevin. Exhausted, no doubt, from continual coughing, desperately using his inhaler and gasping for air...

A general instruction of silence pervaded right across the boarding house life in those early days. Certainly, silence after lights out in the dormitory with the high probability of a detention if caught talking by the resident housemaster or by the boarding house prefects. The prefects were tasked with doing occasional 'ad hoc' walks along the corridors containing the dormitories after lights out, almost hoping they would catch out some unlucky dormitory – or so it was thought by the juniors. Inside the dormitory there would be a hushed whisper as perhaps tomorrow's lessons or the forthcoming weekend was being discussed. Suddenly, the dormitory door would crash open. **"RIGHT, WHO IS TALKING?"** The voice of a prefect would bellow out in a threatening tone. And then – silence. Total silence. 'Silence is Golden', sang The Tremeloes, with their 1967 pop chart hit. It was anything but golden in that dormitory, with a boarding prefect stood waiting for those who were talking to own up. The dormitory light would stay turned off, but sufficient light filtered in from the corridor lights to generally make it possible to discern which faces were looking particularly guilty. The pregnant silence would seem to last for ages. In reality, it was probably no longer than fifteen to twenty seconds. Was anyone going to own up? "Unless whoever was talking owns up, the whole dormitory will be in detention!" The voice of the prefect was always steely and determined. Another short period of silence and then, eventually, a whispered admission from one of the beds, "It was me... I am sorry." The voice from within the dormitory would always be delivered with the intention of pleading for forgiveness. Sometimes an apology offered sincerely was sufficient and no detention would be handed out. At other times it was all in vain, and a detention would be the penalty for honesty. Perhaps it all depended on the general mood of the prefect and indeed, which prefect was on duty. Had he had a good day? Was he feeling magnanimous or spiteful? Had his favourite football team won or lost the previous weekend? Indeed, that could quite often be an important factor in determining whether a detention was handed out!

Is honesty the best policy? It was regularly put to the test in that dormitory, housing up to eight boisterous teenagers, but generally, the guilty were obliged to own up. Staying silent would potentially put the whole dormitory in detention. Friends would then be lost for a period of time. It was always known, of course, within the confines of the room who had been talking when the prefect or housemaster had 'pounced'! Within the dormitory there was a close bond of friendship, and it was certainly not acceptable to "grass" on a friend and tell the prefect or housemaster who had been talking. It was a time to stay silent and rely instead on those who were guilty owning up – always hoping, of course, that they would!

Silence also whilst listening to instructions given out by boarding house prefects. Silence whilst listening to a variety of messages and orders from the housemaster after the Saturday breakfast. Silence certainly whilst he then read out the names of those boarders in detention. Would one's own name be included? These were boarding house detentions, not school detentions. During the daytime, through the week, a school detention would involve, for instance, being given 100 lines. "McCart, I want you to write 'I must not fool around in class' 100 times during the afternoon break and bring it to me in room seven at the end of school." "Yes, sir!" A boarding house detention was dished out within the boarding house during out-of-school time. The names of those who had sinned were read out at the conclusion of Saturday breakfast and included the previous week's misdemeanours – being read out, not in alphabetical order, but in chronological order. This, of course, meant that those who incurred the wrath of a prefect at the beginning of the week just gone would be the first to receive the bad news!

The format remained constant from one Saturday to the next, with the housemaster on duty for that morning's breakfast announcing the dreaded news, well, almost in a matter-of-fact way. It will have been of no consequence to him, but to the juniors sat on the wooden benches, it was critical. "The following boys are in detention this week." The housemaster's voice then droned on, but there was only one name to listen out for whilst the heart fluttered slightly with obvious apprehension. "Denson, Oliver Way, Jeffrey Walton [not Harry, his brother, who would invariably sit grinning slightly and looking rather smug with himself if his brother's name was called out and not his own], Carruthers, Holmes, Payne, Denson (again!), Atkinson, Green." Huge relief – this time, thank goodness, not McCart! Then, for those whose names had been called out, the ruination of a Saturday morning with the housemaster giving the usual instruction, "Can they please wait outside my study at 10 o'clock."

It was often a case of 'pot-luck' with the detention system, particularly for the junior boarders. Quite often, having been told earlier in the week that one had been given a detention (and some prefects had a habit of giving them out like confetti), come the Saturday morning after breakfast and one's name would, mysteriously, not be included in the detention list. Sometimes, the reverse was true and, having no recollection of being told that one had been given a detention, it was then with considerable disappointment to find one's name included. It was a futile process trying to establish which prefect had given out the detention and, more importantly, why. Occasionally, when one's name was called out quite unexpectedly, it initiated a wasted hour or so asking around the prefects after breakfast to try and establish who was responsible for giving the detention. It was generally in vain as, to a prefect, they were reluctant to own up, perhaps realising that the system was, on occasions, flawed and unfair. Had they decided 'off the cuff' (so to speak) to include someone just for badness or because someone had irritated them during the week? Trying to find out was futile. In any case, it did not change anything. Once the detentions had been called out after morning breakfast, they were very rarely, if ever, rescinded.

Some prefects were more considerate than others. Some had a reputation for giving a boarder a detention for some minor infringement and then quietly rescinding it without telling the unfortunate soul. A good number of the prefects were adept at using the system to their own advantage. Having given out a detention to some miscreant, they would then make an offer that one found difficult to refuse. "McCart, can I get you to clean my shoes tonight and I can then possibly forget about that detention?" A nod of the head in reply was sufficient. Once back in the dormitory after prep, a pair of shoes would be waiting by the bedside, ready to be cleaned and polished. The job done, they would be dutifully returned to the prefect's dormitory (and it was obligatory to knock on the dormitory door and await permission to enter) and the thanks would be termed as if the job had been given as part of a learning exercise. Once the shoes had been carefully inspected, there would be a suitable response. "Thank you, McCart. In future, you will never forget how to clean a pair of shoes properly." *That much is true!* (So, to some extent, it was a learning exercise – was it? There is a skill – apparently – to be acquired in cleaning shoes correctly!) Intentionally or not, those prefects from the early years at boarding school – De Gruyther, Austin, Cantrill, Cubit, and others – instilled a sense of fear and foreboding into a young, rather green teenager. To them, it was all a game – and one they enjoyed playing. To young teenagers, it was anything but.

Now the boot is on the other foot. Six years later, that young, rather gullible teenager is a prefect and is about to take on the role of overseeing the detention system as the head of the boys' boarding house. Will the experience of watching with some bewilderment at an obviously flawed system in years gone by help? Should leaders be popular? Do they need to be popular? Last year's 'A' Level Sociology course discussed such issues. What about the boarding house? This boarding experience suggests that the prefects couldn't give a damn as to whether they are popular or not. In fact, in those early years, it frequently appeared that they quite enjoyed being unpopular. They seemed to relish it. Hopefully, the experience of those early years will now help with dispensing a more equitable regime. However, power corrupts – hasn't that always been the case? How easy will it be to dispense discipline fairly?

As a junior in the boarding house then, the detention system and the way it operated always ensured that the period immediately after Saturday breakfast would be fraught with anxiety and some foreboding. Whatever plans one might have for the Saturday could be ruined in an instant. Instead of yearned-for freedom, a detention meant helping the housemaster with what would be some onerous tasks around the school premises. Tidying up classrooms, picking up litter, sweeping the dirt off the tarmac tennis court adjoining the dining room and suchlike. For a period during the winter term of 1966 and into the early part of 1967, a Saturday detention within the boarding house meant being 'voluntarily' enrolled into the team of boarders assisting with the building of the swimming pool. It was being constructed adjoining the south aspect of the main school building. The foundations were dug out each weekend by those in detention, although the digging also formed part of the woodwork lessons during the school week. The problem was that it generally meant that one was involved in the task for far longer than one hour, the normal length of a detention. On occasions, the work would be on-going all afternoon, effectively taking all of the supposed free time available to boarders on a Saturday. Keeping out of detention at that time was, therefore, imperative and a considerable amount of pleading regularly took place with the prefects if one was given a detention. Generous offers would be made, therefore, to assist in any task that they might need doing in order to successfully have the detention rescinded!

Then at the end of Saturday breakfast, with the detentions delivered to the unfortunate souls sitting on those wooden benches who had misbehaved, the obvious disillusionment they felt would only partially be negated by the pocket money for the coming week being handed out. This involved everyone's name being called out in turn, at which point one would walk up to the housemaster on duty to collect the two shillings and sixpence. It was yours to spend as you wished. A visit to Mrs Edmondson, in charge of the school tuck shop, would most likely be the first port of call. But money also had to be allocated for buying the next set of British commemorative stamps that were due out, the details of which will have been gleaned from the last boarding house 'stamp collecting club' meeting. A typical commemorative stamp set from that era would generally cost upwards of what was then a week's pocket money, so a degree of elementary planning would always be necessary to ensure some money had been saved from the previous week. Otherwise, there would be no cash for sweets! Basic economics – yes – but a lesson in money-management, nonetheless. Not everyone heeded the lesson and there would often be a request amongst immediate friends to borrow money, to be repaid the following week.

Mrs Lister, Postmistress at Low Bentham Post Office, would always be ready and waiting for the influx of young boarders who would, without fail, troop through the Post Office door in Low Bentham on a Saturday morning, following the issuing of a set of commemorative stamps. "Are you all wanting a set of the new stamps?" she would ask in a reassuring and patient voice. A collective nod of heads and murmured confirmation would follow from the young boarders all squeezed into her confined customer area. "Right", and she would then confirm just how much of that week's pocket money and savings she needed. "The cost of a set of British Paintings is 2s 7d so if you can have your money ready, please". It was a request delivered in a kindly manner, not at all as an instruction. She would then proceed by carefully tearing off an individual stamp from a sheet for each denomination before handing them over in a small paper bag so that they would not get irretrievably bent, and thereby ruined, on the way back to school. If available funds permitted, then an additional set of commemoratives could be purchased to stick on an envelope to obtain a 'First Day Cover', with the stamps being given a careful imprint, courtesy of Mrs Lister's official Low Bentham Post Office date stamp. In this way, the stamps received a nice tidy frank from Mrs Lister and meant that the envelope did not have to be sent through the postal system and be subject to any type of random frank by the Royal Mail. The (unofficial) use of a 'Bentham Grammar School' envelope added to the 'First Day Cover' interest and – yes – excitement. Whilst the covers would, almost inevitably, only ever have a token value, they formed part of the whole stamp collecting craze within the boarding house at that time. The collecting 'bug' was impossible to suppress. It formed an integral part of boarding life.

The interest in collecting both stamps and train engine numbers at a young age satisfied some strange inner urge, with any attempt to explain it to the uninitiated doomed to failure! Why doomed to failure? Well, precisely because there was no logical clear-cut reason as to what benefit accrued from collecting stamps or engine numbers other than it was rather good fun. And innocent fun for all that. For some reason, it satisfied an inner yearning for collecting which was particularly strong as a young teenager. Now, as a young adult (as the school terms the 6th form pupils), that urge has receded somewhat, being replaced by pop music and a growing interest in the opposite sex! Back in the early years of boarding school life, it was a close-run thing as to which was more popular – train spotting or stamp collecting. Most certainly, though, both were well ahead of any interest in girls.

The school had actively encouraged the stamp collecting hobby in an era when it was still a relatively popular pastime in society and indeed, that popularity cut across all age bands. The school stamp collecting club, the membership of which was most specifically linked to the boys' boarding house, was at that time organised and overseen by the then resident housemaster and geography teacher, Mr Philip Sydney Jackson.

Known throughout the school at that time, and indeed in the current era, by the simple nickname of "Jake" – or more bluntly as "fat Jake" – his familiar, almost rotund, figure was a reassuring and kindly one, particularly for fresh-faced boys commencing life in an unfamiliar boarding school environment. Rather than walking, he always appeared to glide along the corridors and for reasons never quite clear, pupils would let out a chorus of "beep-beep" as he was seen approaching or passing by! Jake took it in his stride with the faintest of a knowing smile on his face.

Teachers almost inevitably have reputations attached to them, mostly unfairly (but not always) it must be admitted, by scurrilous schoolchildren. Fat Jake, it was widely believed and accepted, lived almost entirely on a diet of Mars bars. This was why, in the view of those in the boarding house, his bodily shape had an uncanny resemblance to a beach ball. Rotund or corpulent might be more specific, albeit unkind, adjectives! This fixation that the boarders had with his extraordinary diet was based solely on intermittent visits to his room in the attic of the boarding house, generally to be admonished following some minor infringement of the rules. There would almost certainly be two or three Mars bars on his sideboard. In addition, spread indiscriminately around the confectionary in that bachelor abode, would be an array of fossils – all different shapes, sizes and colours – testament to his first (and only?) love, Geology. With regard to the Mars bars, one surmised that they were definitely not languishing on his sideboard ready to be given to the residents of the boarding house and so it was blindingly obvious to all that Jake consumed them on an evening after dinner.

Once this type of reputation has been given to a teacher, for better or worse, it is never lost. Jake, presently still the school geography teacher but no longer resident in the boarding house, is to this day still thought to have a yearning for the popular chocolate bar. Quite clearly in the here and now, with Jake living away from the boarding house premises, the confidence among the pupils regarding his devotion to Mars bars must be mere conjecture. Accurate or not, it is a reputation that will undoubtedly remain with him until he relinquishes his teaching post.

The school Mars bar fanatic! Geography teacher and one-time boarding house master – 'Jake'. His enclave in the attic of the boarding house would be home to an array of fossils, the famous chocolate bar and a cane he nicknamed 'Jemima'!
(Photograph: J. Hebblethwaite)

*[**Mars bars** -- as an aside, it has been alleged that whilst Jake was in the process of moving out of the boarding house at the end of the school year in July 1971 and being assisted in the process by some of the senior boarders, he had volunteered the fact that he did not particularly like Mars bars! How can such a protestation be believed? In the words of a sceptical 6th form lad, "he would say that". The Mars bars reputation has to – and will – remain, whether it be justified or not. It has become part of Bentham Grammar School lore.]*

Notwithstanding the humorous reputation attached to him, the stamp collecting craze and attendant membership of the stamp collecting club with Jake was always enjoyable. He invariably passed on his enthusiasm for the hobby to the juniors in the boarding house. Indeed, geography lessons with Jake for the junior boarders also had there humorous moments. How, one imagines, he must have smiled to himself when teaching the third year about the land mass of the South American continent. The study of the topography of Peru would always include Lake Titicaca, the highest inland lake in the world. It caused much amusement to juvenile teenagers with its obvious slightly vulgar overtones. The mere mention of the lake in class was sufficient to cause a ripple of laughter, giggles and silly faces being pulled, and not just from the boys!

The vast majority of pupils who have been taught by Jake, and indeed, those who are still being taught by him at the school will, without doubt, be familiar with that slight purse of the lips, the merest hint of a smile and the piercing eyes displayed by him, all accompanied by a "mmmm" from the back of his throat. It was at that point that one knew full well that a geographical answer given during a lesson was somewhat wide of the mark. He would hardly need to utter a reply as his facial expression told all. Alternatively, if a pupil was not paying sufficient attention or was misbehaving, then a piece of board chalk would soon be winging its way towards them from Jake's hand. He had a good aim, from years of practice no doubt! Whilst his keen eye for geology was indeed legendary throughout the school, his aim with pieces of chalk was also renowned. His aim was rarely erratic. Nevertheless, being hit by chalk was always preferable to being hit by a flying board rubber, far larger and harder than chalk, which one might be on the receiving end of in some of the other teachers' lessons! At least Jake kept the board rubber for its specific purpose rather than launching it as a missile towards unsuspecting pupils.

Teaching Geography up to 6th form level is Jake's specific school subject, but his passion is firmly with Geology, which he also now teaches to 'A' Level standard. His rounded face will light up at the merest mention of layers of rock strata. Teaching at the school within sight of the Pennine range is clearly manna from heaven for him. If an explanation is needed for the weird and wonderful rock layers that lie within the Pennine district to the east of the school, then our Geography teacher, as the resident connoisseur, is an obvious point of contact.

As time has moved on, with the 1960s being replaced by the present, supposedly more modern, early 1970s, the stamp collecting hobby at the school and indeed, in society at large, seems to have gone into a steady and seemingly terminal decline. At the school, this is partly, perhaps, because of the recent departure from the boarding house of Jake and the fragmentation of the stamp collecting club as a consequence. Notwithstanding this, there is no doubt that the hobby is beginning to be seen as somewhat 'unfashionable'. Perhaps this is a shame. At this grammar school, it gave young teenagers a rudimentary grounding in various subjects which were not, at that time, necessarily covered in the basic school curriculum. The fairly recent introduction of Culture as a school lesson for the junior forms has helped in providing a general understanding of some aspects of life not specifically covered in the core school subjects – for instance, nature study, debating and local history. Before Culture made its appearance in the school timetable – an early innovation of Mr Kaye, the new Headmaster appointed in 1967 – stamps partly performed the culture function and played their part in a pupil's assimilation of general knowledge. The *'British Paintings'* UK stamp set issued in early July 1967, for instance, introduced the boarding house, young and old, to George Stubbs and his magnificent horses, as well as L.S. Lowry, with his rather strange looking matchstick figures. His 'Children coming Out of School' 1s 6d value stamp depicted a school in the midst of an industrial landscape, quite alien to Bentham Grammar School and its surrounds. This clear difference in the vastly differing landscapes of two educational establishments was perhaps lost on young teenagers. Now, over five years later, looking to the west on this Sunday afternoon with the railway disappearing into rural Lancashire and with the Pennine chain and the Yorkshire Dales to the east, it is easy to be more than grateful for an education in a truly rural landscape. It is a vista that, for this particular boarder, feels very much like 'home territory', even though 'home' is nominally a considerable distance away.

A wider general knowledge of the world around us could also be obtained via the collecting of stamps and with being an active member of the once thriving school stamp collecting club. There was indeed some excitement in obtaining stamps, for example, from Rhodesia & Nyasaland, Pitcairn Island (bringing with it memories of watching, as a child, the feature length film 'Mutiny on the Bounty' at the cinema), Nigeria and Trinidad and Tobago. Where were these countries? A school atlas faithfully provided the answer. With the school providing a surrogate home to a good number of boarding pupils whose parents lived and worked overseas, there was always an opportunity to obtain stamps from all the main continents with, perhaps, the exception of Australia. There would, therefore, always be considerable excitement among young teenagers at the start of a new term when stamps from other countries could be bartered for, not necessarily with a straight exchange of stamps, but sometimes in exchange for food from a well filled tuck box or by offering other 'collectables'!

CHAPTER V

KEEP STILL, McCART!

What then of corporal punishment? The growing nostalgia felt for those early days in the boarding house does not extend to the painful memory and experience of receiving the cane, whether it was justified or not, for wrongdoing. Whilst the use of this form of sanction was not widespread in the main school or, indeed, in the boarding house, it nevertheless existed. It will have done in a majority of public and private schools. Perhaps there was nothing malicious in it being metered out to boys in the boarding house when they had transgressed. It was clearly considered necessary on those occasions when it was used. (No cane, of course, for the girls, who received, instead, a ruler across the palm of the hand.)

Within the boarding house, it was dispensed by the resident housemaster or his deputy whilst, during the school day, it was the headmaster's prerogative. Fighting was perhaps the most common cause of the cane being administered. Cane or no cane, it was always safer and far more interesting to be a spectator rather than an active participant with a fight, whether it be in the school playground or in the boarding house. The start of a fight between boys (and it always was boys) would spread around the playground surrounds like wildfire. "Fight, Fight!", would ring out from those near to the fracas and within a few moments, a large crowd would be in attendance, cheering on one or other of the lads involved. It was never too long before either a teacher or prefect would intervene, much to the disappointment of the overly enthusiastic audience who would then quickly and silently disperse. The two who had been involved in the combat would then be led away to the headmaster's room to face the inevitable. It would involve a backside and a small thin flexible rod! Thus, an innocent lad – perhaps defending himself against a bully – would face an unjust punishment. Indeed, one lad unfairly accused had, apparently, argued his case vehemently with the headmaster and, in desperation, had snatched the cane from the headmaster's hand (just prior to the strokes being administered!) and broken it in two! Clearly, the passion displayed had been sufficient on that occasion and the lad was let off with a stern warning – successfully escaping six of the best!

Perhaps, looking back, with the practice of caning having been all but eliminated, it was not the fact that the cane was experienced, but more often the inherent unfairness of why it had been given in the first place. That was what rankled. There remains still the abiding memory of a *Jaffa* orange that went "missing" from the bedside cabinet belonging to J.... W..... The simple case of a missing orange would not, ordinarily, be of any undue concern, except on this particular occasion, he claimed that it had been stolen. Would anyone in that dormitory really want to steal an orange? Really? Everybody had their own tuck box, kept in a downstairs cloakroom below the dormitory, all of which would hold varying amounts of food, including fruit. Why then would anyone, therefore, steal an orange? Had someone, perhaps, done it as a prank? Had he already eaten it? He claimed not and J....., clearly feeling that the loss was sufficiently grave, duly reported the missing orange to Jake, the duty housemaster. The perpetrator was given twenty-four hours to own up. Otherwise, warned Jake, with that familiar purse of his lips, "the whole dormitory will have to see me tomorrow evening." Stalemate.

So, seven young teenagers – the whole dormitory, excluding the erstwhile owner of that *Jaffa* – were lined up outside the housemaster's study after dinner the following evening. The procession was then instructed to walk in – one at a time – to receive three strokes of the cane. Punishment from a cane that, allegedly and perhaps rather perversely, Jake called 'Jemima'! "Trousers down, bend over!" Then the immediate searing pain as the cane and one's delicate bum made contact. It was impossible not to sob and in addition, to jump away with an involuntary move from where one had been bent over. Worse still, there was going to be another two strokes to follow and there was an irresistible urge to keep moving away before the next stroke was administered. "Keep still, McCart!" Oh dear! After the punishment had been dispensed, one then had to walk past the remaining friends who were still lined up outside the study awaiting their punishment. (Confucius, had he been there to dispense suitable advice – he is now the 6th form has been reached – would without doubt have suggested, "Never be first in the queue for punishment, but neither be last." After all, one does not want to hear too many squeals before one's own turn.) The other lads in the queue would have heard the squeals and they would see the tears. It was most unlikely that it would help them take their medicine. If anything, it made waiting for it worse.

The pain – it quickly subsided – but the evidence, the red lines across the backside, were visible for some considerable time and were always proudly compared between friends when back in the dormitory. With typical bravado, claims would also then be made that one hadn't cried, albeit it was quite evident that most had. Those that *really* had not cried – well, they were brave. Heroes almost!

What about Jake? Had he enjoyed dispensing physical punishment to seven young lads merely because an orange had gone missing? Did he think it fair? Was there one lad within the group who justifiably received punishment for stealing and was it worth six others receiving the same punishment unfairly? Just perhaps, he did enjoy dispensing that particular form of chastisement. After all, one lad had apparently suffered three strokes across the backside every night for five days, Jake administering such discipline until the lad had apologised for his 'crime'! The problem was, he didn't know what he had done to deserve such punishment. Eventually, after the five days, Jake relented, telling him not to run along the school corridors in the future. (So, that was MY crime, the lad had ruefully acknowledged!)

Notwithstanding all the unanswered questions regarding the theft of an orange and the punishment handed out to a bunch of innocents because of it (well, to six of them at the very least), J.... W..... lost, for some considerable time, a nucleus of friends from within that dormitory. The orange? It never re-appeared. Just as well!

Perhaps in some respects, the pendulum has now well and truly swung towards the pupils, with the introduction in 1967, under the aegis of new headmaster, Mr Kaye, of what is termed a 'School Council'. What is to be made of the meetings? The cynical view among the pupils is that they are merely a sop to make it appear that pupils are getting involved with, or are having, an input into school life. These meetings held every three weeks, without doubt generated a good deal of interest at the outset. They were used, almost without exception, by pupils to let off steam about any school rule to which they disagreed. Are the meetings a vehicle to argue the toss with those who have opposing views or a sensible venue and outlet for reasoned debate? The usual topics raised their head initially and continue to figure largely in meetings; length of hair (only for the boys!), school uniform, detentions, etc., but the frustrations and 'needle' that the earlier meetings produced have largely dissipated. At least, the meetings no longer have the feel of a workers' protest group being overseen by shop stewards. (The shop stewards being, of course, the 6th form prefects. The teachers are, obviously, the Management.) Isn't school for learning? Shouldn't rules be obeyed? Maybe so, but only if one is in agreement with them. Have the meetings made pupils more responsible? Probably not and interest in them has gradually waned. In any case, there has been a gradual relaxation of the school rules over the past few years, a direct consequence of a new headmaster and indeed, of the times we now live in. (Any claim that the school council meetings have played their part is, perhaps, slightly disingenuous.)

An enforced visit to the headmaster's study was something to be avoided, if possible, at all costs. The dread of waiting outside his large and ornate room proved almost as frightening as being called in. Oh, the cramp in the pit of the stomach once the door opened and a tall foreboding figure ushered one through to that largely unknown and unseen 'inner sanctum'. The first year at school had been under the headmastership of John Le Plastrier Webb, B.Sc. (London), otherwise known within the confines of the 'Cottage' dormitory as "Plasticine Webb". This nickname was linked to the middle part of his name, which always seemed to be a rather odd addition, such was the haphazard thinking of the junior boys. He had been in charge of the school since 1946, shortly before the subsequent purchase of the rectory from the Church Commissioners, had successfully oversaw the move into the new premises in 1947 and had stayed until relatively recently, retiring in 1967. Throughout his headmastership he gradually and successfully increased pupil numbers, whilst boosting the standard of educational achievement in the process.

Tall, lean and authoritative in appearance with a rather gaunt face, a pointed nose and white wispy hair that was thinning, he appeared as a formidable figure to young teenagers. He was, though, generally a mystery figure whom one would only normally see every day at the morning assembly. Just occasionally he would enter the classroom in the middle of a lesson, seemingly unannounced and with no prior warning. Without being requested or cajoled, the class would then rise to their feet as one and stand to attention. Having received a suitable acknowledgement and a gesture that one could sit back down, he would stand watching proceedings for, perhaps, five minutes before taking his leave. Once he had closed the classroom door behind him, there would be an almost audible and collective sigh of relief from everyone, including the teacher. For what purpose were these visits made? Quite probably it was to watch and assess the ability of the teacher but to youngsters, his unannounced visit always used to make for an awkward and an uncomfortable lesson. Why so? The obvious fear was that a question would be asked and directed at oneself and, horror of horrors, the answer would not be known. The worry was that this might well happen whilst Plasticine Webb was stood watching. It was apposite to keep one's head down and to try and stay anonymous during the headmaster's classroom visits. Head well down, no looking up and hoping against hope that one did not hear the dreaded, "McCart, do you know the answer?" It was a ploy that would not always work!

Mr Webb's imposing and authoritative presence was no better witnessed than at the morning assembly. With a raised stage at one end of the Assembly Hall, he would stand in the middle of it wearing the regulation gown with all the teachers sat behind him in chairs that were arranged in the shape of a crescent. In the format of strict segregation, the schoolmasters would be sitting on the left and the schoolmistresses on the right, cementing the rigid policy of Plasticine Webb, that of formal separation of male and female throughout school life. Nevertheless, the school was advertised as 'co-educational'. This segregation also manifested itself within the classroom with the girls and boys in the same classroom, yes, but on different sides of the room. The wearing of gowns in morning assembly also appeared to be compulsory for the teachers and in consequence, the odd teacher who attended without the regulation gown was considered, by the junior boarders at least, to be not quite as intelligent as the rest. Did they perhaps feel inadequate on display before the school without a gown – a gown being proudly worn by the rest of their compatriots?

Above the headmaster, at the top of the stage, a large ornately made wooden plaque proudly displaying the school crest:

(Digital version supplied by Diane Clements - née Lumb)

With the familiar crescent and wavy lines, a reminder to all of the history of the school. The routine and format of morning assembly was always very predictable, with the concentration on a religious slant and, for schoolchildren at least, hardly interesting. Perhaps the most memorable episode in morning assembly in recent times took place under the headship of Mr Webb's successor, Mr Kaye. The new headmaster made a subtle change to the morning routine by asking that (or making) the teachers sit down on benches beside and facing their form pupils, leaving himself alone on the stage to supervise proceedings. Whilst he was delivering various items of news one particular morning, a fire extinguisher inexplicably fell from its wall mount, hit the floor and proceeded to spray out foam. Unperturbed, Mr Kaye merely picked it up and after saying, "I don't think we need this!" he proceeded to open the stage window and let go of it (so it would drop to the playground below). He then carried on with assembly as if nothing had happened, much to the amusement of the assembled throng!

CHAPTER VI

LET US PRAY

Silence, then, was the order of the day and night. The associated punishments for not observing it pervaded most aspects of boarding school life. With the close link between school and church, perhaps the most important silence of all would be whilst walking in line to a compulsory Sunday church service, after having formed a dead straight line outside the school entrance doors at 10am in formal school uniform. This would always include the school cap and school blazer, although the cap would automatically be taken off in deference as one entered the church.

Before walking to church, the obligatory inspection by the boarding house prefects. Had one cleaned one's shoes? Had one's tie been correctly done up and positioned? Had one's hair been combed neatly? Indeed, had it been combed at all? Are the socks pulled up to the knee? Have all the buttons been done up on the blazer? All part of the church service inspection, whilst the peal of bells sounded out to remind those lined up that it was a 10.30am start. A few fortunate souls were exempt from this weekly ritual by virtue of either a religious belief not in tune with the Church of England creed (most probably they were 'Roman Catholics') or because they or, more specifically, their parents were 'non-believers'. At that time, it did actually seem odd that a few school colleagues were being educated at a school linked to the church when their parents had no time for the teachings of the church. Then again, one's own parents had never shown any interest or enthusiasm for religion. With hindsight, perhaps an exemption from that repetitive Sunday service should have been sought via parents. It is, however, unlikely they would have agreed, despite not possessing any religious fervour. (Probable reply – "Do as you are told.")

Perhaps these days, an exemption is not particularly wanted. In some strange, non-religious way which is difficult to quantify, the church service is interesting, intriguing even. It provides, for better or worse, a regimented order to the weekend activities. In retrospect, the religious side of a boarding education was, most likely, not given any thought by parents who almost certainly belonged to the secular part of society in the (so-called) permissive 1960s. It was, no doubt, sufficient to have found a suitable boarding school, within the framework of fees that were going to be paid by a government employer, which was domiciled reasonably close to relatives by the North Lancashire coast. The religious slant of this school, or any school in truth, was most probably absent from the thought process.

After inspection, the walk to church in silence along the short pathway that linked the main school entrance with the churchyard. This, no doubt, was the path the incumbent rector will have taken umpteen times in years gone by. Now, it was the most recent generation of schoolchildren treading the same route, walking past gravestones in what was undoubtedly the oldest part of the churchyard. Young teenagers had no interest in studying the old tombstones of course, some of which were almost hidden in rampant foliage with the careful tendering of the graves no longer taking place. Had the relatives lost interest? Had they moved away? Had they themselves passed away? Had the local family link with the deceased been lost? Whatever the circumstances, that part of the churchyard appeared uncared for and largely ignored and even for uninterested teenagers, it was nigh impossible not to notice the neglect. The long-time departed in that section of the churchyard were indeed left in peace, save for the motley collection of school boarders who walked past them every Sunday on their best behaviour. Whilst passing by the many graves, did the otherwise truculent churchgoers ever give any thought to the passage of time and to the fragility of life and to mortality? Of course not. Young minds were fixed firmly on what was for Sunday lunch and what the plans were for that same afternoon once a church service had been negotiated. Sunday afternoon was a period of freedom. Freedom from lessons, freedom from homework, freedom from the prying eyes of duty prefects. Sunday afternoons would mean being alone with school friends, walking out along the surrounding country lanes or partaking in that most popular of hobbies – trainspotting. Sunday afternoons were to be treasured. The only problem was that for young teenagers, they just did not last long enough.

The large, heavy, solid wooden front doors of the church would already be open, the church eagerly awaiting the boarding house ensemble. There wasn't much that enquiring teenage eyes failed to notice and there was, therefore, always a quick glance up whilst walking through the church porch to look almost in awe at the enormous church bell, stained a dirty-green, hanging above the entrance. Was it securely fixed in place? Would it perhaps fall one day on a parishioner? Such thoughts occupied young minds. The mouldy-green colouring betrayed the bell's copper heritage, but to teenagers that was quite irrelevant. To a twelve-year-old, it was just a very old and large antique bell – but it has, in fact, been hanging in the porch since a partial rebuild of the belfry in 1891. Unlikely then that it would just fall, but in the minds of impressionable youngsters, well you just never knew. Perhaps it might just suddenly fall. There was, therefore, always an almost imperceptible quickening of the pace to get through the porch quickly and enter the church, often involving giving the lad in front the slightest of pushes in order to speed things up!

St. John the Baptist Church, Lower Bentham
(Copyright: The Frith Collection)

It was the Churchwarden who felt that it was necessary to give teenage boarders the background to this huge bell. "Well boys, I can tell you that this bell dates back to the fifteenth century and has a Latin inscription on it which you boys will not understand," he announced confidently. He was right, of course, as Latin was not on the school curriculum until 5th form. "When translated into English," he continued, "it says: *When rung, I am called Mary, the Rose of the World.*" Such a phrase elicited an obvious question to the Churchwarden. "When was it last rung?" The Churchwarden did not know. Perhaps no one living now knew and that being the case, to youngsters, it was intriguing. Nevertheless, whatever the translation signified or meant, to young teenagers it was, indeed, just a large dirty-green bell. A dirty-green certainly, but it always warranted a furtive glance as one walked quickly into the church. Leaving that Holy place at the end of the service, the priority was to get back to the dormitory to get changed and the ancient bell was then hardly given a second glance.

*[**An aside**: This copper-stained bell hanging in the porch – according to one or two locals, it was used – until quite recent times – during village*

funerals. It seems that when the funeral cortege reached the road bridge over the Wenning – having progressed in the necessary slow manner from Low Bentham village – a member of the church would then start to toll the bell very slowly. A form of welcome one might suppose! No doubt it was to acknowledge the passing from this life into the next for the unfortunate soul involved. To ring the bell, it will require a long stick with a hook on the end which can then connect onto the bell clapper. Perhaps old traditional customs are dying out. The bell has not been heard tolling whilst in and around the boarding house – during or after school time – at least, not since 1966. So, the old bell, stained with the passage of many centuries, has earned its keep! Will it ever be used again? It seems unlikely.]

Another set of doors guarded the entrance into the 'inner sanctum' of the church from the porch, but not this time as heavy or unwieldy as the main entrance doors. These doors would swing open and swing back to shut immediately if not being held open. On walking through them, the nostrils immediately encountered that familiar musty aroma associated with places that have been shut up and have lacked the inflow of fresh air. Not in this instance an unpleasant smell, more a reassuring one inextricably linked with ancient churches. A rather strange austere fragrance. The smell is, perhaps, one of ancient history. Hundreds of years of Anglican history captured in a unique kind of odour. Strangely enticing and comforting. If one was to be blindfolded and then taken on a mystery trip, it would be immediately apparent from the aroma that one had been taken into Low Bentham church. Indeed, the same might possibly apply with any other small English country church for that matter.

Once inside that Holy place, absolute silence, of course, whilst filing in to sit on the right-hand section of six pews facing the altar and the reredos, this part being reserved exclusively for the boarding house boys. Then the boarding house girls would arrive and sit in the left-hand set of six rows of pews, girls and boys being intentionally kept apart during this era, leaving the middle section of pews for the ordinary parishioners. Silence whilst sat in the pews waiting. Waiting indeed for the service to begin but never sat patiently and forever fidgeting and gazing up at the wooden frames on the ceiling or else aimlessly looking around. Young minds were active. Thinking and pondering, whilst looking – but never asking!

Now, six years later, there is still the impulse to look around this ancient church whilst waiting for a Sunday service to commence, but it no longer means looking around without purpose. Glancing around now is to soak up six hundred years plus of history in this Norman church, with various artefacts quietly on display. Ancient stained-glass windows – with predictable religious messages and themes – and on an inside window ledge beside the reserved boarding house pews, part of a Saxon Crucifix found during nineteenth-century restoration work and reputedly over a thousand years old. Even to the non-religious within the boarding house who are compelled to attend the weekly service, there is a slight feeling of awe within these religious surrounds, always with the reassuring background accompaniment of church bells. Otherwise just a pregnant and polite silence.

The boarding house pupils were invariably the first to file into church, no doubt by design, to then keep the church entrance and aisles free for the dedicated Sunday morning worshippers – the regulars. Perhaps there were plenty of sinners in Low Bentham, perhaps not. Whatever, the hard-core of regulars never numbered more than a dozen to fifteen reliable souls coming to have their sins forgiven. (And that remains the case to this day.) The rest of the villagers presumably hoped their sins would be forgiven without the need to attend church. They would no doubt be ready to provide a genuine reason for non-attendance if challenged by the rector, for indeed the Revd Boden Parker would not hesitate to seek them out within the confines of the village in an effort to establish a reason for their (what he might term) "unaccountable absence". A story circulating recently told how a Low Bentham resident (a young mother), on being challenged by the rector regarding her absence at church the previous Sunday, replied solemnly, "Well, there was an urgent need for some baking to be done for my family", followed up by an enthusiastic and more cheery, "I feel sure that the Lord will understand". The Lord may indeed have understood, but the rector most definitely did not.

Reading matter in the church was kindly provided via the *Book of Common Prayer*. Seemingly full of mumbo-jumbo to a twelve-year-old lad – and it was always a puzzle as to why the book continually referred to the 'Catholic Church' when we were sat in a Church of England establishment! – anxious for the service to commence, whilst all the time, the head would be twisted around to witness the arrival of the familiar Sunday parishioners, who would filter in and claim, almost by right, their usual pew, with an individual cushion on the pew awaiting their arrival. Even the seemingly elderly local farmers, sporting ruddy faces that were etched with years of outdoor toil, took advantage of the cushions provided, but for them, one always imagined, generally only as a support for creaking bones as they knelt to pray.

"Head to the front, McCart! And you, Denson!" The voice of a boarding house prefect would sound out in a rather suppressed tone in keeping with the general ambience of the surrounds, but it was always a firm instruction, nonetheless. Only the church bells interrupted the air of silence – a strange eerie, foreboding silence unique to churches, the bells suitably dovetailing in with the surrounding country landscape and strangely consoling and comforting, although sounding somewhat muffled when heard from inside the church. Someone once said that there is a "quality" to the silence in church (however one might define quality in the context of silence) but there was certainly no quality in the silence within Low Bentham church. That, at least, was the opinion of young teenagers, always fidgeting impatiently on the pews whilst waiting for the service to start. And was that eerie silence speaking to the assembled congregation? If it was (and indeed, if it still is) it will surely be ignoring the 'rabble' from the respective boys' dormitories.

When inside the church as a young boarder, there was always the inescapable feeling that, somehow, one was being watched, but not in this instance by the school prefects. Instead, by someone invisible. It was a concept that young teenagers found impossible to comprehend. Was there someone watching or not? Whatever, even to non-religious teenagers wanting to escape the claustrophobic confines of a religious building as soon as possible, there was a feeling of safety within the silence and listening to the peal of bells. It was akin to lying in bed at night as a young child, perhaps, and hearing heavy rain lashing onto the bedroom window, but knowing there was safety being tucked up under the bed sheets. It made the protection provided by the bed, and indeed the bedroom, even more cosy.

Sometimes there would be a request for more bell ringers from within the boarding house ranks. It may have been rather pleasant to listen to the church bells and they gave a strange continuity to the second part of the weekend – but to be involved in learning to pull the bells? No, thank you! Football practice easily took preference on a Friday evening if it was a choice between soccer or being shown how to ring church bells. It was no contest, particularly when one had to keep in contention for the position of goalkeeper in the Under-13 school football team. Not even the prospect of an occasional evening meal at a restaurant for the bell ringers provided by the rector, or sumptuous (allegedly) suppers at the rectory would alter the decision. Football was for the boys. Bell ringing? Well!

Whilst the tenor bell and the treble, two of the six church bells, continued to ring out, there would be no prospect of the service commencing. Eventually, however, the domineering appearance of the formidable Revd Reginald Boden Parker from the vestry, enrobed in a white cassock, prayer book in hand and with what appeared to be a long black scarf around his neck, gave a sure indication that the service would shortly commence. That was the cue to pick up the tatty copy of *Hymns Ancient and Modern*, which the Churchwarden had handed over on entering the church and to skim quickly to the page of the first hymn from the list displayed above the lectern. (Unless, of course, this had already been done in an idle moment whilst waiting.) Once the rector reached the bell tower behind the congregation and had (what was assumed) a small pep-talk with the assembled choir – no doubt in the form of a small prayer – the church bells would at last fall silent. That was the cue for the organist, the ever-reliable Miss Robinson. She would be galvanised into action, vigorously pumping the eighty-year-old church organ, with its 1,900 pipes, (1,900 – really? It hardly looks big enough...) and the first hymn listed on the board by the lectern would commence. Hurrah!

Immortal, invisible, God only wise,
In light inaccessible hid from our eyes,
Most blessed, most glorious, the Ancient of days,
Almighty, victorious, Thy great name we praise...

The singing would be accompanied by the Revd Parker, with his choir now in tow, walking back up the main aisle from the bell tower. Once the lectern had been reached, he would turn to face his congregation with a beaming face, no doubt pleased to see (in terms of numbers) a healthy congregation, courtesy of course of the boys and girls from their respective boarding houses, whilst allowing the choir to filter into the side stalls behind the lectern – girls and women to the left, boys and men to the right. Standing large and with his booming voice, the Revd Parker indeed led the way with the singing, providing a great show of gusto and passion. The junior boarders could only watch, almost open-mouthed, at that weekly spectacle.

To all life Thou givest, to both great and small,
In all life thou livest, the true life of all.
We blossom and flourish as leaves on the tree,
And wither and perish, but nought changeth Thee.

Did anyone in the choir notice, one wonders, that walking up the aisle involved stepping on the tombs of families buried underneath that walkway in the early part of the nineteenth century? Who was he – William Ellershaw buried with his faithful wife Elizabeth? They had been entombed under the aisle floor in 1808 and 1811 respectively. They both reached a ripe old age in early nineteenth-century terms (seventy-one and seventy-five respectively) and will have heard about Nelson's triumph at Trafalgar in their later years. Then, buried inside the church for eternity. They were clearly residents of the Bentham area, holding a position of some importance, one might assume, to have had a burial within the church rather than in the church grounds. However, to young teenagers, their background and position in local society were quite irrelevant, but it was intriguing to think that this couple and their family were buried underneath the aisle. Just how many pairs of shoes have stepped on their tombstone in the intervening years without giving a thought to the passage of time? It is only now, when in the school 6th form, that local history has become more relevant and of some interest. Young boarders were not to know that the 'Ellershaw' name has a history going back many centuries in the Bentham area. Indeed, a possible link there might possibly have been with the Grammar School through Henry Ellershaw and Richard Ellershaw respectively, effectively deputy headmasters of the school in the late-eighteenth century, although the official term in that era was as an 'usher', rather than deputy headmaster. As was fairly common practice at the time, Richard had also taken holy orders, there being a closely entwined link between the church and education at a time when literacy was confined to those in the higher echelons of society.

And then, at the end of the first hymn, the ever-predictable booming tones of Revd Parker, saying for the first of several times during the service, **"Let us pray"**! So, it was time for prayers and the boarding house pupils would give a rather sluggish half-hearted shuffle forward on the hard wooden surface and spend the time in prayer perched on the edge of their respective benches, furtively looking around at each other, suppressing a grin in the knowledge that, if spotted by the prefects, it would mean a certain detention with the associated loss of liberty on the following Saturday morning. Who else had their eyes open during prayers? Most of the boys in the boarding house it seemed. The suspicion was that it was most probably the same across on the pews where the girl boarders were assembled. After all, wasn't it a tad soppy to close one's eyes during prayers? School friends would certainly take a dim view of it. Was it possible to pray without one's eyes being shut? If not, then it seemed clear to a teenage boarder that it was only the loyal local congregation who were actually doing any praying to the Almighty. The rest were seemingly passive spectators waiting impatiently for prayers to finish and for the singing of the next hymn. Would praying do any good in any case? It would still be double woodwork on a Monday afternoon at school and sooner or later, freedom on a Saturday morning would be jeopardised by a detention which, it was always felt, would invariably have been handed out unfairly. What did Milton suggest? *'They also serve who only stand and wait'*. The motley collection of boys from the boarding house most certainly stood and waited (and indeed, they still do) but not for the same thing as a blind Milton waited for. Redemption may, indeed, have been given to a seventeenth-century poet, but to the boarding house in its entirety? Unlikely!

Joining in with the 'responses' whilst the rector read out the canticles during prayers was also somewhat half-hearted, despite the fact that they were known off by heart with the church service following the very same pattern every week. With an identical and familiar format, the pages of the Common Prayer book would be dutifully turned over to the correct place even before the Revd Parker requested the congregation to go to the *Apostles Creed*. Then, as now, it was a case of following the narrative whilst murmuring it very quietly, or perhaps just staying silent. *I believe in the Holy Spirit, the Holy Catholic Church, the communion of saints, the forgiveness of sins...* (Only now in the 6th form is the distinction understood between the Catholic Church and the Roman Catholic Church.) It mattered not that the boarding house made little effort to join in because a couple of elderly local farmers used their almost operatic sounding voices to fill the church with sufficient noise so that the pathetic combined effort emanating from the boarding house almost went unnoticed. Or so it was always assumed and there never seemed to be any complaint about what was, essentially, clearly a half-hearted involvement.

(Half-hearted – except from Helen, a girl boarder, whose grating voice was so awful that she was actually told to refrain from singing!!)

'Glory be to God' – but only, of course, on condition that the names read out for detention on Saturday morning did not include one's own! *'It is he that hath made us and not we ourselves'* – but how was it that a science lesson had already explained to young teenagers that the earth was formed many millions of years ago? How can that be? Why did *'HE'* wait such a long time before 'making' us? Lots of unanswered questions and a young boarder was happy to let them remain unanswered. Indeed, perhaps they remain unanswered to this very day. Notwithstanding that *'HE'* took so long to decide to 'make us', the assembled congregation (or at least, those who had no involvement with the school – excepting, of course, whoever was on duty as the boarding house master) were keen to *'praise him and bless his name forever'*, which they did numerous times whilst giving thanks for all the works of the Lord. And then, as if that was not enough, they were happy to (and indeed, are still happy to) *'magnify him forever'*. Marvellous!!

Once the Revd Parker strode to the lectern to deliver his weekly sermon, with the assistance of a huge antique-looking bible – with what appeared to be most helpful large print – then the service was progressing nicely with only one final hymn and a quick prayer to follow his thunderous delivery. Young teenagers picked up little of worth from these weekly tirades regarding sin and, ultimately, forgiveness. The attention span in that holy place was, for some reason, a good deal shorter than in a classroom – learning, for example, about the Peruvian Andes or how Charles I lost his crown (and his head). Young boarding pupils did, however, pick up the odd pertinent fact from the weekly sermon – the main one being that sinners would be going to

'Hell'! (And why, oh why, did the rector stare keenly at young boarders when he pronounced that diktat in a menacing manner?) It always seemed more than probable from what he espoused, that the boarding house in its entirety would ultimately perish in 'Hell'! Stephen Kirkwood, a boarder in year five during those early years at boarding school summed it up succinctly with a short piece regarding church,

'Lots of pews for us to use. Lots of space to say our grace. But what's the use?'

One might be forgiven a wry smile as, six years later with those young boarding teenagers having progressed into the 6th form, the style and content of the weekly church service is all but identical and the boarding house pews still see the majority of eyes open during prayers, with heads furtively looking around to see who, if anyone, has their eyes closed. No detentions handed out, however, by this Head Boarder for such behaviour. It is not so many years ago since the head of the boarding house would also peer cheekily around at friends, checking that their eyes were open! It is easy to empathize.

When, eventually, the booming voice of the rector commenced his peroration, that was the point at which there would always be a huge collective and palpable (albeit silent) "hurrah" among the assembled boarders. The many gloomy faces would suddenly look quite cheery and enthusiastic! Following the summing up, the sermon would always be concluded with the rectors wholly predictable and very welcome, *"Here endeth the lesson"*, followed immediately (and just as welcome) by, *"Praise be to God!"* – although it always seemed unlikely that God was keeping a close eye on junior boarding house pupils, however much one might have praised him. Everyone then knew the end was in sight. All that remained was the singing of a final hymn before the rector and choir disappeared back into the bell tower.

With the final hymn, just one last traditional event – the collection. Whilst the congregation sang dutifully (including, at this stage, the boarders, safe in the knowledge that the service was all but over), the Churchwarden would deftly sidle away from his pew and miraculously re-appear holding out a large wooden spatula, with a small cloth bag fixed underneath the spoon part, in the expectation of receiving thanks to the Lord – in the form of the Queen's currency. No contribution, of course, from the boarding house pupils – pocket money was far too valuable to be given away. Instead, a single donation from the housemaster sufficed on behalf of the school. It was up to the 'regulars' to provide the lion's share. The Churchwarden would be the one with the knowledge of who gives what – very important in a small village community. (According to a rather cynical father, the ones able to give the largest financial donation will almost certainly give the least!)

The only question exercising a young boarder's brain was what exactly happened to the money once it was handed over to the rector after being tipped onto a large silver tray he would be holding. (No dud coins in there hopefully…) The rector duly offered the tray, with its bundle of notes and coin, up to the Lord – literally – with arms outstretched. (The Lord, of course, quite unable to spend it…) Was it then the property of the Revd Parker for keeps? A young, innocent, schoolboy assumed as much.

Once out of that Holy place, to the accompaniment of a fresh peal of church bells that formally indicated the end of Sunday morning worship, the rule of silence would end. Indeed, on the short walk back to the boarding house, there was no requirement to be strictly in line but, nevertheless, any hint of running would bring an immediate detention.

This then was typical, no doubt, of any boarding school at prayer. In this instance Bentham Grammar School but no doubt mirrored across the country in the mid-1960s at any Church of England boarding school with strong links between the school and the Church. This link remains cemented by a joint representation on the schools governing body, enabling the church to have an input at the very least into the operation of school life. The long-established Church of St. John the Baptist has been on this site since Norman times and will feel more than entitled to play a key role in major decisions affecting the school and the church/school relationship. Any changes at the school will undoubtedly be closely scrutinised by the incumbent rector and it would be, and still is, something they no doubt feel entitled and obliged to do.

That, then, the Sunday worship as it was – and indeed, as it still is. This weekly ritual (for that is what it is) – what purpose does it serve? Does it commit an individual to a life of praise towards the Lord or, perhaps, will it merely cement a continuing aversion towards the church and religion once these schooldays are completed? One suspects the latter unless, of course, the seemingly non-religious colleagues within this boarding house are actually keeping their religious persuasion very much to themselves. They might be. Within the school, perhaps any school, it appears that there is a rather strange embarrassment in acquiescing to a religious creed. It will need a firm mind and a definite lack of self-consciousness to admit to a belief in God. Within that framework, it is perhaps not the 'done thing' to admit to a religious adherence among 6th form colleagues. If one were to do so, one would quickly become the brunt of a good deal of derision. It is, after all, a bit sissy being religious. (Isn't it?) With religion, one of the earth's darkest places was within the recesses of the mind – for boarding teenagers, that is. Even if there was light *('…and, in earth's darkest place, let there be light.')* it could not – indeed would not – penetrate teenage thinking.

*[**An aside**: during the last academic year – with a mind very much on girls and most definitely not on religion – the weekly Sunday service, for a short period, became much more interesting, courtesy of a new teenage choirgirl. Morag, domiciled in the girls' boarding house, sang with vigour and enthusiasm and it proved nigh impossible not to watch her continuously during the hymn singing. Perhaps she noticed the interest being taken in her, for there was always just the hint of a smile when she looked across to the boarding house prefects sat on the back pew. At other times, her singing would be occasionally interrupted by a large grin when she realised that she was being watched. Everyone else may well have been 'praising the Lord and blessing his name forever', during the weekly ritual of the Benedicite, but rather than praise being directed to the sun and moon, the stars in heaven, the showers and dew, the winds, etc. etc., it was instead silently directed towards young Morag – her delightful adolescent build and nicely protruding bosoms belying her years. This then was certainly the time when there were lessons to be learned about religion – but not the one the Lord was preaching! This other religion was a lesson in the female form and the attractions it presented, either by design or otherwise.*

In addition to the meeting of eyes at the weekly church service, there seemed to be regular mutual acknowledgement of each other during normal school activities, with smiles regularly traded. Nevertheless, further advancement proved to be slow and protracted, perhaps partly through lack of confidence (on both sides) and no doubt because of the seemingly insurmountable gap in the respective school years – Lower 6th and 4th forms, respectively. However, there were, eventually, regular meetings which were, by necessity, at the weekend, as neither party had thought of suggesting the possibility of meeting at break times or during the dinner break. Generally, these meetings were in the Assembly Hall – standing by one of the large windows which looked out northwards, giving a view of the cinder path passing by the kitchens and the 'Cottage'. Privacy – there was none – with the hall being used regularly by boarders on their way to and from the environs of the dining room. Indeed, it was through this Assembly Hall that regular journeys had been made, oh, so many times in those early boarding school weekends, always to the accompaniment of the musical tastes of the era, thanks to the boarder prefects as they played (over and over again... and then again!) their favourite records on the stage. Sounding out almost continuously would be, 'Waterloo Sunset' (The Kinks), 'Pictures of Lily' (The Who), 'House of the Rising Sun' (The Animals), 'A Whiter Shade of Pale' (Procol Harum), 'Matchstick Men' (Status Quo), 'Hole in My Shoe' (Traffic), amongst others – and not forgetting 'The Mighty Quinn' (Manfred Mann). In fact, a hole in my shoe was indeed pertinent – as was very apparent in winter when running onto the playing fields, after wet weather, to spend the time trainspotting!

Regarding young Morag, however, sadly, interests did not dovetail sufficiently, personified perhaps by enthusiasm for First XI football versus choir practice and music. A hand may occasionally have been held – but it (that is, the Head Boarder's hand) had no realistic chance of progressing any further, and quite definitely not towards those quite dazzling (on the basis of a close-up assessment) boobs – for as a 4th former, Morag appeared to be endowed quite generously! Frankly, the 6th former's hand had no chance of further progression on two accounts – the obvious lack of privacy and, more pertinently, an unwillingness on her part (or at least, that was the assumption that a slightly reticent 6th form boarder made) to allow a marauding hand to go anywhere else other than in her hand. Would it have been worth a try? Dear Morag - 'He who would valiant be; against all disaster' – and had this 6th form boarder tried, it surely would have been disaster! Or would it?

The meetings, well they gradually fizzled out without either party doing anything to prevent it and school life moved inexorably on. The occasional smile that still takes place whilst passing each other in the school corridors, or when in the queue for mealtimes serves, perhaps, as a reminder of a friendship that never quite got into its stride, but for the loss of which there were no tears shed. There was, instead, seemingly a mutual acceptance that it had finished almost before it had started. A lost opportunity? Perhaps. A painful experience? Not particularly.]

CHAPTER VII

BUT I AM LEFT-HANDED, SIR

That was, typically, Sunday morning and then the afternoon. Sunday afternoon. Free time for a variety of pursuits, but always niggling away at the back of the mind was the dread of Monday. Not particularly the dread of another school week. No, but rather, the dread and the fear of a double period of woodwork on a Monday afternoon. A dread it indeed was. Just the thought of two lessons of technical drawing and woodwork in the wooden hut adjoining the playground the following day would often be sufficient to ruin what remained of Sunday after the Lord had been praised. Pity the woodwork teacher, Mr Lonsdale. Barking instructions to a teenager who did not honestly know one end of a screwdriver from another was utterly futile and only served to exacerbate the issue. "But I am left-handed, sir." "That's got nothing to do with it, boy." "But sir..."

(Well actually, it does have something to do with it...)

An accomplished joiner and a veteran of WW2, flying Blenheims for the RAF, Mr Joshua Lonsdale (known by his nickname, "Lonny") has successfully overseen a variety of substantial construction projects at the school, which has utilised his expertise as an obvious alternative to instructing outside contractors. His achievements include fitting out a new Biology laboratory, a new Physics laboratory and a new Chemistry laboratory in turn. Also, overseeing the building of a cluster of wooden prefabricated classrooms by the riverside. His undoubted *'piece de resistance'*, however, was the construction of the swimming pool, in the latter part of the 1960s, being assisted in this project, as well as with the others, by the pupils.

There is no denying or doubting his joinery skills. However, teaching a group of young teenage boys how to produce a simple mortise and tenon joint with two pieces of wood was, for him, probably a far more complex task than building wooden classrooms and one which, with some pupils, he would never conquer! Lonny, did you not realise that some will use a hand for writing (and not for chiselling) and that a brain will assist some with the written word, rather than assisting them to get a side and an end elevation correctly proportioned in technical drawing? There was indeed skill and justifiable pride in looking at some of the finished articles made by those pupils with practical skill in their hands. Wooden aircraft, bookcases, kitchen utensils, etc. Very impressive – it was easy to be envious. However, the small number of pupils lacking practical skills struggled to complete even the simplest of jobs involving wood. A letter rack, for example, with a mortise and tenon joint that fitted together so badly that the whole thing wobbled horribly. It would have been quite an embarrassment having to take it home at the end of term. Instead, another option was available. It was conveniently and quietly disposed of in the fast-moving waters of the Wenning!

Lonny gave the various ramshackle attempts at woodwork the visual and verbal contempt that they clearly deserved. Surely, did he not realise that his obvious joinery expertise would always be wasted on some pupils? Those pupils lacking the necessary skills and unable to acquire them, despite Lonny's continual bad-tempered efforts to engrain a modicum of skill into disinterested hands, invariably obtained a verbal bashing and sometimes a physical one. The back of the head or the ears being a favourite and regular target for Lonny's hand. There was some schoolboy admiration and respect for a more senior lad who, frustrated at being regularly clipped over the head for being somewhat belligerent, once exacted revenge by sticking a chisel through Lonny's infamous tweed flat cap, then skewering both chisel and cap onto one of the woodwork benches. How to become a schoolboy hero! It really was the stuff of *The Beano* comic. No one would 'grass' on that daring escapade and, indeed, no one did. There were plenty who felt it entirely justified. Indeed, Lonny's flat cap was a regular target for the venting of frustration. Was it Peter Robinson – alias Robbo, the ever-popular train fanatic (at least, with young train enthusiasts) – or was it, perhaps, another lad from his year who waited one woodwork lesson until Lonny had left the room on an errand and then calmly threw Lonny's hat on the floor (a floor strewn with wood shavings, etc.) and then proceeded to jump on it with considerable force? Feeling much better, the lad then duly picked it up, dusted it off, replaced it from whence it had been taken and continued as normal! Ah, the trials and tribulations of woodwork.

Those original start-of-term joining instructions always included a timely reminder to parents that the cost of repairing any damage to school property (caused by any of the pupils) would be charged to those responsible. Would that, one wondered, have extended to Lonny's trademark flat cap, which must, surely, have needed replacing on a regular basis.

A school report showing a position of fifteenth out of sixteen boys in the form for woodwork (the girls, of course, had their own tribulations with Domestic Science) was accompanied with the rather caustic comment, *'Must make more effort to improve his standard of work.'* That rather blunt overview could not be challenged – it was entirely justified. Nevertheless, improvement there was none and many times, Lonny's patience was tested to the limit and beyond. After two extremely difficult and challenging years of woodwork and technical drawing, which involved regular gnashing of teeth by both teacher and pupil, another school report from Lonny proved there had been no progress with a typical biting comment, *'Practical work and technical drawing are both very poor.'* Technical drawing: very poor? What an injustice. It was abysmal. Drawing lines this way and that on a piece of paper and trying to envisage various elevations was nigh impossible. It made no sense and seemed illogical. It still does – the thought process from 1966 has not changed in the interim period.

Perhaps the easiest part of those fearful woodwork lessons to actually cope with was the initial inspection at the start of a lesson. Inspection? Yes – before commencing the technical drawing, Lonny would carefully inspect everybody's pencil to ensure that it had been sharpened satisfactorily. Not an instruction to "Present Arms", but rather "Present Pencils"! Woe-betide any lad whose pencil had not been sharpened to the required standard – a clip over the ear would almost inevitably follow. The reality was, of course, that however expertly this young boarder's pencil had been sharpened, it made not the slightest difference to the standard of work produced.

Whilst managing to be consistent over a two-year period regarding the placing in class – *always* second from bottom – it was most reassuring to know that at least one fellow pupil's skills were not as good as McCart. An achievement indeed for the lad who managed to keep McCart off the bottom. What a great sense of relief and freedom from anguish (again, for both pupil and teacher one might imagine) when, in later years, the subject was no longer compulsory.

Then in 1967, and only marginally less daunting than woodwork lessons with Lonny, the arrival of husband-and-wife team, Mr and Mrs Croft, to oversee games. Their brief was to provide a more dedicated and defined approach to Physical Education (PE) which took place in the Assembly Hall, conveniently serving a dual purpose as a Sports Hall during the day. For the senior lads in the school, it was more the arrival of a young Welsh goddess called Christine and her husband, rather than a man and wife team. Her blonde 'bob' meant that the 6th formers would (allegedly) ask regularly, at least among themselves, "but is she a *true* blonde?" They were, of course, aware that there was only one certain way of finding out – and it was only Mr. Croft who could provide the answer they needed!

With her ever-so-slightly stocky figure and attractive legs, together with a tightly wrapped body produced by a closely fitting dress, there were plenty who wished they could be offered a ride with her in the Croft's easily recognisable red minivan. Not only that, but a good number in the senior school yearned to have the opportunity to offer her a 'shoulder-ride', so that her legs would be wrapped firmly around their neck. The more squirming she did, the better it would be! The most popular adjective being used at that time to describe her was most probably, "stunner". Yes, the Welsh goddess and her amazingly lucky husband (in the view of those same 6th form lads) had arrived to teach games – but not the sort of games that the 6th formers wanted. And why, some of those 6th formers wondered, was it not possible to be allowed to do PE – and games for that matter – with the Welsh Goddess, instead of with Mr Croft. The senior lads had to be content to dream – and dreams never come true. Such thoughts were, of course, well outside the sphere of a young teenager whose inner thoughts were more concerned about the implications concerning indoor PE, rather than with the obvious attractions of a female goddess.

Such worries regarding a more defined approach to PE were well founded. The Croft's arrival, unfortunately, heralded a speedy influx into the Assembly Hall of numerous items of PE equipment. Wall bars, a trampoline, weights and – horror of horrors – a vaulting horse and a horse box. There has never been any problem with sports. Football or cricket, depending on the season, on the playing fields was always enjoyable (and still is) but indoor PE was quite another matter. Once the large protecting mats had been placed on the floor, out would come the horse box and it was then time to get to the back of the queue of the waiting boys. Not only was one expected to get over the contraption in one simple movement, but it was casually assumed that this would be accomplished by a somersault onto the horse and over, thereby ending up on one's feet at the far end of the horse. Some hope! A good majority of the lads (the segregation of the sexes also being rigidly observed for PE lessons) were able to do it with ease. Just how on earth did they manage it? As one moved gradually towards the front of the line of waiting boys, there was a skill in attempting to leave it whilst Mr Croft was watching one of the boys performing his somersault. One then mingled with those who had already jumped in the hope that it would not be discovered that one had conveniently missed a turn. "McCart, have you jumped?". "Yes sir". Untrue, of course, and an early foray into 'white-lies'. Mr Croft will have realised as much. However, he would want to ensure that everyone had their turn. "Well, I don't remember seeing you. Come on, have a go will you..." Goodness me, that horrible horse vaulting box was never conquered, although there were numerous times when an involuntary meeting was made with the floor mats on either side of the horse. The large floor mat on the far side of the horse where Mr Croft stood waiting, ready to steady the balance of those young lads who successfully made it over, remained virgin territory for a young lad and his spindly thirteen-year-old legs!

A quick somersault over the 'horse box'.
Just how on earth do they do that?
(Photograph: J. Hebblethwaite)

There was inevitably a great inward sigh of relief when the equipment was finally moved away so that the remaining period of the PE lesson could be dedicated to a game of football. A game played on one's haunches with an absurdly heavy medicine ball, which one could only kick a distance of three or perhaps four feet... at best. Any attempt to kick the ball harder seemed to have no impact on making the ball actually travel any further. The only impact was rather more long term, with the painful experience of a rather sore left foot for the rest of the day.

Problems with woodwork and indoor PE indeed, but no such problems with drawing and painting. Art was under the supervision of an attractive and bubbly Mrs Piper, in a classroom domiciled at the end of the wooden 'prefabricated' buildings, built by the pupils under the close supervision of Lonny in the mid-1950s. These classrooms stood alongside the river which, when in spate, provided a spectacular distraction from the mechanics of mixing various coloured paints together in an attempt to produce a specific shade. When the River Wenning is heavily in flood, the water level is sometimes only yards away from the art classroom and this inevitably provided a constant distraction during those early years. Indeed, during the summer holiday break, in August 1967, such had been the flow of water (and in summer to boot!) that the classrooms alongside the river, including the art room, had been inundated with water. Further downstream, at the village of Wray, a road bridge had been swept away. In retrospect, it seems nothing short of a miracle that these classrooms were able to be repaired and cleaned up and ready for use again by the start of the autumn term 1967. Young teenagers would be ignorant, of course, as to the work that had obviously taken place to get the classrooms ready for re-use. For that, credit must be given to Lonny and his maintenance team, particularly as the repair work was carried out during what might nominally be termed as the holiday period. Credit where it is due!

It always seemed quite in order to 'mess about' (so to speak) in Art, when a large A1 piece of brilliant white squeaky-clean paper waited on the desk for the not-so-confident starting strokes of the paintbrush. But the messing about was all part of the creation of a particular painting. At least, that is how it seemed. Irrespective of the end result, it was not necessarily a failure. At least, not according to Mrs Piper. She possessed seemingly endless patience in finding the positive out of a quite ordinary attempt at drawing and painting.

"Ian, can you not sketch anything else other than trains and ships?", Mrs Piper would ask regularly. (It seemed an odd tradition that all the female teachers from that era addressed their pupils by their forename, unlike the male teachers who would only use surnames with the boys, whilst using forenames with the girls...) Trains and ships? The continual challenge with art lessons was to ensure that, whatever the subject matter might be, it would have to involve – somewhere on the canvas – a picture of a train or a ship. Why was that? With the railway line passing along the school playing fields, a sizeable majority of the young boarders were dedicated trainspotters. Drawing trains in art was merely a logical extension to what was already almost an obsession.

Why draw ships then? Ships rekindled the memory of the time just three years before the commencement of boarding school. Then, the experience of living for two years in Aden – a British Colony and a staging post for shipping, situated as it is at the entrance to the Indian Ocean as ships leave the Red Sea – meant watching a daily changing diet of ships of all shapes and sizes, both arriving and sailing. One could stand enthralled at the Chapel Hill RAF school, situated at the top of a hill, and look down on the full sweep of a scenic crescent-shaped harbour bustling with all kinds of shipping – from the large modern passenger liners to a huge variety of cargo ships and also, British naval vessels. (Someone had suggested that up to 500 ships used to call every month at that time.) There was no traditional dockside. The ships would anchor within the harbour basin and to young eyes, they appeared to be scattered with abandon with no regimentation. It made it even more exciting and interesting.

*[**An aside:** there was always considerable enjoyment in the journey – which was made daily in the small, regulation-grey Air Force bus up to that hill-top school, always involving a race with the other buses bringing in children from different areas of the colony. Overtaking another school bus always brought forth a huge cheer and waves of triumph within the bus. The bus driver willingly entered into the spirit of it. Not only that, but he appeared to enjoy it as much as, if not more so, than the kids. There was a badge of honour to be gained by being the first bus to arrive at the hill-top school and to then stand watching with childish pleasure as the other buses turned up – always, of course, at the same time keeping an eye on what was happening down at the harbour.*

Plenty of laughter also on the bus journey to school, as the bus would regularly reverberate to the singing of, "She'll be coming round the mountain when she comes", but it wasn't a white horse she was riding but instead, what she was wearing – pink knickers! So, it was a case of singing, "She'll be wearing pink knickers when she comes." The innocence of youth.

Ah, this thought process. One wonders how many of our lovely 6th form young ladies will be regularly wearing pink knickers during this new school year. There is a challenge, indeed. Will any be prepared to admit it. Will they even discuss it? Well, according to those 'in the know' within last year's 6th form, young ladies now quite commonly wear fancy-coloured knickers, rather than boring, plain regulation white. How do they know, one wonders? Regulation white knickers! Hadn't one of the 6th form lads – who was it? – asked a 6th form girl for a copy of the school's 'Girls' Uniform List' last year, to see if knickers, with a specification of colour, were included? But no, nothing about knickers, only "White Knicker Lining" – eh? – so surely not all the 6th form females will be sporting just the standard – boring – white! Coloured knickers are surely much more – well, sexy. What is inside them, sexier still.]

Many of the ships calling at Aden became so very familiar at that time – including the *Canberra* and *Oriana* belonging to the P & O shipping line, the *Fairsea* and *Fairsky,* belonging to the Sitmar Line (with a familiar 'V' on their funnel), both these shipping companies operating a regular passage to and from the UK to the Far East and Australia. Occasionally, there would be a visit from one of the stylish Union Castle passenger liners, sporting an attractive lilac grey hull and sailing to their regular destination of South Africa but, unusually, down the east coast of Africa, rather than via the more common west-coast route. The multitude of cargo lines also provided endless interest, with the Blue Funnel ships (actually, Alfred Holt & Co) being immediately recognisable by their traditional blue funnel (with black top), whilst their names – based on characters from Greek mythology, always proved intriguing. The names had to be looked up to obtain an understanding of the various mythical figures. Intriguing yes, but also informative.

Almost as common as the Blue Funnel ships were vessels from several other cargo shipping companies. Clan Line, with their familiar red horizontal stripes on an otherwise black funnel. (And what strange excitement there had been among siblings during that time in Aden when news had been received that one of the Clan Line cargo vessels, *Clan Keith,* had sunk after hitting submerged rocks shortly before its expected arrival in Aden harbour – seemingly quite appropriate with an elder brother sporting the same name!) Port Line ships were also regular callers, with their names all being prefixed with 'Port', and Bibby Line, their ships all being named after English counties. Bottle top collecting, stamp collecting and train spotting – yes – and for a period whilst in Aden, inevitably, ship spotting!

It was predictable, therefore, that such recent memories would be sketched out so very often in those art lessons. The various shipping lines enjoying their moment of fame on the art paper provided, albeit that the standard of the finished version rarely obtained favourable marks. Mrs Piper invariably failed in her quest to get other subject matters to take precedence on the shiny clean paper provided, but she always accepted it in good spirit. She would surely affirm to the declaration that "everyone is an artist" – it is just a question of the degree of competence! Quite right.

But success or failure in art didn't seem to matter. The fact is, messing about with paintbrush and paper was enjoyable and her lessons could be looked forward to within the framework of the timetable without the fear that woodwork or indoor PE always generated. If one showed interest and enthusiasm, despite obviously lacking artistic flair, Mrs Piper was quite happy. Comments on the school report for art, such as *'with more effort, could probably do better',* or *'keen, though not all of the time'* were not looked on too dimly by parents who were more interested in the results from what were considered the more important core subjects – Mathematics, English etc.

There was genuine sorrow when Mrs Piper left the school in the summer of 1967 and the arrival of Miss King (who had, as one schoolboy eloquently phrased it, "legs going into next week") to replace her heralded a much stricter discipline, both in class and in the subject matter. No more drawing trains and ships onto every empty canvass and idling away the time looking at the vagaries of the adjacent river or listening for the passage of steam trains during the lesson. These activities resulted in a rather caustic comment on the first school report in art from Miss King, *'Too easily distracted by outside interests.'* A report going the other way (from pupil to teacher) would without doubt have suggested "far too strict and rather too serious". The senior lads, however, would, surely, have wanted to keep taking Art as a chosen subject to keep tabs on those long stylish legs. Forever "going into next week"!

"Sit down, McCart!", shouted Mr Smith, his face scowling half in laughter, half in frustration. "Have you never seen a train before, boy?" "Sorry, sir – but it is a 9F on the Heysham oil tank train, 92009." At the mention of the locomotive number, a good proportion of the boys within the classroom would be jotting it down, generally on the inside leaf of their biology notebook, to be transferred that same evening to a 'spotting' book in the dormitory. The diversion from biology to logging engine numbers would only be a short one, but it might well occur several times during the lesson and Mr Smith's patience was hardly inexhaustible. Of course, one saw trains passing by the school on a daily basis, but the important thing was not the train, but what was pulling it. That is, the number of the steam or diesel locomotive, as one might not have seen that particular engine before.

With hair combed straight back over his forehead – rather than more commonly to one side – Iain Smith could, one always imagined, quite easily have auditioned for the part as Dracula in a horror film produced by Pinewood Studios. His middle forename was Amundsen – a link in some way on his maternal side to the Antarctic explorer, or so it was believed. He was what might be termed 'a man of the people' except, in the context of the school, one could quite easily replace 'people' with pupils. He was popular and good-natured. His bark was a good deal worse than his bite. That fact was well known, and it was, rather perversely, quite enjoyable being the brunt of his bark!

As the biology teacher, it was his misfortune to have his laboratory fronting the school and directly facing the railway viaduct crossing the river, which was in full view. It was a biology classroom that frequently entertained the youngsters with the rancid smell of dead animals – a fox or a rabbit perhaps – which were occasionally left to gently rot on a table-top, awaiting the dissecting skills of the more senior pupils. The geography teacher, Mr Jackson, suffered from the same fate regarding the frequent disruption of lessons by the train spotters, with his classroom adjoining the biology and physics laboratories. It was even suggested that Mr Smith might have had a secret passion for steam trains himself – although if so, it certainly did not rival his huge enthusiasm for motorbikes and with anything to do with taking them apart. (Which, surely, would be just as difficult and complicated as those Woodwork lessons.) Whilst he was no doubt frustrated by boys leaping out of their chairs when a train hove into view – particularly if in the middle of explaining the finer points of the workings of the kidneys or liver – it was rare for a detention to be handed out through the sometime frequent distractions. Jake was similarly tolerant of such behaviour.

Of course, if one was able to 'bag' one of the seats in the biology classroom linked to the long Formica desk looking straight out of the window, then no need for jumping up. Nevertheless, one still needed to stay alert for trains, albeit that a steam locomotive could generally be heard climbing for several miles up the gradient from Wennington. However, trains heading west on a falling gradient could not be heard or seen until suddenly appearing when crossing the viaduct and within a matter of seconds would disappear into the cutting. It was this that made it necessary to jump up from the benches unless one had indeed 'bagged' a window position. As a bare minimum, at the very least, one had to ensure that the train engine had been seen even if the number had not been obtained. The relevant steam or diesel locomotive number would often then be provided the following day by one of the day boys, Stephen Lister, whose father methodically logged down the information from a vantage point at High Bentham railway station.

With his laboratory looking out directly to the school entrance, Mr Smith was well placed to watch the comings and goings of pupils. Just try sneaking out of school without wearing the school cap – there would be the sound of a booming voice from an open biology window. **"Where's your cap, boy?"** "Err, in my pocket, sir." **"Put in ON, boy, put it on."** (Well, after all, it was a school rule to wear a cap to and from school.)

He could also use the advantage of watching pupils entering and leaving the school for his own benefit. One day pupil, about to cycle home to High Bentham during the lunch hour, tells of being harangued down by a booming voice from the biology classroom. **"You boy, come here."** Fearing the worst, he did so.

"Where are you going?"

"Home for my lunch in High Bentham, sir."

"Here is some money, can you pick up a copy of *Motorcycle News* from Forster's newsagent please?"

"Yes sir, certainly sir!"

Thank you, Mr Smith, for being so patient and humorous with all those frequent interruptions. Perhaps you secretly enjoyed all the camaraderie and banter. Your familiar Dracula appearance has been much missed since you left the school to take up a teaching post overseas. What isn't missed, however, is the rather dastardly trick you had of giving young teenagers, on the weekly school cross-country run, a helping hand (that is, a push in the back) down the steep embankments within the wood across from the school, on the opposite side of the river. The predictable complaint from the teenage boys, "Sir, that's not fair, you pushed me", would bring one of two ever predictable retorts from Dracula. He would reply, without a hint of remorse, "Nonsense, you fell!", or "I was just giving you a helping hand", always accompanying the comment with his wicked Dracula-type smile!

CHAPTER VIII

YOU WILL ALL BE SPOTTING TRAINS

Trainspotting. If the thought of double woodwork at the start of the week could be put to the back of the mind, albeit temporarily, then this most popular of school hobbies could be enjoyed during Sunday afternoon as well as at all other times throughout the week, school lessons notwithstanding. It was a hobby, of course, only for boys. The school playing field acted as a magnet for the 'train spotting' boarding house lads. Saturday and Sunday would almost exclusively be dedicated to residing at the side of the railway line waiting for the expected passenger service trains (the times of which were known by heart) and the unexpected freight trains which, seemingly, could come at any time. If it was raining at the weekend, then refuge was taken in rooms six and seven, with their windows fronting the school and looking across to the railway viaduct. If the weather dictated staying indoors, the housemaster on duty would rarely have to ask what the boarders would be doing or, indeed, where they would be. The 'Exeat Book', which had to be completed without fail to say where one would be and what one would be doing at the weekend, would have the same two words opposite a good number of the boarders' names – TRAIN SPOTTING! "I have no need to ask you lads", the Housemaster would say, before looking at the book. "No doubt you will all be spotting the trains. Make sure you behave yourselves."

These two classrooms, rooms six and seven, were part of the 'new block' single story building built in 1962 and ready for use early 1963 – the finance for the building being provided by numerous fund-raising activities and several large grants from local businesses and charities. All the classrooms and laboratories within this block were linked by a corridor, enabling one to gain access to whichever room was needed.

On the wall of the corridor, as well as a photograph of the official opening performed by the Archbishop of York in November 1962, which if nothing else, confirms the close relationship existing between the school and the diocese, there was also (and indeed, it is still on the wall) a photograph of this school's only holder of the Victoria Cross. In actual fact, he was a previous headmaster – not, as one might have expected, an ex-pupil. The Revd T. B. Hardy was head of the school 1907–1913. The framed photograph on the corridor wall shows him receiving his VC from King George V in France in August 1918. Every school will have a 'favourite son' and in this school, it is perhaps this ex-headmaster who has been given that mantle. Youngsters paid scant attention to this cameo from British history whilst on their way to the various classrooms either for learning or for trainspotting. With budding maturity, the photograph has indeed generated a good deal more interest. This is particularly so as the photograph has a poignancy attached to it, as pictures often do when depicting the progress of war. Reading a brief history of the Revd Hardy will confirm that only a couple of months after receiving his VC from the King on foreign soil, he sadly died from wounds received whilst the British forces were attempting to cross the River Selle in France. Sadly, it was only a matter of months before the ending of hostilities of World War I.

From rooms six and seven (which have a partition separating them so they can be opened out into one large room as necessary), steam and diesel locomotive numbers could then be obtained with the assistance of a pair of binoculars. There were generally several pairs in operation among the 'spotters' assembled in those classrooms. Everyone wanted to take part. There was, inevitably, some confusion from time to time when the many using binoculars picked out differing numbers, leading to a learned discussion on who might be most accurate! And in between the trains, the usual skirmishes took place among restless teenagers in the two classrooms, effectively made into one room with the partition always pulled back, playing tricks – on whoever it was decided should be 'picked on' (generally for no particular reason). It was always appropriate to be on the lookout for flying bits of chalk or elastic bands, etc.

When out on the school playing field, a distant column of smoke from the west always gave early notice of a steam-hauled train, whilst a 'lookout' was always posted at the crest of the playing fields to watch for trains from the east. This was necessary as, with a falling gradient from High Bentham and a railway cutting adjoining the fields, they could not always be heard or indeed seen until the very last minute. In time-honoured fashion the almost universal habit of placing money, generally only coppers – 1d being the favourite, on the railway line was practised, if only to see into what weird and wonderful shapes they would be distorted into. To young teenagers, there always seemed to be the illogical worry as the train was approaching that it might somehow be derailed by a 1d coin fouling the line. Did the bogies from the Diesel Multiple Unit passenger train lift slightly into the air as the 1d coin was squashed? Several of the train spotters always fancied that they did but it would, of course, be a case of seeing what one wanted to see – or, perhaps, what one expected to see. In any event, it was exciting to think that the train had kept itself on the rails despite a selection of coins fouling the permanent way.

The steam locomotives were always the most welcome, with the driver and/ or the fireman generally giving a friendly wave from the cab in accompaniment with a short blast on the locomotive whistle as the train passed by. It was invariably the young fireman, the junior in the partnership, who provoked the most interest, often wearing a trademark knotted handkerchief around his head to capture the sweat from continued shovelling of coal into the firebox. In sharp contrast was his senior, the driver, who almost without exception would be a good deal older and would always be wearing the regulation British Railways driver's cap – worn, dirty and rugged but perfectly suited to its purpose. The two men, operating in unison, always seemed to be in full control of what looked, to young teenagers, to be a most complicated piece of machinery. The sight, the sound and most importantly, the pungent intoxicating smell of oil and coal left teenage train spotters transfixed. Is it any wonder that a good proportion of boys yearn to be train drivers?

Even afternoon games on the playing field would be temporarily halted by the passage of a steam train, although it helped enormously having the football pitch for the juniors adjacent to the railway. Any game in progress would suddenly come to an immediate halt as the steam engine approached, much to the frustration of the sports master, who would always realise that it would be a fruitless exercise attempting to keep the game flowing. With a captured and enthralled audience, the driver and fireman were always happy to take the plaudits offered to them by way of the obligatory hand waving from the group of enthusiastic teenagers, always providing a whistle and a return wave as acknowledgement. The excitement on a few selected afternoons reached fever pitch when it was known that the most famous steam locomotive of all, *4472 Flying Scotsman,* was due to come past on a special commemorative train. No less interesting was another special train, headed by a preserved A4 Pacific *60019 Bittern* which, with it being in the same class as the famous *60022 Mallard,* made it a rather special visitor – as well as being a 'cop'! It was most unusual to see a *'namer'* on what was, and still is, essentially a secondary country line linking the two important main lines, the East Coast and West Coast routes. The one exception would be the quite frequent sighting of 'Black 5' *45156 Ayrshire Yeomanry,* which had a rather attractive military style nameplate. This engine was regularly employed on mundane freight duties in and around the surrounding area towards the end of working steam on the railway. It was an end that eventually came in August 1968.

Those days on the playing field by the railway line certainly had their moments. During the era of steam traction on the railway, firemen would frequently throw out red hot embers from the locomotive firebox to control vegetation on the lineside cuttings and embankments. Also, on occasions, sparks and ash from out of the locomotive chimney would be blown by a prevailing wind onto the lineside. It was during a period of dry weather that the railway cutting immediately behind the rector's house was set alight by a passing steam engine. The general consensus among the teenage train spotters was that the fireman had been seen intentionally chucking burning lumps of coal out from the locomotive (to control the vegetation) and within five or so minutes, the whole cutting was fiercely ablaze. To teenage boys, it appeared that the rector's house might be at risk and there followed a race back into school to advise the housemaster on duty. Then back onto the field to watch the spectacle. Even more exciting was the arrival, in due course, of the fire brigade, although rather disappointingly, the fire had started to subside by the time of their arrival – so much so that it perhaps might well have been slightly embarrassing for the housemaster when showing the fire crew exactly where the fire was (or where it had been). Nonetheless, within that group of youthful train spotters, it was felt that a public service had been done and that the rector's house had possibly been saved from certain destruction!

Trains, with either a steam or diesel locomotive at the front, posed no real problem for the generally large number of young boarders domiciled across on the school playing field next to the railway line. The number could easily be seen and agreed by those present. However, there would at times be some considerable frustration with the dreadfully stained working condition of some of the steam locomotives that were seen passing. They would invariably be in their last months of operational service and in consequence, would be so filthy that the locomotive number on the side of the engine would, on occasions, be totally obliterated by dirt! Even at close quarters, it could sometimes prove impossible to read part, or indeed all, of the number much to the chagrin of the 'spotters' present. Sometimes there was salvation by being able to see the number of the engine from its front smoke box cover. However, in those final eighteen months of steam operation, smoke box number plates had often been taken off. (Or gone missing – "liberated" one might term it although, perhaps, that is the rather gullible way of phrasing it!)

Getting the numbers of the diesel multiple unit (DMU) passenger trains also proved problematical. These trains had no single locomotive pulling them, but were trains formed by up to as many as eight coaches, operated from a diesel engine which was an integral part of the front coach. This entailed getting the number of each particular coach (for instance, E51270 being one vehicle coach) and with some passenger trains comprising six or eight coaches, remembering all the numbers as the train passed by was nigh impossible. The solution, therefore, was to task specific 'spotters' with obtaining individual unit numbers. (Someone to get first and second unit numbers, someone else to get third and fourth unit numbers etc.) Even this seemingly foolproof system did not always return 100% results. Why? Well, once the train was passing by, everyone tried to be clever by getting and writing down all the numbers and not just those they had been tasked with writing down. It was impossible not to. All part of the rough and tumble of what some might have termed a pointless, albeit harmless, exercise. Nonetheless, it kept young boarding house teenagers captivated and ensured one had a close-knit group of friends with the same obsessive interest.

How to make sense of the variety and type of locomotives? It was a veritable minefield working out exactly what was what with regard to engine classes and numbers, both steam and diesel. Help was at hand. What was the favourite Christmas or birthday present received when one was a child? An impossible question perhaps? Was it a solid tome outlining the 'History of Britain'? Was it perhaps a toy fort, complete with soldiers, or an imitation hand-held gun that fired automatically? (And a gun, incidentally, that had broken by Boxing Day!) Perhaps it was that board game that involved firing small ball-bearings into holes, thereby giving one the opportunity to build up an impressive score in points – Bagatelle is it, or some such futile game? No. Eclipsing all these was the birthday present in March 1967 received from an elder brother. An *Ian Allan ABC British Railways Locomotives Combined Volume* (price 12/6d). This pocket-sized book (commonly shortened and referred to as an *Ian Allan Combine*) listed every locomotive operating on the British Railways network. The number, the class, the weight, the name – in fact, anything and everything relating to a locomotive being used at that time on the railway system. This small hard-backed book was the last word as a reference point for young train spotters. Indeed, it was the bible of the railway world, far more relevant and understandable than the one the school boarders opened rather reluctantly every Sunday in church!

There were, of course, unwritten rules to be observed with this locomotive combine book. It stayed safely in the bedside drawer in the dormitory. No taking it out to the playing field or classroom. It was far too precious. Train numbers would be scribbled down by the side of the line on pieces of paper or in a rough book and even perhaps on the inside cover of a textbook if a number was obtained whilst in the classroom. The railway combine came into its own, so to speak, once back in the dormitory. One could then, in the comfort and warmth, slowly check through the engine numbers seen that day to see if they had been seen before. If the locomotive had not been seen before, it was designated a 'cop' – specifically a railway term to denote seeing an engine for the very first time.

But how would one know? The tried and tested system (from when the Combined Volumes were first introduced, one imagines, in the 1940s) was to underline the locomotive number once it had been seen. The only issue to be decided was what colour biro to use. Some would use blue. The vast majority preferred red. A red line under the number was adequate proof that the engine had been seen. Some of the older lads in the boarding house had been able to gain access to the footplate (with steam engines) or the driving cab (with diesels) by a kind-hearted driver, most likely whilst spotting at a railway station. Having been in the cab, they would often have a green line under the locomotive number, with a small 'c' by the side of the number (c = *cabbed*) to show which engines they had been on! Tips like that were picked up on the hoof so that all spotters understood 'what was what' when looking through an *Ian Allan* combine belonging to someone else.

Did anyone cheat and underline engine numbers they had not really seen? Perhaps, but surely that would defeat the object of trying to see all the locomotives of a particular class. There was a strange satisfaction in getting all or a large part of a locomotive class underlined. That collecting gene was in its element!

This was an era when locomotives and sometimes whole locomotive classes were allocated to specific parts of the United Kingdom, so if someone claimed they had seen a locomotive locally that was based in, say, the West Country, their claim might well be viewed with some suspicion by fellow spotters. The hobby did not tolerate cheats! At holiday times, such claims were more acceptable. Philip Denson would migrate to his parents in Scotland for the school holidays and on a return to school, his list of Type 1 Clayton diesel cops was more than readily accepted, as this class of diesel engine was largely based in Scotland and in a few small pockets of northern England. However, one would not expect to see a Clayton diesel on the Southern region of British Rail. If someone suggested they had done so, their claim would immediately be viewed with some considerable suspicion by fellow spotters. Such were the intricacies of engine spotting, or as it was (and is) commonly termed, 'trainspotting'.

Suddenly, a jolt. The sound of a distant horn and then the familiar outline of a 'Cravens' two car diesel multiple-unit heading up the grade, with the late afternoon service from Lancaster, jogs the mind back to the here and now. These twinges of nostalgia – recent reminiscences so fondly thought about, even the rather nasty unfair bits – need to be put to one side. That is all in the past.

Across at the school gates, there is now most definitely the telltale signs of activity, with cars slowing down to turn in to the school, bringing back young and old. The Housemaster, Mr Russell, will, no doubt, be in the thick of it, trying his best to create some sort of order out of the visual chaos surrounding the stylish and almost gothic entrance porch to the school. Time to move – a new school year awaits.

MICHAELMAS TERM

CHAPTER IX

A NEW ACADEMIC YEAR

On the return to the boarding house, then, on this first week of September whilst, as always, there would inevitably be some changes, at first glance, nothing visually appears to have altered. Such continuity is always welcomed. Someone once suggested that "change is perpetual". The name of the guilty party who propounded such a claim is buried deep within one of the 'A' Level Sociology study books. The name of the person responsible for such concise dogma has been forgotten, but it is of little consequence. If change must be continuous, then let it be gradual, unassuming and perhaps not noticeable. Someone else suggested, "leave such change unchallenged if it cannot be influenced." To leave it unchallenged. Impossible!

So then, change continues apace, does it? A change there certainly has been in the boarding status from the previous year. This new academic year means a step up to the Upper 6th form and, in addition, occupying the study/dormitory allocated to the Head Boarder. This will no doubt bring with it a certain level of kudos, yes. It will also inevitably mean greater responsibility and, by obvious extension, maturity. It is going to involve an element of discussion and planning regarding the on-going operation of the boarding house with the resident housemaster. It might well, therefore, represent a poisoned chalice. Time will be the arbiter. Sometimes responsibility is welcome and enthusiastically embraced. At other times, it is accepted wearily and reluctantly. It depends, of course, on exactly what is involved. At least, that was how responsibility was espoused during the first year's 'A' Level study. For the academic year now commencing, our housemaster will no doubt want to see his Head Boarder enthuse and embrace the former of the two options. There could well be, and there most likely will be, the odd occasion when he will be somewhat disappointed. After all, the 'adjusted' motto for this dormitory holds good – 'Never ask for a job and always refuse one' (if at all possible)!

The Upper 6th form students have already been split into two groups from the first year's study. The split being roughly based on a Science group and an Arts group. It is assumed that this split will continue into the second year. The housemaster, in a rather helpful way and in preparation for the start of term tomorrow morning, has kindly provided a list of students in each group on the desk in the dormitory room. It needed to be studied straight away. The split between the two groups has survived the summer break, as anticipated. Good!

Of the two groups, the Arts will continue to be mentored by Mrs Fife, the senior mistress at the school and one of the English teachers. She doubles as the wife of the Head of the English Department. Only recently married, the nuptials – when announced to the school via the morning assembly – caused a distinct ripple amongst an unbelieving gallery. Almost open-mouthed astonishment. Total astonishment! It had not been expected. Neither had it been predicted. And Mrs Fife (or Miss Smalley as she was) had come, as all at the school could plainly see, straight out of a Jane Austen novel – a middle-aged spinster, stoically accepting her lot in life, starved of sex, whilst others around her – married of course – were leading a 'normal' life. Then suddenly, here she is – a married woman and enjoying the pleasures of the flesh. (Well at least, that is now the obvious assumption among the 6th form brigade, who also confidently suggest that she has good thick kissing lips.) Miss Smalley married – so, when the 6th form Arts group had their daily morning roll call with her in the form room during last year's study, there was always an almost irresistible urge after saying, "Good morning, Mrs Fife", to follow it up with a cheeky, "Did you enjoy rampant sex with Mr Fife last night?"

The Science group will be in the hands of a capable – but really, rather too serious – Mr Southwell, the deputy headmaster and mathematics teacher. A quick glance down the alphabetical list of names on the Arts list. Hay, Hird, Lister, Lumb – and there we are, McCart! Thank God – a very promising start to the new campaign. No one ever really wants to be in the group overseen by the deputy headmaster. It would surely be utterly humourless. Certainly, with the one at this school it would. Two colleagues from the school First XI football team are also in the Arts group. Iain Ross ('Rosco'), also a boarder, and Michael Pearson, a day boy. Ah, Pearson – always immediately recognisable by his huge head of frizzy hair which one would ordinarily expect to see on a member of a pop group from the Tamla Motown label! How on earth did he manage to head the football so competently with his mass of tangled hair, whilst providing the backbone in the centre of midfield in last year's so successful football campaign? Even more intriguing, how does a barber manage to tackle that head of hair? Indeed, during the previous academic year, the question that was continually asked was, "Does Pearson ever get his hair cut?" It did not appear to be the case. These two football friends from the First XI will, it is anticipated, ensure sufficient laughter within the Arts group, as well as providing ample opportunity for discussions on tactics for the forthcoming soccer matches, with the goalkeeper, left back and centre back all in the group. Last year's First XI record – played 12, won 10, drawn 1 and lost 1 – might prove difficult to better. Particularly so with the promise that has been made of more matches to be played this season – and against stronger opposition.

Day boys and boarders. There has always been a closer tie during the school day with one's boarding colleagues. Inevitable perhaps. Whilst there has never been rivalry between two distinctly separate groups (apart from the annual Day Boys v Boarders football match – generally won by the Day Boys), and whilst there is scant evidence of any 'us and them' culture, nevertheless, there is always a sympathetic leaning towards boarders. They are well known to each other, not quite as siblings might be, but tending that way and are, thereby, more conspicuous in school time. They are lived with, mealtimes shared, a bathroom shared, even the laughter – and sometimes the secrets! The boarders discover their colleague's idiosyncrasies, and they plan together, they talk together. They live their lives together morning and night in the boarding house and in the dormitories. So, whilst it is not quite boarders against the rest, it might well occasionally look that way to a casual outsider. In that context, Rosco is a kindred spirit, Pearson is a fellow member of the soccer team. The assessment is unspoken and invisible, but it is present, nonetheless.

There are thirteen second-year 6th formers in Mrs Fife's group, nine of whom are female. It might very well turn out, then, to be an interesting academic year! There will, most certainly, be something innately engaging – perhaps even intriguing – being in continuous close proximity with half a dozen and more females. All of them, of course, making the transition away from girlhood to young womanhood and, no doubt, dealing with it in different ways. They will perhaps be anxious to show that they have negotiated what for them will most probably be a significant step. Indeed, some will not hesitate to give visual evidence, helped enormously by the current fashion for displaying a generous amount of leg above the knee. Indeed, if the regulation girls' skirt is not showing enough leg, then an adjustment to the hemline seems to be a common enough procedure. Who is complaining? (Confucius says, "If you have got it to show off, then show it off" – good old Confucius. He is full of relevant and sound advice within this boarding house!)

For the lads in this Lonsdale dormitory complex, these young ladies will very quickly be re-assessed at the start of this second 'A' Level year. Not on their educational capabilities, although no one of course will want to have a girlfriend who is far too brainy and in the category of being a "swot". After all, it is beyond the pale to have a girlfriend who is brainier than oneself. No, the assessment will be made as to their 'rateability' – the current in vogue phraseology within the Lonsdale complex. This 'rateability' is based on three essential criteria, none of which has anything to do with intelligence. It is instead an assessment based on:

1. Looks. Yes, certainly, a pretty face is obligatory (always remembering that beauty is in the eye of the beholder!), but also:
2. The shape and size of their legs. Not too big and ungainly. "Tackling thunder thighs is a skill that requires some expertise", in the words of a 6th former – although it is by no means certain he is speaking from practical experience! Not too big then – but also, not legs that are matchstick thin, with nothing to grab hold off.

Last, but certainly not least:

3. The size of their chest. In blunt layman's terms, which senior boarders revel in using, "the size of their tits!" (Variously also described as boobs, bazookas, mammary glands and sometimes, if one wants to be posh, bosoms. But who wants to be posh?) Yes, within this assessment, perhaps personality will be a feature. Only, however, on the periphery and after the main assessment.

Daily contact then with these nine young ladies will no longer make it always necessary to be enthusiastic about watching the girls' hockey matches on the sports field where, traditionally, the skirts worn are always that bit shorter than school uniform skirts. Then again, why not enjoy the best of both worlds? Senior girls' hockey on the playing field and 6th form legs and bazookas being displayed in the classroom. And what about the ladies themselves? They will know, within their inner conscience, that they will be receiving admiring looks from their male counterparts. At seventeen-or-eighteen years of age and wanting to feel and look attractive, they surely will be – or at least, they should be – quite pleased. Ah, the female form and growing up!

Glancing down the list of Mrs Fife's charges, there are the brainy ones – that is, the naturally brainy who never seem to have to break into a sweat to obtain first class marks. Perhaps predictably, they are from the female side. (Of course, as Mr Fife pointedly made clear to this supposedly ignorant 6th form boarder last year, "Ladies do not sweat, McCart, they gently glow. Horses sweat, gentlemen perspire, and ladies gently glow – if you read more widely, that is something you would know." Yes, okay!) Isn't it strange how some have the brains to do well without really trying, whilst others – including this new Head Boarder – will have to work hard to attain the same standard? So, the naturally brainy? Well, Clare Hird, Christine Fournier and Diane Lumb for starters.

A NEW ACADEMIC YEAR

*Four brainy young ladies from the Upper 6th form enjoy relaxing on the wall opposite the church.
L to R: the smiling Diane Lumb, Claire Hird, Janet Hall and Christine Fournier. The male 'interloper' is 'Cess' Hargreaves.
(Photograph: J. Hebblethwaite)*

*[**An aside**: an imaginary letter to Miss XXXX*
Dear XXXX,
You have such an engaging innocent smile and pleasant personality – and rather a nice pair of prim tits with the hint of a delicate pair of nipples, ever so gently pushing your school blouse out at the front. And those enticing bazookas (my dear, that term is THE favourite Lonsdale dormitory concoction for bosoms) accompany a rather lovely petite frame. No ladies tights for you, XXXX. Instead, white socks pulled up to the knee, giving you a definite sex appeal and displaying bare white flesh above the knee. But a different sort of white to your knee socks. Flesh white – lovely!
Everything about you XXXX is petite – yes, including, no doubt, your bazookas. Isn't it suggested that all good things come in small packages? And always grinning. Do you only grin and smile for the benefit of the Head Boarder? Is there a mischievous sense of fun within that lovely smile? Are you always happy? By the way, there is nothing wrong at all with small bazookas – but oh, would you still smile if asked to display that little pair to a 6th form male colleague? A shame, certainly, that you were not one of those Embassy children in Tehran holding up your swimming costume. Would you have been willing to pull your towel to one side and reveal all? A father would exclaim, "Hell's bells!" – just the thought of it!
Whatever, it is hard to believe the amount of brainpower that is obviously stored behind your wonderful grinning façade. Intelligent yes, but please XXXX, not too intelligent. And by the way, do please look after that dainty little body. From an admiring classmate.]

Ah, these individual dormitory rooms. They are made for dreaming! Never mind the school's recommended two hours per night study for 'A' Level pupils. A two-hour study of one's 6th form female colleagues will always be far more productive… at least, in the short term.

All these three brainy young women – Claire (friendly, but not that friendly), Christine (a bit too thin and gangly) and happy-go-lucky Diane (has the Zambian Weed got something to do with it?) – had excelled in last year's Lower 6th form and will no doubt do so again this year. But it wasn't a contest against each other last year – or was it? There will be no placing in class this year. No one is going to be 'top' or for that matter 'bottom'. No finishing well down in the markings this year. The only challenge is against oneself. At least, that is how it is supposed to be. Nevertheless, it will be clear to all, following last year's Lower 6th form 'A' Level study, who the leaders of the pack are regarding intelligence. If it were to be compared to a 200 yards sprint, then Claire Hird would be well out in front as soon as the starting gun was fired – and there would be no chance of catching her. She will undoubtedly be going faster and faster along the final straight, whilst the rest of us will be gasping for breath and perhaps even, perish the thought, slowing up well before the finish line! No matter, it is not about finishing first or even being in the top half dozen. Is it?

Notwithstanding brain power, there is little doubt, however, that this Arts group – to be cajoled and persuaded to study hard whilst being looked after by Mrs Fife (who will always be Miss Smalley to those resistant to change) – has the pick of the bunch with regard to female representation. Several of the young ladies will surely be awarded a high 'rateability' factor. (And yes, that includes you XXXX, with your ruddy complexion and rather lovely petite frame.)

In the group overseen by Mr Southwell, it is a similar picture regarding brain prowess, with one well ahead of the rest. Timothy Goldsack will certainly leave his class colleagues in the shade. They will accept it stoically and most probably think to themselves how glad they are that they are not so damn brainy. Two friends from the first year's 'A' Level study, Stephen Hargreaves ("Cess") and Paul Casson ("Cass"), will most probably be bringing up the rear – although that will be something Cass will not be unduly concerned with. By all accounts, a family farm awaits his ultimate attention after 'A' Levels. How convenient! Having a family job lined up once one has finished with schooling. Surely, because of that, little or no pressure on the learning process.

Perhaps vying for a position at the back of the 'runners' in the 'Boffins' group will be Peter Lethbridge ("Lefty"), a strangely solitary lad with a slightly awkward gait. As with life in general, some pupils wish to be private, others need to be gregarious. Lefty definitely fits in to the first of these two options. He is, without doubt, a nice lad – but having a decent length conversation with him about anything in particular was, indeed, a challenge during the last academic year. There seems little doubt that the interaction with him during this second year of study will be any different. That is surely a fact, however determined one might be – well eventually, it is easier to give up. Perhaps he wants people to give up. Many do not even bother trying in the first place.

Here, then, the first week of September bringing with it – as early September invariably does in educational circles – the beginning of another school year. An autumn term that always coincides with the evenings gradually being enveloped by dusk and darkness, earlier sunsets making continual inroads into daylight. This time, the start of this school year – September 1972 – will be, yes, different, so very different. This Michaelmas term about to commence is the beginning of a final year of study at boarding school. With the start of this term, it appears on the surface as though nothing has changed – but in life, the only constant is change. Sociology has already taught the new Head Boarder that. Things have to change and do change. Why does it always have to be so?

The Russell family, thankfully, are still here – in charge of the boarding house, having arrived at the start of the previous school year. Their two eldest children, a son and a daughter, were already boarding at the school. They certainly brought with them change – but in this instance, welcome change! Previously, looking after the boarding house and the varying needs of its occupants had been the sole preserve of a series of male bachelors. Until the arrival of the Russell family, the boarding house had been the preserve of Jake, with his infamous Mars bars. Now, in an attempt to create a more engaging family atmosphere, here is a family – parents and three children – overseeing events. It has proved to be an inspired bit of recruitment by the headmaster, with certainly more of a tangible 'large family' atmosphere, the boarders almost being a (very) large extension to the Russell's three children.

One of their most immediate and most celebrated decisions on taking up residence in the attic of the boarding house, in autumn 1971, was to introduce Corn Flakes for breakfast. A step-change indeed from lumpy porridge and, in addition, there was the introduction of a new mealtime, which has become enthusiastically known as evening supper. This has proved to be just as popular. Now Corn Flakes for breakfast – yes – but they also appear on the menu at suppertime. [An abiding memory that may well last a lifetime – a jovial Mr Russell emerging from the school kitchen at evening supper with a *mega-size* box of Corn Flakes. Yippee!] The addition of chips as an accompaniment to the main evening meal has obviously proved successful and only marginally less popular than the new breakfast and supper menu. And there is now always the opportunity for extra chips – an absolute treat – or indeed, the ultimate extravagance, chip butties! (And my, don't they taste nice in butties, liberally plastered with tomato ketchup? "Do you enjoy chips with your tomato ketchup?" That might well be a 'tongue in cheek' comment these days, but it is not too far-fetched!) Having extra helpings was not something previously contemplated on the boarding house menu.

With the arrival of the Russell family, then, things quite definitely changed and changed for the better. No more gluey semolina or atrocious steamed ginger puddings now. Even the toast is no longer cold, miserable and bendy – and quite impervious to being cut in half. A knife frequently failed to cut a piece in half – and quite often, nor did a set of enthusiastic teeth! *'Bend me, shake me, anyway you want me'* – (Amen Corner) – has, at least until recently, been the euphemism for boarding house toast – thankfully, no more! That line from the pop charts in 1968 now serves as an epitaph for toast at breakfast. Under the new regime, toast is prepared at the appropriate time (that is, after the bacon/eggs etc.), rather than at the outset of the meal. What a good idea – why didn't Titty think of that?

Mr Russell has an obvious and generous enthusiasm for keeping the boarding house well fed and, if for nothing else, this has made him extremely popular within the boarding dormitories. It is, one suspects, the reason behind a very noticeable clash of personalities between Mr Russell and Titty, who remains in overall charge of catering. Titty, no doubt, sees it as her responsibility to stay in charge of food and the boarding house diet. There is no disputing where the boarding house loyalties lie. Corn Flakes for supper and extra chips being key factors in deciding which side to support. Whatever goes on behind the scenes, with the very obvious and often visual differences of opinion between these two 'heavyweights', it is, indeed, now a fresh new era with the boarding house having been introduced to a new kind of 'haute cuisine'.

In addition, there has been welcome change within the school kitchen as new modern equipment has been installed, thereby negating the need for the dreaded 'washing up' rota within the boarding house. No longer is there the inevitable conflict between impatient boarders and an unforgiving Belfast sink that always took an absolute age to fill. Frustratingly, it took just as long to empty and that was the time when those on washing up duty wanted to get away to the dormitory as quickly as possible – before they were given other duties from within the kitchen.

*Mr Russell, Housemaster 1971–73 and Mathematics teacher.
His ethos of 'work hard, play hard' was appreciated by most, as were
his generally successful efforts at improving the boarding house diet.
(Photograph: J. Hebblethwaite)*

Charmingly Scottish and with an accent to match, Mr John Logan Russell supports an ample frame, is jovial and stern in equal measure and enthusiastically encourages the 'work hard, play hard' ethos. Even to senior boarders who can, at times, be cynical towards those in charge, he exudes an interest and enthusiasm for looking after the boarders in his care and is, by virtue of this, a popular housemaster. Perhaps most importantly, although at times a hard taskmaster, he is a fair advocate and has been more than willing on many occasions to place his trust in his 6th form charges on the assumption that it will not be abused. This trust is certainly sorely tested from time to time by bolshie teenagers but, in fairness, has never knowingly been intentionally flouted. A suitable motto for him might be, 'I don't care what you do, but don't frighten the horses.' (Or something to that effect – who said that?)

To the 6th form students in the boarding house, however, his wife undoubtedly generates greater interest. Mrs Rae Russell is Matron for the boarding house, having in a previous life been a professional nurse. Her energetic style and vivacious character will forever be endlessly intriguing to male adolescents, with her attractive short-cut grey hair turning white and her mildly bossy manner, which might quite easily be mistaken for flirting, particularly in the manner her requests or instructions are delivered! Attendance at the sick bay is to be almost welcomed when it involves being cared for by this engaging middle-aged lady. She provides a constant reminder, if one was needed, of the film *The Graduate*, which previewed in the cinemas a few years ago. (A film that has not been watched but is, nevertheless, talked about regularly in conjunction with what middle-aged ladies have to offer rather 'green' adolescents.) It is often thought, by testosterone-high 6th form males specifically, that the very noticeable 'spring in her step' is as a consequence of looking after the medical needs of adolescent males who require, on occasions, a surrogate mother to hold their hand. Mrs Russell is ever present to do just that – and it is always dispensed with aplomb. To those who enjoy having a lady looking after them who is both bossy and humorous in equal measure, then Mrs Russell has been sent from heaven and has an attractive build to match. A Hattie Jacques – the caricature of a typical dragon-like matron perhaps – Mrs Russell most definitely is not. [Oh, the series of 'Carry On' films with Kenneth Williams, Sid James, Charles Hawtry and Hattie Jacques – superb, corny, slightly bawdy, British comedy. Compulsive viewing.]

Oh, what joy to be a prefect and on the evening duty-rota – overseeing with the assistance of Matron, always elegant and busy, the junior dormitories getting ready for bed. Have the boys washed their hands and face? Have they cleaned their teeth? Have they made their bed properly from earlier in the day? (With the regulation hospital corners, of course – and, hopefully, no apple-pie beds!) Matron is efficient and industrious and oh, she is so exciting! It is always a pleasure to be with her and to see her in action. Not only that, but she is always a welcome visitor to the large communal bathroom within the network of dormitories, where variants of the male torso will be readily on display. A scurrilous invitation was once made suggesting that she might want to scrub a 6th form boarder's back – whilst he was in the bath. The proposition was gracefully declined, albeit being accompanied by that familiar wry and knowing smile which she displays when it might be thought that the banter is just starting to get slightly out of hand. She knows when to rein it in – even if the 6th form boarders don't!

CHAPTER X

A ROOM WITH A VIEW

An instant attachment from the beginning of this term has been made with this enclosed and private dormitory. A welcoming environment where one's room is no one else's sphere. This carefully guarded privacy is only relinquished for and by the housemaster, matron and Mrs Wills – our redoubtable laundry queen. Otherwise, one's fellow students by invitation only.

During the first few weeks of term, the view from this dormitory window has quite readily eaten up not only idle minutes during the early evening, but sometimes longer – with schoolwork being pushed aside, enabling autumn to be fully appreciated. Gazing out at the very edge of Yorkshire – with Lancashire across on the far side of the river – is endlessly captivating and the various moods have been captured in verse. (How else, when the skill of art is only within one's imagination?)

The low evening mist is already with us,
Bringing a stillness, broken only by a
Half-hearted caw from above and
A gentle trickle from a lazy river:
A leaf glides silently along, pulled by
The secret and silent undercurrent.
The trees are rigid and stark,
No wind to give them movement.
A rabbit races across the spacious field,
So open, so scared.
By the riverside, the church of St. John the Baptist,
It's flagstones watching, protecting, standing silently
Over graves as the clock tower still chimes.
And are those ever-reliable chimes asking,
As all of us might sometime need to ask,
Were their human sins forgiven?

Moist grass discharges an aroma,
So sweet yet so sour: a bird hangs in mid air
And then glides afar to join its flock.
The sky gives not a word: above the mist,
Its spacious and unending blue is
Thought provoking: a solitary cloud
Appears to have lost its way: all is silent.
A tree, already bare, is a reminder of mortality:
Others turning brown, yellow, rusty:
Be thankful some stay green.

The river foam, collected in the hidden corners,
Where the riverbank twists its painful way seaward,
Suddenly splits into spinning balls and glides
Downstream; as though initially reluctant,
Although this is its inevitable fate.

Summertime is at its end:
A chilly breeze begins to blow.
The light, which outstays its welcome in summer,
Now departs more swiftly, but it has a message…
Only think ahead is what it seems to say.

Think ahead! To some, these days and weeks may seem much the same. Out of bed, breakfast, morning assembly, a day of learning, dinner, prep, supervising the junior dormitories, and then back into bed. And so, it goes on – and so it will for the next nine months or so. But every day is different, even though it appears that life within this boarding house has continued seamlessly from the previous school year.

No change then in the routines of the boarding house for this new autumn term but change at the very top there has been. The previous Headmaster, Mr. Edward William Thornton Kaye, always appearing splendidly detached from events – as academics often do – but clearly very learned by appearance, has departed to an eminently more prestigious independent place of learning – Hitchin Grammar School. At the beginning of term, the school has 'welcomed' certainly a more mundane looking head of school. Appearance is everything! It is easy to gain the impression that Mr John Francis Day Hagen hardly seems to visually warrant the wearing of a mitre and gown to which he is entitled and which, of course, signifies an appropriate level of intelligence. The Governors have, it is assumed, ample faith in his ability to effectively look after this independent grammar school, with an eclectic mix of boarders and day pupils of both sexes.

To the boarding house, Mr Hagen most definitely hails from the aesthete section of Society. There are persistent rumours of an underlying pacifism lurking within his mantra. That by itself is almost an anathema to 6th form boarders wanting to be 'macho' and favouring the use of force to settle any dispute both within the school sphere and, indeed, in society at large. His fondness for 'theatre' has merely cemented the pacifist credentials given to him. With a love of acting, his theatrical abilities are to be regularly displayed during the morning assemblies. He will quite suddenly and without apparent reason 'blow his top' over some minor misdemeanour committed within the confines of the school by some poor unfortunate individual. The frequency of these verbal explosions in assembly has meant that, within the short space of time since the beginning of term, their effectiveness has proved to be almost negligible. However, they always provide an interesting spectacle and have become a talking point for days afterwards. Not, however, for the content of what was said but rather, for how deep the shade of red has been on the headmaster's face at the end of his 'rant'!

With facial features readily mimicked, a cluster of senior boarding house boys have suddenly become instant impressionists as quasi 'Mr Hagen's'. They enthusiastically walk around sporting a screwed-up face, with one eye shut and with a pointing finger, imitating most realistically the 'dressing down' which many will have been on the receiving end of, following some minor infringement of the school rules. This mimicking and clowning about has become an art form in itself. The winner will be the one who can get the squint in the eye exactly right, whilst at the same time providing a realistic voice to accompany it! A common enough experience it is now in the evening to hear a knock on the dormitory door and on confirming entry, a face will appear around the door with a screwed up left eye accompanied by a pointing finger, "McCart, have you got a minute?" Such stupidity – but hilarious, nonetheless. One might suppose that this acting about will run its course. Not so. With the headmaster's facial features providing such an invitation, it seems highly likely that the mimicking will more than likely run and run. It is irresistible!

In addition, an on-going battle between the senior boarders and Mr Hagen is now playing itself out throughout the school with regard to appearance. Hair is grown as long as is possible, sideboards left to flourish and even beards attempted, merely because all are frowned on by authority. An uneasy peace will be negotiated, only for it to be ditched when rebellious youth again will attempt to flout convention, if only to see for how long the insurgency can prevail. To paraphrase Shelley, 'a great war between young and old' – well, sort of! A war being fought quite unseen in a tiny outpost of the West Riding. Rather a 'David and Goliath' war – but who is who? "It is a battle that you cannot win, McCart!" is the deputy headmaster's assessment. Okay, but that will not stop the fighting. Some relaxation of hair length has been allowed, yes, but where is the line drawn? When is long too long? Modern fashion creeps in – as it must, but very slowly.

The war will always be lost, yes, but the individual battles are keenly fought and provide good spectator sport within the boarding house and, indeed, for the school at large. This, it seems, is all part of the growing up process. Perhaps it is the most visible way the boarding house males have of being seen to rebel against authority. (A most necessary part of all of us becoming responsible citizens – at least, according to 'A' Level sociology books!) It is a way of showing the teaching staff that the boarding house is actually, well, grown up. It wants to be grown up and have its own independent thought. In reality, or at least according to some of the teaching staff, it displays just how much more learning and teaching is still required, as the ignorance of youth is laid bare. Frustratingly, a father has recently expressed a similar view, his advice being to, "Toe the line, you are there for learning." No meeting of minds then regarding length of hair, sideburns, etc. Nor is there likely to be any time soon.

A new headmaster causes change. A change in procedures. A change of emphasis in the various aspects of school life. A change in educational ideas. A change of outlook, etc. Never mind. The stability needed during these changes is being provided by the 'second in command' – the mathematics teacher and deputy headmaster, Norman Southwell. He has, it is alleged, been resident at the school since "God left Chorley" and that is, understandably, thought to be some considerable time ago! [Question: why the hell would God visit Chorley…?] A cold, steely exterior hides what seems to be a cold steely interior – that is unless one happens to be a mathematics genius which then give both teacher and pupil a common interest or bond. (And within the second year 6th form, there would only appear to be a solitary mathematics genius – Goldsack.) An apparent lack of a sense of humour is, perhaps, understandable from someone charged with sorting out the potential chaos of school timetabling with regard to lessons and form rooms, whilst also being responsible for school examinations. Local folklore continues to maintain that the inevitable complications of a school timetable have been regularly resolved by the timetable template being packed in his suitcase when holidays are taken. It can then be studied in the peace and quiet, far away from the school premises. Sporting rather cold, austere facial features, it is easy to imagine that the most enjoyable part of the holiday for Mr Southwell will, indeed, be sorting out the complexities of the school timetable – whilst the rest of his family enjoy the beach, or whatever!

Lost in the midst of time is the origin of the slightly vulgar nickname given to the deputy headmaster – the nickname "Snot" being used universally across the school. It is a nickname which has clearly been handed down by successive generations of pupils who have revelled in the certain knowledge that it is an accurate reflection of the character of the deputy headmaster. No doubt Snot has been known to laugh on occasions, but no one, as yet, has ever volunteered that they have actually witnessed it happening. His appropriate nickname has also been given to the road that climbs steeply uphill away from Millhouses – a hamlet between Wray and Low Bentham. Buses frequently have difficulty with this hill, particularly in the winter. The only correlation that one can draw between 'Snot's hill' and Snot is that they are both bloody awkward!

The 6th form boarders' study block, built as an addition to the main building in 1969. The Head Boarder occupied the top left room (window open), looking down to the swimming pool (the steps in the right foreground lead directly to the pool).

As always and, indeed, as one might anticipate in such an enclosed (school) community, the rumour mill was in full operation towards the end of the last academic year. Those in the know (or should it be – those who think they are in the know) suggest that there is "something going on" between Snot and Mrs Jagger, the French teacher who came to the school in 1967. The suggestion of a secretive liaison between them is explained (the rumour mill suggests) by something as simple as how they look at each other. Alternatively, in the absence of any hard evidence, in the words of the 6th form girls who perhaps have an eye for these things, "you can just tell". If, seemingly, the pupils can "just tell", then what about the teachers and/or our Headmaster? In a school of some three hundred and sixty pupils, such rumours spread as an out-of-control fire might and are never easy to dampen down. A comparison? – a bit like distant thunder, rumbling away! But now, who was it that said, "there's no smoke without fire"?

(Oh yes, and whoever it was that nicked Snot's wrought-iron gates at his Low Bentham house, one thing is for sure – it was nothing to do with those in the boarding house!)

So, although it is consoling to think that nothing has changed, the truth is that indeed it has changed. Is such change necessary and desirable? Whatever one feels, the privacy of a dormitory study room acts as a refuge. As in previous years, on the often calm and balmy September evenings, there is still sufficient daylight to enable one to sit and gaze out of the dormitory window. To see the lush green school lawns laid out alongside the riverbank, where girl guides meet twice weekly in huddles of three or four for 'secret' talks, fully aware, of course, that they are being watched. Then they will be on their way, but not before invariably having a quick glance up at the Lonsdale dormitory room windows in the certain knowledge that they are in the presence of watchful eyes, each of them taking a cue from their leader and offering a rather shy goodbye wave.

In this enclosed private world, with a study dormitory of one's own and with the door firmly shut to preserve privacy – a privacy which was yearned for all those years ago when as an innocent twelve-year-old life in this boarding school commenced – it is easy to be cocooned from events elsewhere. The horrors of the darker side of human nature have been displayed for all to see at the Olympics, taking place in Munich. But here, in a peaceful backwater in the most westerly reaches of the West Riding of Yorkshire, it is possible to watch the individual seasons as they come and go and everything else can be successfully shut out.

Scattered across the lawns adjoining the river, bunches of snowdrops will, in due course, give a welcome signal of approaching spring, generally in late January and sometimes even earlier if the winter has been mild. The snowdrops will be closely followed in February and March by clutches of golden daffodils (to coin a phrase!) and only thereafter, once they have flowered, will the unmistakable sound of the sizable 'sit-on' *Dennis* petrol lawn mower be heard in the seemingly capable hands of the janitor, an unsmiling Mr Heal – otherwise known, rather appropriately, as 'Chopper'. He will be watched, in a fit of laziness, from the safety of and in the accompanying privacy of the dormitory room, following a day's classroom study. Whilst looking ancient, the petrol mower has done its job effectively for virtually a quarter of a century and Chopper would not look out of place steering it confidently, as he does, around a cricket pitch in the process of being prepared for a forthcoming test match.

In the spring and summer, with the foliage by the edge of the riverbank having claimed the area for itself, a peaceful walk can be taken along the narrow stretch of lawn between the river and the adjacent churchyard. This area has always been commonly known as 'The Wilderness'. An apt description as the summer growth is, it always appears, left to its own devices in this most western aspect of the school grounds. Previously, this had been an area exclusively for the girls, but more recently, it has been made available for boarders and it is ideal for those wanting some quiet contemplation. A dry-stone wall separates this wilderness from the neighbouring churchyard, effectively protecting the gravestones from potential flooding from the river when in spate. However, the wall separating the two is low enough in places for the various headstones to be seen whilst walking along the narrow thoroughfare. Some of them must be all of two centuries old. Time has long passed them by and, unlike more recent graves which are well tended and kept pristine and display fresh flowers as evidence of remembrance, the older headstones are leaning at seemingly impossible angles and covered in many decades of moss, giving the area a general sense of neglect and an aura of sadness. The churchyard, always quiet and lonely, provides the opposite end of the spectrum to the customary noises of a sometime riotous boarding house. For those now being cared for by a motley collection of headstones and buried in abandoned graves, the question is often considered: were their sins forgiven? No answer has been forthcoming and nor will it ever be. However, the stark contrast between that silent final resting place and a boisterous boarding house regularly proves thought provoking. By the churchyard, the river – ever present – is a permanent companion but forever changing its mood, whilst the churchyard itself remains impassive to the various quirks of nature and to the passage of time.

Next to the well-manicured lawns, by the riverbank and directly under this dormitory room, the Swimming Pool. Unheated and therefore only for the brave. Indeed, only the very brave will tend to avail themselves of it in the autumn and winter terms, although with the onset of cold winter weather, the pool takes a seasonal 'break' and is emptied. Occasionally, some unfortunate soul from the boarding house will be unceremoniously thrown in fully clothed, generally under cover of darkness – not necessarily as a punishment, but rather out of boisterous good fun. For the victim, of course, it is not remotely funny! Quite the opposite. Nevertheless, great fun to watch! (Perhaps in time future, the unlucky souls will look back with some nostalgia at getting an unfortunate drenching. Or perhaps they might wish to forget!) Whilst sat in the dormitory room, industriously wading through pages of prep, a sudden loud splash of water with accompanied laughing will always give the game away and the boarding house prefects are immediately galvanised into action. The perpetrators would be rounded up to be punished – but by then, of course, the deed has been done, the laughs have been had and one cold and very wet pupil would be away to a dormitory to change!

The pool was built some five years ago with the help of generous donations from parents, local businesses and through various fundraising activities. Plus, of course, the 'volunteered' labour of the junior forms – such labour having been utilised in its construction. The boys were taught how to hold a spade and, more importantly, how to start digging with one. (Actually, it always seemed that the majority preferred digging a large hole in the ground to woodwork lessons!) By the summer of 1967, the building of the swimming pool was all but complete and ready for use. (After some last-minute alterations to the structure.) It spawned a wave (oh dear...) of enthusiasm, with swimming sports hotly contested. There have been, and there still are, several within the boarding house ranks who possess a natural flair for swimming. In particular, those who regularly disappear abroad during the holidays to overseas countries, where the hot climate makes swimming a natural and enjoyable pastime. Swimming as a pastime? Really? What is the point of swimming back and forward from one end of the pool to the other? It is rather akin to lying idly in the sunshine at a beach doing absolutely nothing. Boring! Nevertheless, with the advent of the school swimming pool, it was, predictably, only a matter of time before the challenge of distance swimming was attempted. The honour of being the first person to swim a mile in the pool went to Blas Nadramia, a lad in the boarding house. Whilst a good number of boarders had been patient enough to watch this record developing, most lost count or gave up counting the number of lengths Blas had successfully completed on the way to accomplishing such a feat. Just how many lengths was it? A lot!

*[**An aside**: Swimming! It was all so different as an eight- and nine- year-old whilst living in the sweltering heat of Aden. The wide sandy beach at Tarshyne proved an irresistible urge for an elder brother and "the twins" – that is, once the sun had passed the midday meridian, thereby ensuring that the heat was manageable so that fair skin did not have cause for complaint come the night-time. On the beach, the rollers would come surging in, easily pummelling over a rather weakling child and pushing one back quite easily up to the edge of the surf line, despite the frantic fight against the waves - but therein was the excitement. One could then run back down into the water and fight against the incoming tide and the seemingly huge waves, or alternatively wrestle with a brother to gain control of the family lilo. (Although his four-year age advantage always made it rather one-sided.) All that enjoyment within the safety and protection of shark nets at a suitable distance out in the bay, keeping the barracuda and other sea predators on the seaward side, thereby enabling carefree children to mess about in the warm Indian Ocean quite safely. The Indian Ocean – it was indeed pleasantly warm and to save the hassle of leaving the water when ablutions were required, one could nonchalantly pee into the underwater warmth – as if it were quite normal to do so whilst swimming around. Strangely, the warmth*

engendered within the swimming trunks was different altogether from the warmth of the water...

The sand, yes, it wangled its way into every nook and cranny and most certainly, as Betjeman suggested in his autobiography on childhood, there was 'sand in the sandwiches' – but not in the drinks, which were provided, icy cold, from a huge cylindrical flask – that is, providing there had not been an explosion within the inner casing of the flask, meaning cold orange juice would be intermixed with thousands of shards. (An exploding flask – always an enjoyable accident in the view of the children who were then able to buy a bottle of ice-cold Fanta or Pepsi-Cola from the beach NAFFI store.) An acceptable irritant the sand undoubtedly was and only just tolerable to a child who, even at that young age, liked to have everything neat, in order and in its place.

In the midst of such entertainment, there out at sea in the middle-distance, the comings and goings of the regular passenger and cargo ships, on their way in and out of Aden harbour – a harbour hidden from the beach by a headland which kept the bay suitably private. Their passage backwards and forwards on long ocean voyages gave a natural continuity to those afternoons and evenings spent on the beach and many of the passenger ships became familiar friends, immediately recognisable by their shape, structure and funnel design. Their names would be looked up in a brother's Ian Allan ship combine and underlined, a precursor to the train spotting at the commencement of boarding school life.

Scant wonder then that art lessons had been exclusively turned over to the drawing of ships and trains. The P & O shipping line became a particular favourite, most probably because a passage to and from the Far East (in this case Southampton–Singapore in 1957 and the return home in 1960) had been undertaken on a ship from the P & O Line, the SS Carthage. It perhaps whet one's appetite for that particular shipping line, with its passenger ships sporting an attractive white hull and buff coloured funnel. That bond was further strengthened on the return home from Aden in 1963 on their liner SS Himalaya, eventually berthing, after a fourteen-day voyage, at a cold and windy Tilbury dock. Fourteen days of carefree entertainment and, not only that, but a homeward bound passage in the first-class section of the ship. However, any 'one-upmanship' that might have been engendered by being in the 'posh' bit was largely lost, of course, on a nine-year-old child!

There were occasions when the beach at Tarshyne doubled up as the venue (after dark) for an open-air film show. The films were always watched to the rather exciting accompaniment of the continual sound of waves pushing up the beach. With the darkness, there was always the recurrent urge to look over one's shoulder to see whether the water was likely to encroach on the array of chairs and their occupants whilst the film was showing. It did, just the once necessitating a swift operation in chair removal to further up the beach. (Had someone got the tide times wrong?) As a child, it was always quite thrilling being sat on the beach at night watching a film on a makeshift screen, totally in the open air, with the constant lapping of water never quite out of hearing range.

Some of those memories from Aden, ingrained at that time into a young lad's memory, remain in adolescence as vivid as ever. Watching an open day at RAF Khormaksar when a Hawker Hunter jet failed in its attempt to 'Loop-the-Loop' (or whatever such manoeuvre the poor pilot had in mind) and ploughed into the ground, causing a huge fireball. The crowd, initially silent for a few unbelievable seconds, before the inevitable screams began. It has remained in the sub-conscious ever since, as vivid as the day it happened. It may well stay lodged in the memory forever as, in the words of W. H. Auden, 'one thinks of a day when one did something slightly unusual...'

Other memories: the street beggars – almost everywhere, generally missing limbs (legs more often than not), always asking – pleading – for money. Pulling at the heart strings, particularly those belonging to a sympathetic mother who would invariably hand over some coins - much to the dismay of a rather more sceptical father, who would steadfastly refuse to be – as he would term it – conned! For a mother, it was always worthwhile, as her gesture of generosity engendered a beaming smile from one of the regular beggars, shorn of legs and moving about with the help of two large wooden planks tied to his hands. A life, surely, of torment, temporarily lightened by the generosity of a stranger from a foreign land.

The amazing sight, and one which still brings a smile, was that of watching literally hundreds of local Arabs running down Maalla straight, the main thoroughfare within the colony, divesting themselves of their shoes/sandals as they ran. (Why were they running? Where were they running?) Shoes and sandals going in all directions – then, perversely, a couple of Arab men walking calmly behind the 'mob' collecting up all the footwear. Into a large container the shoes and sandals went. How would they be re-united with their respective owners? Would they ever be re-united with the same pair of feet? A *father, seemingly knowledgeable on matters such as Yemeni footwear, had suggested, rather sarcastically, that they would be re-sold back! Surely not.*

And then there was "the walker" – christened as such by that same sarcastic father. Every day without fail, "the walker", – a tall thin Arab in traditional Arab dress – would stride up and down the dead straight half-mile or so of the Maalla thoroughfare. A firm wide stride, no stopping, whilst at the same time he would be shouting away in Arabic, generally to himself as it always seemed to be the case that no one else was listening. He was left to his own devices. And all the time whilst walking – eating or chewing some strange substance, which a father called 'khat'. It was, a father suggested, most likely the cause of his rather strange behaviour and would be doing him no good! ("But why does he eat it, Dad, if it does him no good?" A young boy was rather puzzled.) Indeed, a lesson in learning for siblings, witnessing it all from the safety of a first floor flat. Surely, a lesson also for Sociology study with regard to human nature. Quite obviously, though, a quite different set of unwritten rules governing everyday life in that Middle East outpost – a world away from studying Sociology in the UK.

There may be unwritten rules here, in our westernized culture – in Aden, there was a distinct lack of what was taboo and what was not. This manifested itself in the local Arab men (and it was always the men – just where exactly were all the women!) thinking nothing of stopping in the street and 'performing' their ablutions in the public domain, including what is comically termed a 'heavy job' within the confines of the Lonsdale complex. At least their Arab 'skirts' were ideal as recommended clothing for such activity – notwithstanding as to what they were wearing, it was an eye opener indeed to a youngster from the 'civilized' world! Such activities were soon accepted without comment, as the norm, in that dry, dusty, sun-scarred British colony.

Not quite so funny as a mob flailing their shoes in all directions – although perhaps it was for young children at the time – was watching as an elder brother dropped his hand made water bombs from the balcony of that flat in Maalla onto local Arab traders on the street below, or else he would be shining a torch down on them whilst they were sat passing the time of day on a roadside pavement. Parents were not amused – neither were the traders particularly and there was immediate retaliation with stones hitting the window of the flat. Most definitely not amusing – indeed, more worrying – was the explosion at an electricity sub-station on Maalla, very near to the flat, courtesy of a bomb thrown from a passing vehicle. It was a time when the initial yearning for independence was beginning to show itself visibly.

For a child then, the British colony of Aden, for all its sweltering heat and subsequent problems, culminating in that British withdrawal some four years later, had seemed an idyllic existence, albeit that there was always a struggle between fair skin and sunshine. Indeed, it was idyllic, notwithstanding the heat and the regular tingling on legs, arms and on a freckly face, at the end of a day when too much time had been spent in the sun. (On with the Calamine lotion – YUK!) But nothing can or will last forever, and a father's two-year posting came to an end as 1963 came to an end. Aden was left behind and life moved on. Within a few years, the harsh reality of boarding house life presented a complete divergence from that of the former colony, both in terms of the experience of day-to-day life and in the entertainment available. That is, of course, when one was not in the 'straight-jacket' of learning.

A final reflection on Aden – an elder brother would like to return to Aden in the future to 're-live' the recent memories. Someone once said, 'Don't ever go back to the places where one was happy as a child'. Why not? The passage of time can change one's perspective – is that possible? A younger brother, ensconced in this very western outpost of the West Riding, is in any case, rather unsure about a return, however brief, to that Middle Eastern outpost – a very different one indeed compared to this West Riding outpost and the environs of Low Bentham.

Swimming – well, okay. But sunbathing? It has always been somewhat of a puzzle as to why one's parents and siblings were forever obsessed with sunbathing whilst the family lived in Singapore, Aden and Iran! What is the purpose in it? A satisfactory response has never really been provided. The verdict? Too hot, too boring and rather lazy!]

Below this dormitory window, gusts of wind from the west (the eastern side of the swimming pool being protected by a high screen – essentially a wall of breeze blocks behind a façade of stone to give the appearance of a stone wall) will often push ripples of water against the sides of the swimming pool and sometimes over, giving a continual impression of it having just rained, leaving a patchwork of wet concrete surrounds, as if drying in the warm sunshine. During the worst of winter weather, when gales come sweeping across from the Irish sea, the water in the pool will often be whipped up and instead of modest ripples, will resemble quite respectable waves. Once they have formed high enough, they then crash against the sides of the pool and gush over, completely covering the surrounding concrete. Fascinating to watch and mildly hypnotic. Always a pleasant break from homework. A solution during inclement weather will often be to completely empty the pool, with a tarpaulin then being tied over the top of the pool for safety. Once ready to be re-filled, this will be achieved with two standard garden hose pipes and it will, therefore, be an operation that inevitably takes some considerable time. From the dormitory window, it is always difficult not to be spellbound, watching the water literally dribbling in and the process would still be on-going well into the following day. When glancing out of the window during the process, a mental note is unconsciously made as to the progress with the re-filling, involving upwards of 43,000 gallons of water. Allowing the mind to wander and to take an interest in what is essentially a mundane operation regularly proves to be eminently successful as a required break from the drudgery of the boring parts of study material.

To the immediate east of the swimming pool and just visible from the window, the area which has been, over the years, traditionally reserved for boys and used as the playground. The prefabricated 'temporary' classrooms to the south (although just how temporary the classrooms, built with the aid of pupils under Lonny's supervision in 1968, actually turn out to be, when there will always be a myriad of other pressing building needs in a private school remains to be seen) provide a barrier from the river and the north border is the dining room building. Cutting the playground directly in two stands a high stone wall, probably upwards of a height of ten feet. In those early days of the mid-to-late 1960s, when the segregation of the sexes was rigidly adhered to (albeit that Bentham was a co-educational school – in the classrooms at least), this wall acted as the defining line or border between the play areas for the girls and boys. The girls' area, between the wall and the dining room, was strictly out of bounds to the boys during break time and at lunchtime. If a teacher on playground duty was not there to ensure the segregation remained secure, then the fact that straying into the other section was taboo sufficed as a restraining factor. Not being able to play in the girls' section was not, however, of any consequence to teenage lads, whose main concern during break times was to succeed as far as possible in the game of 'British Bulldog'. Perish the thought of being one of the first to be caught. There was a good deal of kudos being one of the last and managing to escape the clutches of the many – they who had already been captured. They would be lined up, determined to stop you passing through the line of 'Bulldogs', standing there looking horribly aggressive because they had been previously caught. That was the time, of course, to take it out on someone you didn't particularly care for – it would be assumed that it was all part of the game!

If it was not 'British Bulldog' that was taking up the playground space and keeping teenagers occupied during break time, then it would be the game that, at that time, had recently been introduced by Mr Ratcliffe, then a reserve or 'stand-in' housemaster. The game he introduced was coined 'Off-Ground'. The aim, of course, was to avoid being caught and so one had to find within the (boys) playground area anything that was raised off the ground and that could be stood on, however precariously, at which point, one could not be caught. If it was raining, then the game was transferred almost seamlessly to the Assembly Hall, to the exclusion of anything else that might have been proposed or planned in the hall by other pupils.

Mr Ratcliffe was considered a schoolboy hero. Certainly, he was to the trainspotting boarders, with his legendary middle of the night recordings of steam trains heading past the school. All done from the comfort of his private room, within the attic of the main boarding house, with his window wide open. This was, in many ways, the catalyst for the thrill of watching the passage of steam engines in the night from the 'Cottage' dormitory in 1967, despite those regular protestations from Titty requesting an immediate return to bed. Mr Ratcliffe was indeed a champion within the boarding house ranks and it had, therefore, been all the more inexplicable when suddenly, he was no longer at the school. No reason given, no understanding why. He had just left without any prior notice under unexplained circumstances. Plenty of rumours. Suggestions of a secret assignation with a married member of staff, or perhaps with the history teacher, Miss Clarke – but she was not married – so surely, no problem! Had he been too persistent with his attentions? (Or, in dormitory language, did he "try to have it off" with her?) Miss Clarke, herself, left at the end of the same school academic year. Lots of conjecture, of course, but regarding his unexplained disappearance, the rumour mill failed in its primary task – that of finding out the facts! Yes, it was a puzzle and indeed, it has remained so. The world has kept on spinning, yes, but the boarding house lost, at that time, one of its most enthusiastic proponents.

Looking out of the dormitory window now, early evening, this playground area will generally stand empty and silent. There is the occasional game of impromptu football (after homework), involving the more junior dormitories, providing a familiar vocal background from that area of the school, whilst revising or whilst tackling, quite reluctantly, a Sociology essay. For 6th formers, any early evening entertainment following dinner, when not in hibernation in the dormitory of course, will most likely involve chatting to the female boarders before they make their way back up to Collingwood and Ford House, on the High Bentham Road. The girls always, predictably, making good use of the school minibus, rather than utilising their feet. Well, they would, wouldn't they? Those lovely female legs are NOT made for walking. [Despite what Nancy Sinatra may have said – well okay, perhaps that was with boots – but their graceful legs will be inside the boots!] Why walk when a lift in the school minibus is on offer?

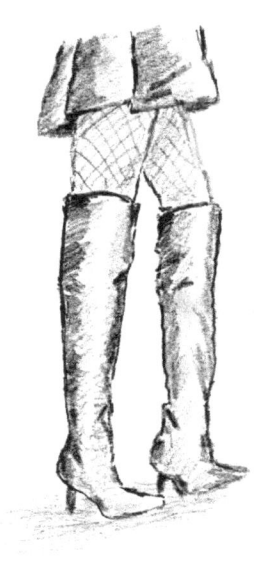

Absolutely no possibility of the 6th form boarders accompanying the senior girls up to Ford House. Sadly then, it is only the day boys who have, *it is alleged*, watched in awe from the roadside pavement as a daring young lady (she remains anonymous) gets changed in front of the first-floor bay window at Ford House – no doubt fully appreciating that, with her room light on and her curtains open, it presents an enviable combination (that is, for those watching on the pavement)! Fully changed? Surely not (the day boys are not telling…) but certainly down to knickers and bra – which would assist enormously with the Lonsdale dormitory rateability test. Typical! Missing out on such enjoyment. Life can be (and is) so unfair for boarders!

The river, surrounding the east and south of the school, acts as a natural border. The Wenning, a tributary to the River Lune, traces its source back a mere four miles eastwards, at the confluence of Clapham Beck and Austwick Beck near Clapham village and in the shadow of Ingleborough, one of the Yorkshire 'three peaks' – Whernside and Penyghent being the other two. Take a walk inside Ingleborough show cave, approx. a mile from Clapham village, on the way to the famous Gaping Gill pothole on the flanks of Ingleborough, and the crystal-clear waters that flow through the channels within that cave commence the formation of the Wenning. Making its way via a series of 'hair pin' bends, the river passes through High Bentham and Low Bentham, before running a course beside the school grounds to eventually have its meeting with the Lune five miles westwards, near Hornby, Lancashire.

At times, particularly in the summer, it might appear as a small stream barely managing to make its way westwards towards the larger Lune. However, following periods of wet weather, it never fails to impress, with a surging water flow which frequently floods the school land which it borders. Whilst only small in length, the river, nevertheless, has provided over several years many hours of free entertainment for the boarding house – be it fly fishing in the gentle rapids or casting a fishing line into the numerous deep pools of water away from the main current. Within the fishing fraternity, there is the everlasting hope of catching either brown trout or sea trout – or whatever swims in freshwater rivers! For the younger boys, there is sufficient interest in searching for bullheads under the small rocks and stones in the shallows.

In addition, the river provides a predictable refuge for wildlife and, with luck, the view from the dormitory window will include the occasional sighting of a heron, stealthily and with purpose moving along the river shallows, as if walking on eggshells, ready to pounce on any unsuspecting fish. A keen eye may also, apparently, spot kingfishers and dippers (and indeed, it will need to be a keen eye – the eyes looking out of this window are not quite so 'eagle-eyed'!) whilst an open window in the evening will confirm the presence in the wood, adjoining the river, of woodpeckers and tawny owls. The giveaway presence of the woodpecker within the wood being regularly provided by the constant sound of high-speed drilling, interspersed by short silent gaps before another burst of drilling is heard, as the woodpecker makes a successful insertion into the bark of a tree. By contrast, the tawny owl sounds suitably laid back, with its occasional hooting in the darkness echoing across from the wood, giving notice of its presence within its territory to any prospective interlopers.

A long hot summer will invariably see swimming in the river as a preferable pastime to doing the same thing in the swimming pool. Local folklore has also suggested that the river has been used as a makeshift ice-skating rink for the boarders during very severe winters and at other times boarders would build temporary dams (although this ceased after intervention from the water bailiffs). When the volume of water in the river was low, it would be a test of skill to see if any boarder, willing and brave enough, could manage to get across the river on foot to the adjoining wood – to then return to the school side, again crossing the riverbed. There would, of course, be the inevitable fall if a step was misjudged, to the accompaniment of a round of applause and cheers from those watching by the riverbank! In recent times, such enjoyment has ceased...

Indeed, the school cross-country runs threaded a course across the river at one time. It was always rather a daunting prospect for young, hesitant teenagers – the successful way to get across the river was, by all accounts, to start running fast and not to stop – and not to look down. Easier said than done! That particular route for the cross-country runs was eventually discontinued on safety grounds. All in all, the river – ever present – has played and continues to play a large and continuing part in boarding house life. Well, almost. Rather sadly, it is difficult to shake off the general feeling that the significance of the river does seem to have lessened somewhat in recent years. One no longer sees a regular line up of fisherman boarders along the riverbank, casting their lines into the deep pools, hoping to catch, well, something – anything! Hope, as the saying goes, springs eternal and it still does. But in this case, with fewer and fewer keen fishermen from the boarding house.

Across on the opposite bank of the river, stands a small wood. It is riddled with paths, some authorised walking routes, others not – but, nevertheless, used regularly as short cuts during games lessons when the cross-country runs are routed through the trees and vegetation. The correct route for cross-country runs goes down some fairly steep banks within the wood – hence, in the absence of the watching eyes of a games teacher, the unauthorised routes would be searched out as an easier option. If a teacher was indeed there – and especially if it was Dracula – then a helpful hand from him in the small of the back would assist an unfortunate pupil on his way down a steep gully on the authorised route!

At the far edge of the wood, a minor unclassified road, winding its way up the surrounding hillside. Known locally as the Millhouses Road, it threads a route, heading westwards towards and through the tiny hamlet of the same name. This road will take vehicles almost exclusively to surrounding farms. That is, unless the traveller wants to take a relaxed and casual journey to the west, across the modest hills. Alternatively, this minor road can be used to travel south to gain access to the Forest of Bowland, an area consisting primarily of high moorland and designated an 'area of outstanding natural beauty', sitting primarily in North-East Lancashire but nudging ever so slightly into the West Riding. Ordinarily, motor traffic heading to the west or South-West would use the main thoroughfare, the B6480, an old turnpike road passing in front of the school entrance and the church – this road linking Lancaster with the market towns of Settle and, further eastwards, Skipton.

With the fading autumn light and winter darkness, there is always the occasional sight from the dormitory window of car headlights on the minor road behind the school, heading one way or the other as people get on with their individual lives. As W. H. Auden succinctly phrased it in 'Musee des Beaux Arts', [they]... *'Had somewhere to get to and sailed calmly on'* (but driving, in this instance, not sailing)! The occupants of a car always oblivious, of course, to the watchful eyes of a restless adolescent in a dormitory room, who is rarely thinking about the future – notwithstanding that, very shortly, there will be a lifetime ahead to not only think about but, far more crucially, to plan for. Looking out of this window – always slightly ajar, on these balmy autumn evenings with the scent of freshly cut grass filtering in – any current or, indeed, any future plans beyond summer 1973 are not on an agenda – if indeed, an agenda of any worth actually exists. If it does exist, it is nowhere to be found in this private dormitory room.

An agenda? There will most certainly be an agenda in place from the school's perspective for this 6th form pupil, involving a degree course to follow 'A' Level studies. Precisely the same thought process is in place, surely, in the mind of a father who is now fully subsidising the boarding and tuition fees. In the absence of any other logical alternative, a degree course is an obvious progression. (Assuming suitable grades are obtained and who knows what they are likely to be. That will become clear once a discussion with Snot has taken place.) But progress to a higher level of educational learning is surely just deferring to a later date the choice of a career, is it not? In any case, what type of career? Do some people actually wake up one morning and decide they want to be a doctor, a policeman, an accountant? Nothing like that has yet happened in this dormitory room. Some things are, nevertheless, set in stone. For instance, a future occupation, whatever it might be, will certainly not involve woodwork or, for that matter, art and design. Neither will it involve becoming a lighthouse keeper as one ex-pupil has become – a private study room yes, but a lonely lighthouse! You prospective architects and joiners – and lighthouse keepers – sleep easy in your bed.

CHAPTER XI

I THOUGHT YOU WERE FAIRLY GROWN UP

As the days shorten, the lights are switched on for evening prep in each of the boarding house dormitory rooms. These south facing rooms enjoy the morning sunshine when the sun rises over the nearby rolling hills but, consequently, miss out on the beauty of any sunsets which might form and be displayed from the west. As compensation, perhaps, for missing the 'western glow' of sunset, these individual dormitory rooms, whose sole purpose often appears to be merely for sitting at a desk for evening prep and thereafter, for sleeping, have a birds-eye-view of the river. The river – ever present, but never the same – making its torturous way westwards in a series of bends, trying its best to form an 'oxbow' lake, which no doubt it would eventually achieve in the absence of management by the human hand. The twisting riverbank enables batches of river foam to form in the moribund corners. These get gradually larger and appear to be seemingly immobile at the river margins beside the muddy bank, with a flow of water that is sometimes hardly noticeable at the river edge. Then suddenly, without warning, water will be pushed into the corners, take hold of the foam, split it into several parts and each individual section will then float away, carried gently by the river current, as if taking part in some organised river race. The foam then disappears around the next crazy hairpin bend of the river – and then gone. Gone forever! It makes compulsive viewing.

This is the view that, for a period of time during the first year's 'A' Level study, had been replaced by a dormitory room on the first floor, at the front of the original rectory building. Situated away from the Lonsdale dormitory complex, it was a move necessitated by the larger number of 6th form students boarding at that time. That room had been the one that, when the property had been the residence of the rector, had served as a bedroom for one of the servants. A grand room it indeed was – far bigger than the present dormitory, which provides privacy but limited space. It enjoyed a north facing aspect and an immediate view from the window of the main school driveway and of the side door into the school, used by pupils moving between classrooms and by those going into the Assembly Hall. It was a view that also took in the front manicured lawn and was the catalyst for taking cuttings of tulips flowering on the front flower beds during the spring of 1972, before placing them in water and then they would take pride of place on the shelf within the dormitory. An adolescent 6th former would then wonder, in silence, at their beauty. They were, of course, soon withered and the search was then on for new blood. Did the teachers or Chopper ever wonder where a good many of the tulip heads had disappeared to?

In terms of keeping an eye out on what was going on at the front of the school, the room was without competition and its size was welcome. But it did not enjoy the south facing aspect – the meandering river, the adjacent wood or, indeed, the pleasant area of lawn beside the river. Strangely, neither did it feel as private, with continuous activity below by the main school entrance always invading the quiet. The river, the wood, the lawn – all these provide a calming influence, giving a constant reminder of the rural surrounds. Whilst it is so easy to take a private dormitory for granted and to feel that it is, at the very least, an entitlement, spare a thought for the 6th form boarders prior to 1969. They had the dubious privilege of sharing a dormitory with several others, at a time when adolescence is being replaced by the concept of being grown-up, with the almost obligatory attendant requirement for occasional solitude and privacy.

The river, with its flow of water sometimes restless, at other times calming and occasionally in full flood, the coppice beyond with its criss-crossing of paths, the gentle lapping of water in a swimming pool, the playing areas of grass – all of these can and, indeed, do easily catch the wandering eyes of an Upper 6th form boarder looking out of a dormitory window, conveniently ignoring a large pile of textbooks sitting neatly in order on a study desk. (Not only neatly stacked but also arranged within each stack by size!) These three stacks of seemingly complicated reading material incorporate the 'nitty gritty' of the first year's 'A' Level study in three of the Arts – or the "easy" subjects, as Rosco calls them. No complicated Physics or Mathematics for the wimps in the art group! Instead – History, English Literature and Sociology.

These worn and well-thumbed books incorporate the various intrigues of those in charge of this island nation via medieval 'A' Level History. In this case, a comprehensive study of the Tudors and their successors, the Stuarts, and their counterparts in 'near' Europe – with the 'Diet of Worms' cruelly being compared to the standard of food being produced in the school kitchen by Titty, whose bawdy nickname is always spoken with relish and slight disdain within the boarding house, because of the general assumption that she continues to resist attempts by Mr Russell to improve diet. The 'Diet of Worms' involved the possible nemesis for Martin Luther at the hands of the assembly of the Holy Roman Empire, with strife and division at the centre of European religious faith. Boring it is, interesting it is not. The only thing to be learned, it seems, by the exploits of Martin Luther and his accusers is that some 500 years later, in the world at large with regard to religious faith, nothing has essentially changed! It might well be the case that religion, irrespective of whatever faith, has been, and is still, the major common denominator in the cause of war. Whether that would be relevant in an answer to a test paper question on fifteenth- and sixteenth-century History 'A' Level is open to conjecture. Perhaps, somehow, a way might be found to incorporate this theory into an answer on European history, bearing in mind that the period being studied seems to be awash with religious fervour.

*[**An aside:** and studying the Stuarts includes, of course, Charles I – "off with his head" having become a trade-mark exclamation in the senior echelons of the boarding house, whilst to some, the name Oliver Cromwell is inextricably linked with a famous British steam locomotive rather than a rebellious Parliamentarian whose face was covered in warts…]*

This stack of 'A' Level history books is complimented by a similar number of tomes on the core social problems facing Britain and the society we live in, since the beginning of the twentieth century. More crucially, they discuss how these problems might be solved (if only everyone could agree on how and why they were caused in the first place – if only, indeed!). Such discussions come under the group subject name of Sociology and the entire first year's study material seemed quite woolly to a disinterested seventeen-year-old boarder. Does it really matter how society is structured, what the prime causes of delinquency and graffiti are and whether poverty will ever be eliminated? Before even attempting to answer the contentious question on the potential elimination of poverty, many hours of verbal 'sparring' has already taken place between the sparse number of 6th form pupils brave enough to take on this seemingly pointless subject – three pupils commenced the two-year course – and the Sociology teacher, Miss Shirley, who, it is often thought, seems to be on a permanent crusade to promote the ideology of Socialism as a panacea to all ills. This is the same Miss D. A. Shirley who had leapt to fame (literally) for just – well – the briefest of moments in the 1960 Olympic Games, obtaining a silver medal for Great Britain in the high jump competition. It is something she reminds both pupils and staff about on a very regular basis. How many times does the story need telling?

[There is a story to tell linked to her silver medal! Three athletes had finished level in second place, having successfully jumped the same

height – Miss Shirley gained silver by virtue of a successful jump at the first attempt. Three attempts were allowed at each height and, if successful, one moved to the next height level. Miss Shirely and two others all failed at the next level, but one athlete had only succeeded at the previous level at the third attempt – thereby enabling Miss Shirley to gain silver – jointly with one other!]

There is no leaping about for sure with the 'A' Level Sociology course, quite the opposite in fact. It seems hard enough in discussion to even agree or decide on a definition of poverty, never mind getting to the 'nitty gritty' of deciding on the best ways to eliminate it. Here we are a good way through the twentieth century and society still grapples with problems of delinquency, graffiti and indeed, poverty (however it is assessed). A key question might well be to ask if poverty will ever be eliminated – would that be too obvious as an exam question in next years 'A' Level exam paper?

Exam question: Will poverty ever be eliminated?
Exam answer: No.
Exam result: Fail.

Ah, well…

There is no escaping the sneaking feeling among the three students involved in tackling this subject that there are no right or wrong answers to such complex problems. In theory, therefore, providing one presents a reasoned argument to whatever solution one enthuses over, then an 'A' Level pass will be in sight. 'In the bag', one might even suggest! This, by itself, perhaps, provides the sole justification for spending another year of study grinding away at insoluble problems. But why do our textbooks have to be so excruciatingly long-winded and complex in telling us what we sometimes already suspect? That is, that there is no solution to some problems within a complex and ever-changing society. With a probable pass already within one's grasp for Sociology 'A' Level (sometimes one feels compelled to count one's chickens – this is one of those occasions!), Miss Shirley's pet subject, (she 'doubles' as a Games teacher…) it is, perhaps, just as well that thoughts of abandoning it last year in favour of something 'meaty' like Geology had been quickly forgotten.

With the Geography and Geology courses, there seems to be adequate opportunity to spend days out in the nearby Dales on what might be termed 'field work'. Sociology, however, is virtually confined to the school desk, in the company of complex workbooks – albeit during the first year's study, there was a solitary visit away from the school premises to the Calderstones Mental hospital near Clitheroe. The most enjoyable part of that day's field work was undoubtedly stopping off on the way back to the boarding house at Farleton, near Lancaster, at the home of Mrs Atkinson. She was, in a previous life, Miss Lewis – the rather attractive young music teacher at the school prior to her leaving in 1970 to start a family. Miss Lewis was one of the few teachers that one could identify on her approach to the classroom even if one could not see her. This was by virtue of the regular beat and frequent clicking of her heels, the noise of which seemed to rebound off the walls of the corridor as she approached. It always sounded as though she was late and in a desperate hurry. Ah, Miss Lewis (as you were)! The music workbooks told us about Beethoven and Brahms, amongst others, and about quavers and semi-quavers. However, you told us more – albeit quite innocently – about attractive ladies, bouffant hair styles and rosy complexions!

Mrs Atkinson was sufficiently attractive to have almost warranted tackling Music 'A' Level had she still been at the school at the commencement of 'A' Level studies. Well, were it not for the fact that there would be almost certain failure at attempting to learn a musical instrument, coupled with the total inability to read and understand music and, most important of all, studying the subject would have witnessed a massive drop in respect from one's male – and macho – peer-group. Could one cope with being seen to take on such a soft subject? Music is, surely, for the girls! Sociology it is then that is being persevered with, a natural reticence for change also responsible to a degree for preventing a quick flip over to a Geology course during the last academic year.

Perhaps this pile of boring Sociology books, accumulated during the first year of study and taking up valuable space for writing essays and letters on the desk in the dormitory, might have been better used last year, for example, as a door stop to keep the dormitory door open, enabling the distant sounds of 'Argus', by the British rock band Wishbone Ash, to be heard wafting through the compressed air of a claustrophobic hallway, from a dormitory room further along the landing. However, the door will always have to stay firmly shut if the strained and morbid tones of Leonard Cohen are detected from the opposite end of the hallway. ('Once More with Felix' – not likely!) A real case of 'one man's meat'– and a reflection of the diverse musical tastes emanating from a motley collection of a dozen-and-a-half 6th form students. With the door closed as necessary to avoid the musical treats on offer elsewhere, the sound of the pages of Sociology textbooks being quickly flipped over can always be accompanied by the ever so slightly rebellious lyrics of Lindisfarne, with their 1970 LP release 'Nicely Out of Tune'. To 6th form ears it is anything but out of tune. With two poignant lines from that LP's 'Scarecrow Song' sounding out:

Your Saturday nights, they are sober,
And your Sundays are too long.

It is, regretfully, easy to agree with the first line. Saturday nights in the boarding house are indeed sober. As far as Sundays are concerned, after a compulsory Sunday church service (and the rector's sermons are quite definitely too long – someone needs to tell him!), the rest of the day is just not long enough, with no free time (or is 'freedom' a more appropriate word?) until after church and lunch. Sundays are just not long enough.

However, the content incorporated in this third pile of reading material sitting on the desk has already proved to be far more enjoyable than the rather boorish behaviour of the Tudors and Stuarts and considerably more interesting than the complexities over how an enlightened society might be better structured. This pile of books has become precious – to be read and re-read until the pages have been left tired and "dog-eared" with continual use. 'A' Level English Literature is to be nurtured, longingly pored over late at night and early in the morning. Before school, after school, during school – and if it was feasible, even whilst in the bath! The study of poetry and classical literature has opened up a world of imagination, often blurring the lines between make-believe and reality and nurturing an appreciation of the surrounding Yorkshire Dales countryside. It has given a speedy impetus to the creative juices of romance, which have lain dormant and are now ready to be awakened by an array of attractive female students in the Lower and Upper 6th form. There can be no flunking English Literature.

This third pile of books, easily forming the highest pile, might well have formed a 'sub' (or fourth pile) if there was the space available on this study desk. The school study books for English Literature have been supplemented at regular intervals by individual purchases from pocket money, carefully saved up from when, in time-honoured fashion, the cash is handed out to pupils on Saturday morning after breakfast. But now, at the senior level of the boarding hierarchy, pocket money can, if necessary, be an issue for discussion with Mr Russell, so that one may have what one requests if it is for a specific purpose. Always providing, of course, that the pocket money 'pot' is being regularly replenished by parents. (Regular letters are sent reminding them that it needs to be frequently topped up!)

The school's textbook on John Keats is now ably supported by the purchase of *Keats, Poetical Works* (now an entire collection of poems can be studied and not just a select few). The *Collected Shorter Poems* by W. H. Auden has provided a far clearer insight into a twentieth century poet (and a living poet at that, here in 1972) than the school study book available. Similar purchases have

I THOUGHT YOU WERE FAIRLY GROWN UP

followed, with John Donne, Milton and Wordsworth, together with a clutch of 'literary critiques' covering the authors and poets in the 'A' Level curriculum. To fail in English Literature has, from the outset, been unthinkable.

A delicious mix of ancient and modern literature has been provided for study. Henry Fielding produces a hero in *Tom Jones* to whom aspiring 6th form male students, looking for romance, can easily relate to and perhaps emulate. (Well, the ladies in that novel were not slow at stripping off and Tom was never slow to take advantage! Who suggested the Victorians were boring and prude?) In *Villette*, Charlotte Brontë's character Lucy Snowe shows quite the opposite, with a sort of reserve that, whilst acceptable no doubt in select sections of nineteenth-century society, is certainly considered somewhat boring in the late twentieth century 6th form common room. Surely, hopefully, the young women in the 6th form, with their protruding bosoms, curvy hips and slick, lithe legs, are not like that! Even *Paradise Lost* and *The Canterbury Tales* (abridged version, this is despite the fact that 6th form students are nominally considered 'grown up') have been enthusiastically devoured. In addition, such an oddity (to 6th form students at least with a previously restricted knowledge of English Literature) as *The Playboy of the Western World* by J. M. Synge has been given a cautious (but studied) welcome. That was still the case even when it was established that the Western World depicted is the western fringe of Eire, not quite the most obvious venue for a playboy!

Perhaps the only exception to such enthusiasm for English Literature involves the most famous bard of all, William Shakespeare. Tackling *King Lear*, whilst necessary, is being studied rather painfully and almost as a form of penance! Does anyone enjoy Shakespeare at school? Is it supposed to be enjoyed? If anyone enjoys studying it, then certainly there must be something wrong with them. As a father would say, "They need their head seeing to"!

There has been no wish to cut corners in 'A' Level English Literature. It was natural to feel aggrieved, therefore, with the 'throw away' comment which had appeared, without any prior warning, on the school report under English Literature at the end of the previous term, immediately prior to the summer holiday break – viz: *'hopefully, this young man will very soon start to take this subject more seriously and so benefit himself to the extent he deserves'*. Just perhaps, with a modicum of thought, that sort of comment might well have been predicted. Why? Contained within the English 'A' Level end of term report immediately preceding Christmas 1971, after only one term of 'A' Level study, was the simple, but stark, comment, *'too fond of oral objection: he will be good when that has worked out of his system'*! A leopard doesn't change its spots – or so the saying goes. These two comments, in some respects, mirror the form teacher's comment from the form IIIA school report in spring 1967, *'he often seems oblivious of all authority'*!

Ah, the form teacher responsible for those comments from early boarding school years. Mr Warbrick – school librarian, a teacher of the languages and a study in poise and presentation! Tall, very tall, thin as a beanpole, always seemingly sporting brown shoes and what to teenagers seemed to be rather posh, patterned suits. And then, to top it all off, a bow tie – nicknamed by pupils as a "dicky" and looking somewhat incongruous within the confines of the classroom. But this was a teacher just starting out on a career, not at the end of it. One might have accepted a bow tie being sported by an 'old timer', winding down to retirement. Would one expect it with someone fresh from teaching college? After all, this grammar school is not exactly Eton or Stowe. Never mind, figuring largely on the plus side, Mr Warbrick was, and still is, a railway enthusiast. For that, he can be forgiven his religious adherence to strange-patterned suits and a "dicky".

Notwithstanding any obvious shortcomings, the urge to succeed in English Literature has been, and still is, as strong as ever. Failure in English Literature is not an option. Indeed, there exists an insatiable appetite for literature, perhaps less so for history. Such youthful enthusiasm for learning is, though, sadly lacking with the bland statements from Miss Shirley extolling the virtues of Sociology and, by extension, socialism.

It would, however, be fair to say that the two seemingly fatuous comments included in the respective term reports for English Literature were not entirely without some foundation. There is no doubt that the comments expressed have their roots in a strange kind of long running and, at times, seemingly secretive feud that has played itself out during the first year of 'A' Level English Literature study. The comments on those school reports perhaps give credence to that old saying, 'he who laughs last, laughs longest'. The writer of that English Literature report at the end of the summer term 1972 has on the face of it obviously laughed the longest. The protagonists in a rather childish feud throughout the 1971/72 school year were the Head of English at the school, Mr John Graham Fife, and a lower 6th form pupil (at that time) who occasionally decided he would try to flout authority, particularly if it was thought he could get away with it! In any case, isn't a challenge to authority part of the 'raison d'être' of 6th form study?

What of the senior of the two exponents involved in this feud? Mr Fife is known throughout the school by his nickname, obviously handed down through successive generations, of "Ducky" – at times extended to "Ducky Bicky". Exact origins unknown but thought to be a derivation of the rather slang term which John Fife uses (slightly harshly it might be added), that of "thicky bicky" to describe pupils who have no idea about the correct answer to a particular question or problem posed within English Literature. This particular nickname,

I THOUGHT YOU WERE FAIRLY GROWN UP

Ducky, of which Mr Fife is well aware (as, no doubt, are all the other members of staff), generally plays itself out when he enters the classroom at the beginning of a lesson. At that point, various enterprising pupils will start whispering "quack, quack" under their breath… quite quietly… but loud enough to be heard in a silent classroom. Ducky most probably gets fed up with hearing it, but ignoring it is perhaps the correct reaction as it is always done, of course, to get him frustrated. The class will always know they are onto a winner if there is a clearly visible reaction! Getting him needlessly frustrated is, of course, rather pointless, as it always has ramifications on the rest of the lesson. Nevertheless, many still find it impossible not to give out a brief "quack" when he enters the classroom, to the accompaniment of suppressed giggles.

To pupils, he can quite rightly be described as slightly eccentric. (Par for the course at an independent grammar school perhaps. Does it go with the territory?) He will reply or exclaim "fishboxes" if a pupil's answer to a literary question is wide of the mark! At other times, he will address a pupil of either sex as a "nitbox". Clearly not a complimentary adjective and whilst one will struggle to find that particular adjective in a dictionary, nevertheless, its use around the school has become widespread with pupils as an alternative to, perhaps, calling someone a fool. Sometimes his gown will be pulled over his head and he will be bent over, presumably deliberating on how to react to an answer given in good faith but plainly quite wrong. He also has a rather strange habit of addressing all pupils as "George", for no specific reason other than, perhaps, his memory for names is not up to the same standard as his teaching.

He has been known, at times, to bring the learning within a lesson to a temporary halt if things have become a little 'stale' regarding pupil interaction. He will then send everyone in the class outside to run a circuit of the school perimeter in order to liven things up! This is primarily with the juniors one might add and at one time it became quite normal whilst in the middle of a lesson, or whilst in the library, to see the pupils from one of the junior forms go running past the window. One knew without asking that they would be enjoying an English lesson with Ducky. What the other teachers make of it, goodness knows. It is easy to imagine the likes of Mrs Jagger, always very strict and demanding and insisting on deadlines for work and prep being rigidly adhered to, being rather puzzled and not particularly amused. (Something to do with her being a teacher of French perhaps!)

Ducky also often has a frustrating habit at the start of class of asking as to whether those present would prefer the lesson to cover some poetry within the curriculum, one of the set fiction novels needing to be studied, or alternatively an examination of the various types of writing styles within the syllabus. Having obtained a consensus, he will then progress the lesson with one of the options not actually chosen by general agreement within the classroom. It has developed into a real 'cat and mouse' game. Perhaps that is his intention: does he derive some satisfaction out of it? Yes, most probably he does. Unfortunately, the cat invariably wins, despite occasional attempts by the 'clever' 6th formers to circumnavigate his ploy by agreeing beforehand to choose an option that they do not actually want. It occasionally works. Maddening? Yes.

Notwithstanding all these idiosyncrasies, which provide much amusement, and also considerable gnashing of teeth and at times derisive comment amongst the pupils, the quality and standard of his teaching, one perhaps has to admit begrudgingly, is not in doubt. It is, at least, teaching with some entertainment, ensuring that lessons are not pedestrian and predictable. Perhaps on the 'non-teaching' side, when he was for a time responsible, along with Jake, for looking after the boarding house, Ducky's forte was displayed at the annual bonfire night celebrations. He clearly revels in organising and overseeing the firework display. The bigger and more spectacular, the better! He is most definitely in his element, arranging and being responsible for setting in motion the various fireworks. If he had long straggly hair (a BIG if, as he is virtually bald on top) he would not look out of place, with his craggy facial features, re-enacting The Crazy World of Arthur Brown and singing 'Fire', whilst setting the bonfire alight! Almost as dramatic is to watch him hurrying along the school corridors – his gown, gained by virtue of a degree, flowing up with abandon in his wake.

'Ducky' – otherwise Mr Fife, the Head of the English Department, enjoying a reflective moment on the school wall by the playing field.
(Photograph: J. Hebblethwaite)

It may well be true, of course, that 'he who laughs last, laughs longest'. If so, the abiding memory of Ducky from winter 1967, during the second year's study at the Grammar School, remains that of seeing this English teacher, turned auxiliary 'sports master', being laid low by 3rd formers on the sports field. It was Ducky who had the misfortune to be at the sharp end of a football kicked at him inadvertently (one likes to think) and from close range, the football making a direct hit with his nether regions (or his "bollocks" – as that area is colloquially termed within the Lonsdale dormitory complex). It laid him low – metaphorically and physically! Naturally, this brought a temporary halt to the football match in progress and was the subject of some mirth among the aspiring teenage footballers. Ducky, sadly, did not seem to share the obvious amusement of the event. With hindsight, he would probably not have been able to raise a smile even if he had wanted to laugh it off as an almost inevitable consequence of boisterous teenagers having an organised kick about! And so, the question often pondered is, who really has laughed last (and longest)? Yes, we want to be grown up, but there are times when being childish is rather satisfying.

So, sadly, the suspicion of each other's motives ensured that the two protagonists in this pointless feud – teacher and pupil – played out a rather tetchy first year's 'A' Level study. Perhaps it is an unfortunate clash of personalities. Perhaps teacher and student share a similar temperament. A question: is the onus on the pupil or the teacher to adapt and seek to improve a relationship? Whatever, mutual respect there was little, and it came to a head towards the end of that first year's English Literature 'A' Level study. Ducky had asked for a detailed essay on 'Fashion'. On *Fashion*! What, one might ask, has an essay on Fashion got to do with studying Henry Fielding, John Keats and Wystan H. Auden? (Christ! Who calls their son Wystan, of all things?) An essay, for example, on whether it was easier to sympathise with Milton or Satan (in *Paradise Lost*), or an essay on the style of the poetry of Keats was fair game. But an essay on Fashion! It was clearly acceptable requesting, as he had done towards the end of last term, a detailed compilation of the authors and poets studied during that first year and indeed, that was eminently logical for an essay request. It related directly to what was being studied. The request for an essay on Fashion however opened the floodgates to frustration. It spawned a quite childish and most definitely not a detailed essay effort, hardly linked to the subject matter, but more aligned with complaining about having to toe the line with an irrelevant subject. Childish it may have been, childish it was (but only on reflection) but a stand had to be made! Stand by one's principles and suffer the consequences. The rather hurried, (Confucius might have suggested, "Never do an essay in a hurry and whilst feeling peeved") semi-erudite manuscript merely came back from marking with a short caustic comment, *'I thought you were fairly grown up.'* Well, you thought wrong! One hopes that, with such enthusiasm for English Literature, this second year of study, now having commenced, will prove to be much more fruitful so that this student can and will, as the previous report also hoped, *'benefit himself to the extent he deserves'*.

This study bedroom is awash with books, the majority of which, however, are of course the property of the school. Only the few privately purchased English Literature books are personal possessions. These are complimented by a small collection of books on the Yorkshire Dales which have been bought locally. There is, mind, a rather pleasing and comforting feel to possessing and owning these books that have been purchased independently, both to supplement the 'A' Level study and to learn about the surrounding countryside. They are mine! Mine to keep.

The ownership of books is a reminder of the occasional visits during this boarding school education, primarily at half-term breaks, to an auntie and uncle living just to the south of Lancaster. There, at their farmhouse, in numerous display cases, was a veritable collection of books. Fiction, non-fiction, biography, autobiography, large books, small books. Spellbinding and impressive.

I THOUGHT YOU WERE FAIRLY GROWN UP

[An aside: Certainly, much more impressive than their outdoor "bog" – i.e., privy – which had to be used during visits. A particularly unwelcome necessity, indeed, at night-time in the wind and the rain! Notwithstanding the privations linked to the call of nature, there was always a feeling at that time that it must have been almost an idyllic lifestyle on their farm. Cousin Anne, the middle of three daughters and of a similar age as her contemporary here at boarding school, was almost a tomboy and seemed to enjoy helping out on the farm. Getting stuck in on their pig and cattle farm – she was not a bit frightened of that. To a teenager who had become regimented into the boarding way of life, it was easy to be envious of her childhood, growing up in a pastoral setting. Perhaps Anne looked at the other side of the coin and thought to herself how privileged her cousin must be having travelled "half-way around the world" whilst growing up. On reflection, this Head Boarder, despite all the bluster amongst boarding colleagues, would have hardly been suited to 'getting stuck in' with the farming way of life. For starters, he was rather too scared during those visits to even enter the pigsty, where a sow would be settled on the floor with a dozen or more piglets milling around – and absolutely no chance of going anywhere near a large and unfriendly looking bull ("he is really quite friendly" – oh yes!), much to the amusement of an uncle and Anne herself. Collecting the eggs every morning from the various hen houses was more in keeping with the capabilities of a boarding pupil! At least he could be relied upon to tackle that errand successfully.]

But the books at that farmhouse. The thought process was always the same whilst gazing at the numerous rows of reading matter. Have they read them all? It must, surely, be a lifetime's accumulation and how satisfying it must be to own such a feast of reading. Such an impressive collection of books had never been on display at home whilst growing up. Whether this was as a consequence of frequent moves of home, as overseas postings broke up the continuity of a stable home life, or whether it is just a simple case of parents who do not particularly enjoy reading is not clear. From a child's perspective, it always appeared to be the case that a father was what might be termed a "workaholic", with little spare time in any case for reading. Whatever, the very modest book collection in this dormitory room is going to be treasured. If they end up looking ragged, well, all the better. It is adequate proof that they have been pored over, read, re-read and, more than likely, enjoyed!

Underneath the study desk, another small pile of books, the importance of which is plainly obvious by them having been pushed, albeit tidily, out of sight which, of course, helps keep them out of mind. General studies. What of General

Studies, or Minority Time Subjects, as the school likes to call them? They are the brainchild of Mr Kaye, who introduced the General Studies concept into the 6th form on his arrival in September 1967, when he took over as headmaster. To provide the 6th formers with a 'grounding' in subject areas that are not covered within specific 'A' Levels being taken is no doubt a worthy cause. Perhaps for the students, however, it is seen as an unnecessary diversion and the inevitable consequence is that they are not deemed important or a priority. There is no 'A' Level exam in General Studies at the end of the school year. In fact, there is no examination or test of any sort. Perhaps a wider general knowledge is all that there is to be gained and the question that continues to be pondered without a satisfactory reply is whether it is worth spending time on these extra subjects, such as Divinity, Arts (which might be better termed Music) and General History when there will be nothing tangible to show for it at the year end.

At least during the first year's 'A' Level study, the choice taken up of Ancient Greek History for General Studies held out the promise of an 'O' level examination, which was successfully obtained, and this made the study time and work effort seem worthwhile. In addition, it was an interesting and intriguing subject, be it the various developments of democratic rule under Pericles or the seemingly constant ebbing and flowing of the Greek Empire, fighting both themselves and the Persian Empire with varying results. No doubting, however, the fate of politicians in ancient Greece who would, almost without exception, be either killed in battle, murdered whilst in office, executed or, (perhaps) the 'least-worst' option, merely ostracised! As it is, with the two subjects within the General Studies umbrella that are being transferred seamlessly to this second year of 'A' Level study, there is, in particular, little appetite for any further tribulations within Divinity, with the Sunday morning compulsory church service being more than sufficient in that sphere. These schoolbooks for General Studies can (and will) remain hidden under the desk until they are (quite reluctantly) needed.

I THOUGHT YOU WERE FAIRLY GROWN UP

So now, this second year of 'A' Level study has commenced. The message from all the four subject teachers is consistent. Ducky and Mrs Fife in charge of English, Mrs Taylor in charge of History and Miss Shirley (Valentine) in charge of Sociology. Now is the time, they say, to get stuck into some serious study.

There appears to be no substitute, then, for hard work – unless you are naturally brainy! In the words of Ducky, "Success is the result of hard work." Well, of course – of course it is! On these three subjects, then, the so-called "easy" ones eminently suitable for wimps, rests the future, whatever that might hold.

*[**An aside:** a claim to fame for each of our esteemed tutors:*

Miss Shirley -- nearly (not quite) a high jump champion.
Mrs Taylor -- having been tutored by A. J. P. Taylor
*   (Some big knob in historical circles).*
Mrs Fife -- nineteenth century icon. A celebrated virgin.
*   (Until married.)*
Mr Fife -- Tetchy eccentric!

How can it be possible to fail with such a select group?]

CHAPTER XII

THE FINEST OF THE YORKSHIRE MOUNTAINS

It has never really been established as to who it was that introduced the 45rpm single by B. Bumble and the Stingers into the 6th form common room. There are rumours that it had been lying about in the room for many years – in fact most probably since 1962 when the 6th formers at that time might well have purchased it once it had reached No. 1 in the UK hit parade. This American pop group specialise in a rock and roll arrangement or perhaps, one might say, a rock version of classical music pieces by famous composers. It seems improbable, however, that it has been lying around for ten years! Nevertheless, the common room walls now regularly rebound during term time to the sound of 'Bumble Boogie', a derivation of Rimsky-Korsakov's 'Flight of the Bumble Bee', and 'Nutrocker', a pop version of the 'Nutcracker Suite' by Tchaikovsky. By co-incidence, the pop group Emerson, Lake & Palmer have released their own version of 'Nutrocker' in 1972, although the B Bumble and the Stingers version is certainly more raucous and obviously, therefore, eminently more suitable for a 6th form common room. Perhaps the most recent version by Emerson Lake & Palmer had been the catalyst for this particular 45rpm single to be resurrected and played continuously in the common room along with 'Roll Over Beethoven', a rock song by Chuck Berry from the early 1950s – suggesting that classical music should make way for the new genre of music, which was getting itself established, i.e., rock music. Such a suggestion – that rock/pop music will replace classical music – has brought forth a simple retort from a highly sceptical father, *"Rubbish!"*

Whatever the origins of these specific music tracks, it makes speaking normally in the common room most difficult at times and frequently, one can find oneself shouting above the cacophony of sound. That is, not only from the 45rpm single being played, but also from a group of crazy 6th formers who each think they are able to give an accurate rendition of the music, also at high volume. At varying intervals during the school lunch breaks, the common room door will be opened, and a request (from a passing teacher) will be made for the volume to be turned down and indeed it is. But then the volume control button will be surreptitiously turned up in stages, until the noise is again loud enough to ensure that it was impossible to talk without suddenly realising one is shouting! It is exactly the same in the evening when the room becomes the province of the boarders, although Mr Russell is perhaps more patient and understanding. The request for a lower volume of sound is not made in quite the same curt or demanding fashion as during the school day. Mr Russell seems to possess an empathy with his 6th form charges, if not being sympathetic towards their choice of music.

So it was that the question to Cess had been delivered, by necessity, in the high decibel range, "Who are they then, Hawkwind?" A simple enough question one might suppose. "You have never heard of Hawkwind? What! What do you mean, you have never heard of them? Surely, you *must* have heard their music on Radio One with their smash hit, 'Silver Machine'." Not only was his voice incredulous and repetitive, but it was also, by necessity, loud and high octane! "Well, whatever, I can get tickets for Friday 17th November", Cess had continued in a reassuringly loud tone, despite the obvious ignorance of his boarding house friend. "Find out from Mr Russell whether you can get out for the night", he had suggested before adding as an afterthought, "and a bit of pleading wouldn't go amiss."

Now, it is early November 1972 and there are, indeed, many other issues, arguably more pressing and important than a proposed rock concert at Lancaster University to consider and deal with. Vis-à-vis (1) Best man at a brother's wedding on the 11 November. This will involve a period away from school, with a journey down to the south coast this coming Friday for a long weekend. (2) The dreaded *King Lear*, to be swotted up on in preparation for a mock English 'A' Level exam which has been programmed into the school diary for later in the month. (3) During the day on that very same Friday, 17th November of the rock concert, a confirmation service at Low Bentham church with the head of the boarding house being a participant. A willing one? Well, at the very least, a participant.

All these forthcoming events have already been preceded, on what is clearly going to be a busy month, by a walk (perhaps it might be more appropriate to describe it as a 'hike') up to the summit of Ingleborough on this Sunday just gone, the first weekend of November. Ingleborough, at 2,373 feet high, is the second highest mountain in the Yorkshire Dales – in England, it is the seventh highest. Arthur Raistrick describes it in his *The Pennine Dales* (Arrow Books 1968 – a copy is in the rather proud ownership of the Head Boarder) as, *'the finest of the Yorkshire Mountains'* and indeed, its features are most impressive. Its familiar outline with a flat summit, almost a mile in circumference, can be seen from the school, standing in splendid isolation at the western edge of the Pennine range and almost inviting those agile enough to test their fitness. It almost shouts to be noticed – it cannot be ignored, standing prominent on the

Pennine skyline. Jake would no doubt tell anyone who is listening, with his inherent enthusiasm for geology, that its shape has been formed by horizontal layers of limestone, shale and grit. The flat summit of millstone grit has, down the centuries, defied erosion, unlike the immediate surrounding area and this makes Ingleborough an appealing conquest.

Ingleborough; 'The finest of the Yorkshire Mountains'

The idea to climb it had been hatched by Stephen Pugh, a boarder in the first year 6th form (with his nickname being quite simply, Pugh), most likely suggesting the idea because he wanted or, more accurately, needed a companion and had not been able to find one elsewhere in the boarding house with sufficient seniority. Several weeks earlier, his familiar rather whitewashed face with pudding basin hair cut had appeared around the dormitory door and a rather posh voice had asked enthusiastically, "How do you fancy a climb up Ingleborough Mucca? I am going on Sunday 5th November, you can come along if you wish" and before receiving any sort of reply, he added, "Don't worry, I have checked and the First XI play on the Saturday, you are at home to an Old Boys XI. I expect you will get beat" (he wasn't wrong) and, after a slight pause, he added "and we will, or at least we should be, back in plenty of time for the bonfire… and fireworks." Then, hardly waiting for an affirmative answer and with a grin on his rather baby schoolboy face that perhaps suggested that he was pleased that he had found a walking companion, he disappeared back into the adjoining dormitory. Pugh. In the adjoining dormitory, albeit he is only Lower 6th. Almost certainly in pole position and in waiting for the Head Boarder role in the next academic year. But perhaps a tad too compliant.

Rigid adherence to the internal rules of the boarding house is not always to be applauded. Sometimes there needs to be a challenge to the accepted routines. Doesn't there? (This diary poses the question…)

So it was that a weekend had rather conveniently been planned out in advance – playing football on the Saturday and Ingleborough to be climbed on the Sunday. Fireworks on the playing fields on the Sunday night there certainly was. But no bonfire! A sudden and prolonged downpour in the hours leading up to the night's entertainment meant that, despite a concerted effort, the bonfire refused to burn. It was abandoned as a failure, with the fireworks enjoyed on their own. Not a problem, however, for Ducky who, as always, revelled in being in overall charge of the fireworks, organising, directing and heroically taking charge of the blue touch paper. The fireworks – exciting? Perhaps, but not as spectacular and as compulsive viewing as that witnessed many years ago when, as a young lad and enjoying a fireworks night with the family, a stray firework landed in a box full of them (but fortuitously, the box was in the garden next door – thank goodness!), setting off an impromptu and dazzling display… once one had, of course, taken cover from the 'Jumping Jacks' and 'Catherine wheels' spinning and jumping about haphazardly! But really, isn't bonfire night very much in the same vein as Christmas? An exciting prospect with great anticipation leading up to the event, but invariably, being rather a let-down – a bit of a damp squid.

The evening of 5th November with fireworks, yes, but no fire and the evening had certainly not matched the standard of mischief night the week before when, on the morning after, a bed had mysteriously appeared, nicely made up, on the flat roof of the science buildings! Which dormitory had it come from? If there is no dormitory sporting a spare bed, then who slept the night without a bed? More to the point, who had been involved in putting it there? Naturally, the powers that be were not impressed, but it caused a good deal of hilarity across the school. What a good job there had not been any rain through the night after the bed had been left abandoned on the roof. There were suspicions and suggestions re the miscreants. A lot of questions asked, numerous interviews, but guilt was never determined with any certainty and the culprits evaded censure. There are some, no doubt, who will be all too aware as to who was responsible, but in the true spirit of comradeship, it would not be the 'done thing' to "dob them in"! There are times when it can be quite in order to 'snitch' on wrongdoers' – this was not one of them. Nevertheless, whether putting a dormitory bed up on the roof overnight comes within the remit of harmless mischief night fun is certainly open to conjecture. Whatever, within the school it proved a popular stunt with the exception, of course, of the teachers. (Although perhaps, secretly, some of them may have managed a wry smile to themselves or to their colleagues whilst in the staff room. All part of the rough and tumble of school life, they might feel.)

So, a day out fell-walking with Pugh had been arranged and, rather surprisingly, it was most successful. It was hardly a natural alliance with Pugh. He looks anything but athletic and, to make matters worse, he is an active church bell ringer, which at 6th form level is just not considered sufficiently 'macho' – whilst First XI football and rock concerts are quite definitely not his scene. Nevertheless, on a sunny and blustery early November day, the trek was made along the well-trodden footpath from Ingleton village, nestling at the base of Ingleborough and christened by the Victorians as the 'beauty spot of the north' – notwithstanding that it was a pit village until 1937 and indeed, still has a local stone quarrying industry. The London, Midland & Scottish Railway gave the village the title 'Land of waterfalls and newly discovered caverns'. Waterfalls indeed there are within the immediate vicinity, a locally recognised walk including Thornton Force, a notable waterfall and landmark. Ingleton village is perhaps the most logical starting point for the commencement of a walk up the mountain, at least it is when approaching from the west, albeit that there are several other well-trodden routes up to its flat summit. The strange thing is that, because the village is directly below the mountain, there was no sign of Ingleborough at the commencement of the days hike. Initially, the walk was up Storrs Common and then along what is most likely an old drover's path between two dry stone walls, the walls being such a common feature in the Pennine Dales that it is easy to take them for granted, before reaching the remote '*Crina Bottom*' farm. At the farm, the mountain towers above looking formidable and forever changing colour in the winter light. From there onwards the trek involved numerous steep escarpments. Deceiving indeed they proved to be, with several false dawns thinking the summit had been reached, only to find on reaching the top of an escarpment that another lay ahead. It was akin to a gigantic staircase with no obvious end in sight. The only answer was to keep going. And keep going is what two 6th form boarders did! Giving up was not on the agenda.

Eventually, the summit was reached and on that flat heady height of over 2,300 feet, there is indeed a stark beauty. At the same time, there was an inner acknowledgment that, as a youngster, a period had been spent living in that Iranian capital at an altitude somewhat higher than this flat summit. This fact makes it more plausible, indeed, to accept and believe that in ancient time, man made his home on this summit plateau. Somewhat implausible yes, but true, nevertheless. Towards the east, crouching across North Ribblesdale, is Penyghent – its shape more rounded than Ingleborough and not as high. To the North-East, the watershed of Ribblehead where, as the name suggests, the

THE FINEST OF THE YORKSHIRE MOUNTAINS

infant River Ribble commences its torturous journey to the Irish Sea, which it meets at Preston. At Ribblehead, the imposing mass of Whernside (just slightly higher than Ingleborough) straddling the north side of the large 'U' shaped valley of Chapel-le-Dale, cut out cleanly by an advancing sheet of ice during the Ice Age, leaving what is now a verdant valley bottom between the hills. (For Jake, raw and unbridled geology.) At the head of this valley and taking a railway across the valley floor at some considerable height, perhaps upwards of 100 feet, a long curving viaduct with twenty arches or more – Ribblehead viaduct – and from the top of Ingleborough, looking more akin to a miniature model railway. To the southwest and into Lancashire, the unmistakeable shape of Pendle Hill and at the coast, Morecambe Bay and further south, Blackpool Tower. What a vista it is from the summit! [Thank you also to whoever suggested taking binoculars…]

This area is a land of caves, streams, fissures, potholes, dry stone walls and limestone pavement with only an occasional twisted tree, its growth stunted by the strong westerly winds and lack of nutrient in the soil, breaking up the barren landscape. The rainwater – and there is plenty – finds a convenient home in the porous surface, disappearing into a myriad of small fissures only to re-appear at a lower altitude, eventually forming numerous small becks that pre-empt the commencement of the two rivers flowing westwards, the Greta and the Wenning.

The mountain, the area, the walk, have all left an incredibly strong impression and this landscape is here, on the doorstep of our school. This limestone landscape, the limestone country of Ingleborough, has a rough, jagged beauty and somehow, it seems to be a romantic beauty. Just perhaps an 'A' Level in Geology might have been more meaningful than the concept of a 'poverty-free' society with everyone earning a fair wage for a fair day's work. Sociology and Miss Shirley, recounting once again her high jump exploits, is going to seem so boring after the geographical quirks of nature experienced on an eight-mile journey across thousands of years of natural erosion! Scant wonder that Jake goes 'glassy-eyed' at the mention of the various types of rock strata that infest this Pennine range. Indeed, there is also a clear link between this wonderful landscape and the English Literature 'A' Level syllabus. W. H. Auden, born in York, clearly knows this area well and flipping through the pages of *Collected Shorter Poems*, yes, there on page 238 is his acclaimed poem, 'In Praise of Limestone'. Hadn't that particular poem been studied during the first year of study in English Literature? Yes, indeed.

Mark these rounded slopes,
With their surface fragrance of thyme

> *And beneath, a secret system of caves*
> *And conduits: hear the springs*
> *That spurt out everywhere with a chuckle,*

Who else could have thought of and used the word 'chuckle' to describe the fresh flowing water of the Pennine Dales? It fits seamlessly... sitting here in this dormitory, one can almost imagine the fresh glistening water urgently pushing its way in and out of the numerous crevices and recesses...always, *'with a chuckle'*.

Ingleborough (not only the mountain but including the fells that surround it) has been called an 'institution' and perhaps locally it indeed is. It has been climbed – conquered one might suggest – and a mental note has been made. It will have to be climbed again someday. Thank you, Pugh, for persuading me to accompany you. Although in no way 'macho', you made an ideal unassuming companion on a hike across and through thousands of years of geological history. Jake will be impressed when the climb is discussed with him, no doubt displaying the slightest of grins and being not at all surprised that such intriguing geology should interest an arts wimp!

Awaiting the breakfast bell this Thursday morning there is, as always, adequate time to gaze out of the dormitory window with morning ablutions finished and much time to spare. Except, on this November morning, the fog encloses and is likely to take some considerable time to disperse. The view? The surrounds of the swimming pool are all that can be seen, and the thick fog brings with it an eerie, strange silence – no sound from the river, no sound from the adjoining wood. A rather disconcerting silence which would most probably be appreciated by those living in the hustle and bustle of a city, but out here in the country, where are the sounds of the countryside? The fog has blotted out everything, even the familiar sight of occasional vehicles using the Millhouses Road by the school wood. The only sound is from within... from various dormitory doors being opened or slammed shut as the Lonsdale dormitory is on the move.

A knock on the door. A short pause and Mrs Russell's face appears around the door. "Good morning to you Ian. I sort of knew you would be ready by now", she said grinning broadly. "A new toothbrush for you; choose pink or red. [Pink – Christ. What on earth is she thinking!!] And a railway ticket, young man, from the bursar for this coming weekend. As you are ready, can you please pop around the junior dormitories for me to make sure they are all out of bed and getting up. Thank you, Ian." Then she is gone – smart, splendidly efficient and industrious, with a rather engaging twang incorporated within that lovely Scottish accent.

Lancaster Castle to Southampton Central return, via London. Train journeys hold no fear, but perhaps the London Underground might. Euston to Waterloo, is it straightforward? Hiring a suit for the wedding will be the priority on arrival at the south coast. No time before the weekend to have a haircut. Snot has been nagging about the 6th formers getting their hair cut and, no doubt, an older brother will also now be nagging about his best man and the fact that he needs a haircut. He'll be lucky!

Ingleborough climbed. The author sits on the summit cairn, November 1972. (Photograph: S. Pugh)

CHAPTER XIII

INSIDE, A BATTLE NOW RAGES

November now has gone and the cold dry days of early December leave both the lawn by the swimming pool and the trees in the neighbouring wood, on the far side of the river, lifeless. For the time being, this dormitory window stays firmly shut and the radiator firmly on! There is, thankfully, a plentiful helping of continuity here at boarding school, safely ensconced in this private room. Ideal, of course, for a slightly reserved, secretive and somewhat anxious personality. (Although anxious about what?) Sometimes, there is the feeling that there is a sadness with life. Well, there is. Isn't there? Even when there is nothing to be sad about – unexplainable, illogical.

Whilst sitting here and thinking, it also becomes so incredibly easy to be nostalgic. A reminder of the past was provided recently when, whilst across on the sports field playing for the First XI one afternoon in less-than-ideal weather conditions (a 2-1 win at home to Myerscough Agricultural College. A team of thugs – what else would one expect from an agricultural college?), an oil train came along the railway line announcing its presence to everyone with an ever increasing and impressive roar, a suitable reminder of the climb involved up the grade from Wennington. It was diesel hauled, yes, not steam hauled, as the oil trains had been back in the period up to 1968. The interest in railways is still flitting around somewhere in the psyche, but it was always the steam locomotives, taken out of service in 1968, that demanded and attracted the absolute attention of a young teenager. Watching that diesel hauled train, climbing steadily along by the school fields, immediately sent the mind spinning back six years to one very cold and snowy morning in December 1966. With the memory rekindled, the brain was in overdrive – six years. Hardly time to catch breath!

A December Morning: 1966

On this winter morning, the thermometer will most probably stay below zero all day.
   The scene, looking eastwards towards brooding Ingleborough
   Is bathed in harsh year-end sunlight, yesterday's heavy snowfall

Frozen hard and uneven across horizons near and far.

Certainly, no games today on a sports field transformed by dunes of snow,

All the warmth of learning today must surely be indoors:

It is still early, before morning assembly, but after the lumpy porridge

That will keep stomachs filled until mid-morning milk and on to lunchtime,

And with the church clock chiming the half hour on this crisp December morning,

The distant sound of a steam engine can be detected by several young boarding pupils.

Faintly, quite faintly, at first but quite defiantly the sound of a steam engine

Clearly struggling when heard initially, probably due to a signal check,

And then slowly but surely beginning to find its feet on frozen steel

On the long and testing gradient eastwards from Wennington station:

But, at this stage, still no train in sight, only an increasing cloud of smoke

And a short high-pitched whistle and the regular 'beat' becoming ever more frequent:

That whistle was the catalyst to run across the snow-covered playing fields,

To stand alongside the fence separating field from railway track

And it was from here, surrounded by the cold, that the train could finally be seen:

Looking westwards along dead straight track, there it was, engine and train

Heading purposefully towards us, its 'beat' becoming louder and more powerful.

This is the morning heavy freight train, pulling oil tanks from the harbour at Heysham

Through to the mills and factories of the industrial West Riding.

Now fully in control of its train and working with authority and purpose,

Despite showing clear evidence of neglect and belching steam from

Every available orifice, it has four teenagers gazing in awe:

Soon, almost too quickly, this mighty class 9 freight engine is upon us

And 92167 storms past, the driver giving a short sharp blast on the whistle,

And his fireman giving a friendly wave from the cab side, immediately

Cementing what would become a lifelong bond between railways and spectators:

Then it was gone, working purposefully eastwards with a tantalising

Glimpse of the firebox and flames as the fire was stoked for the continuing climb:

Gone all too soon, away into the cutting and towards High Bentham,

Leaving only a smell in the air, an unforgettable, infectious, pungent smell

Of oil and coal which generations before will have experienced and savoured,

Leaving clouds of smoke high in the sky; smoke that begins to evaporate slowly,

So very slowly in the freezing air of this sub-zero December morning.

Then the walk back across packed snow with hidden dips and shoes

Not sufficiently robust enough to protect the integrity of dry feet,

Whilst to the east, the raw sound of working steam fades gradually into distant terrain.

And then to a morning assembly that fruitlessly attempts to provide culture

With music from Grieg and his Peer Gynt suite No. 1:

But all the while, all the while, the sight, the sound and the smell

Of that work-stained steam engine shows itself as a continuing real-life canvas

Which cannot be removed from a teenager's teeming brain.

A desperately cold morning it was that December day, but perhaps it is easier to deal with the cold when younger. And the shoes, they let in the wet – and with the wet, the cold. Dealing with cold as a youngster is okay but dealing with wet feet when cold – not easy! A nostalgic memory, yes, but the overwhelming memory is of a filthy, grime-ridden steam locomotive still earning its keep against all the odds. Six years ago – really? Perhaps in reality, only yesterday.

What now of November? A pivotal month. The confirmation service officiated by the Bishop of Bradford and a 'stand in' vicar, the Revd Winstone (the rector, good old Reginald Boden Parker, having retired at the end of the previous school year) had passed uneventfully, as might be expected. The Revd Winstone, though, both amused and shocked in equal measure with his garish technicoloured non-matching shirts and ties. Little wonder that he has very quickly acquired the nickname of "the rocking vicar". Vicars should not be modern, surely! Shouldn't they be "fuddy-duddy"? His well-publicised period of contemplation in a nearly naked state on a bed of nails (for a charitable cause, rather than for the fun of it. There is no doubt among the lads in this Lonsdale complex that he will have exclaimed – "I demand to be put through pain on a bed of nails", or some such ludicrous request – and Christ, that hairy chest!) also raised numerous caustic comments and laughs within the boarding house, albeit that it was recognised that the rather strange feat was being done in a good cause. How did he get on the bed? More pertinently, how did he get off without jabbing his rear end somewhat? The rocking vicar's period of glory looking after the pastoral needs of Low Bentham and school boarders has, though, only lasted a short period. He has now returned (with the fancy shirts) to his permanent patch, that being as the vicar of nearby Clapham church. He does, however, have a small on-going teaching roll, so the shirts still make an occasional splash within the school corridors!

Mid-November witnessed the induction of a new permanent incumbent – the Revd John Bradberry, an altogether different 'kettle of fish' to what had been the heavyweight presence of Reginald Boden Parker. Revd Bradberry differs not just in stature, being no-where near as tall as the previous incumbent, but also in speaking. Whilst good old Reginald always had a seemingly booming voice in normal day-to-day speech (always sounding as though he was standing at the lectern delivering his Sunday sermon), the voice belonging to our new rector is quite definitely lacking, both in decibels and authority, so much so that it is quite easy at times to lose track of what he is actually saying. This, by itself, provides a good enough excuse to stop listening. In addition, whenever he says a word which includes the letter S, it is delivered with a subtle, but nevertheless noticeable, whistle. Eventually, one is perhaps paying more attention to the regular delivery of the whistle rather than to the content of what is actually being said. All in all, not an authoritative presence within the day-to-day life of the boarding house. A situation, however, which the 6th form boarders are more than comfortable with. The less intrusion from a man of the cloth, the better for all concerned!

So yes, the Head Boarder has now been confirmed. Confirmed into the Church of England indeed. It will make no material difference to the mandatory Sunday service, with no particular urge or requirement to regularly taste a bit of strange 'plastic' paper (masquerading as bread) or a sip (and it IS a sip...) of rather oddly coloured red wine. Is it really wine? Watered down wine perhaps? So, during the service, when the time comes for all the believers (well yes, the congregation does include some) to queue for Communion, the bulk of the boarders who have been confirmed (including this Head Boarder) sit firmly on their respective wooden benches. They do not budge. Why should they? There seems little or no need to take part. Queuing for mealtimes is bad enough, never mind queuing for makeshift bread and wine. And why be confirmed? It seems as though it had been expected – not only that but also, needed (by the school, not the Head Boarder)! A head boy in the boarding house really "should be/ needs to be" confirmed. (Or at least, that was the direct message from several luminaries. All on the teaching staff, *of course* – mind you, the head girl in Ford House got away with not being confirmed. How did she manage it?)

So, this most recent confirmation provides, does it, salvation for the Head Boarder? Is that from here onward and for evermore and is it dependent on taking regular 'bread and wine'? If salvation is indeed provided, when the 'Day of Judgement' finally comes (as the Sunday service tells us incessantly that it will – one day…), then the Head Boarder will, surely, be provided for and be protected by a host of angels in the sky. Ah well, one can always hope!

The Hawkwind concert at Lancaster University has also been and gone, but not without incident. After some careful deliberation and some specific timescales regarding a return to the boarding house following the concert, Mr Russell had consented to the request, but not without a slightly bemused look on his jovial face. The juxtaposition of a church confirmation service and a rock concert on the same day was not lost on the boarding house master. He was understandably somewhat puzzled as to how the senior boy in the boarding house could indeed reconcile these two widely divergent events. If he had been aware, of course, that the rock concert group Hawkwind included within their act a rather different performance – that is, the services of a stripper, the authorisation to attend (albeit given perhaps a little grudgingly… Mr Russell, if you are going to agree to something, agree with appropriate grace!) would most likely not have been given. On the contrary, it would most certainly have been withheld. There was, fortunately, no real inquest from Mr Russell after the event as to how enjoyable the concert had been. Just as well. He might well have looked on in disbelief had he been told about that most interesting part of the concert. Advising him that the most compelling part of the act (and perhaps the reason for the attendance of a good number of the audience) had been missed through enjoying a short sleep whilst Hawkwind played out their 'Silver Machine' 1972 smash hit to the accompaniment of psychedelic flashing lights and with singing and shouting from the assembled throng, would no doubt have led him to assume there was an element of untruth in the statement. Sadly, there wasn't and the opportunity to witness a lady – calling herself *'Stacia'* – divesting herself of her clothes was missed! By all accounts (well, if Cess and Clarky are to be believed) *'Stacia'* had pretty impressive tits! What about the rest of her youthful flesh – what about the bit down below? Why did she not go "the whole hog" (as the Lonsdale dormitory term it)? Most disappointing, indeed, that her striptease had been missed and that the Head

Boarder did not on this occasion get his "money's worth", enjoying instead a brief period of 'shut eye'!

Despite a brief nap during the proceedings, clearly a late evening rock concert, lasting well into the night, was probably not the best preparation for the First XI football fixture the following day, which involved travelling to Preston to play a very well built and aggressive looking team from Preston 6th Form College. The 0-4 drubbing meant that after an unbeaten run of four games since the start of the school year, two consecutive matches have now been lost. The 1-2 reversal at home to the Old Boys XI, on the weekend that Ingleborough had been climbed, hurt far more, however, than the Preston College debacle. Matches against the old boys are always keenly fought on the basis that there is a badge of honour to be gained from playing and beating previous incumbents of the First XI. (Not only that, but we did not deserve to lose – yes, we would say that…but it is true!) However, to be picking the ball out of the net four times at Preston merely confirmed that rock concerts, booze and playing football are not, and are never likely to be, an ideal mix!

What of a family wedding? Venue: Southampton. The best part? An interesting train-journey. A rather 'posh' suit (in reality, rather too posh) hired for the best man, yes. A suit quite out of keeping with a casual attitude gleaned specifically over the last twelve months because of a school trying its best to teach 6th formers acceptable etiquette. But more crucially, no haircut. A situation that was not at all popular with a brother who, with an eight-year advantage in age, didn't think that the 1972 hair style and *The Onedin Line* sideburns being propounded by his young brother was quite in keeping with the event. An occasion for him, of course, that was far more important and significant than it was for his brother. To paraphrase the words of the pop group The Who, *'he won't get fooled again'*, but more than likely, he will have no further need to call upon the services of this younger brother. Three brothers – two now married with only the youngest still to take such a step – but surely, not for some considerable time. 'A' Level study, the immediate priority. To a boarder just leaving adolescence behind and enjoying the hurly burly of the Lonsdale complex and indeed, relishing the easy-going life in the 6th form (notwithstanding the continual stream of essays and tests), the wedding was rather too formal, dull and rather serious. Ducky seems to think there is still some "growing up" to be done. Perhaps an elder brother will now be inclined to agree with him!

A wedding; a family gathering. They seem rather strange affairs. Well, certainly they do for what one might term the 'McCart' clan. A mother and father, two brothers and a sister – she, being the other part of "the twins". A distinctly disparate group with, it seems, not much in common. How so?

Is it because of the continual travelling across the globe since 1957 being responsible for a gradual breaking up of what should be close family bonds? Parents, indeed, who have never appeared particularly 'close' in word or deed and who might often appear to be quite at odds with living together in harmony, if indeed that is what marriage is all about. The memory – it so easily goes back five years or so to the airport in Tehran and the return to boarding school after one of the main school holidays. A mother and father not together to give their teenage twins a family 'hug', but instead, standing apart – well apart – and giving separate and individual farewells. Whilst not strangers, they could almost have been thought of as such. To teenage twins faced with that situation regularly, perhaps familiarity breeds contempt and such farewells at the ending of the Summer, Christmas and Easter holidays became the norm, rather than, perhaps, the exception and became accepted as such. Maybe there was some consolation after all in being away from home, at boarding school and thereby protected from the frequent bouts of parental verbal jousting.

Parents then not always in tune with each other and perhaps somewhat out of touch, also, with their eldest son, now married. An eldest son always somehow quite remote and aloof, as a brother surely should not be, ploughing an independent and rather private existence (according to a mother) – and so it has always seemed, with little to say and having an unnerving ability to appear disinterested. No such issues with the second son, with a meeting of interests, helped no doubt by growing up together for a longer period and most crucially when young, a joint ability of the two youngest lads to laugh at the silly and absurd… but now, with hardly an opportunity to do so with the one progressing a career and the other still tackling the learning process. Brothers and sisters and parents – all part of the same unit. But a close-knit family group? Hardly.

These various events, then, during November – the ascent of Ingleborough, the confirmation service, a rock concert, family matters, even a mock exam – whilst all important in their own individual ways, have been no real match for the image that has been running continuously through the mind of the boarding house head boy during October and November. What image? The intriguing and enticing image of three always seemingly skittish and exuberant Lower 6th form girls, who, instead of congregating in their dedicated common room, insist on loitering around the self-service coffee machine by the school Assembly Hall during break time and lunch time. Always laughing and eager to talk, it seems as though they quite enjoy and, indeed, almost encourage the regular sparring match which has been taking place almost daily with this Upper 6th form lad, who, in all honesty, is still slightly cautious and wary of becoming too familiar with the opposite sex. (Despite the obvious bravado indicating otherwise when amongst 6th form colleagues.) Perhaps the way to a lady's heart is given a welcome boost via generosity and accordingly, a regular offer has been made over the past few weeks to buy them all a coffee, a sufficient supply of 2p pieces being kept available for this purpose. The almost continuous banter has certainly been more enjoyable than would have been the case ensconced in a raucous Upper 6th form common room, even if some classmates might privately think it rather odd that one of their number is seen to be mixing with Lower 6th form girls, when the Upper 6th form can boast plenty of female encouragement of its own, with bare flesh regularly on show.

One of these three Lower 6th form young ladies – for that is what they really are, even though they might be referred to as girls during normal school activities – displays possibly a slight reserve and a coy shyness, albeit that her voice, with its inherent Yorkshire tone, sounds sufficiently robust. A firm voice, yes, but it never quite seems altogether too confident. Is that because of the nature of the assembled group, with a stranger from the opposite sex breaking in on what would otherwise be the privacy of close friends? And accompanying a resolute voice, a pair of thinking eyes – hazel in colour, large and expressive. Good at watching, with a knack of always appearing attentive. Whilst this young lady is an integral part of the trio, clearly, she is not the ringleader but instead, and perhaps by choice one suspects, is more of a passive listener – albeit an interested one. She is not wanting to hog the limelight or attract attention to herself, leaving her two friends to jostle for the spotlight in the teasing and jesting with an Upper 6th form boarder. Intriguing this young lady is, yes. Overwhelmingly so. This apparent slight nervousness, or perhaps self-consciousness on her part, regularly manifests itself with cheeks which rapidly turn rosy-red if there is a reason, however innocent, to cause embarrassment. Indeed, in the playful 'throw away' comments between friends and an interested outsider from the opposite sex, there is invariably the opportunity for these three ladies (christened 'The Three Musketeers' by the Head Boarder!) to cause each other embarrassment. It does, of course, come naturally with the territory.

This demure young lady, whose face will come alive with bashful laughter, displaying large her sparkling, innocent hazel eyes, when playful comments are hurled back and forward in an effort to embarrass, has been making quite an impression – and a favourable impression at that – with a slightly hesitant Upper 6th form lad who has managed to successfully wangle his way into their daily meetings and discussions beside the faithful drink vending machine. Have they welcomed this intrusion? One Upper 6th form lad versus three Lower 6th form young ladies is rather one-sided, but the banter merely spurs on the obvious enthusiasm displayed and enacted by those three willing participants. Are these three young women aware that there is considerably more interest being shown in one of their number? Has it been so obvious? Do they discuss it when out of earshot or when the Head Boarder is not in attendance? Do they perhaps secretly realise and stay silent? Has that rather shy blushing young lady noticed that she is being admired? If the two main combatants perhaps realise, then surely so must she. Does her heartbeat quicken when laughing and chatting with an Upper 6th form lad from the boarding house? All unanswered questions and inevitably pondered over almost nightly in the privacy of a dormitory bedroom, whilst the advancing nightfall continues its inexorable march into the fast-disappearing daylight.

These three young ladies – Christine Skeats, Judith Greenwood and Barbara Noble – have increasingly become a permanent daily fixture in the timetable, with break times and the lunch hour eagerly awaited. They appear to be inseparable. Even morning assemblies in the school hall are now gleefully awaited and attended with renewed vigour. Locate one of these ladies in the Assembly Hall and the other two will almost certainly be in attendance. It has become most difficult not to stare continuously – an occasional glance has had to suffice. Does anyone notice that the attention span of the boarding house head boy is no longer with the procedures of morning assembly or with the regulation *Hymns of Praise* booklet, but is instead concentrated almost exclusively on a row of Lower 6th form girls on the opposite side of the hall? And every now and then during the morning assembly, this young lady will throw back her head, giving it a little shake in the process, to clear locks of hair intruding onto her face. Does she, one wonders, use that as an opportunity to glance over to the opposite side of the hall to see if the Head Boarder is in school? Is she looking forward to morning break with equal (or more) anticipation than the Head Boarder? Does she lie in bed at night and wonder to herself what the Head Boarder will be doing? Does she, perhaps, wonder which of the three young women he may have an interest in? Maybe she will realise, maybe not. Lots of questions. No clear cut answers. Beguiling, bewitching, certainly.

The inherent interest in this attractive young lady, coupled with a continuing close study of romantic English Literature, is now providing an irresistible combination. It seems logical and common sense to test out the skills one might possess, combined with what one has learnt. However successful or otherwise, the poetry written cannot be handed in to Ducky for evaluation! It will have to stay hidden. A recent study period in the school library had the added and unexpected bonus of Barbara also doing some research and reading. Well, hardly unexpected! Once the knowledge of her study periods had been gleaned, it was odds on that she could be found in the library at specified times. It has been possible to sit at the same table as Barbara whilst in the library but, generally, opposite her so that any interest did not appear too obvious, particularly with others studying in the library. The golden rule of library research and reading – no talking. There has been, however, a mutual acknowledgement of the others presence, with attendant smiles being exchanged. Have you noticed, Barbara, that there has been considerably more interest in you than in the library books detailing, for instance, the events leading up to the end of the French religious wars? The library study periods have spawned the following, scribbled out in this dormitory room at an ungodly hour – but the mind is brimming over – the brain is bursting, in turmoil almost, with the vision of this young lady. Somehow, it needs to be expressed,

> *What thoughts surrounded that pretty-head,*
> *Whilst quietly she sat and mused?*
> *Was her heart firmly implanted on future love?*
> *I envy him: to feel that smooth light inviting skin,*
> *Her light brown hair falling far down her back:*
> *Oh creation, what does she lack?*
> *The firm face matches an excellent figure,*
> *A sturdy stance, an upright walk.*
> *Oh, for a small chat, a private talk with her:*
> *Is that calm temperament so real?*
> *Then to touch those smooth rose cheeks,*
> *To feel her charm.*
>
> *But oh, I am troubled by the most horrible thoughts.*
> *Dear Barbara, are you really as quiet, as tame, as you look?*

This new school year is all but three months old and it is becoming more and more difficult to give priority to the various piles of 'A' Level reading. Reading that will be required to get the pass grades necessary to justify what should be two years of intensive study at school, not to mention the two years of school fees paid by expectant parents and, hopefully, thereafter, to confirm the place that is there in the offing at Durham University. Gazing out into a cold winter darkness from the warmth of a dormitory room, the late-night silence broken only by an occasional distant sound of a train grinding its way eastwards up the gradient, the lyrics from the famous Led Zeppelin track 'Stairway to Heaven' are continuously swimming around the brain. Indeed, they have been doing so for some considerable time in the quiet and solitude… *'and it makes me wonder'*. Is the priority with the vagaries of the Tudor or Stuart monarchs or the French religious wars, or indeed, with the niceties of building a decent society or, more pertinently, is the priority with wooing a young lady from the

Lower 6th form? Not only that, but perhaps a more pressing question – does this captivating, slightly reserved, blushing young lady have any wish to be pursued by a boarder from the Upper 6th form? Inside, a battle now rages, although at the present time, it seems most unlikely that the pursuit of learning will get the upper hand.

Two of the three young ladies who would loiter by the school self-service drinks machine. Judith Greenwood and Christine Skeats. The other member of the 'trio', Barbara Noble, missing!
(Photograph: J. Hebblethwaite)

CHAPTER XIV

WHAT IF SHE SAYS NO?

It was at the end of the week prior to the last weekend in November, on Friday 24th, when four boarding house 6th form boys had been given permission to attend an evening party in High Bentham, organized by a 6th form day pupil. Obtaining agreement from Mr Russell was no mean achievement. However, part of the boarding house mantra is to try and ensure that the residential pupils in the boarding house are not disadvantaged in comparison with their counterparts attending as day pupils. On this basis, attending the party had been sanctioned with the usual caveats – staying within the confines of the venue and returning to the boarding house by 10.30pm. The fact that the party was in High Bentham meant that getting to it would involve a walk of approximately a mile or more up the road. This would, ultimately, have far-reaching consequences for one of the four lads – the one who was the head of the boarding house.

The road out of Low Bentham village, up the steady gradient towards High Bentham, passes a detached bungalow standing by itself on the north side of the road. The agony of decision making! Throughout the week preceding the party, an argument had swung this way and that – an argument that is between the brain and the heart. Should a stop be made at that bungalow to invite the young lady living there with her parents to the Friday night party? The heart said it needed to be done and should be done. Why not let this young lady know that she is admired and give her the opportunity to have a friendship on a 'one to one' basis? The brain, however, suggested caution. The fear of rejection potentially overriding the opportunity that was presenting itself. More than anything else, it was the fear of the "brush-off".

The school play from earlier this calendar year had been a continuation of the annual Gilbert and Sullivan operas, with a (rather professional) performance of 'Iolanthe'. (That is, apart from the Arcadian Shepherd who was rather anonymous and could not be heard!) At night-time in the dormitory, when the tussle between brain and heart was invariably at its high point, that opera was recalled if only for one line from a song within it, which included – if the memory is accurate – *'faint heart never won fair lady'*, or something to that effect! Topical indeed was that phrase from the school performance in March, as it had seemed at the time that a faint heart was part of the reason why the friendship with Morag had failed even before it had chance to flourish. How useless, indeed, shyness is. The fear of rejection was overwhelmingly strong although, without realising it, seeking the opinion of Lonsdale dormitory colleagues to the idea of calling at that bungalow on the Friday night effectively settled the issue – even if, prior to the night of the party, there had been no hint of their planning. Unwittingly (and with some obvious enthusiasm on their part) they contributed towards solving the conundrum that head and heart had caused. It was perhaps just as well they did, because even as late as walking through Low Bentham village on the Friday night, it still was not clear in the mind as to which was going to triumph – the heart or the head. A natural reticence suggested that the head would take the honours. In the event, it was not given the chance!

"Go on!", the chorus of voices in the darkness had said, "Go on, why not? Don't back out now. We are walking right past the front door, you might as well." Another voice from behind had summed it up rather succinctly, "Well, you do fancy her after all, don't you? Tell you what, we will open the gate and wait for you at the top of the drive", continued the voice, brimming with obvious enthusiasm. All very helpful. Fancy her? Yes. Will that fact have filtered through to her at school via the incessant chit-chat among 6th formers? Ordinarily, nothing is spared with gossip rife within the respective common rooms, often running riot. Isn't that what the school common room is for? Perhaps this young lady will already be aware that she is being admired. If so, she may be quite comfortable receiving an unsolicited visit on a November night. That was the thought process. In any case, there seemed no obvious way of getting out of it, with peer pressure being a compelling force. It was easier to simply agree rather than attempting to reel off an array of half-hearted excuses. The most obvious excuse had been suggested. "What if she says no?" That would indeed be the end of it! The consequences did not bear thinking about. No more daily meetings by the coffee machine. It would surely mean the end of that light-hearted banter, with the accompanying laughter and embarrassed smiles. No more checking the Lower 6th form timetable to see where she might be at any particular time in the school corridors in order that a 'chance' meeting would happen, with a few words being exchanged whilst she was on the way to her next lesson. No more looking across during the morning school assembly at the row of Lower 6th form girls to watch her – and being endlessly fascinated by those high cheek bones, shoulder length light brown hair and the 'in vogue' short school skirt, which helps to display a rather inviting stately pair of legs. Legs that are given an attractive brown sheen by virtue of the lady's tights that a seventeen-year-old would feel grown up by wearing. No doubt there are other shades of tights, but the *American Tan* colour is quite definitely the shade to be seen in at school.

"What if she says no?" A voice had repeated the very question that had been posed, although this time it was on a rhetorical basis and not only that, but this time it was several octaves higher than when the Head Boarder had asked the question. As if to boost confidence that was clearly somewhat lacking, the same voice from behind had continued. "Why on earth should she say no?" Why indeed! After all, the blushes and the laughter by the coffee vending machine, the exchange of smiles whenever passing throughout the school, the occasional glance across during school assembly – did they all count for nothing? Why on earth should she say no? By the time this response had been considered, the entrance gate had already been quietly opened, expectant friends waited with their grinning faces conveniently lit up by a nearby streetlight – and from somewhere, a gentle push from behind accelerated the walk down the short drive, which dropped steeply to a garage door.

From the garage door, it was but a short walk along the path at the front of the bungalow until, there, opposite two synchronised cherry trees, was a white wooden door. It was set back in a small porch where the glazed glass protected the entrance foyer inside from prying eyes. A slightly hesitant knock (where was the doorbell? Was there one?) and time had almost stood still! At that juncture, there was no going back. The deed – it had been done. The knock on the door had signalled the commitment to go through with it. Suddenly, the outside porch light was switched on by a shadowy figure on the inside of the front door, illuminating the exterior of the house and displaying a well-ordered garden. Many hours had, it seemed, been wasted trying to imagine what this house might look like inside. Now, at that very moment, the front door had been opened and an opportunity to have a good look had presented itself. Of course, it had proved quite impossible! With a rapidly beating heart and eyes focussed entirely on the lady who had opened the door, the layout of the house was suddenly immaterial. "Could I speak to Barbara please?" A straightforward request, but it had been blurted out, almost incoherently. Name not requested. Name not given. And then the wait – the interminable wait! Was she there? She must be. Surely! Otherwise, her mother would have said she was out. If she was at home then, was she going to come to the door? Did she want to come to the door? Would she want to know who it was before deciding? Would she give an excuse to her mother and stay hidden? So many questions running at random through the brain. The words "young man" could be heard, presumably mother talking to daughter. Yes indeed, there was a "young man" (albeit a nervous one) wishing to speak with her.

And then, at last, salvation! "Oh, hello Ian!", delivered as a rather hesitant and somewhat surprised greeting, but nonetheless accompanied by a bashful smile and with hazel eyes that seemed to display a certain element of interest. Standing at the door was that rather shy seventeen-year-old Lower 6th form girl – the one who would regularly go red with embarrassment with her friends by the school coffee machine. Her long straight light brown hair was tied back in a ponytail, with a large firm forehead fully displayed by virtue of two round hair clips holding the hair back either side of her temple. An imposing forehead, unblemished, clean, youthful. The eyes were questioning, patient, waiting – her chin nicely rounded and her head just ever so slightly to one side, expectant, making it clear that it was the young man's turn to speak. Her jeans were not yet worn out but were heading that way. They showed signs of continual wear with a lighter denim shade around the knees, together with a multitude of creases cutting across the jeans below her midriff, at the top of her thighs. Her lemon flowery blouse hardly matched a pair of bright red socks. Nevertheless, the combination added seamlessly to a casual style one might fully expect to see from a young lady relaxing at home. Particularly so when not anticipating any visitors! Slippers absent, no doubt left behind in the bedroom. After all, for a young lady, lounging about in her bedroom surely would not involve the wearing of slippers. Here was a Lower 6th form lady not suitably attired in proper school uniform, but instead enjoying the relaxation of informal wear at home. Informal or not, she had looked enchanting – and her countenance had been one of enquiring interest and friendliness. Whilst her face spoke of a slight shyness, modesty even, it also showed calmness and was almost thoughtful and slightly inquisitive in the way her eyes looked upwards, for without any footwear, her height was conceded, willingly or not.

The question had been straightforward enough. It had to be. Such a simple, closed question. "Would you like to come to a party in High Bentham, Barbara?" It had provided her with a question that had to be answered one way or another. However, instead of eliciting a "yes" or, heaven forbid, a "no", the question itself had produced a question in return. "What, now?" A nod of the head had confirmed that it was, indeed, now. That very moment in fact! A slightly apologetic and pained expression followed. "But I haven't washed my hair." Saying that it looked just fine was, perhaps, rather a naïve response even if genuine and well intentioned. (And indeed, it had looked "just fine".) After that rather 'green' response from the Head Boarder to what had been a logical and, in the circumstances, a legitimate rider, Barbara had continued, "and I would need to get changed. I am really so sorry, but I cannot come with you, Ian", and after a momentary pause she continued, qualifying her response with a most important stipulation, "but I would have liked to." So, it was not an outright "no", but neither was it a "yes"! It was, perhaps, a qualified "no".

WHAT IF SHE SAYS NO?

There had followed the very slightest of pregnant pauses before, as a suggested alternative, that rather shy and well-mannered Yorkshire voice had continued, "Well, instead of coming with you to the party Ian, would you perhaps like to call on me this coming Sunday afternoon and we can go out for a walk together? Will you be allowed out?" Allowed out! Allowed or not, it had been an invitation immediately accepted. It was an opportunity that could not be turned down. In overdrive, the thought process had determined there and then that one way or another, Mr Russell would have to agree! It was imperative that he agreed. Sunday afternoons are nominally free time. Any internal prefect duties Sunday afternoon would have to be re-allocated. They had to be. Mr Russell would understand. Well of course he would – surely! Yes, he might well repeat that mantra regarding responsibility, "You cannot have the privileges available to 6th form boarders without the duties of a prefect, McCart." And yes, there may well be a reminder that the green 'prefects' badge fastened on the school tie means something. Yes, of course, but on this one occasion he would hopefully understand and, no doubt, be intrigued (even mildly surprised, perhaps) that his Head Boarder was taking a young lady out for the afternoon!

To the grinning 6th form students standing expectantly at the top of the drive, walking away from the door alone had meant only one thing. It was clearly a case of abject failure. But just possibly, the reality was that it might well have been the very opposite! Surely, only ignorant male adolescents can expect a young lady to come straight out to a party totally unprepared and with no prior notice. To have even contemplated asking seemed nonsensical, but the deed – it had been done. The heart had triumphed. In any case, would a group party event have been the most appropriate venue to get to know a prospective girlfriend? The thought process, perhaps to justify the non-attendance of this young lady, suggested not.

The party was attended – the venue, The Brown Cow, High Bentham – yes, but only with boarding house colleagues. A miserable affair it turned out to be, sitting alone and being unable to take the mind off the enduring picture of that attractive young lady. There she was, standing at her front door with nothing on her feet other than bright red socks and smiling sweetly and looking for all the world as though she was actually quite pleased to have been called on. The sight of her – her smile, her countenance – it had played continually on the mind throughout the evening. Presenting what was clearly a melancholy sight, Susan Hornshaw had attempted to secure interest with the offer of a dance (if she fancies the Head Boarder, she is going to be disappointed…), but all that mattered that evening was the excitement of what Sunday afternoon was hopefully going to provide. For the success of the Friday night was, of course, in what had been arranged for the forthcoming Sunday. Whilst the thought process had rather hoped that there would be 'butterflies' in a young lady's bedroom for the next day and a half, there were certainly continuous heart palpitations in a school dormitory room over the same period!

There only remained an annual school Speech Day to negotiate on the Saturday, with the guest speaker, Frank Duncan, a celebrated radio actor whose distinguished voice had been used in 'The Mouse on the Moon' (1963) and 'Far From the Madding Crowd' (1967) amongst other radio plays, telling the assembled throng how knowledge can be expanded, and relationships developed through involvement. Sitting in the Assembly Hall with the other 6th form students on the Saturday afternoon (a *Saturday* committed to a speech day… a terrible waste of part of the weekend!), the interest was not with a guest speaker and how knowledge can be widened (although his content regarding relationships and involvement, particularly with the opposite sex, seemed entirely appropriate!), but instead, was with a young lady on the opposite side of the room, whose eyes would periodically cast a furtive glance over with the hint of a shy smile. The scene was, it seemed, all set.

How does a young child feel when going to bed on Christmas Eve? Excitement and anticipation. It was just like that in the Head Boarder's dormitory room on the Saturday night. Would the Sunday exceed the reality of those Christmas days whilst growing up? The brutal reality was that December 25th was, almost without exception, somewhat disappointing. Would a Sunday afternoon walk with a young lady deliver that same disappointment?

CHAPTER XV

I SUPPOSE I AM A REAL COUNTRY GIRL

And so, to the Sunday morning. The compulsory Sunday church service had been, for a change, something to look forward to and whilst not to be enjoyed, at least embraced. The quicker it concluded, the better. Additional gusto was evident in the '*Te Deum*' and perhaps that sermon did not last quite as long as usual – at least, it didn't seem to! The words to *Psalm 100* are known by heart – to be recited without a need for the hymn book as it forms, without exception, part of the church service every Sunday. Indeed, it has done since September 1966. This Sunday, more than ever, it was certainly a time to be, '*Thankful to him and bless his name*'. Praise to the Lord our God was given, certainly, on this one occasion at least. Glory be to God! But not for the same reason as the Revd Bradberry, rector of this ancient parish, was praising the Lord on a bright and sunny Sunday morning!

Whatever the substance of the sermon, it had not registered. It was never going to register – the mind had been elsewhere until those familiar words, "Praise be to God", gave notice that his address had concluded, and the Revd Bradberry had then duly extracted himself from behind the lectern. (Leaving, as always, the pages of the outsize bible open at where he had finished reading – and strangely, the bible is *always* left open even in-between services. Is it tradition, superstition, laziness? One always fully closes a book after finishing reading part of it – doesn't one?) Then, with the commencement of the final hymn, he led his choir out of their stalls and back down the main aisle towards the bell tower, walking once again over the entrapped tombs of the Ellershaw family (if only they knew) and effectively giving the green light to a speedy exit once the singing of the final hymn had been completed.

Leaving the church at the end of the service, it was impossible not to gaze at the large wooden plaque on the inside of the north facing wall listing, as it does, all the previous incumbents of the diocese since the year 1300 – 670-plus years of history. There, at the foot of a clearly esteemed list, is the name of the previous incumbent, our mate Reginald, rector of the parish from 1964–71. Yes, a man of booming voice and stature, putting fear – inadvertently one always liked to assume – into the hearts of all the juniors in the boarding house. A different character completely from the present incumbent who, one could be forgiven for thinking, seems as though he wants to keep as low a profile as possible, which is indeed a challenge when a large part of the job specification is dealing with the pastoral care of perhaps upwards of 130 boarders, male and female – particularly as the footfall count at the church services during school holidays will more than likely be under double figures. What would the indefatigable Boden Parker, large in stature and thunderous in voice, have made of thanks being given to the Lord because an afternoon walk had been arranged with, hopefully, a new girlfriend? What indeed. Whatever else, it most certainly would not have left him speechless. He would have had something to say no doubt, most likely jovial in content and involving (of course) gracious thanks to our Lord!

No worrying these days about whether the huge, green-stained, copper fifteenth-century bell is likely to fall when one is passing through the entrance porch! Leaving the church behind – and the school – a walk through Low Bentham had provided adequate time for several emotions to swim around the brain, endlessly competing with each other. Anticipation, excitement, slight apprehension, a quick surge of confidence which would then evaporate just as speedily. In some strange way, meeting up with this young lady, away from the presence of her friends, was also quite a daunting prospect – all these emotions and feelings competing in equal measure. A 'one to one' – and no one else to interrupt or be involved in the discussion. Would she, one could not help wondering, be disappointed after several hours alone with the head of the boarding house, the First XI goalkeeper, the guy always acting the fool by the coffee vending machine (a good antidote to nervousness, but at least it regularly made her laugh). Would we, perhaps, run out of things to talk about? Oh God! Also, those parting words from Mr Russell, after a greatly rushed school lunch, became lodged in the back of the brain. "Now make sure you behave yourself, McCart, and show Miss Noble that you are a true gentleman and a credit to the boarding house." A true gentleman! What indeed is a "true gentleman"? Then the walk – through Low Bentham, past the 'Nip In' (closed for the Sabbath), a brief glance at the all too familiar slightly jaded post office window display and then up the gradient away from the village towards a young lady's parent's house. The thought process had been in overdrive. Would Barbara be watching from the window? Would she be ready? Hopefully, she will be looking forward to a walk out with the young man who had been brave enough, thanks to the insistence and badgering of friends, to call at her house on the Friday evening just gone.

Was it possible, perhaps, that the 'Almighty' had organised the weather for a late autumn day, Sunday 26th November 1972? A day that is now drawing to a close. A clear blue sky had provided a sharpness of light that can only be experienced in the autumn and winter months, when the haze from the high temperatures of summer cannot blur the horizons. The distant hills of the Pennine chain always seem so much closer in the clear, clean air and stand firm and proud in the razor-sharp light, with the scattered farms on the hillsides looking idyllic in the year-end sunshine.

On such a day, to be well insulated against the cold was clearly advisable and indeed, sensible. The young lady, sitting patiently outside on the garden seat at *'Benwick'*, looked enchantingly demure with her hair spread out across her back (recently washed no doubt!), and she had indeed been well 'wrapped up'. A large duffle coat with a hood entwined – and almost covered by her hair – would surely prove more than adequate protection, accompanied by brown corduroy trousers, a pair of dainty black gloves and knee-high boots. This time, opening the garden gate and walking down the steep drive had not been fraught with self-doubt or fear and there had been a confidence boosting, refreshing smile in the welcome from Barbara as the suggested plan for the afternoon was outlined. "Well, hello you, I thought that we could perhaps have a walk around the 'square mile', Ian", said a quiet but confident Yorkshire voice. The suggestion was almost made with the assumption of approval, which it duly received. Barbara had then continued, "and my mother will have afternoon tea ready for us when we return."

Splendidly demure, certainly, but also perhaps exuding a quiet and rather controlled confidence. The meeting, after all, was on home ground and had been mutually arranged. Barbara had arisen from the garden seat whilst talking and had then walked around to the back of the house. "I will just let my mum know we are going. I will introduce you when we get back from our walk, Ian" and so saying, she had briefly disappeared. Time there had been then, albeit briefly, to look around! The property, a detached bungalow, stands almost in splendid isolation on the north side of the High Bentham Road, with only one detached house a short distance away on the same side of the road. To the rear and both sides of the property, a farmer's field of considerable size, suitable perhaps for the grazing of stock, leading down to Ellergill Beck which meets the River Wenning in Low Bentham village. From the back garden, a particularly fine view on the horizon of a distant Ingleborough, with its familiar flat top, perhaps seven miles or so to the east. Enticing and beguiling is the mountain, even though it has been climbed. And this young lady living here at *'Benwick'* – she is also enticing, but in a totally different context! Ingleborough is to be climbed again sometime and its caves explored and with Barbara, there is a need to find out all about her. Her likes, her dislikes, her hobbies – to find out all there is to know. Would she be willing to tell?

Silently and subconsciously, within a slightly nervous frame, praise was still being given to the Lord our God! Praise the Lord, indeed – this young lady actually wanted to spend the afternoon with the head of the boarding house. Walking back along the garden path in front of the bungalow, the name of the property had elicited an obvious query. "Why *'Benwick'*, Barbara?" She had given a shy smile as though it was slightly embarrassing, before explaining the origins to the name of the property. "My father was born in Bentham and my mother was born in Barnoldswick. So, you see, they used the first part of Bentham and the last part of Barnoldswick to form the house name. My mum and dad had this property built six years ago. We used to live down in Low Bentham village, which is where I was born". Walking out of the front gate, Barbara had then skipped across the road before adding with obvious enthusiasm, "I will show you the house where I was born if you like, Ian, as we will be walking right past it." And then, she had simultaneously scrunched up her nose and her shoulders as if to indicate that it would be quite exciting. Indeed, the prospect was going to be exciting for both – the Upper 6th Form boarder wanting to acquire as much information as possible and the Lower 6th form day pupil, clearly anxious and willing, and more than happy to provide it.

No. 2 Ellergill Cottages, opposite the Post Office in Low Bentham, is a terraced house with a very modest front garden facing the road. "This is it!" Barbara had said excitedly, "and my bedroom was at the front on the left," she continued, pointing a gloved finger up at a first-floor window. She had then continued somewhat mischievously, "When I was a little girl, I used to sit on the inside of the window ledge in the evening and wave at all the local people who passed by. I should have been in bed really. My mum used to tell me off if she found me by the window." Following the story, Barbara had given a rather fetching nostalgic smile. "I have lived in Low Bentham all my life, Ian. I was born here in the Dales. I suppose you could say that I am a real country girl!" she had exclaimed with laughter, giving another quick scrunch of her nose before continuing down the street to the road junction in the village centre.

A country girl certainly – perhaps enthusiastically admitting the fact, partly in mitigation to help explain a slight shyness that had been exhibited, intentionally or not, over a period of the last six or seven weeks. Perhaps the confession had been made with her being acutely aware that the young man, with whom she was spending an afternoon, appeared to be the exact opposite, with parents working and living abroad and the potential boyfriend being therefore, by necessity, well-travelled. Whatever, the admission was endearing and added to her charm. Despite any obvious differences in life experience up to young adulthood between this country girl and a seasoned traveller, there had been no sign of it in the innocent happiness on display. Perhaps you thought, Barbara, that being well travelled might produce a young man with a sense of superiority. If you thought as much, then you would have been quite wrong. Despite all the travelling, there is within this jumbled psyche a continual feeling of insecurity. Goodness knows why.

"Okay, up the Burton-in-Lonsdale Road now, Ian. It is quite a steep climb up to the top of the village," Barbara had directed, with a gloved right hand pointing northwards. Afternoon walks from the boarding house, particularly in the formative boarding years, involved the back road – that is the Millhouses Road – behind the school, which winds its way slowly but surely around numerous bends whilst gradually increasing in altitude until the first or second signpost is reached. If the outing didn't involve this back road, then it would be an afternoon walk onto the moors to the south of High Bentham to eventually reach what is known locally as the 'Big Stone', although officially it is called 'The Great Stone of Fourstones'. It has always been a mystery, however, as to exactly where the other three stones are situated as they do not appear to be anywhere within visual or striking distance of the 'Big Stone' itself, situated as it is on the unclassified road heading south out of High Bentham towards Tatham fell. Rumour has it that some local farmers took away the other three stones – really? It is assumed that this stone was conveniently deposited at its site by the shifting ice flows during the ice age, leaving it in splendid isolation in the middle of a deserted heather moor. A previous and rather helpful generation has kindly chiselled some steps into the solid stone (sacrilege, perhaps – what would Jake have to say about such desecration?), enabling one to walk to the top of the stone for a scenic view which incorporates, to the east, the vista of all the three famous Yorkshire Pennine peaks – Ingleborough, Whernside and Penyghent.

So, the route this Sunday afternoon – that is, the road northwards out of Low Bentham to Burton-in-Lonsdale – had indeed been new territory. The road climbs steeply and bends left, passing 'Woodys' general stores before turning sharp right and continuing boldly upwards, so that by the top of the hill, on the northern fringe of the village, a panoramic vista is provided of the surrounding countryside to the north and east. Across on the near horizon, the lower slopes leading to Whernside – and to their right, Ingleborough, splendidly isolated. On this Sunday, a faint sheen of snow had covered their upper slopes where the temperature had obviously stayed below freezing, giving the hills an authoritative and imposing presence. "My mum and dad took me and my brother up to the top of Ingleborough quite a few years ago but I haven't been up since then," Barbara had said, giving a rather nostalgic sigh. She had stood with a gloved hand resting on an old rusty farm gate, with her stylish boots carefully avoiding the churned-up pasture surrounding the entrance to the adjoining field. Seemingly slightly in awe of the majestic view, despite it being one she will encounter almost daily, she had gazed across to Ingleborough whilst remaining silent. "Perhaps we could go up some time," she had then suggested before adding rather thoughtfully, "but it really would have to be on a nice warm sunny day." Indeed, we could! Ingleborough had only recently been climbed with Pugh, but another opportunity to walk up this iconic mountain with a new girlfriend could hardly be declined. Barbara stood, again silent, obviously thinking for a few moments. Then she looked across from the gate rather wistfully, possibly realising the implication of what she had said. With a cheeky smile lighting up her eyes in an instant, she had then added a little hesitantly, "Well, that's assuming we want to stay friends with each other." And then, without waiting for any sort of confirmation, she quickly added, "I am sure we will, don't you think?"

Approximately a mile up the Burton-in-Lonsdale Road, at a crossroads, a right turn was made, and a further right turn a mile thereafter, at which point the road, twisting this way and that whilst rising sharply, passes High Bentham golf course on the outskirts of the village. (Which is where, no doubt, Titty plies her golfing prowess.)

The walking had been relaxed, casual and invitingly slow. It wasn't a route march! The slow pace was about right. It provided adequate time to gaze around, to chat and to ask all those questions that could, of course, have been asked over recent weeks had either party been confident enough. So High Bentham village was ultimately reached, by which time a slender gloved left hand was being held. A left hand? Yes. The correct etiquette taught by a maternal grandmother whilst staying with her during the regular half-term breaks had been faithfully recalled and followed to the letter, viz. "If you ever walk out with a young lady along a road that lacks a pavement, Ian, always make sure that she is on the inside and protected from the traffic, with you on the outside." Thank you, Nanny Parkinson, for that valuable advice.

Whilst walking, Barbara would occasionally lift up her left hand and move it back and forward playfully, making sure the two hands, entwined, stayed together. "Right, Ian," Barbara had said excitedly when High Bentham was reached, "I do have lots of relatives in the village, but this last house of the left is where my grandmother lives. She lives downstairs and my auntie and uncle live upstairs," she had said as she looked across to a large end terrace house called *'Westward View'*, next to High Bentham junior school and very nearly into the village centre. "We had better not visit them today as we have to be back for tea of course, but perhaps we will be able to visit sometime in the future," Barbara had added confidently in the expectation that her suggestion would illicit a favourable response. Of course, it did! How could one decline? It gave the promise of future meetings.

By the time Low Bentham had been reached via the main road from High Bentham, it was the middle of the afternoon, and the winter light was fading rapidly. The welcome sign of smoke emanating from the chimney at *'Benwick'* meant that afternoon tea would almost certainly be with the accompaniment of a coal fire. When Barbara had opened the front door to the bungalow and enthusiastically motioned for her new boyfriend to follow, it was indeed to the sound of a thriving open coal fire with its attendant warmth. In addition, in the combined lounge and dining room and diagonally across from the fire, a dining table was neatly set, awaiting five people, whilst in the kitchen, a middle-aged lady with short cropped black hair containing just a hint of grey entwined therein and wearing a flowery pinney, busied herself with the trappings of a Sunday buffet. And what a buffet! On the kitchen table tops, numerous plates of varying sizes all generously filled with food – a large salad dish, a platter containing different sorts of meat, an attractive Lakeland slate cheese board and several plates of cakes and buns, the bulk of which most definitely appeared to be homemade. Nothing posh however in that genuine Yorkshire household. No dainty sandwiches shaped as triangles with the corners cut off and placed carefully on doilies, as one always expected to see on the occasional visits to an elderly (and slightly formidable, at least in the eyes of a young teenager) paternal grandmother in Morecambe whilst growing up! A mealtime with Nanny McCart invariably meant a trolley being wheeled into the living room with the 'posh' sandwiches on the top level with various (shop bought) cakes, whilst underneath, on the bottom of the trolley, would be the very predictable large bowl of fruit salad. The tinned variety, always accompanied by a tin of *Carnation* milk.

Nothing like that in the Noble household. It was food for eating, for enjoying – not for looking at. Not only that, but it was a display most definitely a world away from the neatly packaged, rather bland convenience food provided when living at home in the UK with parents (whilst abroad, servants were always provided, which included a resident cook) that had normally presented itself in the form of Vesta meals – chow main, paella (with prawns or was it, perhaps, with chicken?), beef risotto and the like. Nothing like that. This was welcoming and homely – a welcome indeed. Whether intended or not – impress it indeed did.

"Hello Mum, we are back. This is Ian from the boarding house at school and this is my mum, Ian. She has been looking forward to meeting you – *honestly*!" As she spoke, there had been a slightly mischievous grin across her face, pushing out and highlighting cheeks that were rosy-red from the November cold. Barbara had spoken with confidence and with an assured manner, gained almost certainly from an afternoon walk with a new boyfriend. Her slightly cheeky introduction had the effect of putting her mother somewhat on the defensive. "Well, this young lady has been telling me all about you," she said in mitigation, shifting the onus back to Barbara. With a hand willingly offered up, it seemed most appropriate to seal the introduction with a handshake.

What of a new girlfriend's mother? Straightforward, sporting a kind, patient countenance. Short hair, yes, and simple but stylish nonetheless and combed or pushed up off her forehead. Mother and daughter being a similar height – a daughter slightly taller perhaps – and both displaying the high cheekbones and a comparable build. Welcoming as she was and interesting to converse with, it had almost seemed as though preparing a buffet for the family, with the intriguing addition of her daughter's boyfriend, was, for her, all part of just another normal day in the kitchen. If it was quite special for her to be welcoming a young man that her daughter had brought home, she nevertheless appeared to take it in her stride.

With the arrival back at *'Benwick'* and following the introduction, Barbara's mother had opened the freezer compartment at the top of the fridge and had taken out an Arctic Roll, which she then placed delicately onto a waiting plate by the kitchen draining board. An Arctic Roll! Good heavens! Something of a special treat and the type of dessert that one could only dream about here at boarding school where the puddings are, by necessity, more basic and nowhere near as luxurious. "Right, we can let that defrost whilst we eat the first course." Turning around, Barbara's mother had continued, "Fetch your dad and brother, Barbara, the food is ready, and I will brew the tea." Down the corridor towards the bedrooms and with the confidence which comes with being on home territory, the sound of a positive full throated Yorkshire voice could be heard, "Come on you two, tea is ready, and I want you to meet Ian!" (A younger brother had, of course, already met Ian at school, although this was now on home ground for brother David and in quite different circumstances. This was not a 6th form prefect to pupil relationship, but instead, a sister's boyfriend relationship. Two very different common bonds and might, one wondered, they perhaps become interrelated over the course of time if the friendship with this lady stands the test of school and time.) Ian, meanwhile, had been only too glad to offer to assist in transferring the splendid fare from the kitchen and onto the dining table via a rather cleverly designed serving hatch linking the two rooms. It was very important, after all, to make a favourable impression with the most important person in that household – well, after, of course, a girlfriend – that is, a girlfriend's mother! Nanny Parkinson, in her own inimitable style, would no doubt suggest, "Start as you mean to go on".

It was a dark and cold November evening when the front door of *'Benwick'* had once again been opened, but this time it had been for a walk alone down through Low Bentham village and back to the boarding house. Barbara had not stayed by the front door, however, but instead, she had walked along to the garden gate and then skipped across the road, with her delicate small hand, this time devoid of a black glove, willingly offered up. It had been gratefully accepted and two hands remained clasped together for a few moments, but it had felt more like thirty minutes! "It's such a shame you cannot stay a bit later so that we could have watched *Dad's Army* together, Ian. It is one of my favourite comedy programmes", Barbara had said before continuing, "never mind, I have really enjoyed today, Ian. I hope you have." There was hardly any need to answer, but for a girlfriend an answer would be expected – an answer indeed needed if only to calm any possible worries. Enthusiastic confirmation had been gladly given. A regular look back was made whilst walking down the hill towards Low Bentham village and there, under the glow of a nearby streetlight, Barbara had been stood, giving an occasional wave until the curve in the road took her gradually out of sight.

Now, in the quiet and welcome solitude of the dormitory, it is almost impossible to take it all in. Something has been released from the inner self. When Keats first read Chapman's 'Homer', he was full of wonder and the poetical lines he penned are akin to the feeling that is experienced now, whilst sat in a dormitory after having spent an afternoon with a new girlfriend. Keats wrote,

> *Then felt I like some watcher of the skies*
> *When a new planet swims into his ken;*
> *Or like stout Cortez when with eagle eyes*
> *He star'd at the Pacific --- and all his men*
> *Look'd at each other with a wild surmise --*
> *Silent, upon a peak in Darien.*

How does one measure success? If it is measured by the holding of hands and by the certainty of an agreed meeting tomorrow at school break time, then the day has quite definitely been a success! What excitement there is in sheer simplicity. The questions, the queries, the answers, the laughter, the facial expressions, the admissions ("I've had butterflies all morning", said in that endearing Yorkshire voice) and the squeezing of hands. *'What peace there may be in silence'*, a suggestion in 'Desiderata' (a poem by Max Ehrmann, written in the 1920s), was certainly not appropriate here as the talking had been almost continuous. Strangely though, there had been a calming 'peace' in the talking, with neither party wanting it to stop. The rather splendid home baking that comprised afternoon tea indeed stopped the talking temporarily – the pregnant pauses whilst food was consumed being punctuated by the meeting of eyes and the hint of a smile. And did a girlfriend's mother notice the occasional secretive smile traded across the table, along with the silent gaze into a pair of eyes opposite? All in between, of course, mouthfuls of food? (And the audacity of asking for an extra slice of Arctic Roll had been happily accommodated, Barbara herself volunteering to get it for her new boyfriend.)

Everyone – mother and father, their proud daughter, for she had brought home a young man to introduce to them, her younger brother and a 6th form boarder – all on their very best behaviour, trying hard to make a good impression with the niceties of mealtime being obediently observed. (Although father might well have been given some gentle advice by his daughter after the boarding house visitor had left regarding putting his knife into his mouth! Not only that, but this new boyfriend was indeed rather puzzled to watch Barbara's father tucking into an interesting and intriguing combination – a hunk of crumbly Lancashire cheese with a wedge of fruit cake!)

All days end. They must end. Tomorrow will be another day, yes. In a dormitory room at the end of this most significant day, the lyrics of a Cat Stevens hit on the LP 'Teaser and the Firecat' have been running continuously through the brain,

> *I need to know you,*
> *Need to feel my arms around you,*
> *Feel my arms around you,*
> *Like sea around a shore.*

Village life is insular. Without doubt, Barbara's neighbours will have noticed that she now has a boyfriend. What will they be saying? "He is a lad from the grammar school." "He is a boarder at the school." "I saw them both out walking last Sunday afternoon", and suchlike. Nor will it go unnoticed with the teaching staff, particularly with Snot, living directly across the road from *'Benwick'*. What will the all-important teachers be saying in their common room? That is, those who are trying to teach this young man the basics of the various 'A' Levels, once they are aware of this new relationship. "Perhaps he should be concentrating on his studies." Ducky, perhaps, will be wondering whether it might make his English student a tad more grown up! Within the boarding house, there will also be the inevitable chitchat – "Mucca has got himself a girlfriend. It's a lass from the Lower 6th form, Barbara Noble." And with Barbara's two school colleagues, Christine and Judith, it is perhaps only what they suspected all along. For the time being at least, you might say that

I SUPPOSE I AM A REAL COUNTRY GIRL

Barbara and Ian are going to be, if not quite the 'talk of the town', then most certainly 'the talk of the school'.

For all this, perhaps thanks should be quietly given to the previous headmaster, Mr Kaye, who, upon his arrival at this school in September 1967, espoused proper 'co-education' within this school. This enabled girls and boys to mix naturally during school life rather than being segregated, as had previously been the case under the somewhat authoritarian rule of Mr Webb. Mr Kaye, learned in appearance and in deed, thank you!

A new girlfriend from 'Benwick', Low Bentham, putting on the style by pretending she is at a Paris fashion show! November 1972.

CHAPTER XVI

IN IT, CAN I PLANT MYSELF?

30th November 1972. Less than a week has now elapsed since last Sunday. The enjoyment and the thrill of that day has not waned one bit. Each new day is full of excitement as a child might display when presented with a bag of sweets from its mother! What is it then about confidence? Where self-assurance is lacking, the joy and warmth of starting a relationship can inevitably be affected by a strange melancholy. A worry (perhaps a needless worry, but a worry nonetheless) that the mutual friendship and attraction may not survive. And this despite there being no outward sign that things are not going to work out. Whilst sat in the dormitory, there have indeed been occasional – albeit brief – bouts of melancholy, brought on merely by the thought that this new-found relationship may not last the course! Will it succeed? Will it fail? As Keats reminds us in his 'Ode on Melancholy':

But when the melancholy fit shall,
Sudden from heaven like a weeping cloud,

And melancholy, that leads to a strange form of depression, *'Doom is dark and deeper than any sea dingle'*. That is Auden's take on it. Perhaps the English Literature study material is partly to blame, with the likes of John Donne and John Keats writing eloquently of unrequited love. But this is not unrequited love – not yet it isn't! Why the worry that it might end up as such? Both these two poets – most particularly these two from all those being studied within the syllabus – have encouraged the writing of poetry, albeit on a much less grand scale and in some strange unexplained way, the most powerful expression and output is invariably the result of melancholy. Why should this be? Keats was perhaps an incurable romantic. Is that the point? Is the yearning to be looking for and hoping for romance that much sweeter, rather than to actually finding it and then enjoying it? Surely, that cannot be the case. It would be nonsensical.

Having now been attracted to the young lady who would turn so easily red with embarrassment by the drink vending machine, a foray has already been made into writing romantic poetry. It is now an unstoppable urge and a way of expressing a feeling which cannot be given to this young lady verbally (even if it had been obvious, merely from the day-to-day banter with the three ladies, that Barbara was the attraction). Now, after last Sunday's afternoon walk, a poem has been written almost as a plea to keep the relationship going. Lack of confidence to the fore again. John Donne wrote *'Go, and catch a falling star...'* and in that style following a November walk – whilst holding a tender gloved hand, where the leaves of autumn were scattered across the roads, had been blown onto the verges, were spread liberally across the fields and also had been watched with a new girlfriend being pulled along by the river current – the following has been written as a cry of hope, of expectation, or perhaps of anticipation – maybe all three!

> *Go catch that leaf.*
> *It holds the sweetness of life from your touch,*
> *Let it not drift away*
> *Towards oblivion:*
> *This clear November day could smell*
> *No finer than that simple branched piece.*
> *And that grass,*
> *For you have trodden upon it*
> *Leaving an imprint along the way of life:*
> *In it can I plant myself?*
> *Such a fool as I am.*

Composing such verse helps to expunge the doubt and the melancholy (until the next time)! However, the time is not right to let Barbara have sight of such scribbling. The verse is, perhaps, too intense. Anyhow, it is surely far, far, too early to be pondering on long-term plans. This dormitory room is, without doubt, the ideal place for dreaming.

The daily sparring by the school drink vending machine is now taking place with renewed vigour. No longer three girls against one boy. Now, it is two against two – one of the 'three musketeers' has defected! With a boyfriend and girlfriend fighting the same corner, there is, inevitably, an increased impetus from Judith and Christine to cause as much discomfort as possible to Barbara. The aim, of course, to provide some enjoyment in seeing her cheeks turn red and by association, hopefully embarrassing her boyfriend at the same time. All in good spirit, despite an occasional (well, frequent...) slightly scurrilous suggestion that the 6th form boarder might want to be aware of a rather interesting mole on a particular part of Barbara's anatomy. And a specific part at that – which *surely,* they could only know about by all three of them sharing communal showers after the 6th form ladies have played hockey or, more likely, netball. (In view of Barbara's dislike of, in her own words, "running aimlessly around a games field carrying a hockey stick!") Oh God, Barbara in a communal shower naked – nothing on, being seen by all the other 6th form girls. Just imagining it sends the mind into a sexual frenzy! Is it just a young male fantasy to imagine witnessing a group of naked young 6th form girls bathing in the school showers? All the lads in the Lonsdale dormitory complex would certainly relish the opportunity to witness such a display, surely. Who can blame them? Would the same principle apply in reverse? Would Barbara accept an opportunity to see the First XI football team in the showers after a match? A difficult one to answer. Perhaps not, or is it that one would like to think not? Are young ladies maybe a little more reserved? Would they feel slightly awkward agreeing to witness such a spectacle? Are they interested in seeing nude males? Would they even admit wanting to?

> *[**An aside:** this, then, is the Lonsdale complex 'take' on such problematic questions:*
>
> *The boys – they will, surely, to a man stand in awe and with some considerable yearning – to be there amongst it all – whilst viewing a group of naked 6th form ladies in the communal showers.*
>
> *The girls – they will stand giggling – and perhaps even screeching – whilst viewing a group of 6th form lads in the communal showers. Giggling? Definitely! Who would blame them looking at a motley collection of appendages on display?]*

Interesting conjecture and pondered on, to be sure, within the framework of the male bastion of Lonsdale dormitory. No problem in this environment discussing the female form, interspersed with a generous helping of bravado. A discussion frequently circulates around the 6th form ladies' bodies. In particular, deciding who has the biggest boobs etc. Without doubt, within the wide variety of upper and lower 6th form bazookas, Barbara does not (on the basis of a general assessment during normal day to day school life) appear to have the biggest boobs. A view of them in the communal shower (hell!) would without doubt confirm that – but hey, so what? She is still an attractive young lady with such a pleasant personality, so who is bothered? The girl with the biggest boobs might well be vindictive and spiteful and will, more than likely, surely, be a show-off, yes? This young lady is incredibly engaging with such a sunny personality, and it is on that basis that an attraction has been formed. In a similar vein, it is hoped that Barbara has taken a liking to the First XI goalkeeper due, in part, to his personality. (What personality?) Hopefully, Barbara would say, in her own measured and thoughtful way, in a style that she frequently uses when being ribbed by Judith and Christine by the coffee machine, "Well I like you Ian, but most of all I like you for being you."

Yes, all conjecture. Sociology 'A' Level would be a tad more interesting with discussions of this nature rather than the travails of examining poverty. Would Miss Shirley be astounded, shocked even, by how the mind of this upper 6th form male works, as indeed do the minds of the bulk of the other Lonsdale dormitory residents, regarding naked females? Perhaps not. Someone in the common room suggested, "You blokes are all the same." Perhaps so – is it something to do with biology?

With Barbara then, no amount of cajoling will elicit any further detail about that strategically positioned mole. Perhaps no knowledge would have been preferable to being given a snippet of information, but what, after all, are school friends for? It has inevitably been the subject of sporadic ribbing from Judith and from Christine, but far more valuable and re-assuring was the comment from Barbara regarding last weekend, "I was thrilled when you called to ask me if I wished to go to the party." And yes, when her mother had announced with some charm and with a knowing smile that Friday evening at her bedroom door, "Well Barbara, there is a young man at the front door asking to see you", indeed, Barbara did wonder! ("I was rather hoping that it might be you.")

These boisterous colleagues in the boarding house, who had cajoled an apprehensive lad into 'going for broke' with an unsolicited house call are, at least, now aware that it wasn't abject failure attending a Friday night party without a girlfriend. Far from it! It was most probably a blessing, as the 'one-to-one' walk around the 'square mile' on a beautifully sunny November day was eminently preferable to a raucous 6th form party. A party where, without doubt, a private chat would have been quite impracticable and, even if it had been possible, certainly nowhere near as intimate.

CHAPTER XVII

PERHAPS WE CAN ENROL IN DANCING LESSONS

December has moved swiftly on. Today – Friday 15th December – is the last day of this autumn term. One term over – two to go. The view from this dormitory window has changed considerably since that first week in September. On this December morning, the adjacent wood appears stark, many of the trees shorn of their leaves. The flow of water in the river gives testimony to the fact that the month, after the first few cold dry days, has been miserable, cold and wet. Cold and dry, acceptable – cold and wet, wretched. The grass running along the riverbank and into the wilderness has, over the last couple of weeks, had the appearance of being permanently soaked. Indeed, at times, the grass had been totally covered by the substantial outflow of water running off the Pennine fells, which the river has been unable to cope with. The tarpaulin over the swimming pool is an ungainly permanent fixture.

Nevertheless, now, on this final morning at school before the Christmas break, it feels as though a good deal has been accomplished during the term. Even the rather fragile relationship between teacher and pupil in English Literature has seen a modicum of mutual respect develop. Indeed, so much so that the term end report has, rather pleasingly, confirmed, *'Ian is making good progress, his thinking is usually sound, and his expression is improving...'* Praise indeed. Perhaps the Head Boarder is becoming a little more responsible – yes? An element of stubbornness still, perhaps, manifests itself in studying the morass of ideas contained within the Sociology syllabus leading to, one might suggest, a measured compliment in the term report, *'He seems a little less rigid in his attitudes, which enables him to see, if not to sympathise with, opposing views...'* Slightly odd, perhaps. Of course, one can see other views (even if it is difficult to understand them), but that is not a reason to sympathise with them, never mind deciding to support them. That comment might, perhaps, be construed as suggesting that the views held are, indeed, still somewhat intransigent. So what? What if they are?

The 'one-to-one' relationship with Mr Russell has been, without doubt, a success story. Mutual respect, there is plenty, and he has been extremely flexible in permitting regular visits to *'Benwick',* not only for these last two weekends just gone but also on weekday evenings, after dinner, but always on the premise that "it doesn't impact on your studies, Mr McCart!" Of course not, sir – ha! By now, at the end of this term, he has become well versed in anticipating the usual letter being handed over, without fail on a Thursday, from Barbara's mother asking permission for leave of absence for the Head Boarder on either the following Saturday (providing the First XI have not got an away game) or Sunday.

"I always know that I will be getting some post on a Thursday, McCart", he now remarks with a broad grin on his face, as the letter from Mrs Noble is handed over. The relationship between Housemaster and Head Boarder has developed, and continues to develop, very satisfactorily. There is a friendly mutual understanding of each other's situation. It was immensely rewarding, engendering a feeling of pride, yes, to read his comments in the end of term report, *'As head of [the boarding] house, he takes his duties seriously... and sets a good example to the younger boys. Keep it up'*. What he did not say, albeit that he might well have been tempted to, was that discipline can be administered without the frequent need to shout. Those in the junior dormitories might well agree with that suggestion.

Looking back, the last fortnight has been a hectic period. Not just on the educational front. Friday 8th December had seen the school annual cross-country race taking place and, as always, the route over the moor to the south of the school sorted out the competitors. In the senior race, it was casually accepted by all that Paul Wood would lead the pack and he did – from start to finish. There was little point in trying to keep up with him once he was out in front. And he was out in front from the very start, treating it almost as a sprint race. If he became aware of another runner gaining on him and threatening his domain as leader of the pack, he merely increased the pace to ensure there was good headway between first and second position. At least this year he took the correct route, rather than 'allegedly' being shown the incorrect route – which just so happened to be a shorter route – across the moor by a race marshal, as was the case last year! (Why was everyone sceptical then?)

Why take part in cross-country when it is a punishing schedule and drains the energy? It is quite simply the challenge. Last year's position of seventh place was there to be bettered. As an early riser, the training for this most recent senior cross-country competition involved a morning run of twice around the sports field. Perhaps a distance of a couple of miles, followed then by a quick shower, then a short cramming session on one of the 'A' Levels being studied. All prior to breakfast and school. Oh, the advantages of being an early riser and being full of beans from the word go.

The relationship fostered with Barbara brought about an immediate and mutually agreed change to the well-established morning training run. The amended training routine involved a run up from the school, through Low Bentham village, to *'Benwick',* where *Bendy* (a little rubber toy soldier – a memento from travelling overseas!) would be put through Barbara's slightly ajar top window, to be collected again from Barbara at school break time. It gave a purpose to the training run and made it infinitely more enjoyable. So much so that it has been continued every morning, even with the cross-country race having come and gone. With these dark winter mornings, there are few prying eyes. This morning escapade is quite often made more exciting by tying little messages to *Bendy* for Barbara to read when he is retrieved from the bedroom floor and there are also quite frequently messages tied to the window latch for collection by the early morning runner. Sometimes, the messages are supplemented by various little treats in the form of sweets. Here onwards, the Head Boarder has been christened 'The Phantom Road Runner' by his girlfriend!

Ah, what sights one can witness jogging through a small village in the hours of the early morning. The school games mistress (yes, as well as the Sociology teacher), Miss Shirley, keeping herself 'in trim' with a morning run. (No pleasantries exchanged, merely a nodding of heads which is, frankly, sufficient for both teacher and pupil.) Much more intriguing, the Low Bentham paperboy doing his deliveries. Nothing particularly noteworthy there. Except, this paperboy must, surely, hold the record as the oldest one in the country. Edgar Lister, brother-in-law of the Postmistress, cycles calmly around in the dark of the morning delivering the newspapers, whilst in years he must surely be over seventy years of age! Possibly well over. Commitment? Yes. Admirable? Yes indeed. An example of dedication? Indeed. But also, of course, saving the cost of paying a 'traditional' paperboy! Yorkshire thrift at its best. (Why else would he be doing it?)

Also, the milkman, Sid Hogg. (NOT the fastest milkman in the west. Doesn't that accolade belong to Ernie – and Trigger! Yes?) Whilst delivering to *'Benwick'* and the nearby properties, Sid has clearly been perplexed at witnessing a young man running through the front gate of *'Benwick'* in the early morning. Indeed, sufficiently puzzled to have felt it worth mentioning to Barbara's mother who, fortuitously, had already been made aware of the ritual by Barbara herself. In Barbara's words, her mother is comfortable with the arrangement, providing "the house brickwork separates the runner from his sleeping girlfriend!" Ha, yes, and the thought of a girlfriend inside that brickwork, tucked up in her bed is rather exciting. An intrigued mother is without doubt watching the firming up of this relationship closely and with some interest. She understands there is no harm being done with the early morning jog to *'Benwick'* and perhaps has in mind that popular dictum – 'you are only young once'! (According to the 'oldies'...)

What of the cross-country race itself? A punishing pace across some sodden moors and farmland but, strangely, rather perversely and difficult perhaps to explain or understand, most enjoyable! It hadn't been easy to determine what position one was holding in the race until running back into the school by the side entrance and on towards the finish line. There, with no one in hot pursuit, Barbara confidently held up five fingers on her hand to confirm fifth place was 'in the bag' so to speak, also providing a welcome little wave. (And far better than putting two fingers up as it would have been quite obvious that she wasn't confirming second place. Yes, very funny from an idle spectator, who suggested she had actually put two fingers up! She is far too nice a girl to play that kind of prank.)

An improvement, then, from the previous year and the highest placing from within the boarding house. A satisfactory run, certainly, with a feeling of exhaustion and being totally knackered only apparent once one has stopped running. Only four others in the school who are more accomplished long-distance runners. Impressive? Well, indeed, it felt impressive. Cess had come in one place ahead. He has done well. He was regularly in sight up ahead during the race, but it was impossible to make inroads into the gap separating fourth and fifth place. Perhaps only fifteen or so paces ahead, but it was sufficient. He was used instead, quite conveniently, as a marker for running at the required pace. Ah, the joys of cross-country running!

The senior cross-country race December 1972. 'Cess' Hargreaves (in fourth place) keeps an adequate distance ahead of the author on the approach to the Punch Bowl Hotel and the finishing line at the school. (Photograph: J. Hebblethwaite)

Anyway, what about the female cross-country race? In particular, the senior girls. A shorter course – well, of course! Good to see the girls returning, quite predictably, with legs covered in mud, tops splattered, hair all over the place and looking generally bedraggled. (Strange, the boys never look like that!) And Morag, there in fifth place for the senior girls – perhaps there might well have been something in common after all… A young Miss Southwell (deputy headmaster's daughter) and a young Miss Jagger (French teacher's daughter) also finishing in the top ten. No doubt under some parental pressure to do well! However, none of our second-year 6th form ladies there in the leading pack –

they have, no doubt, better things to occupy their school time. Who can blame them?

The cross-country race was followed the day after by a difficult encounter on the football field with traditional arch-enemy Settle High School. Settle School and Bentham School – an ingrained persistent rivalry, perhaps because, historically, local pupils would have the delicate choice (if indeed it be so) of studying either at this grammar school *or* Settle High School if they could pass their 11-plus examination. Ingleton High School was the ultimate destination if they failed the exam. This choice, offered to the brainy locals, has inevitably been the cause of historical local rivalry – rather like a local 'derby' football match. A 3-2 victory against Settle, then, was hard won, involving two penalty saves by the head of the boarding house. As one of the penalties had been awarded against the goalkeeper for a foul, it was perhaps just as well that that penalty, as well as another, had then been saved. (Well, one just couldn't let the player dribble past a stranded goalkeeper on the ground. His legs were there to be grabbed!) And was the other penalty award *really* hand-ball? Two penalty saves and subsequent fame – well, for a day at least. Perhaps for a bit longer with the juniors, who are always anxious to have a hero that they can aspire to on the school football pitch.

At the end of the match, it had been time to take stock. Filthy, mud caked just about everywhere – the face, in the hair, legs without a hint of white skin (a wet December day had seen to all that) – but nevertheless, a tinge of pleasure in the total discomfort of it all. Evidence, if it was indeed needed, that the goalkeeper had been fully involved in a match – and a hard-fought one at that.

Ample compensation for such a hard and bruising match was offered at full-time by perhaps the most important spectator, Barbara. She suggested a walk up to *'Benwick'* so that some badly cut, and very grubby knees could be properly washed, hair cleaned, face sorted out (and all by her fair hands!), with Dettol then being applied to sore knees. Who would – who could – refuse such an offer? It had also involved happily dispensing with school showers, opting instead for some tender care from a young lady anxious to give a visual show of affection. Indeed, it had been a relief in some respects missing the communal showers. They invariably end up as raucous affairs, particularly after being victorious in a game. Several of the team always anxious, whilst in the showers, to compare and even measure their manhood against the acknowledged 'standard bearer' and 'all-time great' from last year's First XI team, M….. V…... The rest of the team always feel the need to try and match his prowess in that department, but all fail miserably! (Had he been a boarder rather than a day pupil, matron would most definitely have been impressed, notwithstanding that she has "seen it all before". She might well have then

FROM A DORMITORY WINDOW

appreciated the fact that, in actual fact, she had *not* seen it all before…) No one person can excel in every department and whilst he may have only collected modest exam results, he will, surely, always be allocated top marks for the size of his 'appendage'!

A cruel nickname that had been given to one of the First XI defenders (who must, possibly out of pity, stay anonymous!) last season was the unfortunate title of 'Midget'. This nickname most definitely did not relate to his height. Perhaps more appropriate as a suitable moniker for him might well have been pinched from last year's chart success from the pop group Sweet with their song, if indeed that is an accurate term, entitled – 'Little Willy'! Whatever, the nickname of Midget for one of last year's team players became entrenched in the daily school life until he left. Did the girls understand or realise, one wonders, what the background was to the particular epithet given to him?

Oh dear, nicknames. What would this school, and indeed schools in general, do without them? Without doubt, the most recognised and well used girls nickname around the school is 'Tank' – given to a lass on account of the size of her frame. It would be a reasonable bet that not many, outside her own class, will be aware of her correct name, other than those who are close friends. Some nicknames given are logical. Lanky needs no explanation. Fudge, well perhaps that does. Noggin Park, Spinner Hall, Acker (nothing to do with a clarinet), and Piggy Gardner – Piggy most definitely a nickname for 'fat'! And nicknames for the First XI goalkeeper? Mucca is the acknowledged (and acceptable) nickname throughout the school, although previous incarnations have included Tivvy (from early days as a junior in the boarding house – albeit that it is difficult to provide any logical explanation). Also, more logical perhaps, Muck Cart and rather more unkindly, 'MacFart'. The secret, of course, is to take nicknames in one's stride – not that easy to do, however, when one is young. At least the nickname of 'butter fingers' has not been needed when stood between the goalposts for the First XI. Not yet, in any case!

Matches against local rivals Settle are traditionally hard-fought and the victory was indeed sweet and deserved. However, a heavy defeat in Preston several days later, 2-5 – again at the hands of an aggressive Preston 6th Form College – restored reality.

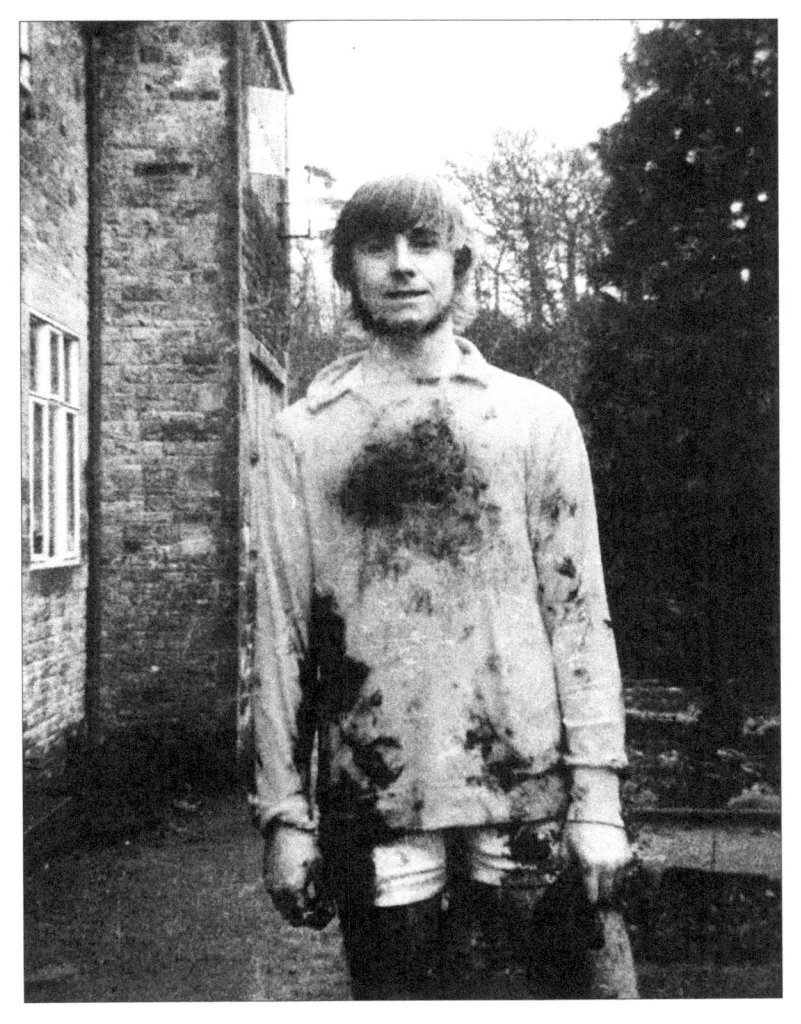

Aftermath of the infamous 3-2 victory over Settle High School.
'A tinge of pleasure in the total discomfort of all the dirt...'
December 1972

With this autumn term now ending, the weeks leading to the 6th form Christmas party had been spent trying to sort out arrangements for the holiday period. Eventually sorted at the party. Ah, school Christmas parties masquerading as discos. Not something that has ever been looked forward to with any great enthusiasm, irrespective of age. The party last year was a rather pedestrian affair, particularly when there was little interest or eagerness for dancing. Occupying a dormitory room at that time at the front of the original rectory building, the most entertaining part of the evening had been watching all-comers trooping into the Assembly Hall. Dolled up in their finery (well, the ladies at least!) and for some, with the safety of a partner. (Very helpful. It made it possible to be certain about just who is "going out" with whom.) What a transformation though for the ladies – from pedestrian school uniform to fashionable evening attire. Even the ordinary can suddenly be quite appealing. Alas, the prospect of dancing last year only succeeded in making attendance distinctly unappealing, despite the elegance of female flesh and fashion on show.

This year, however, quite different. The infamous disco for the senior forms. The Christmas Party. It culminated in the 'rant of all rants' at the very next school assembly. Mr Hagen at his finest and in full flow. A spectacle indeed! One can feel quite privileged to have witnessed it. After having the junior forms ushered out at the end of morning assembly, he exploded. Not immediately, no. He wound himself up to it but somehow, you just knew it was coming. The inevitability of it garnered the suspense. Eventually the balloon went up. So, what about the Christmas disco? A bit of smooching, girls sitting on boys' knees – nothing desperate. But what had been happening outside the Assembly Hall? That, indeed, was the headmaster's theme, although it was slightly confusing as to what that actually had to do with him making love to his wife in public! Well, in his words, "I wouldn't do it." Thank God for that! And good heavens, do they really get up to that sort of thing? At their age?!!

[Well now Ducky, you would, surely, be less than impressed with that punctuation…?!!]

"What was all that about?" A common enough question doing the rounds after the headmaster's fighting talk in morning assembly. It hadn't gone unnoticed, however, by a small number of those attending the disco that the odd couple or two had 'disappeared' during the evening. How had our Headmaster described them? "Adolescent exhibitionists"! They were, predictably, the usual suspects who necessarily remain anonymous – but the boarding house is in the clear. It is one thing being full of 'talk' – and the Lonsdale complex generally is – but action is quite different from discussing it, thinking about it! Those amorous couples who left early, but hadn't really left – just exactly where did they go and what did they get up to? No bicycle sheds in the vicinity, but plenty of conveniently dark hiding places in this rabbit warren of a school. They were obviously 'found'. By the time they were, had trousers fallen to the ankles and more pertinently, had knickers been pulled down? Rumour will elaborate and exaggerate. It will remain in 'overdrive' for a good while. Of course, it is a matter of personal opinion as to whether those miscreants are assessed individually by their peers as true heroes or classed as foolhardy. But are we not expected to 'look up' to heroes?

Notwithstanding the obvious excitement after the event, the disco had this year been something to look forward to. (The prospect of dancing, however, had been a constant worry beforehand...) A boyfriend was more than willing, as Barbara had requested, to wait her arrival at the entrance to the Assembly Hall and to then walk in together, hand in hand. It was a non-verbal notification to the other 6th form lads essentially saying, "this 6th form lass is with me tonight, so keep your hands off"! It was important to make not only that statement of intent but also to continue to make a favourable impression with Barbara. The word in some quarters is that she has recently had one or two other prospective suitors – local lads by all accounts – all of whom have, in her own words, been given "the bum's rush"! ("the bum's rush" – where does she get these sayings from?)

Barbara came to the dance in an attractive coloured dress, very nearly navy blue and covered in very small white spots. The dress was invitingly short, without being too short, enabling her to show off a rather lovely pair of shapely upper legs, nicely coloured by the ever-predictable *American Tan* tights. (What other shades are there!!) Chairs had been positioned all around the perimeter of the Assembly Hall, with the rest of the floor then available for dancing. Oh dear! Some dancing with Barbara there had to be. It would be a travesty to say it was successful or indeed enjoyable. Rather ominous was a comment from Barbara as the evening wore on, once she had fully appreciated just how calamitous dancing with her boyfriend turned out to be. "Perhaps we can enrol in dancing lessons together, they do hold them in High Bentham." Really? Whoopee indeed. Oh, dear me. (Woe is me...) Can it honestly be expected that dancing lessons will make the slightest halfpence of difference? Those born with two left feet will always have, well, two left feet! You cannot surely want to dance with your boyfriend, Barbara or, far worse, teach him to dance. The passage of time will surely see a change of heart. By a girlfriend, of course, but hopefully only with dancing and not a change of boyfriend.

It was towards the end of the Christmas party evening, whilst still in the Assembly Hall that the subject of the Christmas holiday had been raised, "But we won't see each other for three weeks." Barbara's voice had been heartfelt, genuine and quite desperate. The sentiment and how it had been delivered was more than reciprocated. She was staying in Low Bentham. A boyfriend wanted to do the same! Staying with parents for the holiday period would entail travelling to Europe. Absolutely no chance of visiting *'Benwick'* from there. There had to be a suitable alternative. There was. A subsequent discussion with Cess and Cass regarding Christmas has sorted things out nicely. Cess, living in the west end of Morecambe, has conveniently come to the rescue. Not quite Low Bentham, but near enough. Staying with Cess will be eminently more enjoyable than being with kith and kin but, more importantly, the venue is in close proximity to Low Bentham. Surely, a new girlfriend is clearly going to need some company from time to time from a new boyfriend. (Or so this boyfriend hopes!) To say Barbara is enthusiastic about the idea would be putting it mildly. "We can arrange to see each other, perhaps in Lancaster. Will you please write to me, Ian – pretty please?" Over the next three weeks it is, without doubt, going to prove impossible to refuse such requests. Heavens, writing to a girlfriend. Indeed, that will be a first – rather an exciting first.

"And what about *Teddy*?" Barbara had said with genuine concern. Ever faithful *Teddy*. Sitting here on the dormitory bed. Someone you can talk to, someone who will never let you down, a friend – someone who understands! "What is happening to *Teddy* during the Christmas holidays?" Barbara had continued in a mildly quizzical manner with just the slightest of grins. It was a grin that perhaps suggested that it might well be appropriate to leave *Teddy* in her tender care. This was not the end of a school year so dormitory rooms do not have to be completely vacated. Personal items, then, can be left 'in situ' for the beginning of the following term. *Teddy* was, therefore, going to be "staying put". At least that was the original plan. It didn't quite feel appropriate to be taking him to stay at a friend's house, not least because of any possible fallout if it became general knowledge across the 6th form that the Head Boarder has a teddy bear! (Lonsdale dormitory colleagues know when to keep a secret – credit where it is due. Therein, the benefit of a close-knit community.)

There is, of course, a well-known precedent for having a teddy bear as a constant (and ever faithful) companion. In the novel *Brideshead Revisited* by Evelyn Waugh, the maverick aristocrat, Lord Sebastian Flyte, had his own teddy bear. Sebastian's teddy was named Aloysius. The recently appointed Poet Laureate, John Betjeman, also has a teddy as a constant companion, a good deal older than this teddy, called Archibald. Archibald, Aloysius – stately names, posh even. The teddy that normally sits on the bed watching and listening impassively to a 6th form boarder in his dormitory room is just, well, *Teddy*. Not in any way an original name, but he remains a loyal and constant friend nonetheless and, most importantly, he is a good listener…

> [**An aside:** *Teddy had been a gift some years ago to a young teenage nephew from an aunt. Auntie Maureen (Mo), large in stature, both physically and mentally, always seemed to swish along with loose, flowing clothes. Clothes that to a young lad always appeared quite fancy, maybe almost Bohemian in fashion – flamboyant, and multi-coloured. They were worn, perhaps, to help hide as far as possible her portly frame. However, even if successful in such an objective, her stature and bearing, if only in terms of her presence, gave the game away. Tall and*

formidable, of all the Parkinson clan – that is, of a mother's three sisters and two brothers – Auntie Mo has a justifiable claim to the intellectual crown. She will thrive in a discussion, wanting – for her own enjoyment – to make any subject matter more interesting by putting forward an intentionally provocative point of view. In this way, she would yearn to be controversial, to then sit back and watch the subsequent chaos of any discussion. Her siblings, lacking the same scholarly thought and knowledge, have never seemed quite as enthusiastic for such heady discussions. Her house may indeed have been "a tip" (in a mother's words following a visit), but is it, perhaps, excusable with academics? Freud, Einstein – they are all the same!

For Auntie Mo then, sadly, she was born too late to fit seamlessly into the Bloomsbury group, which flourished in the early part of this century. She would, indeed, have been a worthy paid-up member.

The making of soft toys is, according to a mother, a sideline – almost a serious hobby – which perhaps provides a bit of spare cash, the soft toys generally being sold for profit. Teddy was an exception, being provided 'free gratis', which perhaps gives credence to the well-known line from a 1920s song, 'the best things in life are free'.]

"Would I be able to look after *Teddy* over Christmas?" Barbara had asked. "He shouldn't be left on his own for the holiday. I might even buy him a Christmas present," she continued, grinning broadly. "Please, I will take care of him, Ian, and I am sure he will behave himself! In fact, I will let him share my bed, he will keep me company and remind me of you." (Christ! Sharing a bed with you, Barbara, behaving himself will indeed be most difficult.) And so, *Teddy's* holiday has been settled. He is now spending Christmas at *'Benwick'*. (You lucky *Teddy* – sitting in bed whilst watching a young lady get undressed at night! Cover your eyes, you naughty *Teddy*.) Hopefully, he will not mind coming back to boarding school after the Christmas break…

So, the bags are packed. The breakfast bell sounds – the last day of term. Nothing serious to be learned in class today. A journey thereafter with Cess to Morecambe. A Christmas holiday in a seaside town.

FROM A DORMITORY WINDOW

A Christmas holiday sat on a girlfriend's bed – cover your eyes, you naughty Teddy!

CHAPTER XVIII

NARROW CHANNELS OF WATER, GLINTING IN THE WINTER SUN

The tide is out. It always seems to be out in Morecambe Bay. If you ever visit Morecambe, it is odds on that the tide will be out. Perhaps only Weston-Super-Mare in Somerset has a further tidal range, taking the sea many miles out into the Bristol Channel. When it is low tide in Morecambe Bay, the water is nowhere to be seen. It disappears from the view, sucked along by the pull of the moon far away into the distant horizon. And then, even when it is high tide and the bay is awash with the incoming sea, it is almost immediately on the wane before the view can be fully appreciated... or so it seems.

This Saturday morning, the tide is most definitely fully out. Looking out across the bay from the lounge window of 10a Heysham Road, better known locally as the Battery Hotel, over to the north towards Grange-over-Sands, the low tide has enabled the winter sun to expose large tracts of wet glistening mud, idyllic looking – but extremely treacherous. With scant time to fully dry out before the next tide, the shining mud hides many areas of quicksand, invisible to the naked eye. Occasional narrow channels of water, glinting in the winter sun, streak across the wide bay, threading an ever-changing route between the sandbanks as the River Kent empties into the bay the water it has collected, as it follows a course, southwards, through the nearby Lakeland fells.

This is the view then, a constantly changing one, from the Battery Hotel on the morning of this winter Saturday in December. Saturday 16th December 1972 to be precise. Thoughts drift back and forward from this scenic splendour of Morecambe Bay to that village on the western edge of the West Riding of Yorkshire. The autumn term ended only yesterday. This, then, the first day of the Christmas break and the thought process is already in overdrive. What will be happening at *'Benwick'* this Saturday morning? Perhaps Barbara will be still in bed asleep ("I am not very good at waking up in the morning, Ian") and if so, *Teddy*, bless him, will no doubt be cuddled up and keeping a close eye on her. Perhaps she will be washing her hair sometime today ("I always want to have my hair looking nice") and then maybe sometime later she will be taking a walk up to High Bentham to do some shopping for her mother. Whatever is happening in Low Bentham – albeit that it is the ordinariness of everyday life – it is still infinitely more interesting, intriguing even, than events on this cold, stark Lancashire coast. Barbara has a part-time job arranged at Thornbers wool shop in High Bentham during this week prior to Christmas, so she will be there at the shop from this coming Monday helping out. No staying in bed late and cuddling up to *Teddy* in the mornings next week then. It is almost impossible to concentrate on the here and now, with *'Benwick'* and Low Bentham continually swimming around the brain.

Even on an early morning walk along the promenade seafront, there was a reminder readily provided of that West Riding village. After walking past the iconic and grand *'Art-Deco'* Midland Hotel and along the seafront, a view to the east revealed, quite surprisingly, the familiar shape of Ingleborough, standing proud on the distant horizon. The mountain is perhaps all of 20 miles inland from Morecambe Bay – maybe more – but on the walk this morning, it had looked so incredibly close. Very close indeed and providing a reminder, if indeed one was needed, of the same view – albeit one that is considerably closer – that can be enjoyed from the back garden of *'Benwick'*. What was it that Simon & Garfunkel sang – *'that is where I want to be'*, or something similar?

*[**An aside:** (1) The 1930s-built Midland Hotel – regretfully, now looking rather worse for wear, standing in faded grandeur – and where, as a teenager in the mid-1930s era, a father had wheeled holidaymakers' luggage across from the adjacent Midland railway station in a pram, successfully adapted into a luggage carrier, for the price of a 1d. In his words, "an early example of entrepreneurial skill" – always doffing his cap on receipt of payment from the rather 'well-to-do' guests. Presumably, it would not have been good form to have made the passengers aware of a dedicated underpass linking the railway station to the hotel. Valuable income would have been lost!*

(2) An early morning walk on the promenade – there is a gene inside that automatically tells the body to wake up at circa. 6am, sometimes earlier, irrespective of the time of retiring the previous evening – in this case, definitely "like father, like son". At times, the gene is most welcome as it enables revising to be done or essays to be finished before breakfast, in the dormitory. At other times, though, somewhat frustrating – once awake, there is no going back to sleep!]

This, then, the first weekend of the winter school break. Less than a week away from the shortest day and the light that streaks across the glistening mud will, in a few hours, be setting across on the far side of the bay behind the Lakeland fells and the darkness will usher in the chill of winter. This morning, the large private lounge in the Battery Hotel is looking rather tired and worn, with the wallpaper stained and the paint having peeled off in places, leaving bare wood looking strangely damp. It is clearly in need of being totally redecorated. There is a strange odour redolent in the room, suggesting that the windows have not been open for a good while and the lounge has consequently been deprived of fresh air. Nothing at all like the musty smell from inside Low Bentham church. The smell in this lounge is mouldy and dank and most unpleasant. In complete contrast, the lack of fresh air in Low Bentham church makes for a pleasing antique sort of smell. What a strange paradox. The ambience in the lounge is not helped by the smell of stale draught beer from the previous night, which has seeped through from the public bar downstairs. No amount of cleaning at the end of the night in the public bar area seems to have succeeded in combating the strange smell this morning. This pungent aroma has combined with the rather faint whiff detected of a cooked breakfast in the process of preparation in the nearby kitchen, giving the lounge the look and feel of a typical cheap 'greasy spoon' café, which one can often find alongside the seafront in run-down seaside resorts. Here though, instead of the usual compliment of two or three customers sitting glumly with huge mugs of steaming tea in their hands, there are two students from the Upper 6th form, prostrate on hard wooden chairs, looking less than enthusiastic with regard to the books spread out across the table in front of them.

A school textbook on *King Lear* lies open on the large wooden table alongside some scribbled notes from recent English lessons. Cess sits across on the opposite side of the table with his copy of *King Lear* on the table, but his copy of this Shakespeare 'masterpiece' (eh?) has yet to be opened. There is a brief period of silence whilst he adjusts to the 'early' morning. (Although after 9am is hardly early – except when you are Cess and have been out drinking the night before.) He seeks to engage with the day with the assistance of regular gulps of strong Maxwell House coffee.

Eventually, after some careful thought and after staring blankly at the cover of his 'A' Level English Literature folder, he exclaims in a rather dejected manner, "The character of King Lear and the play's development. Why on earth do we have to do *another* essay on *King Lear*? We have done our mock exam. We need a break from bloody *King Lear!*", and so saying, he gets up and walks over to a portable record player and proceeds to put on a Beatles LP, 'Let It Be'! This, of course, makes it eminently more difficult to concentrate on the Shakespeare 'classic'. No matter – as Cess returns to the table and takes a final swig of his coffee from a heavily stained mug, his eyes settle on a green folder headed up *'English Lit 'A'*, and scrawled underneath in different handwriting someone has written, *'My Name is Barbara!'* "No need to ask who has written that," he suggested rather sarcastically, before sitting back down and lounging idly on his chair, paying scant attention to his own English Literature folder and gazing instead at the open books on the opposite side of the table, whilst quietly singing the lyrics to 'The Long and Winding Road'. Frustratingly, he is neither in tune nor in unison with the music or the song emanating from the record player!

Regarding *King Lear*, he is, of course, quite right and it is easy to empathise. The last few weeks leading up to the mock examination had involved continuous intensive study of this Shakespeare play. Is there anything else or anything new to be learnt about *King Lear* one might ask? And now, with the Christmas school break, who wants to write another essay about a king and his three complex daughters? This is a holiday, for God's sake, and most importantly, a promise had been made before the school holiday to write a letter to Low Bentham. Now was perhaps the time to carry out the promise. With a convenient excuse that the music makes study impossible, the school textbook is carefully sidelined, and a writing pad and envelope taken out of a battered school briefcase. It is a briefcase that has previously seen many years use with a father who then, rather frugally, handed it down for use with 'A' Level studies to his youngest son. A crafty ploy which saved the expense of buying a brand new one. A well-travelled and battered briefcase it may well be (and it has, like the rest of the McCart family, travelled "half-way around the world" – something a mother is *always* keen to stress) but, strangely, that has added to the sort of authority it gives to its owner. Surely, it looks more authentic in a battered state. Would a brand-new briefcase appear rather too posh? It would, perhaps, look even more impressive without the large red 'smiley face' sticker that had recently been surreptitiously stuck on the side by a cheeky new girlfriend!

The easiest part of writing a letter is, perhaps, addressing the envelope. Miss Barbara Noble, 'Benwick', Low Bentham, Nr. Lancaster. How strange that a property in the West Riding of Yorkshire should have an address linked to Lancaster. No doubt the Royal Mail will readily provide an explanation. Across the table, Cess is still idling away, doing nothing in particular – just listening to the music whilst gazing out at the expanse of mudflats across the bay. Suddenly, having noticed the envelope being addressed, he is galvanised into action. "Why on earth are you wasting your time writing to her when you will be seeing her this coming Monday?" (Yes. A meeting the day after tomorrow in Lancaster...) The promise that had been made only a few days before to write a letter to Barbara made not the slightest impression on Cess. "If it were me, I would have her under my thumb," he continued before disappearing out of the door, quite obviously exasperated that his protestations were clearly not going to have the desired effect. And then, having disappeared, he sticks his head back around the door and adds as a quite unrelated afterthought, "and who decided on the subject for the school 'Public Speaking' competition next term?" Before waiting for a possible answer, he continued, "Sounds like typical Ducky. Who on earth wants to talk about the 'sun' for fifteen minutes?" Who indeed? Nevertheless, that was the chosen subject matter and if Cess wanted something useful to do, perhaps he could start his preparation for that. Some chance! It is certainly going to be a long and winding road for Cess in 1973, as this year draws to a close and the New Year awaits.

*[**An aside**: a first letter to a girlfriend. A letter to Miss Noble. How to start? Letter writing poses no problems. Writing a first letter to a new girlfriend might. The general tone will, surely, have to be light. "Dear Barbara" is surely too formal. Barbara sounds fine in face-to-face discussion but would, perhaps, look a tad serious at the commencement of a letter. 'Babs' is a non-starter. Only recently Barbara had almost pleaded, "please don't ever call me Babs, Ian, because I honestly don't like being called Babs." The request had been delivered without the suggestion of an obvious alternative. What about 'Baba'? Err... no. What would she think of Barbi? Isn't Barbi a doll? At least for now, Barbi will have to do. The fact is a letter had been requested just prior to the Christmas break and a promise had been given that one would be sent. The earlier the better – more chance of a speedy reply. Receiving a letter from a girlfriend – far more exciting than writing one. This 'smiley' writing paper, kindly supplied as a present from a sister, will be used to add to the light-hearted manner and tone, for it is unlikely that anything substantial can be included in a first letter to a new girlfriend. How is Teddy? Are you looking after him? How is your mother? Have you been to see Diana across the fields at Ellergill Farm? (Her best friend – out of school – Diana: according to Barbara, "the original tearaway.") Have you been shopping in Bentham? Questions, questions. Will they provoke a reply by letter? All quite light-hearted stuff then, with perhaps a flourish at the end of the letter. How about: looking forward to seeing you on Monday, your mad boyfriend, Ian – or suchlike? Are kisses appropriate at the end of the letter? Perhaps not for the time being! A bit forward – perhaps?]*

The thought process halts temporarily as Cess strides back into the lounge and, finding that his Beatles LP has run its course, he proceeds to inject even more background noise with his Groundhogs LP and their four-part raucous rendition of 'Split'. Twenty minutes or so of loud heavy metal music is, perhaps, not the ideal backdrop for schoolwork or, indeed, letter writing – the latter of which will without doubt best be completed in the privacy of a bedroom, together with the writing of three Christmas cards. No, not to family! To Judith, Christine and Barbara. (And buying Christmas cards to send to three young ladies really has been a first!)

Cess is keen to talk about his plans for an evening drinking session at a procession of pubs along the seafront. His idea for a good Saturday night out is not reciprocated and, indeed, it clashes head on with the compelling urge to get this letter to Barbara completed. There is a nagging feeling that it is not going to be an enjoyable Christmas break on this North Lancashire coast. It may well be considered macho to be trawling the various seafront establishments, but just perhaps the thought of it in this case is more enjoyable than the action. Particularly so when a letter needs to be written to a girlfriend. Oh, God! Two weeks and the rest to go until the new term and despite the glaring pitfalls of staying in Morecambe, it is still, surely, preferable to an enforced stay with parents in Germany. (Isn't it?)

LENT TERM

CHAPTER XIX

RING ON, RING ON, YOU MORNING BELL

The first week of January. Nineteen seventy-three – a new year. What will it bring? It has a nice rounded, almost calming sound. Slightly less than six months before the end of school year exams. This stark fact will, no doubt, be made plain by each of the respective 'A' Level teachers when the new term commences tomorrow morning. The relatively short time frame remaining through to the exam season will almost certainly be stressed and will then for good measure be repeated many times in the coming weeks. Six months – isn't that ages away? Why the fuss, for God's sake?

From the window of this dormitory, the sky to the east is a golden tangerine as the sun finally pushes its way reluctantly up and over the horizon. Sunrise at this time of year seems to take an age. Dawn is definitely in no hurry. Whilst pondering on the passage of time and gazing towards the eastern glow, eventually the sun manages to claw its way fully above the horizon and its weak rays mix with streaks of cloud. This causes the clouds higher in the sky to take on a strange cotton wool appearance as the sunlight catches hold of them. The vista might almost be mistaken for a range of snow-capped mountains. Capture this moment. An artist would. How satisfying to be an artist. (But only, of course, with traditional pastoral scenes – none of this new-fangled rubbish.) A timely reminder of those mountains standing to the north of Tehran, whilst growing up in the safety of that embassy home, free from worry and fret. It now seems almost a lifetime away. Having spent a good proportion of boyhood living abroad, there is no longer any urge to leave these shores. Any yearning that there might have been has been successfully extinguished. The last couple of months has seen to that.

Christmas over and done with. For the here and now, what a relief to be back in the privacy of this dormitory after a somewhat fraught holiday break. Christmas was, well, hardly a success. Santa Claus may have been coming to some towns (according to the Jackson Five), but he certainly did not visit Morecambe, or indeed, the sea front! Even if he had, it would have made no difference. Spending the evenings in the pub at the end of the pier or along the seafront was hardly productive or enjoyable. But then, what else was there to do? Sat in the company of Cess and Cass – a group of three all looking miserable and drinking Pernod – perhaps was not the best way to have spent the fag end of the shortest days of the year. Pernod – aniseed, what exactly is the attraction? Aniseed balls – different altogether! The only interesting part of an evening spent drinking was watching the change in colour when liquid was added to a colourless Pernod – it turned the concoction pink. Very strange. A rather intriguing practical chemistry lesson, albeit that it was with an alcoholic drink.

A diversion – of sorts – from that Christmas seaside 'idyll'! An 'overnight' party in a house 'abandoned' by God knows who – well, Diane's parents! (She of Zambian Weed fame…) A journey to the southern reaches of the Lake District – arriving in the dark, leaving in the dark. Is there an attraction in partying all night? There was certainly no appeal in sleeping on the floor or being obliged to wait (as patiently as possible…) early next morning for the 'chauffeur' to decide when exactly he was ready to exit Westmorland and head southwards.

A Christmas, then, spent in a seedy, downtrodden seaside town. It was not particularly wanted and was devoid of enjoyment. It was, you might say, a means to an end. The tedium, the boredom, tempered only by no less than four visits to Lancaster to meet up with Barbara and even a day visit to Low Bentham following the Christmas Day and Boxing Day period. But even that – five meetings over a three-week period – was hardly sufficient. It seems as if meeting and chatting with Barbara needs to be daily and perhaps, one rather hopes, that feeling is reciprocated – is it, though? (A question to this diary…)

The meetings prior to Christmas had, by necessity, been on an evening at the Cinema in Lancaster, by virtue of Barbara having that holiday job leading up to Christmas at the wool shop in High Bentham. It was a useful way of earning some welcome cash, enabling her to happily pay for the Cinema entertainment on an evening. (A rather convenient reversal of roles.) But no sitting in the seats at the back of the Cinema ignoring the film – as everyone seems to think you should! She is not that sort of girl, nor is her boyfriend the sort of person who would suggest it! Nevertheless, delightful it was to be just sat holding hands and to be in her presence. And then, whilst holding her hand, the torment and the agony whilst the same question was asked – repeatedly – inside the brain. Will she allow a boyfriend to kiss her? Will she want him to kiss her? It had eventually proved irresistible. It had to be done before a fragile confidence completely drained away. Permission not requested. It could be said that the kiss was, well, 'stolen'. A risk, yes, but one that sooner or later had to be taken. A natural extension, perhaps, of holding hands which is now done almost automatically and somehow by telepathy on meeting away from the school premises. The respective pair of hands clasp together almost in unison, as indeed they did on meeting at the bus station, and they stayed together on the walk to the Cinema and once sat in the stalls. On being kissed, Barbara had provided instant reassurance with a quiet but thoughtful, "thank you", accompanied by a beaming smile, together with the now familiar scrunch of her nose and shoulders. She had then returned the compliment with the briefest of kisses. Her gesture had immediately restored some self-assurance, confidence even, which had then been boosted further by a squeeze of the hand from Barbara. There is a lot of meaning encompassed within a simple squeeze of the hand. What joy…

That particular evening produced an intriguing film in *Butch Cassidy and the Sundance Kid*. Were the two outlaws' heroes or villains? The blunt ending caused a stir and, whilst a Lancaster bus station late at night was bleak and the air cold (but it was dry, so there was no real need to have been singing, "Raindrops keep falling on my head" – a song from the film – much to Barbara's amusement), there was a warmth in seeing Barbara onto the bus bound for Bentham, after those two outlaws in the film had met their untimely end. A brief kiss before she boarded the plush Pennine bus was almost, well, anticipated by a girlfriend – and her parting comment as two hands parted was the cause of some mirth – "I do hope you can get a bus back to Morecambe Ian; you don't seem the type to 'kip' down all night on Lancaster bus station!"

Barbara had been rather disappointed that neither of the two Lancaster 'Picture Houses' had been showing *The Sound of Music* over the Christmas period, which she would have gladly gone to watch. That is even though, as she rather proudly admitted, she has already seen the film upwards of a dozen times since its release in 1965. This is something that her dad, the taxi driver, will apparently (and somewhat wearily, she suggests) confirm. She enjoys and expects happy endings. The 6th formers in this Lonsdale dormitory complex, quite naturally, 'poo-poo' a soppy ending. *The Sound of Music* would undoubtedly be considered far too slushy for a senior lad from the boarding house. Admitting one had been to see the film would most certainly be met with a torrent of derision, perhaps even scorn. Nevertheless, it would have been worth the possible 'flack' from boarding house colleagues to have been able to watch it with a new girlfriend. From the memory of watching it (only the once!) in the company of a twin sister and a maternal grandmother during a half-term early in 1967, Julie Andrews, the children's nanny, was rather attractive. But now, the Head Boarder is six years older, and he has grown up. (Message for Ducky – yes, he has!) Now, Julie Andrews is quite definitely not anywhere near as inviting as the young lady from Low Bentham.

*[**An aside**: Films. This would certainly not be the time to admit to a new girlfriend that at previous half-term breaks during the last school year, there had been visits to the Lancaster Odeon to watch Soldier Blue, somewhat more violent than a musical set in Austria and in addition, The Adventurers based on a Harold Robbins novel. Most certainly too rude to watch with a new girlfriend. Or is that a mistaken assumption? Would Barbara be happy to watch nakedness and sex on the big screen? The sexual antics of Dax, the hero, in successfully persuading a succession of women to strip off for him, would not, surely, be appreciated by an innocent country lass not accustomed to such crudity. Admitting one had been to see such a film is hardly appropriate – she might form the wrong impression about her boyfriend! There is, indeed, a stark contrast between singing on an Austrian hillside and the sex and violence as depicted in each of those two respective films. Then again, there is no wish to take a new girlfriend to a cinema to watch violence (needless or otherwise) and certainly not to watch sex, which might well prove to be slightly uncomfortable, not just for Barbara but, in actual fact, also for her new boyfriend – whilst in her company, at least! Ah! – how this mind works.]*

Christmas Day itself, then, had been spent mostly in a bedroom reading and revising at the Battery Hotel, Morecambe. Christmas Day spent on revision. And why not? Even as a youngster, it had always seemed to be the case that whilst the lead up to Christmas was full of such anticipation and excitement, invariably – for whatever reason, or perhaps for no specific reason – the day itself never quite lived up to expectations. Indeed, it was quite often disappointing – predictably so. Certainly, it was never properly enjoyed. Why? A state of mind perhaps. In any case, Christmas Day and Boxing Day would always be quickly over and done with and life would then move on, returning – one might suggest with some considerable relief – to normal. Is it compulsory to enjoy Christmas? All the razzmatazz, the decorations, a Christmas tree taking over a large portion of a living room and leaving the inevitable mess, an array of 'not particularly wanted' presents and the food – far too much of it! And to cap it all, the claustrophobia of being indoors, with darkness arriving by mid-afternoon. And those Christmases abroad – more daylight certainly, but still rather a 'let-down'. Ah, how many more Christmas scrooges are there out there?

There are those, of course, who seem to thoroughly enjoy such festivities (well, the 'non-religious' aspect of it at any rate). They (and 'they' in this context relates mainly to the girls…) would, surely, have been in their element had they joined the recent boarders' outing by train to the Keighley and Worth Valley Light Railway – just 'up the line' from Bentham and an end of term Christmas 'treat'. Just why would they have enjoyed it? There, ensconced on the steam train between Keighley and Oxenhope, was Santa himself, nestling in his 'Magic Grotto', sporting his regulation white beard, red coat, and oversized boots! (His reindeer were unaccountably absent, left behind, one assumes, somewhere in the snow – in any case, how would Santa have got them on-board?) A somewhat scurrilous suggestion had subsequently been made that some of those from the 6th form in the party had to be "restrained" from presenting themselves to Santa himself – they would most probably have been wanting the inevitable present that would have been provided by Santa. The white bearded man would, surely, have determined that they looked rather too old for such excitement. Certainly, the Head Boarder had not contemplated a 'one-to-one' with Santa, being more interested in the steam engine pulling the party of 'revellers' along the recently opened, rather quaint, preserved branch line. (An LMS Tank engine if you must know…)

So, Christmas 1972 over and done with. A miserable and lonely experience indeed without the company of Barbara. Has there ever been a more wretched Christmas? In the company of a girlfriend, it may well have been oh, so different. Revising on Christmas Day. Yes. Should one admit as much? How many others from Mrs Fife's Upper 6th form charges will have been sat in their bedroom, happily revising on Christmas Day? None, surely…

Yes, some revising, but also a lot of idle scribbling on bits of paper:

If I had the talent to paint and to draw,
Having been granted the appropriate skill,
I would portray the beauty of each tender limb,
Catching in colour her beautiful skin.

In your gaze there is a story to be told,
A story that is ages old,
It lives again in two hazel eyes,
And within my heart is sold.

Let me hold your tender skin,
Please rest always in my arms:
And then, please let me stroke your hair.
Will love, ages old, now begin…

My goodness! Miss Barbara Noble, how is it that you are so beautiful and so enticing?

The absence of a telephone at *'Benwick'* had meant that even talking to Barbara over the Christmas period was at times problematical, depending on whether the public telephone box down the street in Low Bentham was, firstly, operational, and, secondly, not already in use when Barbara had walked down at the appointed time to ring the Battery Hotel. And if the telephone kiosk was in use, why did the occupant(s) carry on chatting when they must have noticed a young lady waiting anxiously outside, wanting to ring her boyfriend? It regularly meant that the telephone calls that were made were a good deal later than the agreed time, with a boyfriend waiting anxiously by the hotel telephone and with Barbara eventually exclaiming in frustration, "I am so sorry, Ian, I have had to wait ages in the cold and the dark to use the telephone." (But surely…wasn't it worth it?) And then there was the slight discomfort Barbara felt whilst standing alone in a dimly lit village in the dank air of the winter evenings, whilst waiting to use the telephone. "I am a respectable young lady, I don't want people to get the wrong impression", she would say half-jokingly, albeit with a hint of seriousness. In a small village, it is important that people don't get the wrong idea and as Barbara herself confirmed, "I have never wanted to hang around on the streets at night" – something to thank her parents for and unlike one or two other local girls who seem to enjoy loitering (with or without intent). Yes, a little awkward waiting around at night in the dark, Barbara – but, you will have realized, of course, that it was worth it… And certainly, no one could form the wrong impression about you Barbara. Surely!

With a combination of letter writing, telephone calls, evening meetings in Lancaster and a trip to Low Bentham, perhaps by the end of the holiday Cess was most likely wondering exactly why a stay at Morecambe had been arranged. Very little time had been spent in his company during daytime and there had been little enough enthusiasm shown for those night-time drinking sessions in the pub. If he did wonder, he was good enough not to mention it. But now, back in this dormitory. What a relief to be back 'home' and not only that, but to have been able to return a day early, with Mr Russell and family being back at school for the start of this weekend. So, a return yesterday rather than today. Be thankful for small mercies... who said that? Whoever it was, it is so true in the context of returning to the boarding house.

How pleasing, indeed, it is to be just looking around at the familiar surrounds of the boarding house. How many others at this school, in particular those in the boarding house, will be glad to be returning? Most, no doubt, are glad to leave at the start of a holiday and are, perhaps, pretty miserable at having to return. With the Head Boarder, for the time being at least, the opposite is the case. What a comfort to return to the intimate privacy of this study room. A return to 'home ground' indeed. How enjoyable to see the familiar array of beer mats adorning the top of the pelmet and, above them on the wall, a poster of Everton football club 1970/71 (league winners!), a reminder of the once fanatical interest in league football which, perhaps, has been waning somewhat over the past two years, even if the enthusiasm is still present for playing with the school First XI team. Playing, rather than watching, has proved far more enjoyable since the commencement of 'A' Level studies.

Welcoming also the other poster hanging on the wall – one of three spaniels looking down towards the bed, where a tidy pile of dry cleaning has been returned by the boarding housekeeper, Mrs Wills. What a true doyen of the cleaning staff she is. A surrogate mother almost, and an absolute treasure to 6th form boarders who are not in any way adept at sewing and dealing with all the other menial tasks associated with laundry. Always happy, always enthusiastic, a lesson in living.

Even this pair of trousers, the white shirt and the blazer hanging up ready for the start of term tomorrow are strangely welcoming. The large red "smiley" face on the dormitory door, always inviting of course, and these individual stacks of study books, a timely reminder that June 1973 is not that far away. But still far enough away to prevent the onset of panic and doubt.

But what of the future? Durham University now awaits, providing suitable pass grades are attained. The school remains confident regarding obtaining pass grades to qualify for admittance – the Head Boarder less so. The enthusiasm and interest originally generated for that educational path has dimmed somewhat over the past six weeks. It is just not possible to shake off the realisation that there is a direct correlation between a cooling in the prospect of a university course and the eagerness to learn more about *'Benwick'* and the young lady living there with her parents. The attachment and the admiration of the nearby Pennine fells has only been strengthened by the friendship developed with a "country lass" and this shows no sign of waning. With arrangements already in place to visit the University for the day (with an overnight stop) during the first week in February, it will, perhaps, be prudent to go and have a look. Nevertheless, some serious thinking will need to be done over the coming months about the progression towards a prospective degree course if, indeed, the blossoming relationship developed with Barbara survives through this spring term and the summer term that follows. At this moment in time, albeit with a relationship that has lasted a mere six weeks, there would seem to be every prospect of the friendship continuing. Dovetailing it with some serious study will have to involve a disciplined use of both school and non-school time. Common sense should prevail – but what is the sensible solution?

With a return to the boarding house, *Teddy* will have to return home. Will he be allowed to return to the dormitory? Will Barbara want to release him? (In her words, "*Teddy* has settled in nicely and enjoys sleeping with me…") Space also needs to be allocated on this inside window-ledge for what was indeed a rather special Christmas present, handed over by a new girlfriend at a meeting in Lancaster just prior to Christmas. A photograph in a frame, showing Barbara as a bridesmaid at her Auntie's wedding in High Bentham in 1971 – she would be nearly sixteen years of age. She stands holding a small bouquet of flowers, with a fresh and confident smile. She looks intelligent, she looks sensible… and she is pretty. Is this really the same girl who will still occasionally turn bright red by the school coffee vending machine? The photograph has been annotated: *'To Ian, all my love Barbara xxx'* – three kisses!! It will now sit proudly on the window-ledge.

Just as welcome as this Christmas gift, however, are the two small white envelopes resting on the table, both addressed to Mr. Ian McCart c/o 10a Heysham Road, Morecambe, Lancs. For, true to her word, Barbara had replied immediately to the letters that had been written to her from Morecambe and each letter had a little message on the back of the envelope: viz, *'Not to be opened until you feel depressed – believe me you'll then feel worse'* and *'Is it possible to reverse the charges on a postage stamp coz if it is, I will do it next time'*. In addition, the first letter written prior to Christmas commenced… *'Dear Ian (and believe me, it is "dear" at 3p a letter!)'* and the humour continued unabated throughout the letter ending with… *'yours till the cows come home… Bye-eeeeeeeeeeeeeee from your mad partner in crime. Barbi'*. And all written on

'Alias Smith & Jones' notepaper. Typical of the humour that has been displayed since that first meeting in late November. However, the ending confirmed that Barbi is an acceptable nickname which can now become common usage, both face to face and by letter. No kisses, however, at the end of the two letters from *'Benwick'*. Perhaps it was just as well that no kisses were added at the end of the letters sent from the Battery Hotel. Or just perhaps, had there been kisses on the *'Benwick'* bound letters, then kisses may have been included on the return Morecambe bound letters – chicken and egg…

The second letter had been written on New Year's Day, perhaps indicative of having nothing to do at home, or alternatively, implying that she was missing the company of a boyfriend. Hopefully, the latter! Letters written to a boyfriend, yes, but also during the Christmas holiday, Barbara had written to Gina, her 'pen friend' in Scotland. Will she, perhaps, have mentioned that she has a new boyfriend who is a boarder and in the Upper 6th form at school? Did she perhaps mention the sideburns? [*"Oh Ian…your sideburns, swoon!!!"* A brother may not have been too impressed by them at his wedding last November, but a girlfriend is captivated by them!]

*[**An aside**: and should this diary be privy to a rather unpardonable sin over the Christmas holiday? The venue: a queue in Morecambe Post Office. (Stamps required for those three Christmas cards and for a letter to a girlfriend!) There, towards the front of the queue, a paternal grandmother and 'step' grandfather. (Is there such a term?) Oh dear! Time, it was, to make oneself scarce until they had transacted their business and taken leave of the post office. Disgraceful? Well possibly, but the fact is, there has always been a slightly awkward – frigid almost – relationship with Nanny McCart. Rapport, there is none. Why not? There had been visits to her home in the west end of Morecambe with parents when younger, but as even a child, one never felt entirely welcome. The warmth of a family reunion seemed to be missing – this despite the extra-large humbug sweets always kindly offered by a 'step' grandfather and despite the constant attention of an enthusiastic Cocker Spaniel. Looking across that living room at the assembled group would be a parrot, ensconced in its cage, obviously interested, but respectfully silent! Even the promise of half-a-crown or whatever to the grandchildren could not make up for the awkwardness of a visit. [Half-a-crown – what a super coin for a kid. Now it has gone.] Did it seem that children were to act as adults? No playing, no messing around – just sit still and behave. What is the phrase? To be seen and not heard – most appropriate for those visits.*

The most amusing part of visiting a paternal grandmother was – and all the family agreed, even a father – that she bore an uncanny resemblance to Thora Hird, both in looks and mannerisms – Thora Hird herself, of course, being a native of Morecambe and from the same Victorian era. They could quite easily have 'doubled' for one another, with a regular question between siblings following a visit being, "Was that really Nanny McCart or was it Thora Hird?" No sitting silently, though, when visiting a maternal grandmother – talk, play, mess about. With Nanny Parkinson, every visiting day was turned into fun. At Lake Avenue, not so.

So, it had been apposite to stay out of sight. A meeting would have meant vague, frivolous chatter and, quite possibly, horror of horrors, an invite around to their property – not that far distant from the Battery Hotel. Surely, it would have been impossible to decline such an invite – so best to ensure that an opportunity to offer the invitation did not present itself. No such issues with relations on the maternal side. How odd. Appropriate, perhaps, not to mention having seen Nanny McCart to a father.]

Outside on this first weekend of the New Year, the river is heavy with water collected from the fells after a period of wet and windy weather and, like teenagers wanting to grow up, the river is in a hurry. The racing, foaming water is sufficient to form small rapids, with small branches and other bits of winter debris collected from the woods and fields alongside the riverbank being pulled along in its wake. Filtering in from outside the window, slightly ajar to allow the fresh Yorkshire air access, the welcome sound of the church bell gives notice that it is a quarter to the hour. The regular chiming has, rather strangely, been missed during the Christmas break. These church bells add continuity, not only to the order of the day, but also to boarding house life. In some small way, they help confirm that all is well with the world... at least, here in Low Bentham. It matters not what is happening elsewhere.

What a difference with the passage of six years. Back in 1966, whilst homesick for the comforts and privilege of a large embassy home, it was anything but reassuring to hear the regular quarter-hour chime, whilst laid in bed in the 'Cottage' dormitory. It was a case of hoping against hope that 7.15am – getting up time – would not come. It had not been easy to adapt to the communal washing and bathing facilities and it was always with an element of dread that the chime of six o'clock was heard. And then lying awake, the regular chime, thereafter, bringing 'getting up time' ever closer. Then eventually, and as regular as clockwork, a rotund and bossy Titty, waking up the others in the dormitory. They always seemed to be sleeping more soundly, and so the communal bathroom was quickly sought out before it became a hive of activity. Privacy – all important.

Now, six years on and having attained an element of maturity (whatever Ducky might think), the regular chime from the church speaks of continuity and safety. To this Head Boarder, it has almost become an institution. It will not be easy to leave it behind when the school year ends. Nor, indeed, will it be easy to leave Bentham, with its obvious attractions, both pastoral and female.

After the chiming of the church bell, within this Lonsdale dormitory complex, the familiar noise of returning students interrupts the solitude and the quiet. A welcome intrusion, nonetheless, with some familiar voices starting to bring back the regular rhythm of boarding house life. With a knock on the door and a shouted request, "Are you in?" the freckled and spectacled face of John Holmes appears, having not bothered to wait for a reply to his question. "I thought you would be. Right, have a look at this, Mucca, what do you think?" and looking rather pleased with himself, he hands over a photograph from a newspaper showing the Leeds rugby league player John Holmes scoring a try. "Same name as me," he continued, grinning broadly, "This is going to be pinned up on my wall. Fame at last!" (Ah, well!)

Once the newspaper cutting had been handed back and the pleasantries of Christmas finished with, Holmes suddenly remembered the other reason, perhaps really the main reason, for him knocking on the door. "Oh yes, I have been speaking with Ian Crabtree and he tells me that he saw you and Barbara Noble six times in Lancaster during the Christmas holiday – six times no less!" Then with his trademark smirk, he added, "And every time he saw you both, you were holding hands. Is it serious then?" Well, it is hardly front-page news, with it being general knowledge that a relationship had been formed, but there can be no holding hands, of course, in or around the school premises. "You know what it will be?" he continued with supreme confidence whilst at the same time pushing his ginger hair, most correctly parted, off his freckled forehead – a parting that gives him a perpetual boyish look, "I bet she will actually fancy the First XI goalkeeper and not Mucca. There is a subtle difference you know. Think of the kudos to be gained by being associated with, and going out with, one of the First XI football team. Just beware, it might soon fade. You heard it suggested by me first. Just think about that." (As it happens, it has been "thought about"!) Well now, what are friends for?

"And another thing, Mucca," (no, he had not finished!), "I bet you haven't told her that you are interested in trains, have you? God, that will certainly put the kibosh on it." Good point. Admittedly, the subject of trains has not yet come up in any discussion, but its absence has not been by design. Or has it? Can it be that there is a slight feeling of embarrassment in admitting to an on-going interest in railways? There certainly should not be any awkwardness in admitting the fact. Surely, there is no problem with having an interest in railways – or is there?

Then, just as Holmes is about to disappear, Rosco strolls unannounced through the open door – his curly golden locks the envy, one suspects, of a good number of the 6th form girls, and looking as though they haven't felt the pull of a comb for several days. He is brandishing a new book purchase. Not, however, a book linked to one of the wimp 'A' Levels, but instead, something far more illuminating, *The Bernard Manning Book of Jokes*. "This should give us all a few laughs, don't you reckon?", by which he no doubt really means that the book will provide many crude jokes, which some might laugh at whilst others would be in no way amused – such are the vagaries of humour. Crude jokes they may well be, but they will, surely, raise a smile even with the most 'strait-laced'. Didn't someone once suggest that "there is an element of baseness in all of us"? "I will let you read it after me", Rosco continued, sounding confident that others would want to read it and that he was doing the two of us – and the others – a favour. His favour is going to be reciprocated. Still to be unpacked from the suitcase is a new book purchase from Lancaster, *Adolf Hitler, My Part in His Downfall*, by that doyen of the *Goon Show*, Spike Milligan. Manning and Milligan, both comedians with a somewhat crude, albeit humorous, style. Is it possible to like one and not the other? Discuss. Perhaps that might fit nicely into an 'A' Level English exam question. (Not quite at the standard of the 'Classical' authors being studied, however. Mrs Fife would not, perhaps, be overly amused by the bawdy, base humour. But – just recently married – surely, she must be getting involved with some bawdy behaviour? If not, why not!) Of course, neither comedian is on the syllabus, and it is easy to understand why.

More heads appear from around the door: Clarky, Michael Oliver (not brilliant at football – but cricket – fast bowler extraordinaire. A bit overweight for football but undoubtedly the Colin Cowdrey of cricket – but as a bowler), but as yet, all is quiet in the adjoining room. Pugh has yet to return and when he does, it will be quietly and unobtrusively – silently! Geoff Whitaker and Mark Daws, deep in discussion at the far end of the Lonsdale landing, look over and put up their hands as a welcome. 'Bessie' Braddock appears at the top of the stairs leading up from the showers, with just a towel around his waist to the accompaniment of a big cheer! A wide grin develops on his face simultaneously with the vocal welcome. "Thank you, thank you everyone. I can take my towel off if you want," and he goads the assembled throng by grasping the top of his tightly wrapped towel. A capable and stylish swimmer he may be, but he is no Charles Atlas.

How refreshing to be back in this crazy world of boarding house banter. It is the continual jesting and joking, etc. and the almost incestuous living with others (figuratively speaking!) – "In the same boat" – (that is, growing up away from home) that surely makes the boarding house existence preferable to home life. Well, certainly so when at the top rung of the ladder. And then, paradoxically, there is also a need for quiet and privacy – time often needed just to think.

Over the cacophony of noise from a dozen or more returning 6th formers, from along the corridor approaching the Lonsdale complex, is the sound of an easily recognisable determined march. No prizes for guessing it is Mr Russell. "Welcome back, all of you! Are you all ready to get back into your studies?" asks a grinning Housemaster before adding, "Lots of hard work ahead for you all I am pleased to say." The answers and reactions in response are primarily in visible form, with a variety of evil smiles and grimaces, rather than responses of the verbal type. "Dinner is at 5.30, don't be late. There will not be a bell today to remind you so can I ask you, Ian, to make sure everyone from Lonsdale dormitory and those from the junior dormitories who haven't yet arrived back are informed. Thank you." With that, Mr Russell does an about turn and marches away, leaving the individual dormitory suites alive with laughter, shouting and the general chatter of returning students. What it is to be back!

A visit to all the dormitories will be made shortly before dinner to let all the returning boarders know – including Parker dormitory, where up on the facing wall, a large portrait of the school's erstwhile rector, our mate Reginald, looks down with the faintest of smiles on juniors who have yet to make their way in life, for better or worse. Do they yearn to be in the 6th form, with the luxury of an individual study room in the Lonsdale block? Are they excited at the seniority it will bring? Is it all that it is cracked up to be? Yes. Compared to the shared dormitories, indeed it is. The fagging has disappeared, the bullying is not as marked. Life is undoubtedly easier for the juniors now than when the Head Boarder was a junior. They will find that, once the seniority of the Lonsdale block is attained, they can enjoy the prestige and the responsibility that comes with it – most of the time. They may even find themselves shouting at the juniors…

How stimulating, indeed, to be back. But, most importantly, to be in the proximity of *'Benwick'*. It matters! To be here in this room in the knowledge that a short distance away, there is a girlfriend ensconced at home, looking forward, as her boyfriend is, to the continuation of school life tomorrow. It helps set the mind at rest and causes a slight flutter within. Tomorrow morning will soon be here. Ring on, ring on, you morning bell for breakfast and then, for assembly.

FROM A DORMITORY WINDOW

At *'Benwick'* a pair of *American Tan* tights will, almost certainly, already have been washed and dried and will be waiting on a bedroom chair to be claimed by a youthful and rather inviting pair of lovely shapely legs, come the morning. Oh, to be sat on that bedroom chair watching events unfold as she emerges from a night of pleasant dreams, delicately takes off a nightdress, slips off a pair of knickers and then dresses herself in smart winter school uniform. Goodness!

CHAPTER XX

DO NOT OPEN THIS NOTE UNTIL LATER TONIGHT

Looking out from the dormitory window on this February morning, the cloud appears as one large grey morass and the steady drizzle, whilst hardly perceptible, is nevertheless persistent, leaving the near woodland on the south side of the river drenched. The surrounds of the swimming pool are saturated and small puddles have formed in patches on the tarpaulin covering the pool where the rope has failed to pull it tight. Rain. A common enough feature to the weather pattern in this part of the north-country, with continual cold fronts heading westwards. Low Bentham is firmly in the path of their trajectory, as they cut swiftly across the Atlantic Ocean and the Irish Sea in turn.

*[**An aside**: those two years spent living in Aden as a young lad just shy of teenage years had been devoid of rain – not even the slightest of showers. Two years without rain! The odd sandstorm (of which there was generally adequate advance notice, which ensured that the family judiciously took refuge within the safety of house No. 398 at the RAF 'Officers Quarters' of Khormaksar camp – although even then, the sand seemed to penetrate the family home) was about the only weather variety experienced other than permanent sunshine which, together with the consistently high temperatures, made for an uncomfortable muggy existence. Little wonder then that there was always – without fail – an enforced period of rest in one's bedroom from the middle of the day until mid-afternoon, effectively being incarcerated indoors until the high temperatures eased. One advantage, of course, was that school only lasted for a half-day and was, therefore, finished just before midday – although the school day commenced at 7.30am, not a problem to someone wanting to be out and about once awake. Continual hot weather can indeed be unpleasant, particularly with fair hair and lightly-coloured skin. Playing on the beach at Tarshyne in Aden was enjoyable, yes (particularly when getting buried in a sand pit excavated by an elder brother!), but constant Middle Eastern sunshine combined with fair hair and freckles was never an ideal mix. An elder brother, four years ahead and sporting a quite different skin pigment – a good deal*

darker in colour – lapped up the sunshine and the indoor confinement was, for him, indeed a huge frustration rather than a required rest. He would quite happily be 'out in the midday sun', with all the 'mad dogs' – and there were plenty of them in Aden! (Mad dogs and Englishmen...) Within that home on the RAF base, even the mandatory ceiling fans made little difference with regard to comfort.

On returning to the UK, experiencing rain for the first time in several years had actually been quite exciting and certainly novel. (And witnessing snow, even more so.) In that context, the continual drizzle this morning with the accompanying mist is, in some slightly perverse way, accepted. Not accepted stoically, no, but instead with an appreciation of the splendid variety of weather experienced here on the western edge of the Dales. It may not be sunny today, but it will be sooner or later. When it is, it will be appreciated even more.]

The occasional cars travelling on the back road behind the school can be traced through the murk by their bright headlights or by tail-lights. Car lights still on, despite the fact that, ordinarily, they would not perhaps be needed at this hour – after breakfast but before the start of the school day. W. H. Auden penned a line in 'As I Walked Out One Evening' – in his words, *'The geese go squawking about the sky',* and this morning, indeed they do, flying in rather pleasing RAF style formation. No doubt refreshed after their winter sojourn in this temperate climate, the geese will soon, one might imagine, be heading back northwards with the pending approach of spring. No sign of spring looking out this morning. Breakfast – in the form of Shredded Wheat – completed, but why, oh why, with cold milk? The comforts of home life, which really are no longer particularly yearned for, at least had the simple luxury of hot milk on Shredded Wheat. Cereals of all kinds, shapes and sizes are greatly improved with the requisite milk being heated. As the Bard should surely have written... 'My kingdom for hot milk' – never mind for a bleeding horse!

On the bed is *Cider with Rosie* by Laurie Lee. It has been read, a little reluctantly admittedly (but only reluctantly, of course, because of being told to read it), as the novel has been suggested as required reading for those taking English Literature. It provides primarily what Mrs Fife terms "additional reading" – that is, it is not on the 'A' Level curriculum but should be read to increase depth of literature knowledge. Was it an enjoyable read? Not really – that is despite the fact that it is a supposed classic in literature. Lee's adolescence is from another era, between the two wars, and was in a largely unknown part of Gloucestershire. Perhaps this is what has made it a little difficult to relate to. Is it believable? Have the events he describes in the book been enhanced somewhat to make the read more enjoyable? Was there really a murder in his village whilst he was growing up? What, and no one reported it! Back in that era – and indeed before Laurie Lee's time – every grown-up boy seemed to be writing about his school and growing up. Does anyone do that anymore?

Certainly, for the moment, there is no urge to go and borrow the sequel, *As I Walked Out One Midsummer Morning,* from the school library for another dose of supplementary English Literature reading. *Titled Trains of Great Britain,* by that railway doyen Cecil J. Allan is for sure eminently more enjoyable as a night-time read, whilst sitting in bed before turning out the light. Then to sleep and perchance to dream… Christ, who wrote that? There are times when the memory can – and will – let you down.

The *Daily Express* newspaper from several days ago has been consigned to the waste-paper bin, after having been passed around a few educated 6th form boarders. Well, actually, perhaps a few 6th formers who think they are educated. Why such a comment? It is obvious that the pages pored over on an evening, after revising and essay writing, (or more likely, perhaps, before revising even) are the back few pages. They are well creased from continual reading and contain, of course, the sports section!

A rather brief article, however, in the foreign news reporting section has recently sparked some interest and discussion. An 'authoritative' (?) report from New York suggests that Chairman Mao Tse-Tung is reputedly dying of cancer and is unlikely to survive for much longer than the end of this year. How many times have we read a similar headline over the past few years? Can we believe everything we read? Political discussion gets scant mention throughout this boarding house and even the History 'A' Level discussions in class tend to keep studiously to the periods being studied. Our entry at the turn of the year into an economic tie-in with Europe has hardly been touched on in discussions within the Lonsdale complex. (But then again, who wants to sit talking about politics after a day of study and evening prep and an essay or two?) Barbara's mother did mention it briefly during a Sunday afternoon visit to *'Benwick',* but specifically in the context of New Zealand lamb, currently plentiful and cheap, and their preferred option for a Sunday roast. Will it remain available in the shops and if so, will it still be cheap? That seems to be the sole concern. For a housewife, perhaps it is.

Sociology lessons throw up political debate (of a sort), albeit with little chance of agreement between teacher and pupil. (With the original three taking this 'A' Level now having reduced to one – no surprise there – from the beginning of term. This remaining 'contestant', the Head Boarder, will see it through to the bitter end. A popular subject it certainly is not.) Perhaps an exception to the lack of interest in political discussion within the boarding house is with this Chinese leader, variously described as either being a people's hero or alternatively, a despot more suited to living in a previous century! Does the truth lie somewhere between these two views? It sometimes seems to be the case that it is the 'done thing' to support Socialist principles whilst in adolescence. A prerequisite of growing up. There appears to be scant support for such views in this Lonsdale complex. It seems highly unlikely that any fellow occupants will have the 'little red book' tucked away (and out of sight) in their bedside drawer.

That little red book (actually, 'The Thoughts of Chairman Mao') – has anyone tried to read it? Do people read it? Didn't a naïve sixteen-year-old make an aborted attempt to read it during the summer holidays a year or so ago? Hard to believe now and, as a mother glibly stated regarding that choice of reading material, "For what purpose?" Indeed, if the *Book of Common Prayer* was full of mumbo-jumbo to a young teenager, then the tome by Chairman Mao was even more confusing. A religion perhaps, but a different type of religion to that preached in St. John the Baptist Church.

Pull someone out of poverty and will someone else not drop in? Certainly, the mantra that everyone should be equal is, surely, nigh impossible to achieve. Was it in *Lord of the Flies* (or was it perhaps *Animal Farm* – same difference) that someone said, 'Everyone is equal, but some are more equal than others', or something to that effect? Wasn't it 'Piggy'? Some are more equal than others. That particular mantra is propounded with supreme confidence in this Lonsdale complex – but specifically regarding the 6th form and adolescent lady's boobs – there is no equality there!

Never mind the Chinese dictator. A far more interesting question for the Lonsdale complex, which has singularly failed to provide a definitive answer. Here at school, can a lad have a girl as a friend without her being a girlfriend? Well, it cannot be the case surely. Some suggest, yes. How can that be? If one becomes friendly with a girl away from a group situation within, for instance, the classroom, then she is your girlfriend. No? So, the question is, 'When is a girlfriend not a girlfriend?' Who started that one?

Ah well, the priority for discussion in the boarding house and the priority when reading the newspapers will otherwise remain with football and who is likely to win the league. Will it be London, Leeds or Merseyside? Far more crucial... if it is Merseyside, then it will most definitely not be Everton – and neither will the title be going to Manchester, with the football discussion currently concentrating on whether either (or both) might well be relegated. *But!* – Barbara has proclaimed (if that is the correct term and most definitely with tongue in cheek, one hopes) in a recent letter that, *'I am yours until Manchester United are relegated and Everton win the league'*. It could be that the relegation part of that promise might just well happen this season. Could both happen? Let us hope not!

Five weeks have now elapsed since the start of this new term. A History test on the 25th of January was a good deal easier than the struggle encountered last term with *King Lear.* How did Henry VII prevent the recurrence of the Civil War? It was a question that provided plenty of scope for 'waffle'. A mark of only 14 out of 25 indeed confirmed that fact. Nevertheless, the ability to write over four pages must be a reflection that some information is being stored inside this brain. Perhaps it is just a question of how it is assimilated from the brain and transferred to the hand, to be written on paper. A good deal of time has been spent on Henry VII over the past eighteen months. It would be nice to think that he will make an appearance in one or other of the two History exam papers in June.

Rather more entertaining at the end of the week prior to the history exam was an evening which included watching television. An occasional treat for the boarding house residents on a Friday night and at the weekend. *Morecambe and Wise* – funny? Yes, but the next series of *Dad's Army* is what the majority of the 6th formers in the boarding house are keenly looking forward to. Don't panic!

Now then, Barbara… This new term has seen some hilarious daily discussions with 'The Three Musketeers', revolving from time to time, and perhaps understandably so, around a certain young lady and her 'vital-statistics'! Are a girlfriend's measurements actually so crucial in terms of knowledge for a boyfriend? Vital – no. Intriguing – yes, most definitely! A visual assessment is easily made, and the imagination takes it forward from there. There is an obsession certainly, within this Lonsdale dormitory at least, with discussing (and guessing, obviously) the measurements of various young lasses in the Upper and Lower 6th forms. All quite academic (in a non-academic sense…), but there is, nevertheless, an irresistible urge to do it with the inevitable sexual link. Who has the biggest boobs? Who has the nicest bum? Hockey is eminently suitable for making an accurate assessment on both counts. All far more interesting than, for instance, Britain's membership of the EEC. Hardly a contest.

By the ever-faithful coffee vending machine, Christine and Judith have been more than willing to provide their respective bust/waist/hip measurements to someone who is a boyfriend of their school friend. Fine! Barbara has been somewhat more reticent. It no doubt resonates more personally when such measurements are disclosed to someone with whom one has formed an attachment. Is there a slight nervousness involved? It has been, over the past couple of months, interesting to ponder and to quiz and to engage in guesswork

– but now, no more pondering, no more quizzing. At the end of afternoon break earlier this week, Barbara slipped (quite nonchalantly and with just the slightest hint of a smile) a folded piece of paper into the top pocket of the school blazer being worn by her boyfriend and earnestly requested a promise of restraint. "Please, Ian, do not open this note until later tonight when you are alone in your dormitory – promise me faithfully. I am not going to tell you what it is, you will have to wait until tonight. *Promise!*" An appropriate assurance was given following which Barbara had said, "And please, Ian, do not show it to anyone else. No one, please." Always easy, of course, to give a promise. Not always quite as easy to keep it. This was an occasion to keep it. It had to be. The request had been made by a girlfriend with complete trust in a boyfriend. It would be impossible to let her down. Had she asked whether it had remained unopened until the evening and once inside this private dormitory, her boyfriend's face might well have told all if it had not been the case, without the need for a reply. The way in which the paper had been transferred over – into a blazer pocket, with an accompanying bashful smile, had surely meant that it was not linked in any way to a ceasing of the relationship. How typical that that should have been an initial thought process within the mind. No, nothing to do with that, but everything to do with a girlfriend's figure. The paper, folded in four, opened out to reveal Barbara's vital statistics. How lovely:

34inches-24inches-36inches

And then, a brief resume underneath the figures from Barbara – perhaps in mitigation, perhaps by way of explaining her own view of her body, but in tone almost lacking confidence, plainly shown by her providing her own self-deprecating assessment of her measurements.

My bust… 34 inches
(I really am quite ordinary, Ian. I hope you are happy with that.)
My waist… 24 inches
(I do actually think that I have a nice thin waist!)
My hips… 36 inches
(a little too big really… what do you think?)

Nothing else, just the explanation with each figure which perhaps hinted at some slight apprehension in case a boyfriend was not happy with them. Not happy? Barbara, you are lovely to look at in school uniform, or in a smart skirt and blouse and in casual jeans and t-shirt. In a dress you look gorgeous. Figures mean nothing – you look nicely proportioned and your countenance is forever sunny and engagingly innocent. Certainly, no Swiss finishing school needed for you, young lady!

Barbara – along with all her 6th form compatriots – has been, perhaps understandably, conditioned to assume that all the 6th form boys want to have a girlfriend with big boobs. No wonder! All the sexy talk within the classroom bases itself around the 'wonder' of big boobs. The girls are not immune to that thought process. Big boobs, big talk – but secretly, the attraction is with personality and attractiveness. Isn't it? (And oh, don't forget about the legs.)

The following day, at morning break, Barbara had approached with a rather embarrassed grin, with her face clearly displaying some slight discomfort. It showed that she was apprehensive. She confessed to having been worried all morning. Her face immediately changed to a look of relief once she was assured that she was "lovely". Not only that, but for Barbara, it was a lot more meaningful to be assured by her boyfriend that she is "lovely just as you are". Whatever, it is rather exciting to know Barbara's personal measurements. Christine and Judith had previously (and rather proudly) volunteered their own, but that information was really of little, if any, interest. The interest is with a girlfriend and knowing her 'vital-statistics' (as she terms them) somehow makes her even more special.

Okay, knowing is not seeing – but it is, perhaps, part (or the start) of the journey. Knowing isn't seeing. But, of course, it works both ways – or at least, it does with Miss Noble. More of a surprise – a shock – was the follow up from this young lady after she had again stressed that her bust (as she terms it – not boobs, or bazookas…) is just "quite ordinary". Barbara had continued with a rather cheeky query of her own, displaying some new-found, swashbuckling confidence – almost outside the parameters of her own "niceness". The courage to ask the question clearly gained from discussing boobs and her bum. (Which she insists is "a bit too big" – but it isn't!) There was clearly some adventure and intrigue in the question.

"Well, what about you?" was the gentle retort to her boyfriend.

"Eh?"

"Come on, you know what I mean!" The broad smile on her face and a quick jab of her finger in the stomach had given an indication that a reply was keenly awaited – and expected.

[Short pause for joint laughter - slightly embarrassed laughter from her boyfriend!]

"Come on, I have told you about me."

Another pause for joint laughter – eventually, amid more nervous laughter from a boyfriend and a blunt – *"Barbara!"* – which proved fruitless, bringing forth the same retort – "Come on now, you know about me". Was it time to concede? An expectant girlfriend suggested as such! It was!

"Do you mean my 'ding-a-ling?"

"YES!" (Another short pause – with laughter.)

"Well, about normal I would say!" (Was there any other possible answer? In any case, what the hell is normal? Besides which, who would admit to having a small willy?) The answer proved adequate.

"Well, in that case, we are both just normal" – which had been said with the familiar accompaniment of a scrunch of the nose and shoulders. Perhaps it is just as well for both girlfriend and boyfriend to be – well, just average!

For a girlfriend, the agony of doubt as to whether a boyfriend would still fancy her has been dispelled, but Barbara, like all other young ladies (or perhaps *all* ladies for that matter), will no doubt continue to anguish over whether her size could be more "ideal". As John Donne might, one imagines, so typically have said in one of his essays regarding one of life's enigmas (that is, the way that a female mind works or thinks), "Show me a woman who is satisfied with her size and weight." A statement no doubt valid just as much in the sixteenth century as it is now in the twentieth century!

Already thoughts are turning to a rapidly approaching half-term. Arrangements for stopping in Low Bentham at *'Brentwood'*, where a local bed and breakfast is available, have been all but finalised. A room has been provisionally booked, but the small matter of cost will have to be sorted out. Pocket money alone is not sufficient and funds from parents are eagerly anticipated – a request having been sent through when the booking was made. If monies are not received in time, then Barbara, via her parents, has agreed to bridge the cost.

Staying in Low Bentham will be eminently preferable to another unhappy sojourn at the Battery Hotel and most probably it will be of some relief, in any case, to Cess. Breakfast will be taken at *'Brentwood'*, but the promise of both lunch and an evening meal being provided at *'Benwick'* throughout the half-term break is indeed something to look forward to. The prospect of a full week away from school, if not from studying, is also greatly anticipated. But no, not because of being able to escape from the boarding house – far from it – but more specifically because it will be upwards of nine days in the company of Barbara, with the days being spent in and around *'Benwick'*. Plans are already afoot to share various tasks in and around the house, with enthusiastic agreement being given to Barbara in answer to the suggestion posed during a recent lunch break. "If you like, Ianey, during half-term, we can practise doing some home baking together and also help my mum with the cleaning around the house." Impressive or what? To help with the cleaning for a girlfriend's mother. Mrs Noble will surely be impressed. (Or at least she should be!)

CHAPTER XXI

I HOPE HE IS BEHAVING HIMSELF, MRS RUSSELL

What of *Teddy*? He did return to the boarding house after Christmas, being handed over somewhat reluctantly by Barbara, it must be said. It is impossible not to think about how lucky he has been to spend the time not only in Barbara's bedroom, but in her bed – being cuddled and kissed by her. Goodness! Lucky sod. (No, he isn't real but – nevertheless!)

Another poem, essentially in anticipation – justified anticipation perhaps, has been penned since which, following a brief return to the boarding house, *Teddy* has returned, at Barbara's behest, to take up permanent residence at 'Benwick' – it is nigh impossible not to be envious. Oh *Teddy*!

Back home Teddy:
Three weeks have these blank walls
Not seen your stylish grin...
You look as though you have something
To tell me with that engaging smile...

What!
You have been sleeping with her,
Smelling her silky skin.
She nuzzled you with her nose,
She held you tightly,
She kissed you gently,
Showered you with sweetly smelling scent!

Well may you laugh Teddy!
Can I but hope, some-day, one day,
She may do the same for me.

On the school front, yet another history essay question, eliciting – surprise, surprise – well, no surprise – a poor mark. (Are poor marks given on purpose to encourage a better effort?) 'How far was James I's unpopularity due to his foreign policy?' (Is anyone out there bothered?) The mark of 52% disappointing, although perhaps just slightly tempered with the comment, which now seems to appear regularly on the essays from all the three subjects,

'A good effort but you need to cut out the waffle.' Waffle – it is not going to fool the examiners then. Maybe not, but it certainly makes a completed essay look impressive. And a recent comment at the foot of an English Literature essay on *The Knight of the Burning Pestle* [Is it a comedy? Discuss] merely said, *'Why use a thousand words when one will do? To be blunt, frank, you write some dreadful English, and you are a long-winded fellow. Beware those split infinitives.'* Eh? What are those? Then as a follow up, a postscript, *'Don't doodle in the margins...'* Thank you, Ducky, for that. Five pages. But doodling encourages the thought process. Yes, it does! His comments – somewhat harsh, but not unexpected. And surely, a rather petty follow up, *'Please use fountain pen and not pencil with your essay answers.'* For God's sake – does it matter? (Anyway – no more cartridges left.)

Those at the senior end of the school – the 6th form contingent – should, of course, exude responsibility. On that basis, getting thrown out of the school library not once, but twice in a week is, perhaps, not the best way to show maturity. Well of course, Ducky has suggested that there is some growing up still to be done. Barbara, bless her, was thrown out at the same time by association. The teachers might just be starting to think that she is keeping bad company. Don't some young women thrive in keeping bad company? Inexplicable? Perhaps, but nevertheless, sometimes the case. It happens here. How is it that the odd *'Blifil'*-like character (re: Tom Jones) gets hitched up with an attractive girl? Baffling...

This 'A' Level study timetable ensures that there is always an element of free time for research and study. The senior school library provides the obvious focal point for reference and reading. It was the comedian Spike Milligan who was to blame for the joint banishment. His fault and his alone. Instead of using the library to obtain some useful in-depth research into the problems between Henry VIII and the established Catholic church (although the issue appears on the face of it to be merely a straightforward case of a King's desire to divorce a rather unfortunate wife, thereby enabling him to obtain a son and heir via another woman), it was far more enjoyable reading the recent purchase, *Adolf Hitler, My Part in his Downfall*, the World War II memoirs of Spike Milligan. As a read, it is indeed both bawdy, base and smutty, utterly crude, perhaps almost bordering on the obscene. Nevertheless, at the same time, it is hilarious with the dialogue accompanied by numerous comical sketches. Perhaps it was rather naïve to have even considered reading such material in a school library, where the norm is silent study. Talking and laughter are quite definitely taboo. Well, there was no talking, but there was unrestrained laughter. It did not take long for the hilarity to get going and with a handkerchief held over the mouth in a vain attempt to prevent uncontrollable laughing, the book had been passed over to Barbara. Her bemused face had elicited an enquiring, 'what are you laughing at?' expression. After a few moments of reading, Barbara was also unable to control her laughter and before a judicious exit could be made from that normally hushed place of learning, an edict was issued from a clearly frustrated library mistress, whose finger pointing to the door was self-explanatory. She was, of course, quite right and those in the senior forms should know better. Yes, you are right, Ducky. There is (only on the odd occasion, mind) still some growing up to be done.

That it should have happened in the library again a few days later, with the same cause and effect was, perhaps, as Lady Bracknell was at pains to point out in *The Importance of Being Ernest*, rather careless! With the threat of a period of banishment from the library, Spike Milligan has, sensibly, now been removed from a battered briefcase.

The law of unintended consequences raised its head this month with a short stay in the school sick bay. A football match, playing away at Morecambe Grammar School, resulted in a 4-3 victory – a famous triumph at that, against a traditionally strong and capable side. Unfortunately, it also produced a couple of bent fingers, with bones sticking out at rather strange angles! All thanks to a football boot belonging to one of the Morecambe thugs who clearly felt he could get the Bentham School goalkeeper, prostrate on the ground, to release the football with a sharp stamp on his fingers. His ploy was not successful, but the fingers, well, they definitely came off second best.

Oh joy, undiluted joy! Yabba-Dabba Do! Well, it would have been at one time, now no longer so. Perhaps partial joy at least, with a brief incarceration in sick bay, enjoying the services and care of matron, who dutifully and carefully examined the fingers every day. Most certainly she handled them with care, almost caressing them – rather nice actually! The two fingers, badly bruised and hurting terribly, soothed then by a matron's kindly hand. But – were they broken or were they just heavily bruised? The doctor confirmed no break. (Then why, oh why, do they stick out at a rather odd angle?)

The enjoyment and the tenderness of regular attention from matron was, nevertheless, tempered by the rule that she does not permit visitors into the sick bay. No visitors? Surely not! There ensued a sort of 'friendly', albeit combatative war of attrition against a firm and determined matron lasting for several days. Surely matron would give way, wouldn't she, when it involved a girlfriend wanting to check all was well with an injured boyfriend? Several times that familiar Yorkshire tone could be heard at the entrance to the sick bay, asking matron if all was well with the patient. "I hope that he is behaving himself, Mrs Russell" – cheeky! What did you mean by that, young lady? But still no agreement to allow Barbara entry.

Persistence. Pleading. Eventually success. Mrs Russell partially relented, resulting in one visit – a victory of sorts – with Barbara being permitted to make a short five-minute stay by the bedside. (Actually, extended to nearer fifteen minutes after matron had kindly gone off to sort out other duties, with her parting words to Barbara being, "I am sure I can rely on you to leave after five minutes, Barbara." However, the look on her face spoke volumes, perhaps providing a different type of instruction…) For both a visiting girlfriend and her bedridden boyfriend – in his pyjamas – it was rather an exciting episode. Just a pity the situation had not been reversed, with a young lady in bed wearing just a nightie being visited by her boyfriend…

Mrs Russell and Barbara Noble: two lovely ladies, but the younger of the two wins the prize. In reality, it is no longer a contest, with the attraction and lively personality of a new girlfriend supplanting the interest previously shown in a middle-aged, albeit enticing, stylish and highly rateable (as the saying goes within the Lonsdale complex) matron.

Whilst there was no shortage of printed material regularly handed in to the sick bay, it was, regretfully, reading material of the wrong type, in the form of history and sociology books. Let's be fair, it provided a good opportunity to do some background reading, but there is only so much reading one can do continuously – particularly so when it is boring. It was a relief to be released back into the hurly-burly of school life, particularly as there was certainly no wish to miss the next First XI football match. However, two bent fingers are, and might well continue to be, a reminder of a short period of 'imprisonment' in the school sick bay.

News, of course, spreads quickly and once the reason for the incarceration in the sick bay had filtered throughout the school, a mantle of God-like status was briefly enjoyed by the First XI goalkeeper, particularly with the youngsters in the lower school years. Predictably, the hero worship did not last long. It never does, even with the considerable success enjoyed this season with the First XI football results. Juniors are conditioned, however unintentionally, to be wary and cautious in their dealings with senior members of the 6th form. There is an issue of trust. It was absent in 1966 and perhaps it is still absent in 1973. The Head Boarder is friendly – except when he is shouting…

And what of Durham University? The familiarisation visit over two days – Monday 5th and Tuesday 6th February – cannot be considered to have been a great success and there is a definite question mark over whether the visit was at all worthwhile. (Hold on! Cross that out – a correction – it was not worthwhile.) The growing attachment to Bentham and the surrounding area is gnawing away continuously at the idea of a university degree course. In the confinement of a dormitory bedroom, it becomes quite easy to persuade oneself that it would be far simpler to obtain employment locally after the exams, thereby negating the need for additional years of study. Surely, a university degree is not the 'be all and end all' – is it? (Isn't that Shakespeare? Rosco reckons it is...)

Advising the school with regard to what would be a significant change of plan will not be easy. The school's viewpoint, understandably, is for as many 'A' Level candidates as possible to progress to further education. It will look impressive on the school's CV, obviously giving kudos to its reputation both locally and, more crucially, with the West Riding and Lancashire County Councils, who allow pupils admittance to what is essentially a fee-paying school. Making the school aware of a change of heart regarding university will have to wait for an appropriate time. Far easier for the moment to continue mulling it over until a final decision is made. More importantly, it would be prudent, perhaps, to find out how Barbara might react to the suggestion, bearing in mind that this relationship – whilst seemingly a close one – is still barely three months old. And who to tell? Snot, who has responsibility for arrangements regarding university entrance and courses? Mr Russell, the Housemaster? Not something, one suspects, that is within his brief... but he might be a more sympathetic listener and offer more understanding regarding the main reason driving the thought process. The headmaster, perhaps... oh dear! The whole issue can, for the moment, be left for another time. In the wise counsel of Cess, "Why decide today when you can put it off until tomorrow"? An effective delaying mantra for sure. (But surely not one that Confucius would be recommending. Or just perhaps, for a hesitant adolescent in the boarding house, maybe he would.)

So, there was no morning run with *Bendy* through Low Bentham and up the road to *'Benwick'* on Monday 5th February. Instead, the National Express coach leaving Lancaster bus station early that morning was rather too hot and stuffy and there had been no particular urge to pass the time of day with an elderly gentleman in the adjoining seat, some of whose clothes had, perhaps, been in the close proximity of mothballs in a bedroom drawer or cupboard. Inexplicably, within approximately thirty minutes of leaving Lancaster, a prolonged stop for breakfast (for those who were interested) was made at the Highwayman Inn at Burrow (or as the village sign terms it, Burrow-in-Burrow, indicating perhaps the name of the village, as well as the name of the surrounding area). The inn has almost certainly, in years gone by, been an old stagecoach stop where, surely, at one time horses (as well as travellers) were fed and watered, or even where, perhaps, a new set of horses were provided for a continuing journey across the turnpike road between the West Coast and the North-East. The inn's eighteenth-century credentials are not in doubt, but frustrating indeed it was having a long meal break so soon after setting off. With further protracted stops at Kirkby Lonsdale, Sedbergh and Kirkby Stephen, it was well into the afternoon by the time the main road crossing the Pennines and heading towards the North-East was finally reached.

The evening lights of Durham had at last advertised arrival and the subsequent evening meal was similar, albeit on a much grander and a larger affair, to what is experienced here at boarding school. Sleeping arrangements, however, were not enjoyable, with a large, shared visitors dormitory, a 'throw-back' to the memories of the commencement of boarding house life in 1966. In that vast, rather grand, antique dining hall of the University, it was difficult not to shake off the feeling that it was almost imitating a Tudor-style banquet, albeit without any carcasses hanging on hooks from the ceiling and without the required attendance of nobility. (Or, for that matter, servants…)

The daylight of the following morning was most welcome after the less than private sleeping arrangements. The city itself is indeed impressive, not only with the castle incorporating a large part of the University, but also nearby, the rather grand Durham Cathedral presenting itself in a somewhat gothic style and also, a dominant railway viaduct crossing the city skyline. An attractive city yes, but nevertheless, it was with some relief that the National Express coach had been boarded for the painstaking journey back across to the West Coast. A return to 'home ground' being eventually completed by late Tuesday afternoon.

No getting off the Pennine bus, on the journey back from Lancaster, at the junction by the Punch Bowl Hotel however – to then take the familiar walk over the bridge to school. No, instead, an obliging bus driver had, with a wise and knowing smile, happily stopped outside the gated entrance to *'Benwick'* and a delighted girlfriend, being obviously aware as to who it would be getting off the bus directly outside the house, came rushing out to provide the best possible welcome home. The motley collection of remaining passengers will surely have smiled inwardly to themselves when a girlfriend, arms outstretched all but leapt into the arms of her boyfriend – or perhaps the older blokes might have thought, "how soppy!", whilst the old 'dears' (bless them) will have loved watching the display. They would be more likely to be thinking, "how sweet!" (Or some of the more elderly, "how forward!"). High Bentham, Low Bentham – we know how it is – more than likely one of them will have declared, "I saw Barbara Noble's young man get off the bus and they greeted each other with a big hug. Rather forward in public if you ask me…"

Durham – an impressive university? Without doubt and indeed, one of the oldest learning establishments whose motto is, 'Her foundations are upon the holy hills'. Indeed, they are – with the University looking down upon the city as it does – but, perhaps more pertinently, they are not the hills of the Craven fault and, increasingly, the heart is here at the western edge of the Pennines. In the words of a song penned by a local folk group, *'It is in the high, high hills of Craven where I'll always want to be.'*

Once back in the dormitory, the letter on the bed awaiting the recipient's return undoubtedly provided the most humorous part of the trip. The 'love' letters that had commenced during the Christmas break have continued into this spring term and they have become a most pleasurable pastime, both in writing them and particularly in receiving them. Yes, they do take up time that, perhaps, might (and should) otherwise be spent on writing essays and on revision, but so what. Barbara had written on the Monday after school to summarise the day she had experienced, a day without being able to meet up with her boyfriend – *'I have been through hell today!!! Mrs. Taylor said right in front of all our form "I don't know how Barbara is going to manage to get through the next two days. She will even have to carry her own schoolbooks home"!!! Meanwhile, I was searching for a comfy hole in the classroom wall or a crack in the floorboards!!! Cess told me to take a couple of Disprins to relieve my look of obvious anguish!!! Some people even had the cheek to ask why you had finished with me!!'*

Funny indeed, although there is, surely, an underlying message within this most recent of letters. If intuition is to be proved accurate, it is saying that neither party wishes to be separated from the other. The visit to Durham was the first time a daily meeting, either at school during the week or at *'Benwick'* during the weekend, had not taken place since the Christmas break and the subsequent start of term. There is a definite feel in reading the letter that Barbara is lost without being able to see her boyfriend. Whilst in Durham, the sense of loss at not being able to meet and chat, talk, laugh and just gaze at a girlfriend meant that the way Barbara felt was more than reciprocated. If for no other reason, the arrangement for half-term to be spent at *'Brentwood'* in Low Bentham is to be welcomed. It will mean the daily meetings can continue throughout the holiday break. More pertinently, it again calls into question the most basic issue of the practicality of being away at university for up to three years. Unthinkable? Snot will not understand. No, of course he won't. "Priorities, McCart, priorities." That is indeed the issue – what are the priorities and who is going to make the decision on them? Not Snot, that is for sure. There is a deep dread at having to tell him that the priorities have changed, perhaps irrevocably so. It will have to be done, but not yet. (The sound advice from Cess still holds good... "why do something today when...")

Having lost track of the time, quite suddenly the familiar sound of the school bell signals the commencement of the school day. Well, actually a buzzer. Unlike the early days in the boarding house, when a hand bell was used to denote mealtime, prep times and when it was time to vacate the dormitories at the commencement of the school day. It was generally a prefect (although if they could not be bothered then it would be a junior to whom they would allocate the task), who would walk all around the boarding house and into each dormitory ringing the bell to ensure they could hear it – no one could then claim they had failed to hear it. (Well, they could, but it would never be an acceptable excuse.)

But now, the dormitory must be vacated in favour of the school Assembly Hall. Wednesday means the weekly dose of 'posh' music, courtesy of Mr Lethbridge, whose sterling efforts at attempting to educate students every week with refined 'old fashioned' music is all but wasted, falling almost without exception on 'deaf ears'. You might say that last week, Mr Lethbridge was *In the Hall of the Mountain King,* but regarding the pupils, there were not that many with him – he was in a world of his own! The assessment of his taste in music? Well, the jury is still out... and is likely to stay out for some considerable time. Which composer will Mr Lethbridge be trying to indoctrinate adolescent minds with this morning? Bach, Beethoven, Sibelius? Whatever, it will all be in vain. He must surely realise as much.

On the landing, Mrs Wills is busy filling three large laundry baskets with boarders dirty clothing. "Good morning, Ian, I know you will have your laundry bag ready at the end of your bed, you are one of the organised ones. I wish they were all like you." On both counts, she is 100% correct – the laundry bag awaits her at the bottom of the bed, and within the psyche, there is an unending and irresistible urge to be tidy and well organized. An inexplicable mild panic makes itself known if things are not left tidy and in good order – a feeling surely at odds with the mantra, 'why do something today if it can be put off until tomorrow'. The mind works in a strange way (sometimes).

Mrs Wills is left gamely manhandling the wicker baskets ready for their collection by the laundry van, which will make its weekly Wednesday call at the school mid-morning. Further along the corridor, whilst passing the headmaster's study on the way to assembly, the door opens and Mr Hagen shuffles out. He is wearing his regulation black gown but, as always, his suit appears somewhat unkempt and, at close quarters, appears rather too large for his frame. "I am glad I have caught you, Ian. I would like to pop to see you tonight, just to chat about the poetry meetings. Should we say half-past-seven, perhaps? I will catch up with you in your room." Well, indeed, that is something to look forward to! It would perhaps be preferable listening to a Leonard Cohen song – well, no, maybe not!

(Mental note to self – back from *'Benwick'* 7pm – prefect duty – meeting with Headmaster – homework, 2 x essays – love letter to write (a priority!) – Corn Flake supper – Christ!)

CHAPTER XXII

THAT KINGDOM BY THE SEA

'I was a child and she was a child
In the kingdom by the sea...'
(Edgar Allan Poe)

'*Brentwood*'. Most probably an Edwardian building – possibly Victorian – and situated towards the western end of Low Bentham village, where the main through road bends slightly in preparation for it crossing the river, after which, the road passes under the railway and heads towards the school. This imposing property consists of three floors incorporating five bedrooms, with all but one of them available for bed and breakfast clients. The establishment is in the seemingly confident and capable hands of the landlady, Mrs Noulton. She appears to have a good grasp of most, if not all, of the local chit chat and gossip – not only for Low Bentham village, but also for the surrounding area. Her knowledge of the school gossip however is not quite so extensive... but she is happy to listen to it!

The vista from this room on the third floor in *'Brentwood'* looks out to the countryside at the back of the property, giving a bird's eye view of the passing railway and, to the south just up the Mill Road, the old Ford Ayrton mill now stands disused, awaiting a future lease of life, perhaps serving some other purpose. Otherwise, the view is pastoral and pleasing and shouts of continuity. The room itself is adequate, if somewhat cold late at night once the heating has gone off, and, therefore, not by that time conducive to late night learning and revision. The problem is that late night revision it has had to be – with the days being spent not here, in *'Brentwood'*, but at a detached bungalow on the outskirts of the village, up the High Bentham Road.

'Brentwood': not at all as comfortable or homely as the boarding dormitory (and it is certainly not as magical as the house up the High Bentham Road) and being here – away from the school – has created a slight and inexplicable feeling within the mind of insecurity. Where exactly is 'home' going to be after the completion of 'A' Levels? Certainly not in Germany with parents. It seems extremely unlikely that a parent's house, wherever it might be located in the future, will ever again be classed as home. The home of childhood has been left once and for all. So where will home be? Not at Durham, either. This

questioning is fuelling a sense of uncertainty. Never mind! For now, remaining in Low Bentham for this half-term break was always going to be a priority. All the trappings of a study bedroom left behind at school, but the photograph of Barbara as a bridesmaid at her auntie's wedding has been brought along and adorns the bedside table. Goodness, how many times has it been looked at?

The biggest surprise, without a doubt, is to find that one of the semi-permanent guests (so to speak) at this establishment is none other than our erstwhile Olympic high jump silver medallist and Sociology teacher, Miss Shirley. Breakfast times, whilst enjoyable for their food content (Mrs Noulton does provide a far better breakfast, as one might expect her to do, than can the school canteen) have otherwise been slightly awkward affairs with the semi-formal nature of the 'pupil-teacher' relationship being uneasily maintained, despite both parties being away from the school environment. In addition, it is obvious that there is no meeting of minds on a political viewpoint, which to some extent plays itself out during the sociology lessons with an undercurrent of hostility. (Rather like an iceberg, the majority lies under a creaking and grumbling surface!)

Occasionally, this mostly silent animosity at the breakfast table bubbles to the surface and is, by necessity and rightly so, rapidly extinguished by the school mistress (rather than by the pupil) and a semblance of normality restored. Miss Shirley clearly has no time or patience with Edward Heath, despite his undoubted leaning to the centre left of Conservative ideology. His political mantra would need to go a good deal further towards the Socialist left, no doubt, to appease her. Is it wholly inevitable that a teacher of sociology will be a fervent Socialist? Is she a Socialist? Teachers will not (or should not) divulge political leanings, but somehow with Miss Shirley you can just tell. There has, therefore, been the odd period of studious silence during breakfast, with perhaps both teacher and pupil wishing the other was not there. The mild embarrassment felt is surely only with the pupil and not with the teacher. Somewhat fortuitously, Mrs Noulton has been helping to keep the general chatter going with interesting titbits of local gossip. Miss Shirley, without doubt, will be pleased to see the end of half-term and this bed-and-breakfast guest returning to school.

There has, however, been one piece of breaking news straight from the horse's mouth. (Or high-jumper's mouth in this case!) Prior to this half-term break, there had been persistent rumours circulating within the school that Miss Shirley was to be leaving. At the very least, these enforced meetings at breakfast have indeed confirmed the rumour as fact. She leaves at the end of this term to take up a post with Oxfordshire County Council. The power of school rumours! Well, she has not lasted long at the school, only arriving to teach at the start of the autumn term 1970. Oxfordshire Council will be pleased, no doubt, to learn first-hand about her recent Olympic feat, but might not be so keen to keep hearing about it thereafter. So, for the summer term leading to the examination in June, the teaching of sociology will be solely with Mrs Taylor, for whom there is already a good deal of admiration via the history syllabus. The respect rightly given to her is warmly reciprocated via a friendly and sensible discourse and her treatment of senior pupils as 'grown-ups' is refreshing and to be welcomed. Mrs Taylor's political leanings appear to be to the left of centre (how easy it is to make assumptions), but in this case, the opposing views of teacher and pupil are accepted (and respected) and there is an absence of any suspicion or feeling of rancour towards the other party.

This half-term break, now almost over, has gone quickly – far too quickly. As Barbara bemoaned just prior to this weekend, "I always hate the last day of a holiday. It is so sad!" Of course, the weekend doesn't count as proper holiday and indeed, this week just gone has had the feel of a holiday, even though it has been spent in Low Bentham. Yes, particularly sad as girlfriend and boyfriend have been together every day. Notwithstanding this, the final day of a holiday is always sad for Barbara. She felt the same, she said, on the last day of the family holiday earlier this year in Stranraer. She terms it a 'bitter-sweet' moment – nice to get back home, but also a shame that the holiday had to end. All holidays must come to an end – and the last day, well, particularly poignant.

So, the return to the boarding house this coming Sunday 25th February will be welcomed, yes, but it will mean the end of the daily visits to *'Benwick'* and spending all day – every day – with Barbara. Is it possible to get fed up with the constant, continual presence of the others company? On the evidence of this half-term week, the answer has to be a categorical no. The week has played itself out largely within the confines of *'Benwick'* and with both Barbara's parents out at work during the day (albeit only until mid-afternoon with her mother, who assists at Low Bentham Parochial School), the house has been the half-term 'playground'.

So has begun, courtesy of Barbara as a willing hostess and teacher, a 'beginners' guide to baking and, to a lesser extent but no less important nonetheless, cooking. Barbara, already possessing the numerous secrets and skills of successful baking – these having been handed down from her mother's generation – is, on the evidence of this half-term week, indeed an accomplished baker. Proud and independent enough to have her own 'Barbara Noble's Recipe Book', with recipes written therein in that familiar large flowery writing that she manages to create by holding a pen/pencil between a second and third finger of her right hand, despite it looking most awkward writing in such a manner. Is Barbara the only person to write in such an unusual style? It appears most bizarre, awkward almost, but effective nonetheless, providing a rather unique and recognisable script. Is it indicative, perhaps, of some hidden talent? (She reckons as much!) Inelegant it may appear to be, but it produces what one might term a 'harmonious' well-ordered handwritten end-result.

The baking sessions have helped to cement a bond that has developed over a period of just under three months and which has been free of even the slightest of disagreements, or indeed any sort of difference of opinion. It is almost a meeting of minds, and an intuition seems to have developed almost seamlessly, so that on a regular basis each knows what the other is thinking without it having to be said. What joy in baking with the kitchen as an arena. "You don't mind spending time helping me with the baking do you, Ianey?" It was a question that hardly needed to be asked or, indeed, answered. Flour is weighed out, then sifted, whilst at the same time, an eye is kept on the black treacle and margarine melting in a pan on the cooker. Greaseproof paper is cut to shape and size, baking tins are lined, oven temperature checked. It almost had the feel of an enjoyable art lesson under the guidance of Mrs Piper, or perhaps really a Domestic Science lesson, were it not for the fact that cooking and baking at school are the specific province of the girls. Whilst these tasks were being completed, Barbara would be busy cutting out ginger biscuits ready for them to be placed in the oven – and all the time, tender little smiles jointly traded, and the occasional sneaky kiss being furnished or received. What heaven! And the other treat in addition to the regular supply of little kisses? Well, being in charge of the washing up meant that the remnants of the various biscuit and cake recipes could be methodically taken up with a finger and eaten before the bowl was plunged into hot water (with the fingers) to be washed clean. Super! Except, the kitchen had, by the end of the baking session, taken on the appearance of a bomb site. But, in the words of the expert, "you cannot have a successful baking session without making a mess." Really?

As well as baking what Barbara terms her usual recipes (Gingerbread, Canadian fruit cake – why Canadian? No-one knows, least of all Barbara, Finnish ginger biscuits – why Finnish?), a foray has been made in this half-term week into bread making, the bread dough being warmed via the coke boiler in the corner of the kitchen. For several hours, whilst the yeast was rising from the warmth of the boiler to its required height and consistency, Barbara was prevented from sitting up on top of the boiler herself. For as well as servicing the central heating system and providing hot water, it was quite obvious very quickly that the boiler facilitated another additional important household task during the winter months – in Barbara's own words, "I like to sit up on the boiler in winter, as it helps to keep my bum warm." (Indeed, according to her mother, Barbara has been known to spend several hours at a time reading a book whilst sitting up on the boiler. She would certainly, therefore, have the comfort of a nice warm 'bum' by the time she clambered down!)

For Barbara, sitting on the boiler has become something of a pastime during this half-term holiday – in-between the baking and whilst waiting for various recipes to be taken out of the oven. Once ensconced on the top of the boiler, she would only move off rather reluctantly, it must be said, when more coke needed to be shovelled in, and once her boyfriend had completed that task, she would then jump quickly back on as if to claim squatter's rights! The height of the boiler is such that it means it is ideal for her to sit on and provide outstretched arms to place around her boyfriend's waist. Then the time would be spent chatting, often about something and nothing, the chatter being interspersed with tender little kisses. A normally anonymous and purely functional boiler has, therefore, proved eminently successful as a bonding exercise. A couple of times, Barbara had put out her arms and legs, "Right Ianey, do you want to carry me to my bedroom, I am not too heavy am I?" said with a steely look in her eyes which indicated that she really *shouldn't* be too heavy, and it better not be admitted that she is. She would then be carried along the corridor in a bear hug fashion (and the proximity of that body – Christ!) and then carefully dropped onto a now familiar blue bedspread.

Barbara's bedroom. Typically, and quite rightly so, a young lady's private space – but one into which a boyfriend is now willingly and enthusiastically admitted. Rather like, when as a young child, one might wish to usher a new friend into one's bedroom to show off any games and comics or wall posters or, perhaps, just to sit chatting in private etc. Her large bedroom window looks out on the front of the bungalow, with net curtains keeping the room private from any visitors walking along the path from the garden gate to the front door. A rather convenient arrangement indeed for watching and identifying visitors arriving during daylight hours but, of course, the visitor on that Friday night in late November last year would not have been seen, with the bedroom curtains closed during hours of darkness. On the wall facing her bed, a large 'family tree' poster of pop music. To its right, a picture of Gilbert O'Sullivan and underneath it, a page cut out from a magazine showing a modern stylish young lady with two large shaggy dogs. Underneath that, by the bedside, a pendant of Manchester United (whisper it quietly), although Barbara has willingly admitted to being a "glory supporter". (Shame on you – there are, by all accounts, far too many "glory supporters" linked to the Reds…) No poster, however, of Che Guevara on the bedroom wall – thank goodness!

Across from her bed, a small bookshelf on the wall, made by her father, displaying an array of current fiction interspersed randomly with classical fiction. The books, perhaps, hint at an appetite for reading. *Black Beauty* and *The Forsyte Saga* prominent (and the former now a serial on television – *The Adventures of Black Beauty* – she will be watching it), but ignoring these, Barbara had instead rather proudly picked up a small green coloured book from the bottom shelf entitled *The Golden Treasury,* compiled by Francis Turner Palgrave, the book being a compilation of (as the introductory page describes it) 'the best lyric poems in the English Language'. Inside the front cover, a brief annotation… *'To the first Head Girl of the Parochial School: thank you Barbara: Mr. Garner.'* She had handed it over with an explanation, "This is perhaps the book I value most highly. Not necessarily for the poetry, but for the memory." Indeed, that was why the book had been proudly offered up. "Perhaps," Barbara had suggested whilst the book was being skimmed through, "if you are allowed to stay over sometime maybe at the weekend, you could read me a few poems from the book once I have got ready for bed, before going to sleep. That would be rather nice, wouldn't it?" Nice? It will be absolute heaven. Christ! Certainly, Keats, Auden and Wordsworth, all from the 'A' Level syllabus, are represented in the substantial collection of verse. The prospect of reading poems to a girlfriend whilst she sits in bed is a wonderful suggestion, far exceeding the travails of the three-weekly poetry readings that take place in the headmaster's house.

Above the two rows of books and on the top shelf, Barbara's *Roberts* radio (a "trusty *Roberts* radio" in Barbara's words) and a small, rather ancient looking, portable record player. *Teddy* sits patiently on the bed by Barbara's pillow (now that he has been commandeered back to *'Benwick'* on a permanent basis from the boarding house – lucky devil!). To preserve his modesty, Barbara has kindly adorned him with a nappy! Both *Teddy* and his new 'owner' seem quite happy with their respective living arrangements. For *Teddy*, quite understandable.

A thin air force blue dressing gown with gold lining at the sleeve ends and around the neck hangs on the back of the door. Directly opposite the bed, a dressing table incorporating an integral mirror. A dressing table that displayed a liberal collection of creams and lotions, with a tube of her favourite *Desert Flower* body lotion cream prominent, together with a small tube of *Aqua Manda* bath lotion. With a couple of small scent bottles also sitting on the table-top, the use of all of these, presumably every morning, combined to give the bedroom a pleasing feminine perfume smell. Plenty of drawers in the dressing table. All fully closed and just thinking about what clothes and underwear there might be in them was, for a boyfriend, both tingling and tantalising. In the style of John Betjeman, an appropriate line for his humorous poetry might well have been:

'And which was the drawer with the knickers in?'

(To fit quite conveniently with:

'Which were the baths where they taught you to swim?'

'Myfanwy': *From Old Lights for New Chancels*: published 1940)

That pleasantly scented bedroom at *'Benwick'* – it is indeed a *'Kingdom by the sea'*.

"Well, now that you have seen my bedroom", Barbara had said, "I wonder if I would be able to have a look in your dormitory room sometime, Ianey, please?" The reply had to be honest and practical. It was. "It will be quite difficult you know, Barbi. The boarders' dormitory rooms are strictly out of bounds to visitors, particularly visitors of the opposite sex, with the only possible exception being close family." The slightest of frowns on Barbara's face told of her obvious disappointment, but her face had also displayed a steely determination. Without her saying a word, her look had almost said – we will have to find a way!

A possible solution to the impasse had been suggested later that afternoon. "Well, perhaps there might be a way, Barbara, and it is only a suggestion mind. If you have a word with Mrs Wills sometime, she may be prepared to take you up to the room when there is no one about. Perhaps mid-morning time when you have a free period, but please, you must not let anybody know and please try not to let anybody see you. The next time I see her, I will warn her that you will be asking." Barbara's smile said it all. Once she has decided on something and her mind is made up, her resolve is firm. There is no doubt that within the next few weeks, there will be a clandestine visit to the Lonsdale dormitory by a day girl, assuming Mrs Wills is sufficiently obliging. With our redoubtable laundry heroine being quite taken with the Ian and Barbara 'match' ["You know, Ian, you two do look made for each other – it's lovely!"], her agreement to such a request will, more than likely, be forthcoming. "Made for each other" – a few people have said the very same thing – including Rhoda Coates, one of the kitchen stalwarts! How reassuring! When that feedback had recently been given to Barbara, she had given a shy smile and just replied, "I know." (Accompanied by the mandatory scrunch of her nose and shoulders...)

One afternoon earlier in this half-term week, once she had been gently dropped onto the bed after being carried into the bedroom from the kitchen, Barbara had then got up off the bed and gazed for a few moments into the mirror. She adjusted herself to stand straight, before turning away from the mirror with her body, whilst looking back around with her head. Her face had been contemplative, the slightest of frowns creasing her full forehead. "Now tell me the truth, Ianey. Please tell me truthfully, won't you? Don't just tell me what you think I might want to hear." Her face displayed a pensive, slightly hesitant countenance. "Have I got a big bum? Thirty-six inches around my hips remember. Please be honest," she had pleaded in a rare moment of serious reflection, looking keenly at her bottom. A bottom which was very nicely rounded from the contour of her brown jeans, which fitted tightly onto her seventeen-year-old frame. By asking, Barbara perhaps displayed a slight element of insecurity and was yearning, even hoping, for a reply in the negative. (But – a boyfriend had to tell the truth...) The jeans had clearly been painstakingly ironed and hung clean and straight, hugging her shapely legs down to her bright red socks. With a big red heart across the right-hand cheek, they fitted her perfectly and helped to display her well-proportioned elegant figure. It had been quite easy to provide a genuine reply confirming that she quite definitely did not have a big bum. It was neither too big, but nor was it horribly small. In fact, it was just about right. Was that, though, the answer from someone who is unashamedly biased? Most probably! No matter, the answer had pleased Barbara. She was, perhaps, merely seeking the satisfaction of getting appropriate confirmation, albeit she had added a little rider, "I think you might be a little biased." (A little?)

The discussion had, however, then been taken one step further, albeit with tongue firmly in cheek, by a rather hopeful boyfriend. (Hope springs eternal remember – Confucius again – unless you ask for something, you won't get it.) "Perhaps it would be easier to decide if you took your trousers off, Barbi." After the very slightest of pauses, Barbara had laughed briefly, "Now that is being rude – don't be naughty!" But, nevertheless, those hazel eyes had danced with excitement. She realises, of course, that she is being admired by a boyfriend all but spellbound by her beauty.

It was not without ample justification that late one afternoon during this holiday, Barbara's mother had stood by the sliding kitchen door and shaking her head slightly in wonderment had said, "Goodness me, you two are just like two peas in a pod!" But it wasn't only baking and the preparation of meals that had given Barbara's mother a respite from the on-going household tasks. She had found, rather to her surprise perhaps, that her daughter's boyfriend was a very willing and enthusiastic helper for looking after the open coal fire. A coal fire – how magical and so alive! The lessons on how to light a fire and how to clean it out the following morning had been provided by a jovial and portly grandmother during half-term breaks from those early days of boarding school. Travelling long distances abroad for a half-term lasting a mere week could not be justified. So half-terms were spent with a grandmother, who always made sure her grandson 'pulled his weight' during the time spent at her house in Galgate, a few miles south of Lancaster. Looking after the open fire was a key task allocated and one that was taken up enthusiastically (and always far more interesting than passing wet clothing, sheets and towels, etc. through the mangle in the outhouse). Cleaning out and lighting a fire, chopping up firewood in the outhouse, filling the coal-hod – these were in no way onerous but, in fact, hugely enjoyable. Strangely perhaps, at least for a young teenager, there was also some satisfaction in actually being a help to an elderly grandmother just as, over this half-term week, the same enjoyment has been felt assisting a girlfriend's mother.

[An aside: life with Nanny Parky. There has always been an attraction indeed in the flames and in the red-hot whiteness of the fire. It is constantly changing and in need of attention. What a super crackling sound ensues on putting another shovel full of coal onto a well-established fire. Watching the flames flicker holds such a fascination. With a roaring fire, it can at times appear as though the flare from the burning coal is somehow divorced from the fire itself – intriguing, spellbinding. There were always a few 'ground rules' given to a young teenager during those visits to Galgate. No firelighters to be used. The fire had to be started with just newspaper and kindling before the coal was added in stages. Using firelighters was "cheating" (and only held in reserve as a last resort) and if the skill of lighting the fire was learned correctly, there would be no need for them. "I really have no time for these new-fangled ideas," said a splendidly old-fashioned grandmother! And the other ground rules? One shouldn't be over generous with the coal ("it cost a lot of money") and the following morning, "always check that the embers have gone cold, and you can leave some of the cinders in the fire but get rid of all those that have turned white." Good old Nanny Parkinson – and thank you! Your teaching has now come in most useful for looking after a coal fire at Low Bentham. (And it must, surely, add to any admiration that a girlfriend's mother has for her daughter's choice of boyfriend.)

Not only that but, looking back a mere six years, there is already a nostalgia for those half-term visits to 'Nanny P' (as she is known within the family circle). They would always include feeding the hens in an adjoining back garden, waiting expectantly for the daily visit from the ice cream van, the arrival of which would be preceded by the instantly recognisable ice cream jingle tune (always after tea-time!) and regular dinners of mince surrounded by rice. Whatever the main dish might be, it would invariably be surrounded by rice. Staying with Nanny P has, over the years, always been a pleasure – providing one did not mind her singing:

> *I could have danced all night,*
> *I could have danced all night,*
> *And still have begged for more.*
> *I could have done a thousand things,*
> *I could have spread my wings...*

...and continuing with (sooner or later during the singing):

> *After the ball is over,*
> *Molly takes out her glass eye...*

or something to that effect. (Was it Molly? Was it a glass eye? Was it, perhaps, the Nanny Parkinson version of a song?) And then occasionally, a complete change of mood with:

> *Was my dreaming all in vain?*
> *Will my love come back again...?*

And somewhere later in the performance:

> *Youth and only youth can steal my heart...*

All this whilst she would be making the meals, baking her own particular 'brand' of Lancashire Parkin, or whilst generally busying herself around the house. Is it, one wonders, just the older generation who feel the need or the urge to be continually busy around the house? And then, by the early evening, the jobs all but completed, Nanny P would be in her element sitting in front of the coal fire (a fire under the close supervision of her grandson, of course), being entertained by Charlie Drake or Alfie Bass with their comedy serials on television, checking that petty crime was under control at Dock Green or else being kept up to date with what was happening in the world of Ena Sharples and Minnie Caldwell, those permanent residents of the Rovers Return public house. (Not even the heroic return of Gypsy Moth IV could justify changing channels from Granada TV at Coronation Street time!)

If not watching television, then the early evenings would always be a good time for her to tell the teenage "twins" various scary stories from days gone by in and around the locality. Nothing as spooky, perhaps, as the tale of the infamous Dr Ruxton, who murdered his wife and maid in Lancaster during the 1930s. Not only that, but he cut up the two bodies, scattering the various parts in rivers and ravines in Scotland. For such wickedness, he was subsequently hanged. (Wrapping the many body parts in the local paper, The Lancaster Guardian, was not a very sensible idea...) Thereafter, whenever in Lancaster with Nanny P, there was a morbid fascination with – and the inevitable need to be shown – the doctor's house in Dalton Square. But, once shown, for teenage twins the horror of the story meant that it was all rather too frightening, which meant running past that Georgian house in the square as quickly as possible. As Barbara was to comment on hearing such a tale during this half-term, "Scary biscuits!"

The occasional shopping trips were also made for Nanny P within the confines of Galgate village and with items such as 'Elbow Grease' and a 'Glass Hammer' on the shopping list, it was a non-too surprised shopkeeper who imparted the news that "the twins" had been led up the garden path. That same shopkeeper also knew instantly that the youngsters in front of him had most likely been sent from No. 25 Vernon Park! Sent on a 'fool's errand'. Thank you, Nanny P. Well-travelled the youngsters may have been, but they were still quite gullible with everyday life. Well-travelled indeed – but young and impressionable.

And then, once the stories were over and the television switched off, bedtime was heralded with the filling of hot water bottles, the fire guard being put in place (after, if possible, putting a last lot of coal on the fire – if Nanny P wasn't looking – as it was always interesting to see if there would still be a few red embers glowing in the grate come the following morning) and a nightcap – usually Horlicks or Ovaltine. (But hot Bovril was also available – oh dear! Nearly as bad as Marmite, which a brother worshiped and duly plastered in layers on his toast. To a brother, Keith, then, a deserved accolade – the undisputed Marmite King!) And then, on opening the lounge door to go upstairs to bed ("okay, let's go up the wooden hill to Bedfordshire"), one was welcomed on the staircase by an icy draught, the house being totally devoid of any upstairs heating. Temperature wise, the bedrooms were freezing cold and visual evidence of the temperature was often confirmed in the winter months by the sight of ice having formed on the surrounds of the bedroom window. Getting up in the morning was never easy in the cold surrounds. A twin sister's solution was to invariably resort to getting dressed whilst still under the warm protection of bed sheets. Ah, Nanny P. Such memories! A product of the early Edwardian era, just after the turn of the century. You might be so terribly old-fashioned, but no less likeable for all that.

Inside, within the psyche, there is now an irresistible compulsion to visit Galgate at some time, hopefully in the near future, and to take along a new girlfriend to meet Nanny P. In effect, to show off this young lady from Low Bentham. Grandmothers are perhaps traditionally hard to please. Nonetheless, she will surely be suitably impressed by Barbara's demeanour and personality, particularly as she seems to possess a soft spot within her portly frame for her grandson here at boarding school.]

So, the open fire at *'Benwick'* has been religiously cleaned every morning and then set ready for lighting later in the day. For that, Barbara's mother has been most grateful although statistically, there will be little doubt that the coal consumption for this half-term period will have seen an increase, with the fire probably being lit earlier than it normally would be and with the fire regularly and generously being poked about with and kept topped up with coal. (Something she seemed to accept, albeit stoically!) Playing with the fire, with the assistance of a poker merely for the pleasure of 'playing' with the fire, certainly eats into a supply of coal, but it has an unending and magical fascination. (Didn't an exasperated mother declare at times that her youngest son was "obsessed by fire" – a belief she had, perhaps, understandably formed when, as a five-year-old, that youngest son had set fire to the curtains in Singapore with, it should be added, the kind help of a maid who generously provided a box of matches when requested! Perhaps the term 'maid' is too English for a servant in Singapore. The local word in that Far Eastern outpost, at least in the 1950s, was an 'ayah'. The assistance of the 'ayah' was not required, however, when a school cap was thrown onto an open fire – merely to watch it burn. The noun 'pyromaniac', suggested by a twin sister, is perhaps a suitable, if uncomplimentary, description for her brother!)

As well as the enjoyment of an open fire – preparing it, lighting it and keeping it well stocked up with coal etc. – and the delight of baking and cooking with Barbara, another hugely enjoyable pastime has emerged over half-term which has been made possible by spending a large part of the day under the same roof with a girlfriend. How might one describe it? Mutual grooming would be possibly the most appropriate term. Isn't mutual grooming a term used to describe monkeys at a zoo, where they spend time looking after their partner's well-being? Can the same terminology be used for humans? Why not? For now, at least, whilst at *'Benwick'* the answer is yes. What is good enough for monkeys is surely good enough for humans…

Barbara's mother had looked on with some fascination and, indeed, with some admiration, whilst her dad had, perhaps, watched with some puzzlement as Barbara's straight, shoulder-length, hair was brushed and combed by a boyfriend, the favour then being returned whilst the television was being watched in the evening. At other times whilst watching television, Barbara would roll up her trousers or jeans to the knee so that her *Desert Flower* body lotion could be applied to the lower part of her legs. Then her toes/feet would be given a manicure. To begin with, a pumice stone would be used to smooth out the underside of her feet (and what pretty, well-formed toes you do have Barbara!) before the anticipated, "You choose what colour nail varnish you want to put on my toes, Ianey," from Barbara, whilst sitting astride the settee with her graceful legs freshly creamed and at the same time, handing over her nail varnish set and varnish remover. Putting nail varnish on her toes has become an art form in itself, with Barbara always having a careful check on how professionally it had been applied. (After all, her boyfriend is not exactly a skilled veteran at applying varnish to a lady's toenails.) In a sometime scurrilous manner, she would suggest that an odd nail or two be re-done to a more exacting standard – but only, one soon realised, so that she could continue to be pampered! ("It is so much more relaxing having it done by you, Ianey!")

In exchange for a general pampering session with her legs and toes, Barbara willingly repaid the favour, being generous with scratches on her boyfriend's arms, legs and back! Receiving scratches is incredibly soothing and satisfying, most probably made more so by having dry skin – strangely, far more satisfying when being given them than when scratching one's own skin. After a regular bout of scratching arms, legs and back one evening, Barbara had exclaimed, "Ianey, are you covered in freckles *all* over?" Well, that would, indeed, be telling! "You even have some freckles on your back that are black. I am going to give all those that are black a kiss from Barbi" – what heaven! Meanwhile, Barbara's dad would sit studiously watching television, trying his best to ignore the various treats that his daughter and her boyfriend were lavishing on each other. Clearly though, he was undoubtedly both puzzled and perplexed by the regular early evening grooming sessions. With a mother, it gave even more credence to her "two peas in a pod" jibe and perhaps she has also started to concur with the view within the school that her daughter and boyfriend are "made for each other".

During the daytime, this mutual grooming has seamlessly extended to mutual washing and drying of hair. As might be imagined, dealing with Barbara's shoulder-length hair is a more complex operation. Plenty of knots to be combed out whilst using the hairdryer, to the accompaniment of occasional squeals from Barbara when a knot proved particularly difficult to untangle. Washing Barbara's hair with her leant over the bath also provided an occasional and welcome glimpse of her bra. Even with her blouse tucked in at the neck, keeping it tight and in place was not always possible, particularly so if she got a bit of shampoo in her eye and turned her head sharply to wipe her eye on the towel she was resting on. At times, the collar of her blouse would work loose naturally and, with Barbara bent over the bath with her arms in the bath supporting herself, it was natural to volunteer to tuck the collar back inside her blouse, sometimes doing it automatically without asking. Barbara, being quite comfortable with the situation would confirm acceptance. "Okay, thank you, love". This invariably meant that a view, albeit a brief one, was provided of her bra. It was fun to then comment sometime later in the day about what colour bra she was wearing. This would bring an immediate retort, "You little monkey, how do you know that?" Nevertheless, the laughter in her face gave notice that she took it in her stride and in fact, thought it rather exciting. (It most certainly is for her boyfriend!)

Shaving Barbara's legs below the knee ("I will let you help me if you wish, Ianey") has also been part of this mutual grooming. ("I like to have my legs nice and smooth to the touch, Ianey.") To begin with, the task meant using some hair removal cream and a spatula in her bedroom. Within a couple of days, Barbara had enthusiastically accepted the suggestion made to her by a boyfriend that a razor (with hot soapy water) would be an easier and more efficient exercise. Cue for regular afternoon sessions in the bathroom, with Barbara happily sat on the edge of the bath wearing a short skirt with her feet in the hot water, her boyfriend soaping and shaving her lovely legs – and lovely legs indeed they are! There is almost an uncontrollable urge to continue the shaving operation above her knees – but, whilst hairs grow on her lower legs (below the knee), her thighs appear free of any hair growth. In any case, how far would one dare to go, never mind the question of how far would one be allowed to go? Dare one go above the knee? Jesus!

Once Barbara's legs were lovely and smooth (and creamed), as a way of repaying the favour, Barbara would always suggest with some eagerness, "Right Ianey, would you like me to shave your face? I will be extra careful, I promise," and indeed she was. It was, and will be in the future, impossible to refuse such a request. Not only that, but it will be disappointing if such an offer is not made regularly in the future. Shaving legs and a chin now form an integral part of the successful and enjoyable grooming sessions at *'Benwick'*.

It would be something of an understatement to suggest that this grooming, being provided by both sides of this relationship, is extremely effective as a bonding exercise. Not only that, but (whisper it so quietly in this bed and breakfast room) it whets the sexual appetite which, for an adolescent male and, perhaps, also for a seventeen-year-old female, is becoming nigh impossible to resist. The sexual desire is becoming ever stronger and more difficult to hold back. Rather like, if a comparison can be made, waking up in the night and needing a pee. It is warm in the bed – it might well be cold once out of bed – and whilst the desire is to stay warm, there will be no getting back to sleep until one has had that pee. However, once the pee, so desperately needed, has been done – what a relief! Then it is possible to get back to sleep. This sexual urge – is it rather like that? Can it be held in check? Can Barbara be told? How did Betjeman term it? – *'Oh, would I could subdue the flesh, which sadly troubles me'* – one might suggest 'gladly troubles me' regarding this girlfriend!

It was whilst shaving Barbara's legs one afternoon (and she wants them looked after, shaved, daily – she enjoys being pampered – and who's complaining?) that she had casually said, "Are we very much alike do you think, Ianey?" but without waiting for any answer or acknowledgement, she continued, "Well I honestly think we are because we enjoy doing the same things and we always seem to agree." But really, Barbara? There is not the slightest hint of melancholy in your nature – only joy waiting to burst out when called upon. A kindly and easy-going disposition. You might well have a temper, young lady, but if so, it is buried deep within, and it does not seem to want to surface. Hopefully, it will have no need to. At least, that is, not with this boyfriend. Ah, Barbara! Most certainly two peas in a pod and with visual evidence regularly provided, Mrs Noble perhaps summed the situation up accurately one afternoon. "A secure relationship is all about give and take," she had said, before continuing, "but as far as I can see, you are both always giving."

Another aspect of spending a good deal of time at *'Benwick'* over this half-term break has been linked to music. Yes, music of all things. Music! Whilst there has not been (and it is unlikely there will be) any sort of 'sea-change' in musical appreciation, with Led Zeppelin, Neil Young, Cat Stevens and Focus well to the fore in the school dormitory, Barbara's mother has, perhaps, rather inadvertently passed on an inkling for an appreciation of classical music. Yes!

Classical music. Not something that had been listened to or indeed, even heard whilst growing up at home. It was a home that was, by and large, devoid of any type of music – apart from Tchaikovsky's 1812 Overture, an odd opera or two by Puccini and that regular favourite, 'Midsummer Night Vigil' by "whoever"! The sole foray into classical music over the past six years has been on Wednesday at boarding school, when the morning assembly provides the usual short 'culture' interlude with Mr Lethbridge playing a classical piece. Predictably, of course, largely wasted on a collection of uninterested schoolchildren whose thoughts are invariably elsewhere. Watching *Face The Music,* introduced by Joseph Cooper on television, with Barbara's mum and dad was perhaps the catalyst. The modicum of interest thereby created has enabled an appreciation of, and a sympathetic ear being given to, Beethoven's 1st Piano Concerto, which Barbara's mother has played, generally during her ironing sessions! Also, Dvorak's 9th Symphony, which Barbara's mother freely admitted had been introduced to her via the advert on television for *Hovis* bread – really? And as her mother also pointed out when Barbara had suggested, "Ian, why not stay here to watch the *The Onedin Line* before going back to *'Brentwood'*?", the introductory music to that series is classical – from, in fact, the *Adagio of Spartacus and Phrygia* by Khachaturian. She is, no doubt, correct in that assertion, but in the context of a television series, the music does not have the classical 'feel'! How strange.

Can musical taste successfully straddle classical music and pop music?

A valid question when the divergence between Led Zeppelin and Beethoven is seemingly vast. Can that chasm be bridged? It seems unlikely. And the momentous question that remains unanswered – and a question that will not be answered for some considerable time. Will classical music outlive the emergence of 'pop' music (which incorporates 'rock')? A father, often fond of ensuring than an argument, once begun, should always be won as a point of principal, has firmly maintained that the modern trend of pop culture (and the sound that goes with it) will, in his words, "fizzle out" over a period of years. Of course, he studiously fails to forecast the number of years, but nevertheless, strongly asserts that classical music will remain unchallenged! Time will tell. As with all things to do with one's parents, it would be most satisfying to see him proved wrong.

Whilst, however, classical music is unlikely to make its way into the dormitory, it might help with an appreciation of the weekly Wednesday morning foray into classical music at assembly time, even if the fact is not admitted within the confines of Lonsdale dormitory complex. Well, perhaps it might, but listening to music within the homely atmosphere of *'Benwick'* with a girlfriend and her parents certainly enables the mind to be more broadened. Notwithstanding the seemingly huge abyss between the two different strands of music, classical and pop (or perhaps rock, to be precise), there is also a gap to be tackled (or perhaps accepted with good grace) with a girlfriend! Barbara is fond of The Carpenters, Gilbert O'Sullivan, David Cassidy and suchlike, a world away from Focus and their instrumental expertise – with some marvellous yodelling from Thijs van Leer – what a hero! – and Led Zeppelin, almost essential listening whilst ploughing through homework. Perhaps the key is a mutual tolerance of quite different tastes, albeit that harmony is achieved with the music of Cat Stevens. Just perhaps, Barbara can, as The Carpenters have suggested, *'make a dream come true'*!

The listening during this half-term has also extended to the radio, with *Your Hundred Best Tunes* last Sunday evening hosted by Alan Keith. On the subject of radio, a recent half hour was also enjoyed listening to a new comedy, *I'm Sorry I Haven't a Clue*, on Radio Four which included some weird and wonderful sketches, although what some of them were all about, no one seemed to be quite certain. The Mornington Crescent sketch specifically seemed to have no rhyme or reason, with the rules being that (according to the compare Humphrey Lyttleton), "there are no rules"! Scatty, for sure, but so funny, nevertheless. More entertaining than the television comedy, *Monty Python's Flying Circus,* which has been broadcast over the last few years and, according to Barbara, has always left her mum and dad (and indeed herself) singularly unimpressed. Something else clearly where there is a meeting of minds between boyfriend and girlfriend. Humour – it is a strange medium and perhaps just as well, therefore, when tastes harmonize.

Cooking, baking, cleaning out and lighting the fire, music, mutual grooming and, of course, window cleaning. Another task that has been learnt via the good offices of Nanny P and put to good use at *'Benwick'* for Barbara's mother. There is a lot to be said for staying in a family home, however enjoyable the boarding house might be. And at the very least, by utilising the Head Boarder to clean the windows (Barbara's mother will confirm that he volunteered himself for the task – no arm-twisting required!), there is the saving of the cost of a window cleaner. A saving that will most certainly be just as welcome as the Noble cost-saving measure of squeezing the remnants of an old soap onto a new bar of soap, so as not to waste any. It certainly sets an exemplary example in frugality – on a par, perhaps, with one's own parents! (Will a girlfriend, perhaps, have inherited that trait?) With the windows, Mrs Noble's daughter's boyfriend gets right into the corners and cleans the wooden surrounds. (As, indeed, he was taught to do by Nanny P.) And strangely, there is immense satisfaction in seeing all the windows clean and 'ship shape'. Mrs Wills, in the boarding house, would no doubt be impressed by the Head Boarder's window cleaning skills, but not necessarily surprised.

CHAPTER XXIII

SHE WILL CALL A SPADE A BLOODY SPADE

Several dry days during this holiday break provided the opportunity for walks out, the 'square mile' having become a firm favourite, together with shopping trips (for mum – Mrs Noble) to High Bentham. The outward journey invariably via the river walk all the way to Bentham, the return journey by the road. With a more relaxed timescale (not, of course, having to get back to school at a specified time, or for a particular purpose), a suggestion was made that it was, perhaps, time to meet Barbara's extended family. To phrase it bluntly – to show off a boyfriend from the boarding house. With Barbara's close family all encompassed within a few miles of *'Benwick'*, it was logical and appropriate – and by all accounts, they were actually wanting to meet this boyfriend. (Who has, apparently, been described by Barbara's mother as a "very pleasant, helpful young man"!) Perhaps, more importantly, it was giving notice that this Head Boarder was becoming, or indeed has become, a semi-permanent fixture.

Barbara's relatives are all within shouting distance. Altogether different from living a considerable distance (which quite often involved being oversees) from aunties, uncles and cousins. Meeting them, more often than not, involved an odd visit every two or three years, generally before a father commenced a posting overseas, or upon a return to the UK after a spell abroad. Whenever a visit 'up north' was made, it invariably involved the predictable few nights at the Lothersdale Hotel situated on Morecambe promenade. For youngsters, this meant that it was the 1d arcade amusements just along from the hotel that gained the attention, rather than the formal visits to relations – although the visits to relations would always provide a gift of a florin or even better, a half-crown. This, of course, would ensure that further visits could be made to the 1d arcades – what else was there to do within the confines of a seafront hotel in the evening? Extended family gatherings were never, therefore, a feature or a normal part of growing up. Quite the reverse for Barbara, with almost a full complement of relatives living, as Barbara terms it, "on my doorstep."

So it was that a deviation was made on the 'square mile' walk one morning so that, instead of turning right at the crossroads on the Burton-in-Lonsdale Road to head towards High Bentham, the road was followed directly ahead and into Burton village. "My auntie Hilda and uncle Jim might appear to be a little old fashioned", Barbara had commented at the top of the road that descends steeply into Burton village. Rather ominous. On reaching the village, a rather small, dainty hump-back bridge takes the road over the River Greta which, in a similar vein to the River Wenning, rises on the slopes of Ingleborough and flows westwards, eventually meeting the River Lune.

The rather cramped and old-fashioned *'Riverside Cottage'* (nestling by a small stream at the extreme east of the village – the stream running into the Greta) was welcoming enough, but perhaps Barbara had slightly played down her comment on auntie and uncle appearing old fashioned. Somewhat of an understatement indeed! It was easy to understand why she had felt it so necessary to make the comment. The inside of the cottage was most certainly retro 1950s, both furniture and décor providing an austere look and feel, perhaps almost dour by design. However, whilst it would be unkind to suggest that it suited the character and attitude of the occupants, it almost seemed to! A cottage crying out for renewal and needing to be transformed from its wartime austerity, both in look and décor, the occupants requiring a similar transformation. Just perhaps, any attempt at modernisation would not suit or indeed satisfy its residents. Barbara's auntie and uncle fitted almost seamlessly into the period piece that their house seems to represent.

One might almost suppose that they enjoy the visual austerity that both house and occupants project and would not want it, or themselves, altered or changed. A pleasant enough first meeting it had been, but slightly formal and rather rigid, perhaps confirming that Barbara (and her boyfriend) will have little obvious common ground with one of her mother's sisters and brother-in-law. An obvious age difference, yes, between the residents and the two visitors, but more than that, a wholly different outlook. One providing optimism and enjoyment with life, the other seeming to offer scant enthusiasm for living, accompanied by a generally gloomy slant on life. As an obvious antidote to auntie and uncle, Barbara's two cousins, Linda and Diane, both younger than Barbara (but not that much younger) seem to be determined to break away from their parents' mould, being enthusiastic and chatty. Perhaps they appreciate that, as bubbly teenagers, their mum and dad are quite clearly stuck in a different time zone and are unable and, more than that, patently unwilling to escape from it. They give some credence to the view (Sociology study again…) that parents and their children are generally looking through the opposite ends of a telescope. For Linda and Diane, not a difficult mantra to achieve and for them, everything is magnified.

Siblings can be so dissimilar and contrasting in character. It was all so very different several days earlier when, whilst in High Bentham on a shopping trip for mum (that is, Barbara's mother, who is now more than happy to be addressed as mum by her daughter's boyfriend. It sounds more natural than calling her Mrs Noble – far too formal – whilst Grace, her forename, is perhaps rather presumptuous and doesn't reflect the obvious age difference), a visit was made to *'Pye Park'*, situated at the eastern end of the village. A private drive, which comes off the road that heads towards the nearby moors and eventually Clapham village, leads to *'Pye Park'*, a large semi-detached bungalow. From the lounge at the back of the property, a pair of large sliding glass doors provide a panoramic view of the countryside and the moors rising to the south of High Bentham village, whilst the kitchen, at the front of the bungalow, provides a suitable vista of what is happening towards the eastern edge of the village. Down in a dip or a hollow between bungalow and the moors, the 'Skipton – Lancaster' railway line runs along the valley bottom, sharing it with the River Wenning, the occasional sound of a train being heard but not seen.

Auntie Edith and Uncle Frank are engaging in manner and speech. Auntie Edith, in particular, displayed considerable enthusiasm for meeting (and assessing, no doubt) her niece's boyfriend. Rather small and wiry, she more than compensated by being engagingly fussy and was an accomplished and interesting talker. She seems to possess a knack of talking or listening keenly, whilst at the same time progressing several household chores within a large and well organised (and tidy) kitchen. This enabled her to delve fully and with genuine interest into her niece's boyfriend's background, whilst at the same time, regularly stirring a huge pan of homemade vegetable soup (which was, by all accounts, going to be frozen in individual portions), whilst also kneading a large piece of bread dough. By the time the visit was ending, the dough had made its way onto the top of an impressive and rather handsome Aga range – which would, no doubt, have quite suited Barbara's bum if she had possessed the nerve to hoist herself onto it before the bread dough beat her to it.

Barbara had suggested that she herself would not have been at all surprised if the weekly washing hadn't also been on the go during the visit. Auntie Edith is clearly adept at dealing with numerous tasks and jobs simultaneously, whilst progressing an almost continuous conversation. Marvellous! Her auntie and uncle were at one time the proprietors of High Bentham fish and chip shop. Barbara had always thought that it was most likely the cleanest 'chippie' in the country receiving, as it did, a comprehensive clean every morning from her auntie, who would be up and about before the rest of Bentham had even thought of waking up. A generous supply of potatoes would almost certainly be peeled and cleaned and ready for 'chipping' well before breakfast, the task being completed whilst Uncle Frank was making the daily early morning drive to Fleetwood on the Lancashire coast for fish, freshly landed every morning.

Were they the best fish and chips in Yorkshire? Barbara couldn't be sure, but they were definitely the cheapest (being provided free of charge to a niece)! A mother, wise to the regular requests from a daughter wanting to visit a cousin at the Bentham 'chippie', necessarily regulated such visits.

Their son Neil, a year younger than Barbara and already known from school, is a competent goalkeeper. Outwardly, he waits patiently (inwardly, perhaps not…) and quite stoically for the opportunity to play in goal for the school First XI football team. There will surely be some frustration with the waiting, particularly as he knows full well that his time will only come at the commencement of the next school year when the Head Boarder will have left (that is, barring any injuries or illness before then). For the time being, the football practice he gets at a formal level continues to be between the sticks for the school Under 16 XI side, with a defence not nearly as competent as the one protecting this First XI goalkeeper. His time will come. As Nanny P has always advised during numerous visits, "patience is a virtue." But at 15 years of age does one possess it?

So, by necessity, a rather enjoyable chat had taken place in the kitchen at *'Pye Park'*, fronting the bungalow and conveniently providing plenty of scope for Auntie Edith to keep an eye on any developments at her end of the village from that large kitchen window. It is something that Barbara suggests her auntie enjoys doing on a daily basis. For Auntie Edith, a simple line from one of John Betjeman's poems is quite appropriate, *'Even the trivial seems profound'*, and in village life, it will no doubt often seem to be the case.

A visit also to *'Westward View'*, a large three-storey end terrace property, next to High Bentham primary school and the home of Barbara's maternal grandmother. Nanny Jenkinson is a widow and now in her late seventies. She has five daughters, one of whom emigrated with husband to New Zealand some considerable time ago, leaving four daughters all encompassed within a radius of five miles: Auntie Hilda in Burton-in-Lonsdale, Grace (mum) in Low Bentham, Auntie Edith in High Bentham and lastly, Auntie Freda with husband Jim living on the top floor of *'Westward View'*, with its own entry and exit independent from Nanny Jenkinson on the ground floor. Pity, perhaps, Barbara's late grandfather negotiating his way through life with a wife and five daughters. (Particularly when a son might well have been a natural successor for father's joinery business.) Auntie Freda, the youngest of the five daughters, straightforward and plain speaking, with husband Jim very much in the same mould (whilst sitting back in his favourite chair puffing away constantly at his pipe, with its attendant smoke drifting lazily and in peculiar patterns towards the ceiling). A persona rather harsh and 'down to earth', perhaps, when compared to her sisters. Plain speaking. Would some term it blunt? They might. This most Yorkshire of these four sisters would not be afraid, one senses, to call a spade a "bloody spade" – and if you took exception, so be it. But for all that, a genuine welcome for her niece's boyfriend.

On the ground floor of *'Westward View'*, Nanny Jenkinson potters about spending a large part of her time (Barbara confirms) in her homely kitchen, singing away to herself whilst she cooks and bakes, her wispy white hair neatly tied back. The gentle humming and singing in her kitchen, however, Barbara suggests, is based on a selection of religious songs from *Hymns Ancient and Modern*, rather than from the West End musicals heard in a maternal grandmother's house in Galgate. Quietly spoken and with her face showing the lines that old age brings, Nanny Jenkinson listened attentively to a granddaughter and her boyfriend, whilst no doubt realising that the present day is something that she cannot get overly enthused about, let alone understand. She did, however, make a boyfriend – hitherto unknown – most welcome in her cosy, albeit old-fashioned, kitchen. Rather poignant was her outhouse around the back, still very much giving the impression of a joinery workshop, with various tools all in their place as if expectant and waiting to be used again. Sadly, they never will be. At least, not whilst laid out in proper formation at *'Westward View'*. Barbara's grandfather died the best part of a decade ago.

Of Barbara's relatives on her father's side, it was inevitable that there would be a meeting with her Uncle Bill and Auntie Joan, if only because their tiny ancient-looking cottage, *'Farmstead'*, is squeezed or squashed somehow in the midst of Bentham High Street and adjoins Ronnie Fleming's butcher's shop. (A required calling point linked to mum's shopping list – New Zealand lamb being on the list – and a joint big enough for five people, rather than four. "Remember to tell Ronnie it is for five people, Barbara!" A boyfriend now gets included...) So it was that Barbara had knocked briefly on the door of *'Farmstead'* and then walked straight in (something that visitors are, Barbara stressed, encouraged to do) with her boyfriend in tow. From the outside, the cottage appeared to have been designed without the advantage of a spirit level – the interior appeared much the same, if not more so! The wobbly lines of the walls, together with a seemingly visual instability, nicely matched the woeful efforts of the Head Boarder in woodwork and technical drawing all those years ago.

Uncle Bill – older than Barbara's dad, but quite definitely not as traditional. He grows his hair long, is tall and heavily built, sports a rather casual beard (what a hero he would be in the boarding house!) and seems to have a totally relaxed and carefree attitude. Almost, it seems, too casual, so that one could imagine him being not too fussed about meeting deadlines. If dinner was ready for 5pm, well, he might turn up at 6pm, having perhaps half-forgotten about the time. Would Auntie Joan be bothered? Most likely not. Nevertheless, he is engaging with it, and easy to chat to, as is Auntie Joan. An interest in folk music certainly, with musical instruments scattered liberally about the main room including, improbably, a jug (a large one!), requiring – Bill studiously advises – considerable skill and puff if it is to be "played" correctly. Also, an accordion abandoned on a chair which is, apparently, Auntie Joan's province. They play in a local band – country and western music predominantly, with one of the other members of the ensemble being Kevin Downham from the Lower 6th.

Another example of siblings being like chalk and cheese. Apart from a facial similarity, it might be thought highly improbable, even impossible, that Barbara's dad and her Uncle Bill are indeed brothers. Chalk and cheese – crass terminology certainly, but nevertheless quite appropriate.

Visiting a girlfriend's immediate family – the Jenkinson daughters and the one Noble – has given a feel of some permanence to this relationship, akin to being given a vote of confidence by a girlfriend. Enjoyable? Yes. Hopefully for those who were visited, as much as it was for the visitor. Particularly enjoyable was the easy-going chat and acceptance up at *'Pye Park'*. Continual talking can be tiring certainly, but with Auntie Edith it wasn't. It was easy and engaging. She could most probably talk forever. Now, at least, the intrigue initiated by near relatives, once they became aware that a niece had acquired a boyfriend from the boarding house, will be somewhat allayed.

(Note for diary: suggest another visit with girlfriend when the plums are ready for picking on the *'Pye Park'* plum tree…)

'Brentwood' – at this late hour, outside is now total darkness – pitch black. But still, the noise of the river with its continual crashing sound as swiftly flowing water heads westwards. Auden once wrote, *'and the deep river ran on'* (From his poem, 'As I Walked Out One Evening.') This river, the Wenning, perhaps not too deep – but nevertheless, ever present and thought provoking. And a continual flow of water – never ending. Mildly hypnotic and relaxing.

What a remarkable half-term, albeit that revising has ultimately taken a back seat. Get the Collins dictionary out – an obsession. The dictionary describes it as 'a persistent preoccupation, idea or feeling' – an obsession with Barbara, there most certainly is. Is it healthy? Whether it is or not, it is certainly a feeling that is being reciprocated and it shows no sign of dimming on either side. Who was it who once said, "Live the life you were born to live"? Even at this young age, has a life already been carved out for two "peas in the pod"? This half-term is ending. An obsession with Barbara indeed, but no longer an obsession with Durham. How on earth can one even consider a period of three years away from this rural setting, with the delights that are now on offer at *'Benwick'*? It is an issue that will have to be addressed – but not yet.

Another outstanding issue once back at school this coming week – that meeting in the dormitory with Mr Hagen had left a couple of questions to be answered. Or perhaps, rather than wanting answers, the headmaster had been anxious for feedback. "What is your personal view of the poetry meetings, Ian, and do they have a future? Think about that will you and let me know." Mr Hagen had then added as a follow up, "And what about Barbara, have you managed to convert her yet?"

A school poetry group had been organised by Mr Hagen (as part of his campaign to involve more of the pupils in areas of culture and drama) at the start of the autumn term, with meetings every three weeks, taking place on an evening in his house, at the far end of the sports field. It had seemed apposite to join the group. (It was, perhaps, almost obligatory for the 'A' Level English Literature students, although to be fair, the 'A' Level English Literature study has already fostered a real interest in poetry.) Active group participation in the meetings has, prior to the half-term break, reduced to approximately seven or eight hardy souls – except when the poet Adrian Mitchell presented an evening reading his own poetry. This swelled the attendance substantially with, one might suspect, a modicum of press ganging having taken place. (And, horror of horrors, pupils from other schools turning up!) However, just perhaps, therein lies the problem. Modern poetry. Is it what the students who regularly turn up to the meetings really want?

During that evening discussion in the dormitory, Mr Hagen had handed over (rather as a 'thank you' gift for the input and attendance at the poetry meetings) a recently published modern anthology of poetry – *Poetry of The Committed Individual*. Reading it has proved quite demanding and a generous helping of commitment is certainly needed to persist with it. (And that persistence is still required, as the paperback continues to be 'dipped' into on an all too brief 'ad hoc' basis.) Why? Is it because the poetry almost seems horribly, well, 'modern'? Too modern – can that be possible? This is the 'new poetry' then, is it? (Or *'virs libre'*, as Mrs Fife terms it.) Essentially in verse form, but non-rhyming. No rhymes – does that make it easier to draft out? Keats would be aghast. A twentieth-century invention – who started it? T. S. Eliot perhaps – now, everyone is at it (excusable, of course, with Auden…), but Betjeman still holds the line. Even Mrs Fife's charges in the 6th form are at it… Oh dear!

The school rumour mill suggests that our headmaster has, in the past, had some of his own verse published. Is it, one wonders, in the same 'modern' format as this anthology of verse kindly gifted? There is no doubting that we live in a modern age and presumably, poetry must match the age in which it is penned – or should it? Whatever, the poems in the book have not the same resonance for 6th form students (or at the very least, not for this one) as, for example, Wordsworth with his... *'It is a beauteous evening, calm and free'*, or Shelley, with that all-time favourite, 'Ozymandias', *'I met a traveller from an antique land'*, or, indeed, Keats and his 'Ode to a Nightingale', *'My heart aches and a drowsy numbness pains my sense.'*

The 'Romantic' poets are surely the heroes. Modern poets are no match. Goodness, that would be a valid (and intriguing) exam question to answer this coming June. As one advances in years, will that view perhaps change as one becomes more experienced or mature? Is this view currently being expounded perhaps the fault of the 'A' Level curriculum where the only 'modern' poet being studied is W. H. Auden – and even his best poetry is now upwards of fifty years old – or is it linked to a romantic association with a 6th form female? Is it, perhaps, that anything in the 'here and now' (that is, modern) is not appreciated? Will the poems in this anthology handed over by Mr Hagen be popular and studied for school examinations in the future? Who knows? Thank you, sir, but choose a better poetry book as a gift next time – please!

The poetry meetings may, indeed, have a future, but it might be just as likely that they gradually peter out. One of those ideas that is sound in principal but not sustainable without on-going commitment from the participants. Realistically, the meetings are probably only ever going to attract a small nucleus of students (those studying English Literature perhaps). Oh yes, and the other part of his question – has Barbara been converted? Well, yes, she has attended. Not quite an answer. Would she turn up without a 6th form boyfriend, who puts in a regular appearance, giving an opportunity for an evening to be spent together? No. If Mr Hagen is waiting expectantly for a conversion, he would do well to liaise with Revd Bradberry, who waits, oh, so patiently, for the 6th formers to embrace Christianity. [His wait will be as fruitless as trying to discover where Noah's ark was deposited after the flood! Don't even bother...]

The headmaster had talked freely during the poetry discussion about his own student days. With Mr Hagen having studied both English Literature and History to university standard, this perhaps provides for him a kindred involvement with a pupil taking the same two subjects at his grammar school. That meeting had presented the ideal moment, surely, to at last advise the school that a university education was going to be 'binned' in favour of paid employment. The opportunity was not taken. It should have been. How could it be, whilst he talked freely and enthusiastically about university degrees? That it wasn't mentioned perhaps says something about character. The advice that had been given by Cess is still being adhered to. "Why do something now when you can put it off until tomorrow!"

(And yes, that is an exclamation mark – not a question mark. After all, the advice was not given as a question, but more as a firm suggestion.)

The debate over the merits of a university education versus immediate paid employment (although in the subconscious – deep within it – has the decision already been made?) might be aided by the school's organised visit next week, for the 6th formers, to the factory of George Angus & Co, domiciled in High Bentham. Will it be a productive visit regarding employment? Most probably the largest employer in the area, it often seems as though the whole of both High and Low Bentham are employed by the firm. Barbara's dad works there on the maintenance side looking after the machinery. Her aunties and uncles work there – everybody works at Angus Fire Armour, bar none. Allegedly, the firm is the world's largest producer of fire hose, however improbable that might seem. The factory floor holds no interest (those painful years in woodwork lessons are still fresh in the mind), but perhaps any work that is available in the admin. offices might be of interest. The big advantage? Staying within this Wenning valley and all its attendant attractions. A few local voices among the day pupils suggest the factory, being so very local, is somewhat incestuous and that, in any case, one can "do better" than a lifetime at Angus's. There has also been an implied 'you can do better than Angus's for future employment' feeling from both Barbara's parents and, indeed, Barbara herself. Notwithstanding the feedback given in a friendly and positive way, it will be worth a visit.

Something that hasn't been done during this half-term – a visit to the barbers. The instruction from Snot just prior to this holiday break is still fresh in the mind, "Get your hair cut over the half-term, can you, McCart?" He had followed up his request, which was more of a firm instruction rather than a request, with, "and that needs to come off: you know very well that a beard is not allowed." Snot had accompanied his comments with his trademark wry and slightly hollow smile. The on-going saga of growing facial hair (as he likes to term it) is really nothing new. Beards are not permitted here at school, but this is the very reason why several 6th formers grow them. No haircut this half-term, but the beard has been tamed into what might now be termed a 'nearly' beard, following a rather stylish shave thanks to Barbara. The chin has been relieved of hair-growth, but the sideburns have been left long with perhaps a two-inch gap between each sideburn at the bottom of the chin (recalling Barbara's words in that recent letter, *'sideburns, long sideburns...swoon'*), rather like the swashbuckling style from *The Onedin Line* television series. It is almost certain that the school will no doubt be less than happy – and one can perhaps anticipate that an instruction will follow in due course to say that sideburns may only be to the bottom of the ears, or something similar. The fight will go on! It should. It must.

One of the benefits of Sociology study (yes, it does provide a few small 'chinks' of knowledge and other ancillary facts in the pursuit of learning – don't let on to Miss Shirley!) and of reading numerous books of erudite literature is the suggestion gleaned from both that the conventions of the society we live in should not be accepted 'willy-nilly'! Indeed, accepted protocol should be challenged whilst one is at an impressionable age – perhaps about the age that one studies 'A' Levels for instance! What difference does 'sporting' a beard have to the mechanics of studying? For that matter, what difference does a regimented school uniform make? To counter the argument however, this madcap Sociology study also suggests that society, to operate satisfactorily, needs to work within a framework of 'unwritten' rules. That is, rules not laid down by law, but which are adhered to with a mixture of convention and by the fact that doing otherwise would be strictly taboo. Ah, Sociology! Perhaps that explains why this Head Boarder is now the only 6th form student left studying the subject. (The downside? No laughing and joking with colleagues. The upside? One-to-one – teacher and pupil – learning. Is that an upside?)

Long hair and beards, yes, the fight will go on – it must do. Ultimate defeat is, of course, nigh inevitable, but not quite yet. Who amongst the second year 6th formers will be the last man standing? An all too brief moment of glory awaits whoever it might be.

But it is late – this foreign bed beckons – and after tomorrow, the half-term comes to an end and a school dormitory will be 'home' again. Sleep is needed, but the image continuously and subconsciously in the head is Barbara. It will not go away. On the 'square mile' walk during this past week, Barbara, with some confidence, had made a mental note of the location of various blackberry bushes roadside, before announcing confidently, "Right, we will do this walk again, Ianey, in the autumn so that we can pick some blackberries for a pie." Then, on seeing the slightest of frowns on a boyfriend's face accompanied by just two words, "a pie!", she had added, "Okay then, a crumble." The little idiosyncrasies on both sides are becoming evident and suitably catered for. Not only that, but more crucially, a girlfriend clearly has sufficient confidence to predict that she will be walking out with her boyfriend this coming autumn – still eight months away. As well as the walks – the holding of hands, the firm squeezing of entwined fingers, the laughter, the smiles, the constant ebullient chatter and then, sometimes, in contrast, complete silence – with Barbara seemingly at peace with her head having found a boyfriend's shoulder to rest upon. And those eyes gazing silently up, peaceful, saying everything without saying anything and being accompanied by a delicate smile.

It was then that it was a most appropriate and comforting time to, as Keats so eloquently phrased it, *"Feed deep, deep upon her peerless* – hazel, kindly and bewitching – *eyes."* (Apologies, dear Keats, for adding those three additional adjectives to your timeless sentence from 'Ode on Melancholy'!) At seventeen years of age and not officially an adult until this coming September, she is so utterly, utterly radiant. She is, you might say, in full bloom and her face tells all – without her having to utter a word. She is happy and contented.

This inner melancholy belonging exclusively to her boyfriend – surely there is no need for it. Can it be – will it be – kept at bay so that the happiness can be shared? Why does the mind waste such time and energy on fruitless – futile even – thought? Why should this happiness not last? Happiness. Despite all, the thought process is still – how long can it last, how long will it last? Could it possibly last a lifetime?

For God's sake, get to sleep, Ian.

Three 'heavyweights' in discussion:
The new Headmaster, Mr. Hagen (centre).
The Woodwork teacher, Mr. Lonsdale (right)
... complete with trademark flat cap,
and, Mr. Riley (left), teacher of Latin.
(Photograph: J Hebblethwaite)

CHAPTER XXIV

WHERE'S THE BLOODY DEFENCE?

Saturday 31st March – a dry day, but breezy and cold. (Cross that out!) A more accurate description? Hellish windy rather than breezy. Particularly so on the fells to the south of the school, where the moors rise gradually upwards along the northern outpost of the Trough of Bowland, the area coming under the general heading of Tatham Fells. With a biting wind came the cold, despite it now being officially spring but there, at the top of the fells, not a great deal of evidence of spring was to be found on the last day of March.

It had been the day of the school sponsored walk, a circuitous route of approximately 14 miles in the lee and on the top of the surrounding fells. Fourteen miles was manageable with no time limit built in and with the walk fitted in, as it was, to the daylight hours. Barbara did find the going a tad tough particularly on the final stretch but, then again, mutual support enables greater effort to be accomplished. The hot soup, at strategic points where marshals were on hand to ensure the correct course was followed, indeed welcome. More so was the buffet on display and ready to be eaten at *'Benwick'* on completion. Certainly, preferable in content and indeed, in location, compared to the refreshments prepared at school by Titty for the returning hoards. Even more important, rather more privacy was available and was gladly accepted at *'Benwick'*.

No doubt about the most enjoyable part of the day. Sitting on the edge of the bath in the bathroom at *'Benwick'*, with legs dangling into warm water, whilst two respective pairs of feet were washed and bathed and then allowed to gradually thaw out. "Isn't this rather cosy?" Barbara had said with a trademark scrunch of her nose, before adding, "Put your feet on the towel and I will dry them for you. Then you can dry mine and if you like, you can put some cream on my legs to keep them nice and supple." With her jeans rolled up to her knees, she looked as though she might well have perhaps just walked off the set of *The Pirates of Penzance*.

A day spent walking the fells around Tatham had provided the ideal opportunity to finalise the plans regarding the Easter holidays, now only a fortnight away. It had been several weeks earlier that the suggestion had been made to Barbara that perhaps the Easter holidays might be spent with parents in Germany. It would be an extension, so to speak, of the recent half-term break because, similarly to *'Benwick'*, out in Germany parents would be out at work during the day and the house would be a playground. Another chance to play at 'house'.

An agreement to the proposal was readily accepted by Barbara, which just left the task of obtaining consent from her parents. "I think I should ask my mother first", she had sensibly suggested, a reflection perhaps of the close relationship between mother and daughter. An indication also, one might suppose, of the nature of her father, who can often appear cautious and pessimistic. He might have felt that a trip to Germany with a relatively new boyfriend would be a step too far. Barbara's mother was always likely be more pragmatic and perhaps view it as a 'getting to know you more' session (away from the confines of *'Benwick'* and school), for better or worse. How sensible you seem to be, Mrs Noble, and accompanying your common sense sits a generous helping of practicality. This relationship with Barbara has been exclusively within the school grounds or at *'Benwick'*. Otherwise, there have been walks out together in the immediate surroundings, but nowhere of any distance. Barbara's mother is, perhaps, understanding of this and she will have seen just how close the relationship is becoming. Without doubt, half-term had provided that proof. She will also realise that her daughter is heading towards eighteen years of age and a trip abroad, away from the confines of home, may help a daughter decide just how serious this relationship really is. It may also determine as to whether it can survive a period away from home ground and, indeed, away from the environs of school.

So it was that the following week, after Barbara had briefed her mother on the plans regarding Easter, that a personal and intentionally private chat had been enjoyed with Barbara's dad. Necessarily private – where did everyone else disappear to? Barbara had already volunteered to tidy up and vacuum her bedroom whilst the discussion took place. Good idea. It was a one-to-one chat and Barbara's mother had studiously commenced the ironing in the kitchen and Barbara's brother, under instruction, had melted away into the background. So it was that all other occupants were, by design, absent from the living room. Barbara's dad had perhaps displayed more than a hint of uneasiness – nervousness even – despite him being sat in the comfort of 'his' chair in the living room and notwithstanding that any discussions between him and his daughter's boyfriend were normally so very informal, casual even. 'Ian' and 'Mick' now being used automatically and quite naturally when addressing each other. (Although his forename is actually Gordon – so quite why he is addressed as 'Mick' remains a mystery. Indeed, a mystery to Barbara and even to her mother, who knew him as 'Mick' even before they were married. A nickname from early days at school – he seems to think – which has been perpetuated by growing up within the close confines of village life.)

The cause of his slight nervousness was readily apparent once he started to discuss the plan that had been proposed for Easter. "Well, Ian, Barbara's mother and I have had a chat. We have both taken to you and we do like you. "In fact," he admitted rather generously, "Grace is fond of you and enjoys you helping around the house. We feel sure you will do right regarding Barbara, so we are happy to let her spend Easter in Germany with yourself and your parents." After the slightest of pauses, during which one sensed that something else was about to be said, Mick had then continued with a visual and audible flourish. "However, no funny business please whilst you are both in Germany." His tone had been firm, more defined and several octaves higher than normal. It was his way, no doubt, of outlining just how important the point was. No funny business! In so saying, Mick had effectively cemented the arrangements for the forthcoming Easter holiday.

No funny business? (That is a question to this diary.) The implication of what that meant was quite clear to Barbara's dad and indeed to his daughter's boyfriend, without any further explanation or discussion. It was that issue and the need to mention it that had clearly caused some slight discomfort. It had, it seems, already been mentioned to Barbara by her mother, without it being made any sort of 'big deal'. Was there a necessity to mention it at all? Barbara is, yes, under eighteen years of age. Girlfriend and boyfriend are sensible – but the pull of mutual attraction is strong. As caring parents with a down to earth Yorkshire mentality, a brief mention was quite understandable and duly acknowledged. The talk having finished, both girlfriend and boyfriend, on meeting in the hallway, had exchanged a sly knowing smile at each other. Later that afternoon, in the bedroom, whilst proffering a kiss Barbara had added playfully, "Don't you worry, matey, I will keep your ardour in check. No funny business, remember!" (Not even a little bit, Barbara?)

A late Easter this year – towards the end of April – and the priority after Mick's amenable 'pep talk' had been to organise a visitor passport for a girlfriend, which was done on a weekday visit to Lancaster. Essentially a day off school, leaving Christine and Judith puzzling over why both Barbara and Ian had been missing for the day – and where had they gone? "We will keep it secret," Barbara had said, "otherwise, they might be thinking our relationship is getting serious."

There were, mind, some additional caveats which Barbara's dad has incorporated into the travelling, whilst agreeing to the Easter visit. "Grace and I don't want you taking a night-time sailing to the continent, Ian. You need to arrange a sailing from Dover to Calais, where I assume you can be collected by your parents." As a further considered and prudent insurance he had added, "I will take you both to Lancaster station and you need to arrange a day-time journey on the train please, is that okay?" It had to be okay. Of course, yes, it was okay. On receiving appropriate confirmation Mick had continued, "Champion! Barbara's mother will liaise with your mother regarding all the arrangements." Thank you, Mick. Whether you were bulldozed into agreeing by Barbara's mother or not, thank you. A whole two weeks abroad with your daughter. A wonderful prospect!

So, the sponsored walk is over. Organising it had been under the auspices of Mr Barr, the physics teacher. Essentially an unknown quantity to all Mrs Fife's art group wimps. He clearly comes into his own with the sponsored walk arrangements and, indeed, with anything to do with lighting at the various school plays. The kernel to the whole concept of parents and locals (and perhaps even some pupils) sponsoring school walks originates, without doubt, from the time of the heavy flooding in August 1967, when that road bridge in the nearby village of Wray was washed away. A sponsored walk had been held locally to raise funds re the disaster. The rumour is that the sponsored walk this year, a bi-annual event at the school since the first one in 1969, will raise upwards of £1,500. The money is, by all accounts, to be put to immediate use in fully covering the cost of putting 'tarmacadam' down on the main school driveway and the adjacent parallel path. Goodness, does that mean the main school entrance doors will no longer screech and squeal when being opened or closed? This is something continually caused by small stones from the gravel driveway getting caught underneath the door. More importantly, perhaps, tiny bits of gravel will no longer get caught in the soles of regulation school shoes. It should also, one might imagine, mean that shoes will not now need to be cleaned quite as often. Hold on – a dubious benefit perhaps and only for those who take no pleasure in methodically cleaning their shoes. Does no one else in this boarding house get perverse satisfaction in cleaning a pair of shoes every night, as this Head Boarder does, and then looking with considerable enjoyment at the result? (Yes! The cleanest pair of shoes in the boarding house... perhaps in the whole school!)

A busy month it has been, indeed, with the last of the current year's First XI football matches played 28th March. A victory, 3-2 away at Nelson & Colne College. A result that means that the team has had an unbeaten run of eight games since the turn of the year. Of those eight matches played, all have been won, apart from the 4-4 draw at home to 'Gig' (as Barbara calls them – a generally agreed shortened term used by all Bentham locals to denote the nearby village of Giggleswick). No fixture this season away at 'Gig'. A pity – it would have been interesting to have been able to see the Giggleswick School

WHERE'S THE BLOODY DEFENCE?

domed chapel – a rather odd green colour and a familiar local landmark – at close quarters. A draw at home! Only drawing against a famous public school renowned for their rugby prowess, rather than for their soccer skills, might be termed rather a disappointment. Also, somewhat disappointing – picking the ball out of the net four times!

Nonetheless, several other matches have been hard-fought with deserved victories. 4-3 away at Morecambe Grammar School in particular, resulting in those bent fingers – and they are still bent – and the motherly care of matron for a few days. Also, the 3-2 home win against Fleetwood Nautical College. A few matches were, surprisingly, quite easy victories – 6-1 away at Kirkby Stephen Grammar School and 5-1 away at local rivals Settle High School – despite it being felt before the match that Settle could prove to be a difficult test following the narrow 3-2 victory at home the previous December. Beating Settle home and away – sweet.

What is by far the most disappointing part of the completion of the football fixtures? No doubt about it. No longer being able to have some badly bruised and cut knees/legs (an inevitable consequence of being goalkeeper in the all too familiar goalmouth scrambles) washed and cared for by a willing girlfriend in the bathroom at *'Benwick'*. There will, however, be one match this season that Barbara will not forget for some considerable time. Home to Fleetwood Nautical College on 24th January. Barbara has become a loyal spectator at the home matches, and she was lucky enough (although she didn't think so) to have the rector standing next to her during the Fleetwood match. The Lord's representative is, of course, aware of the friendship between Barbara and the school First XI goalkeeper. Cue the Nautical College breaking away in attack (after a period of Bentham pressure) and with a distinct lack of defenders to protect him, it was necessary for the goalkeeper to remind them – bluntly and very loudly – "WHERE'S THE BLOODY DEFENCE?"

The after match tending of cut and bruised legs included, "Oh, Ianey, how dreadfully embarrassing with the rector stood next to me. I could feel my face go all red. I dare not look at him – but he never said anything. Goodness knows what he was thinking." Indeed, what was he thinking? Perhaps he was smiling to himself – and silently ruminating on the enjoyment of being young and carefree. Hopefully, the rector could forgive the recently confirmed goalkeeper that outburst – said in the heat of the battle! One might, perhaps, have prayed for forgiveness at the following Sunday church service if it had been imagined that it would make any tangible difference.

The football season has finished then. Played sixteen – won 12, drawn 1, lost 3 – a creditable performance. Goals conceded 35 – approx. 2 per match – at this level, not too bad. (Of the goals conceded, 13 were from just three games – 9 goals from two matches against ruddy Preston 6th Form College!) A sound defence has undoubtedly helped a sometime hesitant goalkeeper. A goalkeeper who has a penchant for punching the ball when it is crossed in the air in front of the goal, rather than catching it outright. With the inevitable presence of several of the opposing team challenging for that same ball, punching is, perhaps, the easy option before being unceremoniously bundled to the ground. Nevertheless, the position of goalkeeper has been the preserve of this Head Boarder for this season and indeed the previous one. So much so, in fact, that it was hardly necessary to check the team sheet when it was posted up in the changing room wall prior to a forthcoming match. Conceited? Yes, perhaps, but several of the team, including the goalkeeper, have been a permanent fixture – and why change a winning side? Overall, a creditable performance for the season. Most certainly an understatement. Mr Allison, Sports Master, suggests that it is the most successful football team the school has had since the record keeping commenced, at the time the school moved to its current site. That is all of twenty-five years ago. In a lot of ways, the end of an era with no more football this academic year. Over the past two years, no less than six of the First XI team have been playing together since 1966, when they were chosen to play for the Under 13's XI.

At least the junior forms and other spectators this season will have enjoyed the decent run of results, unlike the memory of the 1967/68 season, when only the odd game or two at home ended in victory for the school team. It had at times been quite embarrassing, although ultimately not that surprising, watching the First XI go down to some sizeable defeats and it became difficult, when walking out to watch a game in progress during afternoon break or at the end of school, not to ask, rather casually – albeit that it was never intended to be cheeky – "How many are we losing by?" Didn't they once lose by 2-18? The memory bank suggests so. Whilst no doubt they were playing as best they could, the abiding memory is of frequently seeing a dejected team with heads down, resigned to their fate. Certainly, a world away from the performances this season.

With some creditable exploits and results over the past two terms against much bigger schools and colleges (and it must surely follow that, in theory at least, the bigger the pupil numbers at a school/college, the better their sporting performance should be), the team's progress has been tracked within the Daily Telegraph's *'Schools Soccer'* results column. Obtaining the paper, therefore, if only to see a brief bit of fame for Bentham Grammar School in the sports section, has been a priority. So, not in this instance to read the back page, with reporters trying to decide whether Arsenal or Liverpool or perhaps Leeds Utd. will win the league, but instead, the section inside listing the school soccer

WHERE'S THE BLOODY DEFENCE?

results – that has provided the interest for the roving eyes of the goalkeeper for the First XI.

Perhaps the credit for the performance this season, and, indeed, last season, should be given to Mr Stockdale and Mr Allison our sports teachers – not only for their guidance and training but also for their unbridled enthusiasm towards football, in particular towards the First XI. The fact that they have both, one suspects, only very recently left full time education themselves (whether it be university or college) helps enormously with the interaction between pupils and teacher. Appearances, though, can certainly be deceptive. The initial thought process on seeing David Allison might well lead one to think that he is quite unsuited to the games field (he does teach French as well as Games) being, as he is, small, slightly built and in no way masculine. In fact, several of the First XI lads tower over him both in height and physical stature. No doubting in this case that looks are indeed deceptive. Mr Allison has strength both physically and in character and to have him refereeing the home matches is almost a privilege – and that is saying something! To his credit, he is scrupulously fair, even-handed (even, horror of horrors, awarding a penalty – or two! – to the visiting teams) and well organised. He has also always offered constructive feedback – particularly during the half time breaks – which has played its part in producing a team showing flair in attack and resilience in defence.

With this football team, it will indeed be a parting of the ways at the end of the summer term and the camaraderie of the soccer matches, both on the pitch and in the changing rooms before and after matches, will be much missed. Quite sad. The laughter and ribbing in the communal showers after a football match has often been a riotous affair, particularly after a victory on the pitch and when playing away from home – a contrast indeed to the sullen faces from the losing home team. It has regularly provided an interesting lesson in human nature. Amongst a dozen or so naked footballers showering off the accumulated mud from often sodden football pitches, V...... – until his departure – was always the standard bearer that the rest of the team has aspired to match! Not, in this instance, for his playing skills on the pitch (albeit that he fully deserved his regular place), but rather for his well-endowed manhood and his obvious prowess in that department was always confidently displayed for all to see! For him, there were no inhibitions in stripping off to use the communal showers – quite the opposite – for he was always proud to display all he has been endowed with. Out of such situations, leaders are readily identified and, in his case, worshipped.

No matter. Regarding the team, it is reasonable to anticipate that a good number will be presented with the school colours at the annual speech day, in the form of a blue tassel. But with the attractive school cap having been discontinued as part of the uniform in 1968, there will be no showing off around the school with a tassel in one's cap, as had been the case with those who had been awarded colours in the 1960s, right at the start of school life in this boarding house.

There has been a generous element of pride, it is admitted, during the morning assemblies when Mr Hagen, always shuffling around with various bits of paper in his hand, would read out the First XI result from the previous day. "The result of yesterday's First XI football match against George Fox school ended in a 5-2 victory; congratulations to the team." It has always made one feel quite important being an integral part of the winning team, not hopefully in an arrogant way but by being part of the success and contributing to it. Particularly so as one always senses that the junior forms are looking around in assembly to catch sight of the players after a victorious result had been announced. It is indeed easy to feel some pity for the players in the 1967/68 campaign when their latest defeat was announced in assembly – and some thumping defeats there were: 0-7 at home to Morecambe Grammar School and 0-9 at the seaside and 2-13 at home to St. Michael's College. No sense of pride surely when those results were read out in morning assembly. Only embarrassment. (One can still see Nelson, First XI goalkeeper, his head down with embarrassment, after picking the ball out of his goal for the umpteenth time!)

So, a highly successful season then and a shame it has come to an end. Only the defeat to the Old Boys XI last November still rankles. The two defeats delivered clinically by the Preston 6th Form College team being accepted stoically on the basis that brawn and bulk does, at times, have the beating of not only brains, but also skill. (And, in any case, the two results against them have been classed as "glorious defeats" by team colleagues!)

And amid all these events in March, numerous essays have been laboured over within the confines of a dormitory – sometimes in the early morning (very early – before breakfast) whilst watching an ever-earlier sunrise – otherwise fitted in late at night. In the evening, though, always after a letter has been penned to Barbara and certainly only after any letters received from her have been read... and re-read... and then read again! Yes, reading a letter received, but there is also excitement to be gained in finding a coloured envelope *(always* a coloured envelope from Barbara) awaiting its recipient on the dormitory bed and then leaving it there, unopened, for a few precious minutes. What enormous pleasure can be gained from leaving it there on show, ready to be opened and then pored over. Perverse? Perhaps, but oh, the excitement in being able to just to say to oneself, "What will it say?", and wondering warmly as to whether it will be a long letter and most importantly of all, how many kisses there will be at the end of the letter. (One hundred and fifty kisses in the last letter, but Barbara had cheated slightly by drawing little hearts and showing that one heart = ten kisses, thereby having to only draw fifteen little hearts!)

Yes, within the confines of the dormitory, what does go on? Taking time out to consider subjects and concepts within Sociology 'A' Level such as: 'Are some children doomed to poverty from birth?' or 'The poor are always with us – discuss'. Also, 'Is social class determined by income?', requires rigorous use of time and a discipline of purpose. Both are becoming more and more difficult to maintain – the presence of a girlfriend becoming more and more of a distraction, but a charming distraction certainly. Letters to a girlfriend and letters received now take priority over the seemingly endless procession of essays. "Why on earth are you writing to each other when you see each other every day?" – a common enough question – or exclamation even – from the Lonsdale complex colleagues. They just do not understand...

Essays. Yes, they need to be done. All three subjects require them. The issue is getting started with them, particularly where the subject matter holds little interest and there is plenty certainly within the framework of Sociology that does not generate even the faintest glimmer of interest. Sitting at this dormitory desk staring at a blank piece of paper (well, blank other than the heading – 'The poor are always with us – discuss') is to some extent quite demoralising. Somehow, a start needs to be made. Plenty of thoughts and ideas swilling around the brain, but actually getting started and putting it down on paper – therein lies the problem. No such problem scribbling out the draft of a poem and knocking it about, changing this and that – all very enjoyable. Essays are another thing altogether. Rather strangely though, once up and running with the first half dozen lines, then (and only then) does it suddenly become easy – and the waffle, it kicks in. And then, doesn't it look splendid and most satisfying when three or four pages have been written and suddenly, the pressure is off?

What of the visit to the Angus Fire Armour factory? Interesting, yes, but only as an eye opener as to the inner workings of the factory floor, assuming it is typical of the factory workplace generally. Maybe these are the sort of visits that a sociology syllabus should organise. The factory floor – certainly not a suitable environment for an arts group wimp. Barbara's dad perhaps summed it up succinctly when the school group walked past him in the maintenance section, "You don't want to be looking at a job in here, Ian." He is right and the escorted visit did not include the admin section in any case, presumably on the assumption that it would not be of sufficient interest. Employment at

FROM A DORMITORY WINDOW

Ingleborough and the surrounding countryside: it will surely be this view; and a similar one from the back garden at 'Benwick' and, indeed, from the top of the church tower, that will remain as an enduring image in the mind's eye in the years to come.

George Angus & Co is not part of any future planning, but then again, nor is Durham.

March – is it still winter or is it spring? On the regular walks up to *'Benwick'* at the end of the school day and at weekends, it has been fascinating to witness the gradual melting of the snow on the slopes of Ingleborough. It has resembled, perhaps, a patchwork quilt, rather like the different patterns that farm fields display in the Dales when hay time is in full swing, with some fields having been shorn of their grass and showing a shade of yellowy green whilst other fields await the combine harvester. In the case of Ingleborough though, the snow, whilst starting to melt with the warmer weather, remains stubbornly solid in small pockets, presumably in the deep gullies, providing a splendid patchwork which would be ideal for a budding artist. As the temperatures have been rising with warmer and longer days, the snow has receded – it being noticeable almost daily and it is intriguing to follow the melting process.

Now into early April, quite definitely springtime – only tiny pockets of snow remain, a testament to the colder temperatures at the higher altitudes with many deep gullies not obtaining the benefit of spring sunshine. No doubt the mountain will soon be free of winter snow, although Barbara has stated quite confidently that the area just below the summit plateau can be covered in snow sometimes well into April and May and even June.

As well as the variations in snow cover, the different cloud formations that surround the summit of Ingleborough are endlessly fascinating. Sometimes the cloud clings stubbornly to the summit plateau and quite often during rain, the view of the mountain disappears, with cloud completely enveloping it. Perhaps most interesting of all, however, is the almost ethereal view created when wisps of thin cloud drift lazily around just below the summit plateau, creating what can appear to be a bubbling cauldron of steam. The mountain, it stays the same, but it is forever portraying itself in different moods and indeed, in different light – its colour sometimes appearing a rather strange ethereal lilac shade. Oh, to be talented in art. (Apart from drawing ships and trains, of course…)

An interesting discussion also took place last month whilst walking with Barbara back to *'Benwick'* about which view of Ingleborough is the most impressive. Barbara, perhaps understandably, thinks the view from the west – in essence the view from her back garden – is the best one. This view from the west certainly provides an iconic outline of the mountain. However, the road heading in an easterly direction out of Ingleton towards Hawes provides a grandstand view of the mountain from the north. Ingleborough then appears much closer and this perhaps is what makes it look more dramatic. In complete contrast, approach from the south and Ingleborough is hardly noticeable, its shape being quite ordinary – certainly nothing special – and its height appearing to be on a par with the surrounding hills. It will surely, however, be the view from here at the school and from the garden at *'Benwick'* that will remain as the enduring image in the mind's eye in the years to come. It will be a view forever linked with the back garden at *'Benwick'* and the family that live within it.

CHAPTER XXV

BALD MEN ARE THE BEST FOR SEX

Two other events during March deserve a mention, perhaps more so than the 14 miles of slog that was the sponsored walk. The annual school 'theatre' play, *The Importance of Being Earnest* by Oscar Wilde – who is the subject of some disdain within the Lonsdale complex ("That guy was a bloody poofta."), and the school Public Speaking Competition, held on the day before the sponsored walk, 30th March.

What about the Public Speaking Competition held this Friday just gone? Before Easter, now a mere couple of weeks away, several potentially awkward English lessons with Ducky will have to be negotiated. Will there, one wonders, be any 'fallout' from the competition which was held in the Assembly Hall? Hopefully, the weekend will have provided a welcome few days' break, albeit that he was seen fleetingly whilst on the sponsored walk. Keeping out of his way (at least until the next English Literature lesson) is perhaps prudent following the Public Speaking Competition. Why?

An annual event and held in the presence of the senior school and a large proportion of the teaching staff, the competition indeed has a worthy aim. It is to give those pupils who will shortly be entering an occupation in the "world out there" (as it is described by some teachers) some confidence, enabling them to address members of the public. But, as Cess had so eloquently phrased it during the Christmas holiday break, "Who on earth wants to talk about the 'sun' for fifteen minutes?" In truth, the answer is, most likely, that no one did. Nevertheless, that was the subject matter. Many of the verbal presentations duly delivered were splendidly mundane, banal, boring almost. Lefty, however, had provided some laughter with his occasional lapses into hype and overdrive, whilst concentrating on the distance between the earth and the sun, the speed of light and how long it takes the sun's rays to travel to earth. In the words of Lefty, to get to the earth the light must be "fair shifting". Indeed so. He delivered this startling fact in his own inimitable style to ensure the audience was kept awake and given something to laugh at with such light-hearted comments. (Which, just maybe, were meant to be serious…)

And then the next speaker from the 6th form arts group was the one whom Ducky had thought, "was fairly grown up" – that is until the 6th former wrote a highly charged and sarcastic article supposedly on *Fashion*! A talk on the 'sun' was indeed delivered and it did, indeed, discuss the 'sun' – but it was the 'Sun' with a capital S. That is, the daily newspaper of the same name. Quite definitely nothing to do with the sun that shines brightly in the sky. (When it isn't cloudy or raining – yes, okay, it is still shining behind the clouds...) To accompany the talk, a copy of a recent daily edition of the newspaper had been obtained. Well, of course, it had to be in order to discuss the paper's content fully, including, in places, ever so slightly bawdy comments and photographs. Cue then for laughter across the sweep of the Assembly Hall whilst the notorious 'Page Three' was being enthusiastically described, with the detail of a rather rude picture of a young female being shown to the audience at the same time!

*[**An aside:** here is a question. Why do the young women on page three of the newspaper ALWAYS have big bazookas? That, surely, is a possible question for Sociology 'A' Level discussion. Well, they do! No point in trying to obtain a photo session with the Sun newspaper if you have a tiny pair of tits. A sound bit of advice from the Lonsdale complex to any aspiring model – and Confucius would agree – do not go to the audition if you only have small tits. Big tits? No problem, please step this way.]*

The Sun. The various pages of the newspaper were then discussed with the audience before a specific article was discussed in detail, its headline being, 'Bald Men are the Best for Sex'. Ducky, standing at the back of the Assembly Hall (with his bald head there for all to see...) was most definitely not sharing in the hilarity. He was, no doubt, also somewhat irritated by a large section of the audience twisting around almost as one to look at him to see what his reaction might be. To his credit – credit where it is due, etc. – he allowed the fifteen-minute speech to continue to its conclusion. Then considerable disappointment, both for the talker and for what had been a hugely attentive audience. He promptly disqualified the entry, despite the talk receiving a more than enthusiastic response with clapping and cheering. Ducky, in a rather moribund tone (and conveniently ignoring the bald-headed news item from the paper), merely explained that the subject matter had been without a capital 'S', also explaining and outlining the various intricacies of the English language, albeit that no one was really bothered. No doubting, of course, that the whole episode will re-affirm his view that this 6th form pupil still has some growing up to do. Just perhaps, Ducky, you lack a certain sense of humour. Initiative is the thing – always take the initiative. Ah well, congratulations to Elizabeth Norris – *the winner* – but there would indeed have been a different public speaking champion if the audience had been able to decide on a show of hands and without the disadvantage of a disqualification. Clearly, the winner does not always win!

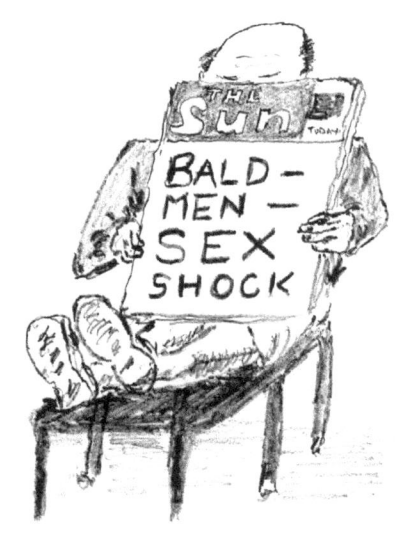

It had, however, been several weeks earlier, when Ducky clearly had sufficient confidence in the ability of the Head Boarder, that he had made a specific request for a 'précis' to be written on the school play, performed on the 16th and 17th March, for inclusion in the *Crescent* (the annual school magazine) ready for its publication immediately following the Easter break. On the basis that two heads are better than one, he had suggested that Barbara should also be involved in the 'critique' and this, rather conveniently, meant two consecutive evenings in her company, being sat together in the Assembly Hall whilst the play was watched – and watched again for good measure.

The Importance of Being Earnest by Oscar Wilde. (Yes, we all know he was a rampant "brown hatter" – nevertheless.) A play just about manageable within the framework of limitations that a school performance will strive to produce with regard to scenery and characterization. It was a significant change from the previous five years, which had seen an enjoyable variety of Gilbert and Sullivan operettas performed every year. Not only that, but they had been performed with considerable professionalism.

*[**An aside**: Gilbert and Sullivan – who indeed can forget the attractive soprano, Margaret Butler, performing as one of the General's daughters in* The Pirates of Penzance *in the 1968 school play? She looked lovely, sang beautifully and captivated the young teenage lads – but, then again, she was indeed rather 'smashing' and her voice sounded magical. Her singing, to young lads, sounded semi-professional and it was impossible not to gaze longingly at her – although from the general gossip flitting*

about the school, it had seemed to be the case that most of the senior lads had been concentrating not on her but rather, on her well-proportioned and nicely presented breasts, instead of enjoying her singing. Perhaps singing and a pair of ample bosoms go together rather like, well, like a horse and carriage?

It was almost impossible not to fall in love with her – that is, of course, if fourteen-year-old teenagers can fall in love! The problem was, quite understandably, that virtually all the other teenage boarder lads were also falling in love with her, not to mention those in the prime position to do something about it – the 6th formers! Had the young lads in the boarding house been aware at that time of Handel's 'Silent Worship' – 'Did you not see my lady'* – then perhaps they might well have consoled themselves by singing it quietly once lights were out in the dormitory, instead of thinking about what steam engines they had seen that day. Lovely Margaret Butler took a leading part in several other Gilbert and Sullivan productions during the late 1960s, so she was there to be enjoyed again... and again. (Rather like, apparently, a prostitute is...) Dear Margaret, now you have left the school, do you still manage to keep young lads entertained? With your singing that is, not with your marvellous bosoms!]

*Decca records, 'Your Hundred Best Tunes' domiciled at *'Benwick'*!

Oscar Wilde's play has been described by critics as a farce and is presented for viewing on that basis. The jointly produced précis for Ducky, whilst trying to be honest and accurate had, it seemed, to be positive rather than negative. A fine balancing act then – a critique too negative would no doubt be consigned to the bin by Ducky, but then again, should a report be written through rose-tinted spectacles? (For the purposes of our school magazine, one might well answer yes, quite possibly.)

There was a particular problem with providing a review for Ducky. For some unknown reason, or indeed for no particular reason, some fellow students are not particularly liked. Indeed, this can frequently be reciprocated – even though there is no logical reason for it. Yes, very strange. So, it was doubly important to ensure that there was something positive to say about the performance of Anthony Calverley (as John Worthing: J. P.) however difficult it had proved to be – on a personal basis that is – to write it. In the event, thankfully, Calverley (Head Boy of the school – is that why there is an unaccountable coolness towards him?), gave a mature and polished performance. One has to be, and should be, magnanimous.

Amid the eating of muffins and cucumber sandwiches (in the play, not the audience) and in between the "bitching" of The Hon. Gwendolyn Fairfax and Cecily Cardew, there was sufficient to be positive about in the précis prepared for Ducky, not least with seeing the vicar played splendidly by Peter Lilley. He looked the part to perfection and his entrance onto the stage as the Revd Chasuble brought forth a cacophony of laughter from the juniors – perhaps that is a prospective career path for him – being a vicar that is, not acting! Also worthy of comment, Roger Batty and Ronald Bentham – two butlers, both contributing to the enjoyment with faultless manners, showing due respect to their 'betters' (only in the play – not within the school!) and with their quintessential 'butler' voices!

Sometimes it can appear that a particular pupil can act a specific part as if the part belonged to them and no one else. It was certainly the case with Alastair McCombie, fitting in seamlessly as Algernon Moncrieff. The snazzy blazer suited him to a tee. One can imagine him wearing it to a school dance or party. McCombie, with his obvious talent for bonhomie and exuberance (sometimes a tad wearing), is also, in fact, one of the stalwarts of the First XI cricket team, as an opening batsman. He provides a perfect example for any aspiring cricketer in the lower forms with his straight bat, upright stance and with his flair for not only getting the runs but getting them in a stylish manner. There is invariably a collective groan across the rest of his First XI colleagues if his innings ends cheaply with the (unspoken) understanding that a good many of his team-mates (including the Head Boarder) are only included in the team to make up the numbers. It is almost certainly the case that, without a solid innings from McCombie, the accumulated run total will be modest and inevitably under three figures. Within the school boundary, he might easily be termed the best cricketer in the West Riding of Yorkshire – but not, of course, the best in the world, as that particular 'mantle' belongs, without doubt, to Geoffrey Boycott!

But back to 'The Importance of Being Earnest'. It had seemed to be the case that the easiest part with both performances was the one taken by Lynva Russell – she, the prompter. As far as could be seen (or should it be heard?), she had little, if anything, to do. There did not seem to be a point in the play when there occurred any sort of slight hesitation, the point at which Lynva could have stepped in – figuratively speaking – and played a starring role.

Lynva (is her name a derivation of Linda or Lynda? Who dares to ask?), in the year below Barbara, but actually similar in look and indeed, in build to Barbara with high cheek bones, an attractive face (even if sometimes appearing slightly offhand – perhaps more to do with confidence), similar facial features, shoulder length hair and good firm attractive legs. The only difference being that Lynva excels on the sports field. (She would certainly make a very formidable fast bowler in the First XI cricket team. Indeed, it would be intriguing to watch a duel, if one were to be set up, between her effective fast bowling and the stylish batting produced by McCombie.) On the other hand, Barbara will try her level best to steer clear of the sports field. Lynva and Barbara – one an enthusiastic sports competitor, the other perhaps best described as "sports averse." (And proud of it!) The nearest Barbara wants to be to a sports field is watching the First XI football team play. The story of her exploits last year during a games lesson cross-country run would, without doubt, go into print in a pupil's alternative version of the school *Crescent* magazine, if one were indeed published.

*[**An aside:** this then is her story, as told to a boyfriend.*

Having run (albeit that there was a good deal of 'walking' in the running) several miles, Barbara and a handful of school friends had to run back down to school from the top of the Millhouses Road behind the school, a distance of perhaps two or three miles. Salvation was at hand for them. Upon seeing a Pennine bus approaching, heading eastwards, Barbara flagged it down to find, to her delight, that the driver was none other than Dennis Mitton, a driver who lived locally and who was a friend of her father. Having no money with them was happily no obstacle, Dennis being more than willing to pick them all up and provide a free ride back down to the Punch Bowl Hotel. And there they were duly dropped off, having only then to run over the road bridge, back into school and to look, of course, rather pleased with themselves – whilst perhaps also trying their best to look tired out. After all, they had all just run several miles...

The plan, it was well thought out (on the spur of the moment, up at the second signpost) and indeed, would have been well executed and most successful. Well, that is, had it not been for the sports teacher waiting for the returning runners at the river bridge by the entrance to the school and watching rather aghast as her charges happily alighted from the Pennine bus! It is, of course, the type of story that will ensure schooldays remain so memorable in years to come. The sports teacher was not amused (no sense of fun you see), but Barbara's dad considered it a good and sensible use of initiative. Perhaps there may have been some sniggering within the teacher's staff room when the tale was related, as it surely must have been.]

So, the report on the school play duly made its way to Ducky. The critical appreciation submitted being a joint effort, making the compilation of it hugely enjoyable. A formal summary prepared in an informal way, but with the joint authors happily and well able to accept suggestions and criticisms of each other's thoughts and ideas. Barbara's assessment of the play, well possibly the more charitable, which is just as well for a report that is to be included in the school magazine. It needs to offer some generous praise. No feedback – yet. No doubt Ducky will knock it around a bit, firming up sentences and punctuation, cutting out what he decides is waffle (albeit that Barbara has already had a go at that), but hopefully, keeping the content largely as written. The publication of the *Crescent* in May will be the acid test.

Yes, March has been a busy month. Not forgetting, of course, a birthday on the 11th, fortuitously this year falling on a Sunday, meaning that the afternoon and early evening were spent at *'Benwick'* after the obligatory church service. On the Saturday, after returning to the dormitory following the 4-0 win away at Kirkby Stephen Grammar School (as a follow up to the 6-1 victory against them in January), Mrs Russell had knocked on the door and with typical panache, she had handed over a bunch of birthday cards. "Good morning, Mr McCart, and a happy birthday for tomorrow. We shall not expect you in for the evening meal tomorrow, but you do need to be back at the school for 7pm please."

Birthday cards from family certainly (with the welcome inclusion of a cheque from parents – a generous cheque!), but the birthday card in a fancy yellow envelope handed over at *'Benwick'* after church was, indeed, the most welcome. Particularly so as it was accompanied by a kiss, a tube of Smarties and two presents. (Wrapped up so methodically and competently that it took some time to unwrap them both. It is a mark of pride for Barbara that any present should be studiously and professionally wrapped so that the recipient savours the moment, whilst taking a considerable time in attempting to unwrap it. She would undoubtedly have excelled in wrapping up a 'pass the parcel' package.)

A tube of Smarties. Why a tube of Smarties? The secret and purpose behind the Smarties will always be to seek out the red ones. Only the red ones. Once a red one has been put in the mouth, it can then be transferred rather seamlessly to Barbara's waiting mouth (or visa-versa), whilst at the same time taking advantage of a little kiss contemporaneously with the transfer. Magic! The simplest of things are indeed magical. The process is treated as a personal kind of togetherness. It is personal, private and meaningful – a statement of mutual attraction. This, of course, was the reason for a tube being included as a birthday gift. Even better if several red Smarties can be taken from the tube, because this most intimate game has developed into being one that involves the same number of kisses as the number of red Smarties transferred across by mouth. The obvious aim? Transferring three or four red Smarties across at the same time. Barbara's lips have a wonderful warm and smooth feel, with each kiss from a Smartie transfer lingering for a few moments before parting, leaving a chocolate residue and taste around the mouth. It provides an almost childlike excitement linked to the mutual enjoyment of playing with the inside of each other's mouths. And sometimes, one can be a little bit naughty by very gently biting the other's tongue, this itself providing a very individual kind of passion jointly shared. Oh Barbara, what wonderful kissing lips you do have! (Mrs Fife, eat your heart out…)

For many weeks now, the regular visit to the school tuck shop has always involved buying several tubes of Smarties, with the relatively cheap purchase price always providing full value for money. A senior 6th form boarder buying Smarties – oh dear. Not only that, but a 6th form boarder also quickly checking on the lid of the cylindrical Smartie box once opened to look for the letter 'B' or the letter 'N'. Currently, two 'B' tops are in possession but no 'N'… Barbara 2, Noble 0 – oh dear!

Oh yes, and the other birthday presents from Barbara? (Confucius says – always open the largest present first.) Firstly, a recently released Lindisfarne LP, 'Dingly Dell', the lyrics of which are certainly more rebellious than their previous release, 'Nicely Out of Tune.' Perhaps the LP cover said everything that needed to be said, '*To Ianey, Happy Birthday with lots of love from Barbi*', and the individual songs are certainly 'anti-establishment', with 'Bring Down the Government' perhaps the most pertinent track with obvious appeal for obstinate youth. Whilst, perhaps, slightly rebellious within the framework of the school and life within the boarding house, there is, however, no inner feeling or urge to be in any way rebellious with the world outside. Is there a world outside?

The music on 'Dingly Dell', rebellious or not, is easy listening and will be guaranteed to liven up the Lonsdale dormitory complex. Perhaps the most poignant track is the final one, which gives the LP the title asking, as it does, *'Will you have my children? Will they grow in the likeness of me? Will they touch the sky?'* Something, indeed, that could quite easily be aimed directly at a young and attractive girlfriend. Best not to tell her…

The other present? Just as efficiently wrapped up as the LP, and from the collection of 'Penguin Classics', a book on the Peloponnesian War by Thucydides. (Translated into the English language – well, of course.) An exciting choice by a girlfriend, who has noticed that her boyfriend continues to have a lingering interest in Greek History. There is now over 600 pages to grapple with during dormitory bedtime reading. Ancient Greek history (and indeed Latin – there is a connection) is no longer being studied, but it remains an intriguing subject and is irresistible reading. The appetite for learning about the machinations of Pericles, Hermocrates, and the others, must rest with our erstwhile Headmaster, Mr Kaye, who himself could almost have walked off an ancient history stage set with his almost military bearing and rather posh diction. He made the subject interesting to learn about and absorbing and, more importantly, the enthusiasm has remained following completion of that 'O' Level examination. That is the secret surely, one might suggest, of successful teaching.

The preferred birthday present – music or literature? Literature undoubtedly. (No, no, stop there – actually, the Smarties. A modest cost but superb entertainment!)

And of course, the other birthday highlight? Undoubtedly a Sunday afternoon buffet, prepared and presented by Barbara's mother, with the usual generous supply of home baking, something never experienced whilst growing up at home when the usual fare was whatever could be obtained in packets or tins, preferably in the form of an 'instant' meal. Can one ever forget those 'instant' meals…?

Another of the 'Three Musketeers' (the inimitable three, who have long loitered with intent by the self-service coffee machine – although only two now actually loiter) has a boyfriend. Christine is now "going out" with Jonty, who is also, like Christine, in the Lower 6th form. The contrast between Christine and Barbara is perhaps highlighted by Christine's illuminating comment. She likes Jonty "a lot", but she is doubtful about the long-term future with him and in any case, they both feel able to quite happily flirt with others whilst pursuing their relationship. How odd. Perhaps that rather strange view highlights the main difference between Barbara and Christine – that of temperament. Barbara has chosen and that choice has been made, knowing Barbara, carefully and with some thought. Having made the choice, it is not in her nature to flirt or mess around with anyone else. Her boyfriend is from the same serving bowl.

With Barbara, if she ultimately feels that the choice made is the correct one – and just how long will it take her to decide that? – then she will be firmly within the monogamous camp (and thank you so much 'A' Level Sociology for an introduction to that clever term) and her loyalty will not, surely, ever be in doubt. That is her character, it is in her DNA. Just perhaps, because of this, the love (physical and otherwise) which will hopefully be experienced will mean so much more. Neither Christine nor Jonty seems to have the ability to be in any way serious towards the other and as a relationship, it cannot, surely, survive the continual teasing with one another and with others – or can it? Not only that, but apparently Jonty will not have a serious discussion about the future, which perhaps confirms the relationship as a casual one. Barbara has summed the situation up succinctly with a reassuring, "I am glad I have got you."

Outside, the moon on this Tuesday night lights up the sky and appears so close. Do other people look up at this satellite of our earth and just wonder? Is there no end to human ingenuity? How on earth (and that is an entirely appropriate pun) were the various ratios worked out to enable mankind to land on the moon and not only that, but to then walk around on that dusty, seemingly arid vast area of nothingness? It almost defies understanding (particularly for a wimp belonging to the arts group) and must surely stand for all time as one of this planet's finest achievements. Does anyone else actually sit and gaze at the moon, wondering just exactly on which bits those brave astronauts landed and subsequently walked around on for several hours? For all those who watched the landing and the subsequent moon walk by Neil Armstrong and Buzz Aldrin, it will be one of those events that will remain in the memory for a lifetime (and it was well worth being woken up at something like 3am to watch it). Incredible! In a strange way though, familiarity breeds contempt and a moon landing last December hardly caused a stir – no longer does it seem to be such an incredible feat. It is, instead, rather taken for granted. How strange. It will, surely, only be Neil Armstrong and his crew that people will remember. The rest of a select band – already forgotten. Rather like, perhaps, the conquest of Everest. Everyone – yes everyone – remembers Hillary and Tenzing – but what about all the rest who followed them?

John Donne certainly spent time looking at both the moon and, indeed, the sun and wrote poetry about them both as a consequence. ('...*unruly sun.*' Rather like a woman, he suggests...) A great many must have marvelled at the wonder of our moon and of space and, indeed, of our place in the Universe. It will always, surely, defy and defeat ordinary understanding. Meanwhile, the moon waxes and wanes and what else can we do but watch it and wonder?

As the light from that celestial body provides a seemingly warm glow around the swimming pool and the adjoining lawn and river, inside on the window ledge, still delivering an engaging smile in a bridesmaid's dress, Barbara looks in at this dormitory room late on this April evening and displays all that is enticing about the female form. Betjeman may have waxed lyrical about Myfanwy, but in this dormitory, the only celebration is with Barbara Noble. Next to the photograph, the familiar miniature lifebelt (a memento from parents obtained when they spent a few years living on the East Coast at Felixstowe), an orange colour which, amazingly, Barbara has said she can see from the Millhouses Road when she is partaking in those, much maligned, cross-country runs. "I will be seeing your room at close quarters before long, Ianey, once I have spoken nicely to Mrs Wills. " Well, young lady, if and when you do make that secret, furtive visit with the redoubtable Mrs Wills, you will certainly find, as you indeed suspect, a tidy, well-organised, study room with everything exactly where it should be and in its place. Quite right too…

CHAPTER XXVI

I AM GETTING TO KNOW MORE AND MORE ABOUT YOU

From within the confines of the dormitory on this April evening, a commotion can be heard immediately outside on the landing of the Lonsdale dormitory. The door opens and Rosco beckons, "Come out here Mucca, and have a look at this," he suggests, grinning broadly. On the landing, several lads are surrounding a figure on the floor. John Holmes has been rather successfully tied up with rope and sits prostrate, his face alternating between frustration and resignation. Harmless fun, yes. Well, that is unless you are the chosen victim. It will, no doubt, be considered good-humoured by the ringleaders of the fracas now taking place. A filling in, so to speak, of the free time following the ending of formal prep and the sort of boisterous fun that regularly takes place towards the end of term. Whittaker, Braddock and Clarky are perhaps the main culprits and justify their action by virtue of being "shocked" (inverted commas are clearly necessary) at Holmes showing them a copy of *Playboy* magazine, displaying two – rather attractive it must be admitted – nude ladies in provocative pose adorning the centre pages. Clearly, in their view, a "dirty old man" such as Holmes needs to be tied up as a punishment – perhaps then, the rest of the complex should also be encased in rope! Whilst only a bit of larking about, it seems unlikely that Mr Russell, despite his jovial nature, will consider it such. A suggestion, or perhaps an instruction, is made to the ringleaders that Holmes is untied before Mr Russell does his evening rounds.

Once released from his bondage, Holmes retreats to his room, none the worse for wear but with his pride perhaps somewhat dented. One suspects (well, not suspects – in this case one is certain) that the rest of the Lonsdale complex will also become "dirty old men" in turn over the next few nights, as and when *Playboy* is offered around and readily accepted. (Yes, and that includes the Head Boarder – and why not?) After all, one can only broaden and improve one's knowledge by reading a wide variety of literature! (Okay, so this isn't the sort of reading that Mrs Fife suggests!) There is a sort of consensus, however, that when the magazine is offered around, it will not be taken up by the full complement within these Lonsdale dormitories. Of course, it takes some bravado to decline such a publication in this enclosed male and macho environment. Don't all adolescent males enjoy looking at naked young women? One can learn all sorts from *Playboy* magazine, the like of which does not feature in the classroom general chat with 6th form females. And quite why would anyone in this Lonsdale complex *not* want to look at naked women? Isn't it an irresistible urge linked to growing up? There are suggestions made as to why some might not want to look at naked women. Is it considered rude? By some, it may be considered so. Others suggest they know the real answer. It might just involve rather lurid and crude ideas involving being, variously, a "Brown Hatter", a "Shirt Lifter", or put in more simple, straightforward language, a "poofta"! Rather kinder, perhaps, would be the term "pansy". Here in the Lonsdale dormitory? Never. No, surely not! It would be appropriate, perhaps, to provide a timely reminder to this Lonsdale complex of the primary difference between the male and the female. (Ignoring for the moment biological issues.) These, then, the words of Kingsley Amis and in the form of a rhyming couplet,

> *Women are really much nicer than men,*
> *No wonder we like them!*

*[**An aside:** those in the know suggest that far more interesting information can be gleaned by obtaining and looking through Mayfair magazine. By all accounts, it is a magazine far more detailed than Playboy, with a more plentiful helping of photographs, including what some term the "interesting bit" down below – and apparently, showing a variety of shapes and colours. Not only that, but also the odd lady – horror of horrors – without hair in that most private area. Isn't it only the seventeenth and eighteenth century paintings, by the Old Masters, that portray such scenes – with naked ladies who are generally, in any case, – to be blunt – fat, with flab hanging out everywhere? For painting, the fatter the better, apparently!]*

Sex. It is certainly not something that was discussed or even mentioned at home by prudish parents. (And did they *really* get up to that sort of thing? Well, yes – but difficult to envisage.) How else does one find out about the more interesting parts of the female form? Silently and privately, one can learn about things that, perhaps – one might assume – sometimes incorrectly, no doubt, that others are already aware of and indeed, which one might have pretended to be aware of oneself in male company. No naughty magazines for everyone then. Neither does everyone take up the offer that was for a time made to a select group regarding a sometime clandestine trip out on a Friday night to the Sun Dial public house in Low Bentham.

Spending an hour or so in the pub at the end of a school term is in danger of becoming something of a ritual, with the Head Boarder and three other 6th formers disappearing from the boarding house (after Mr Russell has done his evening rounds) and returning, well, not too late, around 9pm. Something that is strictly prohibited and at times, the puzzle is how Mr Russell has not caught on to the practice. Has he never come looking for one or other of the participants in the Lonsdale complex? Fortunately, not! Perhaps he has been aware – or has suspected – and conveniently turned a blind eye. What would be the penalty for being caught? The obvious risk involved did not stop a trip being made. Perhaps it is partly the fact that it is strictly against the rules that makes it so attractive and, well, dangerous. In the depths of winter, with the darkness of the nights, the feeling was that it is perhaps less of a risk walking to and from Low Bentham. These lighter nights would undoubtedly make it more problematical. The risk is still there to be taken. Will any of us take it again before the academic year ends? One can always resort to drinking in the dormitory!

What about the others drinking in the pub? As locals, they surely must have realized (or suspected) that the four lads hidden away in the corner drinking their half-pints were from the boarding house – as indeed must the landlord and landlady. How fortuitous that Snot, living just up the road, did not decide to walk down for a pint.

In a few months from now when the school year comes to an end, the bond with these fellow 6th formers in this Lonsdale dormitory complex will, sadly, be broken and the friendships, most probably, will be ending. Individuals will go their own way. Will some contact be kept with these boarding house friends? Experience from growing up suggests not. Friends were regularly made but easily lost when the inevitable move was made by parents at the end of a posting, be it abroad or within these shores.

In the spirit of the affinity created and to recall the occasional carefree evening at the end of a term, which helped to offset the continual pressure of revising and essay writing, the following has been penned to Geoff, Brian and Rosco:

Silently we crept out, into the welcome winter dark,
confident, quietly confident,
always assuming we had not been seen:
across the river bridge, under a railway,
lane narrowing, senses heightened,
a cautious look behind
perhaps hinted at nervousness:
lights of a boarding school behind,
lights of Low Bentham ahead:
now walking briskly in chilly evening air,
on display from every passing car:
finally, the inviting warmth of evening worship
not to God but to 'The Sun Dial' and alcohol:
(God was mandatory only on Sundays)
the same corner, the same bitter and a lager for Brian
chatting, joyful, musing over a week just gone,
dreaming of the days to come, the future:
another drink, more laughter, a final half pint
and with the watch showing nine o'clock
back into the fresh, chilling air towards a school
glimpsed through misty and glassy eyes:
happy, high spirited,
finally, back in the safety, the warmth, of a dormitory room.
Another Friday has drifted on by, the weekend ahead of us.

Where, though, had Barbara been at morning break today? Christine and Judith knew not, but she was at school. She had been seen in morning assembly with her usual cheery smile when looking across to acknowledge her boyfriend, shaking her head regularly – almost automatically perhaps – to keep her hair in place and away from her face. The answer to the puzzle was provided at lunch break. Having joined Christine and Judith, there was hardly a chance to enquire as to the whereabouts of the third (and the most stylish) musketeer before Barbara appeared with a 'guess-where-I-have-been-look' spread liberally across her normally innocent face. She had walked confidently up to the coffee machine and announced with glee, her face changing seamlessly to one of undiluted triumph, "You will never guess where I have been this morning – or perhaps you might", said with a face glowing with satisfaction – akin to a look one might expect from a woman who has just been shown the Crown Jewels, or that of a young child who has just been given a bag of her favourite sweets. "I just knew I would be right, Ian. Really, you are just too neat and tidy for your own good."

A discussion had then ensued whilst Christine and Judith stood watching and listening, almost spellbound. (Quite an achievement, particularly for Christine.) Perhaps on this occasion at least, as silent spectators, they may have just started to realise that the bond that is forming between their lower 6th form friend and the Head Boarder is not in the "here today, finished tomorrow" category.

"Well, Mrs Wills has done the honours then? That is where you got to this morning and without telling me as well. Don't tell anyone, please, as we don't want her to get into trouble. No one saw you then?"

Christine and Judith had stood with lips intentionally pushed firmly together as an acknowledgement that it was to be kept secret, accompanied by a nodding of their heads. (Question: can Christine keep a secret? For one of her best friends, let us hope so.) Barbara had then continued:

"Whilst she led me through the corridors, I said to Mrs Wills that I was expecting the room to be immaculate. She said nothing – but with a 'you–have–certainly–got–the–measure–of–him' look, she just smiled knowingly at me."

"Well Barbara, it's nice that you have been to see where all the letters to you are written. Always late. Very late at night."

"I thought it was very cosy. Of course, I expected it to be prim and proper and it was rather exciting because, of course, it was slightly naughty being in your room. Exciting in the same way that you were thrilled when I first took you into my bedroom at home, do you remember? And how lovely of you to have my photograph on the window ledge. And all the letters I have written to you tied in that red ribbon I gave you. How sweet. And, as I sat on your bed, I gazed at your yellow pyjamas nicely folded up on the pillow. They almost looked silk, quite Noël Coward I could imagine. How lovely. I can just see you in yellow pyjamas sitting up in bed reading Wordsworth or Keats. Wonderful."

Barbara had been enthused. A comparison, however, with Noël Coward is not quite what one might want a girlfriend to enthuse over, but it was possible to understand her thought process. (Anyway, hasn't Noël Coward just died? More importantly, wasn't he a "poofta"?) Barbara had bubbled with obvious elation, only being held back from a more visual and personal show of affection by the venue and the normal decorum, not only expected but required within school premises. Christine and Judith, meanwhile, had been stood grinning with some amazement and, perhaps, thinking and realizing that there was a passion displayed by Barbara in words and looks not previously detected. Maybe they were also a little envious of Barbara visiting a boarder's study/bedroom. After all, it is at times quite exciting to do something that one is strictly not allowed or permitted to do.

Barbara had continued, "Your window was left open, Ian. Mrs Wills tells me that you like it being left slightly ajar for the fresh air. I am getting to know more and more about you all the time, Ian McCart", she had exclaimed excitedly, at which point Christine and Judith had both pulled a sort of 'oh yes – we wonder what that means' sort of look. If they felt a tiny bit like gooseberries, they didn't show it. On the contrary, they appeared to lap up the information, perhaps storing it in their memory banks for future use. In local terminology or dialect, used regularly by those from this West Riding of Yorkshire, they might have been said to be "gob-smacked". So, a dormitory room has been seen, has been visited. Barbara is happy – she has been itching to visit.

A simple, modest (in size and furniture) private room, but for her, exciting none the less, just as her own bedroom, whilst quite ordinary in her view, is enticing and so intensely personal – even sexy – in her boyfriend's opinion. Good old Mrs Wills. What a treasure – and not only with regard to sewing buttons back on school shirts or providing, when required, a new supply of shoe polish, toothpaste and suchlike. She will herself, for sure, have rather enjoyed the cloak-and-dagger visit and she will, without doubt, have something to say the next time she sees the Head Boarder, whilst upstairs surrounded, as she always is, by the requisite pile of bed sheets and pillowcases on bed-changing day.

Keeping this dormitory window open, even if only left slightly ajar, is something that has almost become a necessary habit. These dormitory rooms are small (no swinging a cat around) and whilst not cramped, they desperately require circulation of air, if only to prevent the enclosed atmosphere becoming stale. The dormitory doors are shut during the school day as well as when occupied in the evening for prep and of course at night for sleep – because of this, they can smell. They do smell. A mixture of body smell, stale socks smell, dirty football boots smell, food smell – and goodness knows what other smells! It is something that is noticed when going into some of the other rooms to chat, to discuss essays or prep, to filch (with agreement!) letter writing paper, or indeed, just to idle away the time. They all have their own individual 'pong', some worse than others. It can make going into some of the rooms quite unpleasant. It is most difficult – well, nigh impossible – to tell someone their room stinks and by extension, there is the constant worry that one's own room may have an unpleasant odour (with no one having the nerve to say anything). The solution? Leave the dormitory room window ajar to let fresh air in.

A mental note is hereby made to talk to Barbara when she is alone – to ask her directly, "Did my bedroom smell unpleasant?" And Barbara, you must be honest with your reply. As you, yourself, regularly request to a boyfriend, "tell me the truth, please. Don't tell me what you think I might want to hear". (But dear Barbara, wouldn't you tell me without being prompted if you felt it had been necessary…?) A smell in the dormitory room – the thought process had wondered and rather hoped, that the room might perhaps still have a trace of that unique Barbara Noble smell come the evening – sadly, it did not. It is, nevertheless, a changed room having been visited by a girlfriend. Oh, for a trace of her unique scent to have been left behind, lingering in the room. She has been here, in this room and everything in and around takes on a new feel. Dear Barbara, you have infiltrated the 'inner sanctum', this private space of the Head Boarder, and having done so, you are clearly as pleased as punch. So, indeed, is the room's occupant. Exciting? Indeed so.

[An aside: *The Boarding House:*
April 1973

Proposed letter to our dear Matron:

Dear Matron,

Yes, my dear Mrs Russell, it was ME that you saw walking down into Low Bentham village the other evening as you drove up the road towards High Bentham! And yes, it was, of course, well after the 7pm curfew time that has been mutually agreed for a return to the boarding house. On that basis, it was quite right that you should have wagged your finger and given a disapproving look. But, as you yourself will have been in love when younger, you must, surely, know and realise the difficulties of leaving a girlfriend's house and indeed, a girlfriend, to return to school for a specific time.

To return to what? An empty dormitory room, a (growing) pile of learning, revising and essays. And a return to studious silence, so very difficult and muted after the laughter, the chatter, the kisses and the perfume from a young lady's bedroom. There may well be banter within this Lonsdale dormitory complex, but it cannot hope to compare with the enjoyment of a young lady's bedroom. Mrs Russell, three times the garden gate at 'Benwick' had been reached – three times – only for a return to the front door on each occasion for another kiss, another hug ("Oh, lift me up and hug me tight Ianey – then I will let you go") and a surreptitious exchange of red Smarties. (Which, as Barbara quite rightly points out, provide the excitement of and entitlement to "fringe benefits" – ask me, Mrs Russell, and I will gladly explain this obsession with red Smarties!)

But honestly, Mrs Russell, it is Barbara's fault. She calls me back after the "final" kiss and hug for another "final" kiss and hug. What can one do? What should one do?

Have you read the poetry of W. H. Auden, my dear Mrs Russell? He understood the problem. It is worth repeating. It may help you understand,

> *Consider if you will how lovers stand*
> *In brief adherence, straining to preserve*
> *Too long the suction of good-bye.*

This letter is merely by way of explanation, Mrs Russell – but thank you anyway for not taking the matter any further and yes, you really DO have a heart of gold. Yes, you do! (Everyone says so...)

Just perhaps, both yourself and Mr Russell also think that Ian and Barbara are "made for each other", but no doubt, your husband will be thinking that it could be impacting adversely on 'A' Level studies – well, he might be right. Let us hope not...

Thank you again. Sincerely yours. The Head Boarder.]

(Note to self: take a girlfriend's advice in future and return to Low Bentham village via the farm fields behind *'Benwick'*.)

So, the Easter holiday commences at the end of this week. Accordingly, an end-of-term report has been kindly provided today by Mrs Fife, who sounded genuine with her generous comment whilst handing it over, "This is a good report, Ian, but don't let up!" More importantly perhaps, she also provided a timetable for the forthcoming examinations. Interestingly, the English Literature report has been penned by Mrs Fife rather than by Ducky. One might have assumed the 'Head of English' would do it rather than the form teacher, albeit that they are both involved with the same syllabus. Perhaps Ducky felt it more appropriate leaving Mrs Fife to summarise following the shenanigans of the Public Speaking competition. It is somewhat difficult to put down on paper or even quantify, but there exists a definite "needle" in this relationship between the Head of the English department and the senior lad in the boarding house. In a rather odd, perverse, way it is quite enjoyable. Who can score 'points' off the other? It seems to simmer just below boiling point, with the saucepan likely to boil over at any moment, almost without warning. Perhaps it serves as an explanation as to why Mrs Fife has penned the term report.

She has summarised the good and the bad (but not the ugly!) in one sentence... *'He has worked conscientiously and thoughtfully and, although his essays vary in quality, he has made progress in forming ideas and expressing them. It is his expression that he just needs to improve'*. Reflecting on that comment, it is probably more generous than might have been anticipated from Ducky. No issues with the History report *('...his essays show considerable maturity'*) and even Sociology, soon to be under the sole watching brief of Mrs Taylor, can be considered acceptable (*'...is beginning to achieve a good standard'*). With a developing and all-embracing relationship regularly (in fact, almost always) taking priority over essays and background reading, the results on the school side are, academically, as good as could be expected. In fact, they are quite pleasing. Exams to come – blimey! Will they be easy? Will this fickle memory kick into action? Will the waffle overscore all the good points? No worrying now. At least for the next few weeks, that is for sure, with Easter almost upon us.

The examination timetable. The first exam on 22nd May and then 24th May... both before the half-term break during the last week in May and both Sociology: Papers I and II. Very convenient and handy, getting Sociology out of the way and then leaving a period of revising over the half-term break for the remaining two subjects. Another issue that needs to be sorted – where to stay for the half-term. First day back at school after the break 4th June - English Lit Paper I - then the two History Papers 8th and 11th June, before a final Eng. Lit Paper II, 14th June. Then it is all over. Just six weeks until the first exam – and Easter is going to be with Barbara in Germany. Some revising will have to get done – it will not be easy.

Easter – the arrangements now having all been sorted out. Train tickets, cross-channel ferry tickets, a visitor passport for Barbara, a lift to Lancaster railway station and a parental 'taxi' ride from Calais to Rheindahlen – all organised with time to spare. There is a good deal to thank Barbara's parents for, not least in allowing their seventeen-year-old daughter to travel to Europe with a still relatively new boyfriend.

More than that though, Barbara's mother has sourced an extra bed and, with the constraints of having just three bedrooms, the bed has been placed in Barbara's brother's bedroom – a convenient arrangement (but not, perhaps, all that welcome for her younger brother, who will now, from time to time, find Head Boarder McCart sharing his bedroom), enabling an overnight stay at *'Benwick'* when school breaks up this coming Friday. Then the journey to Germany on the Saturday.

Cases need to be packed and perhaps, predictably with Barbara, she suspects that her suitcase will be filled both quickly and easily with clothes for every conceivable occasion. What about that request which was made earlier today at school? "Ianey, if you have space in your suitcase, could I put some of my clothes in your case, please? They won't take up lots of space, just things like my t-shirts, underwear, bras and 'what-not'." Good heavens. Superb! Yes, my dear. There will quite definitely be space available for Barbara's 'smalls' – even if it means ditching some Easter background reading for Sociology. Priorities McCart! (Don't think Snot would agree that a girlfriend's 'smalls' should take priority over study textbooks...) Opening a well-travelled suitcase once in Germany in order to take out Barbara's knickers and bras. Christ! Just magic – Barbara, let me do it. Never mind, let me do it – a boyfriend will INSIST on doing it!

HILARY TERM

CHAPTER XXVII

WE GET ON SO VERY WELL TOGETHER

It was never going to be a battle between trains and a girlfriend. A girlfriend would have to win hands down, every time. Nevertheless, it was a relief of sorts to hear Barbara say (after having boarded the train at Lancaster for the trip to Dover Marine), "No, I don't think it is silly having an interest in trains, I think it is quite nice actually." Nothing of course was going to usurp the attraction – the involvement with Barbara – but the curiosity engendered by train travel is enduring, even if it has been latent in recent times. Particularly so with the cessation of steam traction, already nearly five years ago.

So it was that some considerable interest was generated by the rail travel at the commencement of the Easter break – and Barbara took it in her stride. The West Coast railway line northwards from Crewe remains the province of diesel traction. The 'Type 4' diesel locomotive (with British Railways having a power ratio for diesels in ascending order from one to five – five is the most powerful) hauling us south from Lancaster on the Saturday morning is still considered to be in the new category, having been built in 1967/8 at Newton-le-Willows in Lancashire and being in part responsible for the ending of steam. These *English Electric* locomotives exude power by both look and sound and in some strange unaccountable way, simply quite unexplainable to others, it felt rather important being hauled by one of these locomotives whilst sitting quite proudly next to a girlfriend. And then a change of locomotive and indeed of traction at Crewe, still the hotspot of the north for train spotters. A veritable Mecca indeed, with trains arriving and departing every few minutes – to North and Mid-Wales, Manchester, Liverpool, to the north and ultimately Scotland, as well as the Midlands and southwards, to London. Situated just to the south of the station, Crewe Diesel Depot, as always awash with upwards of 100 or more locomotives, a trainspotter's dream. But also, a nightmare, as it will prove almost impossible to make a tally of all the locomotive numbers from the window of a passing train.

Electric haulage from Crewe to London Euston then, arriving at a Euston station, now modern and clinical, without any sort of historical past. Also, recently deprived of its rather incongruous, but decorative, Doric arches at the entrance to the station. The electric locomotives are still relatively new and in keeping with a modern London Euston. Built in the mid to late 1960s, contemporaneously with the electrification of the line north from London, the various electric locomotive classes were eagerly spotted on what might be termed 'underhand' occasional visits to Crewe station in the 1967/68 era, whilst staying with Nanny P during half-term breaks.

> *[**An aside**: Nanny P always assumed, incorrectly, that her grandson had spent the day at Lancaster Castle railway station, rather than half-way down the West Coast railway line at Crewe! Those escapades were not attempted alone, however, but were with school friends and a cousin, Chris Parkinson, all of them being welcome travelling companions. It provided the feeling of 'safety in numbers', most necessary when travelling any distance at a young age. Visits were also made to Preston station and Manchester Victoria, where a fifteen-minute fast walk took one to Manchester Piccadilly station – always worth a visit with a guarantee of seeing unusual electric traction hauling the trains to and from Sheffield. Nanny P might well have been aghast if she had been aware of those day trips away from Lancaster. As it was, instead, she would no doubt have been happily singing her favourite West End musicals at home, assuming a grandson was behaving himself at Lancaster railway station. He was behaving himself, by and large, but not at Lancaster.]*

En-route to Dover, the London Underground had been negotiated with relative ease, the mechanics of the journey under an unappealing London (it is far too big…) having been mapped out in advance of travel. It's not at all difficult is it, if you know what you are doing. The final section, from London Victoria to Dover Marine (directly onto the dock for the ferry), with an electric class of locomotive – but not, in this instance, overhead wires but instead, taking the electric current from a 'third' rail on the ground. These 'third rail' electrics had never been seen during spotting days with their sphere of operation solely on the Southern Region and now they are showing their age, having been introduced in the 1950s. All absorbing stuff – if you have an interest in trains, that is. Whatever, Barbara sounded interested by all the information regularly and enthusiastically provided for her throughout the journey, making it, surely, more exciting. And travel, after all, should be stimulating.

> *[**Note to Barbara**: you see, my dear, it is not ALL Keats and Wordsworth that gains the interest of a boyfriend – although your comment on the return from Germany that perhaps your boyfriend's entire knowledge*

revolves around railways and poetry was rather unkind, even if said with tongue in cheek. Cheeky indeed!]

But now having returned from the Easter holidays, a return to the dormitory. Wednesday 2nd May. Back at school after an Easter break. Two months and a tiny bit to go. Once again, late at night after finishing a letter to Barbara and after ploughing half-heartedly through a history essay. 'What were the main causes of disagreement between James I and his Parliament?' (Oh dear, religion again.) It is difficult, mind, not to laugh at the cover of this history file as some comedienne has written on it… *'This is likkle Ianey's history file and no one is allowed to write on it!!!!'* That has been added (in an idle moment, no doubt) during the Easter break. Now who might have scribbled that? Cheeky monkey she is!

In the next dormitory, Pugh is clearly still up and about, with the almost melodic music from his 'Focus' LP just discernible. Instrumentals can be repetitive, but not 'Focus'. The fact that he has it on a low volume is sensible and a reflection of the late hour. Turn it up… Not quite considered musical to some – but to others it is. Catchy as well. It always proves most difficult not to hum along with the tune. It can be easy to get mixed up with the individual tracks with 'Focus', as they are virtually all instrumental. Not only that, but there sometimes seems to be the same underlying beat. It sounds like the track 'Sylvia'. It is definitely one of those LPs that grows on you as it becomes more familiar. Always worth borrowing it – or buying, as an addition to the 'Hocus Pocus' LP already owned.

And then, once in the comfort of bed, as if by magic the music changes and Pugh treats himself to Led Zeppelin. Again quietly, but the melodic tones of 'Stairway to Heaven' can be discerned – ever popular – a quiet, steady beat at first, but gradually increasing in tempo. *'There is still time to change the road you're on.'* No, not anymore. Not after the holiday break. This Easter break, just gone.

Easter in Germany. It was always going to be different and exciting. The first visit home in seven months – but this time, with a girlfriend in tow. It lived up to its advertised billing. It was indeed different and so very adventurous. Just the Head Boarder and a girlfriend. No school. No school friends. No dormitory mates. Away from Barbara's parents. A mother and father in Germany, yes, but out at work. No respite from being together. All day, every day. Whether it was going to work successfully as a relationship or disintegrate instead, Easter was always going to provide an acid test.

The unpacking – Jesus! Oh, the spectrum of coloured bras and, even better, a dainty pair of white knickers with little red hearts circled all around the top.

Magic! To visualise a girlfriend wearing those pretty knickers. Pack your 'smalls' in a boyfriend's suitcase any time you like…

It was certainly not an auspicious start to the holiday. No problem with that train journey south – and oh, how important it felt sitting next to Barbara on the train from Lancaster down to Dover Marine. An unspoken message went out to all those other passengers, "This is *my* girlfriend. Yes, she is with me and isn't she just lovely?" Were those other travellers – the blokes – thinking to themselves, "Blimey, he is a lucky sod?" Yes, they must have been! Then, having threaded under London on the tube without incident and having then watched those white cliffs disappear into the horizon from the deck of a P & O ferry, what should happen? It was the car journey from Calais that provided the only stumbling block to the exciting expedition. Barbara almost immediately, and with scant warning, threw up on the back seat of a father's car, as the French seaport was left behind! (He wasn't too impressed – good introduction…) Barbara had omitted to provide a timely reminder that she does not travel too well on the back seat of a car. No problem with the movement of water crossing the English Channel, but the movement in a car, quite different – oh dear! For parents, therefore, it was rather a brutal introduction to their youngest son's girlfriend.

And then, at the border crossing between France and Germany, Barbara was taken to one side by the German officials as her passport surname, Noble, was different to the rest of the travelling party, the McCart family. Was she travelling willingly and of her own accord? Was she being coerced? Was she happy to continue her journey? She was, she told the border officials, travelling quite happily and without duress. (Phew…) A humorous episode? Perhaps, but an understandable enquiry from officials when a young (and rather pretty) seventeen-year-old female, not quite old enough to be officially classed as an adult, is travelling away from home territory, with a different family and possessing a different surname.

But, more meaningful than anything else during the Easter holiday in a foreign land, was the discussion that took place whilst homeward bound on the ferry from Calais.

[Yes, really -- more meaningful than the numerous sessions of home baking -- the house cleaning -- the ironing -- the preparation of meals -- the walks out in Rheindahlen camp -- the evening meal at a restaurant, organised and paid for by a father, who was not at all reticent, on this occasion, at spending money (and the first time Barbara had been out for an evening meal at a restaurant, with father treating her as a very important lady - well, that sort of thing just doesn't happen to ordinary

"country girls" from Low Bentham) -- more than the visits to the surrounding towns and to see those houses, sitting precipitously on the banks of the Rhine -- more than visits to nearby Holland with its fancy-looking street barrel organs -- even more meaningful than the sound of bath water filling an ancient bath and of visualising a naked young lady stepping into the welcoming warmth, with the imagination running riot - 'peep through the bathroom door: did you ever?' **If only***. – peep through the bathroom door? CCS did in 1971: 'Tap Turns on the Water'!]*

And so, that discussion on the ferry. What was it all about?

"We get on so very well, Barbara. I really hope you have enjoyed Easter."
"I have enjoyed it so much, Ian, I really have."

"Barbara, why don't we start planning for the future? We might as well start making plans to get married. I do love you, but you know that of course, don't you?"

"And I love you as well, Ian – and yes, I would love to be married to you. When we are back home, let's talk to my mum about how we feel. And you know what? I am so glad that you plucked up the courage to call and ask me if I wanted to go to that party. All through that Speech Day on Saturday, I couldn't stop glancing across at you in the Assembly Hall. But I noticed that you were looking at me as well – so there! And you know what, I had butterflies all the Sunday morning waiting for you to call to take me out for a walk."

There we are – that had been casually suggested and easily sorted. A proposal of marriage. Well after all, aren't traditional marriage proposals only made in films? In no way traditional, but practical and in its own peculiar way, romantic. It was really one made jointly. Isn't sea-travel supposed to be romantic? (Well, it is in films. Okay, it was not quite crossing the Atlantic on the QE2, but nevertheless, thank you to *Sealink* and their vessel *Maid of Orleans*, an ideal venue.) In this instance, the shortest of channel crossings had nevertheless provided sufficient time to plan for, hopefully, a future path through life. A simple embrace on the ferry had hardly done justice to the situation, but it was sufficient. Having already mentioned to parents that the university option was being sidelined, Barbara sensibly had added, "Ian, you must speak with the school after the Easter holidays so that they know that you are not taking up the place at Durham." Of course, you are right young lady. It cannot be put off any longer.

So, with exams commencing towards the end of May – in less than four weeks – another priority must now be to consider what available job prospects there might be locally. It is staying within this locality which must be the priority. That, after all, is what has successfully derailed the original plan to seek a university degree. Following exams, time can hopefully still be spent with Barbara. The prospect of regular income will also start the process of saving money towards what Barbara now terms "our future together". (And a natural reticence to spend money – like father, like son – will help with that saving up process.) How will the school react? A father, who has been paying annual boarding and tuition fees for his youngest son, accepted it with what might be termed good grace. Perhaps with stoical acceptance, albeit with some disappointment, as all parents envisage and hope – or whatever – the best for their children. So then, if the school are not happy with the change of plan, well so what?

The return ferry trip was certainly memorable, but the holiday itself was nothing short of captivating. No, not for the various day excursions or indeed for the window shopping trips which involved travelling around Holland and Germany. No, rather for the simple experience of being with Barbara first thing in the morning and last thing at night. Safely ensconced in her own bedroom, she had quite readily enthused at the suggestion of being woken up with a cup of coffee every morning. But then, her jovial warning from several months ago that, "I am not very good at waking up in the morning", certainly proved more than accurate. She had added half-jokingly at the start of the Easter break that any time in the morning before half-past-eight is simply, "the middle of the night, Ianey. Please, no coffee before half-past-eight." This girlfriend has an inherent dislike of early rising!

And so, at the appointed time, the challenge of the waking-up process commenced. A challenge, well it was, although sometimes it was nice just to let her continue sleeping after half-past-eight had come and gone – how can one wake up a sleeping beauty? (A couple of kisses helps…) Indeed, just how long would she stay sleeping soundly if not physically woken up? Goodness knows. The bedside clock had occasionally winged its way a good hour past the agreed morning call time and still no movement. It was generally the case that the coffee was lukewarm (at best) by the time Barbara had woken up properly and was sufficiently alert to drink it. This necessitated the brewing of another fresh cup. The solution? Ultimately, it was expedient to actually wake her up first, before then providing a fresh coffee once she had "come round", as she phrased it.

Even during the waking up process her countenance was, without fail, serene and sunny and somehow, her long straight hair was always smartly in place, laid out by the side of a peaceful face on the pillow. Quite how it stayed so neatly displayed beside her, goodness knows. A reflection of the fact that she does indeed sleep soundly – even in a foreign bed, in a foreign house and in a foreign land! Dear Barbara, if you ever need to rise with the lark or the cuckoo on a morning, it will be a test of endurance for yourself and, indeed, for the person responsible for waking you up. Not only that, but it will surely knock you for six. A morning person? Definitely not! In this respect then, a young lady and her boyfriend are, quite obviously, opposites.

Incredibly, from the evidence gleaned over the Easter holiday, she seems to have a knack for natural morning freshness despite it taking her some while to fully wake up. She neither needs (or, more importantly, wants) make up, the only thing going onto her face first thing in the morning being *Lypsyl* for her lips and some face moisturiser. Anything else would be anathema to her and would, in any case, spoil her youthful freshness. She could quite well succeed in dispensing with a morning face wash, if it was her wish to do so, without it being particularly noticeable.

The commencement, then, of this waking process was identical – every morning, without fail. After giving her a little shake (or two, or three…) and a kiss whilst she lay sleeping, waking up was generally signified by the opening of one eye (only one), a little smile and *always* the initial and predictable question, "What time is it?" Depending on the time and what plans there were for any particular day, once that had been established, there would follow the almost inevitable request, "Please can I just have a little extra snooze [as she termed it], Ianey? Can you give me a further fifteen minutes please… ta?" The 'ta' would be said both in anticipation and indeed, in the expectation of agreement. Impossible to refuse. A little kiss would be proffered as an immediate 'thank you'. Such anticipation of agreement by a boyfriend was well founded. How could such a request be anything other than approved? So extra-time for a short snooze was always made available. Really quite impossible to refuse it. Incredibly, within the shortest of timescales, she was back asleep, her head on the pillow at a slight angle, motionless and serene. Just how does she do it?

All proper behaviour, both in the morning and at night, with "good night" and "good morning" kisses exchanged. Sometimes there would just be the occasional gentle reminder, "Not too many kisses or cuddles, Ianey, as it could quickly get out of hand for both of us." An acknowledgement indeed that with this mutual love, there is naturally a parallel sexual attraction, particularly in a bedroom with Barbara wearing what John Betjeman would describe skittishly as "slumber-wear".

There exists a strong reciprocal trust and a bond, making the relationship strong enough for Barbara to be quite comfortable sitting up in bed just in her nightwear. She was also quite happy to slip in and out of bed ("I need to squeeze my pips"), allowing her boyfriend to help her on or off with the familiar blue dressing gown. She has trust and knows it will not be abused. However, to witness her legs bereft of trousers or stockings and her upper thighs, incredibly appealing and inviting, together with an occasional glimpse of her knickers as she would get in or out of bed was, to say the least, most enthralling and utterly, utterly entrancing. Two words, heard regularly in this Lonsdale complex when the female form is being studiously discussed, sum it up – bloody hell! Such blasphemy was not uttered by the Head Boarder whilst in a girlfriend's overseas bedroom. Nevertheless, it was there at the forefront of the thought process when a pair of eyes could only focus on two delicate white upper thighs that were displayed, along with regulation white knickers, albeit briefly. Too briefly in all honesty. Dear Barbara, if only you knew what effect your half-naked figure has on a boyfriend's 'appendage'! In consequence, the morning and evening bedtime routine was always eagerly awaited. The enjoyment of that twice daily event far outstripping the rest of the Easter 'entertainment'.

Before travelling this Easter, there had been an underlying anxiety about the time to be spent in Germany, with neither the cause nor the fact that it was a worry being relayed to Barbara. The reason for that slight disquiet? The knowledge deep down that home life when younger and during school holidays had not always been what one might term 'sweetness and light'. If *'Benwick'* could be compared to the 'Sea of Tranquility' (figuratively speaking), then home life (wherever that might have been at any particular time) could only be compared to the mountains of the Pyrenees. That could mean some extreme variations in the general ambience within the family home. Peaks and troughs, certainly. Whilst there were times when family life, as one might ordinarily expect, was lived quite normally, regretfully, there were also times (far more frequently than one might wish as a child) when arguments and disagreements between parents permeated throughout the house. This would result in a long period, often lasting a week and quite easily longer when silence was an undisputed champion. An unwelcome by-product of the original altercation. Do children ever get used to it? Some will, others will not. Perhaps some will come to expect it and therefore just accept it as the norm. Somewhere in one of these compellingly boring Sociology books on the study desk, a suggestion is made that with young children, they will feel safe and loved at home providing they sense total unity between their parents. It sets them up for a feeling of security as they grow to adulthood. Perhaps there is some substance in the concept as postulated. Ah, Sociology! How would society cope without it?

With quarrelling parents, where does the fault lie? Quite firmly with the *Floral Hall* at Morecambe, where a whirlwind romance took place amid a global conflict. The Morecambe sea-front certainly has a lot to answer for. Perhaps the wartime years produced a good number of marriages with partners who were ultimately incompatible, with little opportunity being available to get to know and understand each other. Where are we? Five months into this relationship and it feels as though each of us has got the true measure of the other. No doubt there will be more to learn. All part of the thrill. Whatever, the stark contrast witnessed between a home life whilst growing up, compared with the general calm and peaceful atmosphere pervading within a girlfriend's home could not be more marked. There is a refreshing lack of aggression at *'Benwick'* and a more trusting, family atmosphere.

But all that worrying and apprehension before the Easter holiday – there was no need for it. Parents were, thank goodness, on their very best behaviour throughout the Easter break with no hint of conflict. (With a father even whispering quietly to his youngest son, "That girlfriend of yours, Ian, is a very sensible and attractive young lady." Praise indeed!)

There has been so much laughter shared over Easter – most of it spontaneous, some of it silly, some of it (in private) just slightly coarse, bawdy perhaps, with Barbara often taking the lead (so much for being a "country girl"), but all of it being given and taken with so much enthusiasm. For a boyfriend and girlfriend, it can be deliciously mischievous to be suggestively vulgar in private, saying things that will not be heard by anyone else. Such naughtiness frequently ending with Barbara pulling a slightly embarrassed face and exclaiming, "Goodness knows what my mother would say if she could hear us now!" What indeed. Have you been tainted by your boyfriend, young lady, or has that mind of yours always been rather rude? Humour can be different and divisive to different people. As with so many other things, though, there is a meeting of minds on humour, saucy or otherwise, with two "peas in a pod." Oh yes, and another issue where two minds merge into one – that German (or is it Dutch?) habit of cold meats and cheese and suchlike for breakfast. That was a 'no-no' for the Head Boarder and his girlfriend. There was a joint request, bluntly put, to a father – valiantly and willingly – acting as waiter, "Breakfast cereal please!" [He failed miserably in trying to convert the two visitors to a 'continental' lifestyle!] Meat and cheese for breakfast is rather strange. But also, a curious bathroom. The less said about the rather peculiar low-lying sink in the corner, the better. (It is for washing your bum apparently!) And what about the rather odd 'ledge' in the bog which, according to a father, enables an inspection of 'droppings' to be carried out. Christ!

Early in the holiday, Barbara had purchased an umbrella. Not of a standard design, but instead a hard plastic 'see-through' umbrella with which one can completely encompass the head for total protection from the rain. Enthusiastic as ever and wishing to try it out, she was quite happy to walk along in a foreign country in splendid sunshine, her head fully enclosed within the umbrella. Even better, at times encouraging her boyfriend to squeeze up inside the umbrella with her – which left the respective faces within inches of each other. Marvellous, especially for the inevitable kisses that ensued. Her actions certainly provided some strange looks from passers-by, but was she bothered? No. In a strange and liberating way during those days out in Germany, there had been a complete reversal of perceived roles. Barbara seemingly the one who had travelled abroad many times and was quite at home visiting a foreign land with, perversely, her boyfriend representing, almost completely, the caricature of 'an Englishman abroad'! How strange, but the role reversal worked a treat. Most certainly, a metamorphism of sorts is slowly but surely taking place – that is, from a seemingly shy and bashful 6th form girl into a young woman with confidence and stylish panache – and considerable self-assurance.

Easter had also been the time, although it had not necessarily been by design, to share with Barbara the by now growing collection of poems written mostly, but not exclusively, since the start of this school year. (Flirting with poetry writing commenced during last year's 'A' Level study.) There had not been any intention to let Barbara read (and assess) them. At least, not until this friendship had developed so that they could be handed over with some confidence. They are, perhaps, an alternative form of personal diary and as such, can be considered intensely intimate, an outpouring of inner thoughts or feelings. It all happened quite by accident, but then, having seen the collection of poems and read through them, Barbara wondered quite why they had been hidden away. An understandable reticence caused by a naturally diffident nature. "But Ian, good heavens, why?"

Whilst a Sociology folder and several revision books had been happily ditched from the suitcase (to free up much needed space for more important stuff – knickers, t-shirts and bras...), History and English Literature folders had been included in the holiday packing. The continuing belief is, of course, that these two subjects are more important, as well as being more interesting, than Sociology. It still might be the case that Sociology proves to be the Cinderella of two years' 'A' Level study. That is, providing sufficient reasoning is provided to what might well be, according to Mrs Taylor, "Open ended examination questions." Whatever, there had been no Sociology revision on the agenda for Easter and none was done. In all honesty, a minor miracle it was, certainly, that other revision had been done.

It was by chance then that the history folder had specifically attracted Barbara's interest and attention. It is, of course, always more interesting to look through a boyfriend's school folder – or a girlfriend's come to that – rather than one's own. So, Barbara had wanted to, as she eloquently phrased it, "Check on how proper essays should be written!" (She will soon acquire the knack of ignoring the waffle...) At the back of the folder, after all the boring machinations of Medieval European history, the collection of poems had been paper clipped together, representing some eighteen months of writing, having been painstakingly typed out on the trusty portable *'Brother'* typewriter – a simple piece of machinery that is almost as valuable as a loyal friend. A typewriter that had been presented as a birthday present during teenage years by a mother who considered a request for that particular present to be rather odd. "Why on earth do you want a typewriter for your birthday, Ian?" The urge to write and the desire to be neat was already prevalent from early teenage years.

"Oh Ian, I think your poems are lovely – how sweet!" was sufficient acknowledgement. And indeed acceptance – if acceptance of them from Barbara was needed. (It was – and is. And surely, she knows her boyfriend well enough by now to give a genuine considered appraisal. But then, would you have said, Barbara, if you thought they were crap?) Faithfully typed out – but prior to that, written on scrap paper, words changed, sentences altered, stanzas jettisoned, then added to. All that before a final written draft which is then religiously typed out with suitable care and precision. And even then, odd words might be changed involving a further dose of typing. A laborious process? Not at all. On the contrary, hugely enjoyable. All part of the overall process. What a pity one of the 'A' Level English Literature questions will not cover the work involved in the formation of a poem and how the whole is linked together with the parts. Using, of course, a poem of one's own as an example. Mrs Fife did not seem to enthuse to the idea.

One of the poems inadvertently 'unearthed' by Barbara is, well, not naughty but perhaps suggestive. Barbara picked up on how her boyfriend's mind was working almost immediately,

That which you surely take for granted,
For you see them both every day -
They belong to you – they are uniquely yours – they
Advertise, through cotton finery, your womanhood
And are, as you yourself suggest, just "average".

But for another, whose eyes never catch
Sight of the prize, they are valued so highly:
They are priceless and will remain so!
This is how we wish it to be:
Patience and true love inseparable.

"Oh Ian, how naughty, you are a little monkey. A poem about my bosoms. How rude – and for your information, they are going to remain out of bounds. Well, they are, certainly, for the time being!" (Okay – but what about "priceless"?)

And in between the process of writing poetry and endlessly messing about with unfinished versions within this dormitory, the continuation in the evening of essays and reading (many times over) love letters from *'Benwick'*. Then, writing love letters in return, the contents of which, sadly, never quite match the same standard of humour displayed in arrivals displaying that familiar flowery scribe. In writing love letters, Barbara has indeed found her forte, flipping effortlessly from humour to sarcasm, to leg pulling, to genuine affection, to school gossip and for good measure, always giving the slightest hint at being just ever so slightly naughty or suggestive. *('If you could see me now in my see-through knickers... but you damn well can't matey; so there!')* See-through knickers, really? And all encompassed within a typical six sides of letter writing.

So, this ever-growing collection of poems has been given approval from a rather flattered girlfriend and with her natural passion for laughter and living, there were perhaps just three words of disapproval with regards to some of the verses. "Why so sad?" A good question. What is the answer?

Monday 7th May. Undoubtedly, the junior lads in the boarding house have got the measure of the on-going relationship with Barbara. This Monday evening, a letter to Barbara had been started earlier whilst in the dining room looking after the junior forms during their prep period. In one of the lighter moments, they were asked, "Right lads, tomorrow morning, the most fantastic person in the school will be doing the morning reading in school assembly. Who do you think that is?" The question elicited some humorous and perhaps predictable responses. "Is it you Mucca?" "It's not you, again, is it?" "Do we have to go if it is you?" What other retorts might one expect? "No, it is someone from the opposite sex, lads. Now can you guess?" They had been left guessing but most seemed to have their suspicions. "I bet it is your girlfriend, Mucca, isn't it?" "It must be Barbara Noble." etc.

And during the supervision of prep in the dining room, the young boarders might have wondered what the Head Boarder was doing spending time cutting out individual letters of the alphabet from the daily newspaper. What indeed. (No, nothing to do with golfing tips aka Titty!) Once back in the dormitory, the letters have been carefully arranged and stuck onto a letter being written to Barbara and the message in newspaper type is, 'I loVe bARbAra nOBle', in a splendid variety of capital and small letters! A succinct message, even if it is something she is already aware of. Certainly aware. But still rather nice (and comforting) to read in a letter. Can it be written or spoken to a girlfriend too many times? With a boyfriend, the same message coming from a girlfriend can never grate. It needs to be heard and read repeatedly, continuously, to allay that illogical fear lurking in the psyche that a girlfriend no longer loves the Head Boarder.

Despite concerted and continuing efforts, it is difficult to match the humour and sense of fun that the letters from Barbara invariably display. It is as though she can be funny despite hardly trying. For the recent Easter holiday, Barbara had packed several *Woman's Own* magazines and also *Woman's Weekly* to read (her mother buys both magazines, but they seem to cover a readership age range from young adults to middle age) and the magazines provided great fun, particularly the submissions to the 'problem page' with two Marys' –Marryat and Grant – providing suitable answers.

'Dear Mary, I'm fifteen years old and in love with the driver of the school bus.' (What, one wonders, does the school bus driver make of it, assuming he has an inkling? Ha!) *'Dear Mary, I have recently passed my driving test and have a soft spot for my instructor. We have had the odd kiss although he is married...'* Perhaps waking a seventeen-year-old girlfriend up in the morning with a cup of coffee is not so daring after all. With the perverse enjoyment obtained from reading the various problems submitted to the magazines (are

they genuine? Barbara seems to suggest they are) and the inevitable interest in the (more often than not) sternly worded replies, the letter received today from Barbara (which has been answered whilst supervising prep) had its own 'Barbara version' of a problem letter, as follows,

Dear Ian,

My boyfriend and I have been going out together for seven years. Last night, he held my hand for the first time. Do you think he is being rather foreword in his intentions? Yours 'desperate'!!!

Oh, yes – letter writing. No written reply from our lovely Matron to the Head Boarder's 'thank you' letter! As anticipated, however, she took it in the best spirit and had an enjoyable laugh – albeit that she had suggested that the Head Boarder was "rather cheeky" in sending it! (But said with a big, knowing smile on her face.) Really, Mrs Russell, how wonderful you are – surely, the best matron *ever*!

Some ideas are good – some not so! These council meetings for the boarding house – held on the landing of the Lonsdale complex – are they a good idea? They cause some considerable angst for the Head Boarder, who is in overall charge of proceedings! A general moaning session? Perhaps. When the moaning turns inward and specifically at the Head Boarder, not so funny! The music ("the loud music"!) emanating from the room of the Head Boarder is (it now seems) a bone of contention. Okay, the volume needs turning down – why didn't anyone say (Yes, they just have done!) Music when it is enjoyed, it doesn't seem loud; when it is disliked, it is too loud! Strange.

Dovetailed in with all other events immediately following Easter was the inevitable meeting at lunchtime today with Snot. At last. It could not be put off any longer. Barbara had – sensibly, it must be admitted – said, "No meeting today at lunchtime; you must go and see Snot and tell him. Promise me you will do it and I will see you at afternoon break." Barbara, always sensible and practical. She perhaps senses that there is an inherent flaw in her boyfriend's temperament. Lack of self-confidence and the unerring ability (or uncanny knack) of putting something off until another day. It is easy – almost too easy – to put off doing something that is going to be unpleasant and awkward. It was an issue, however, that could not be left any longer without causing problems with administrative issues.

"Are you sure that is what you want, McCart?" Snot had asked looking somewhat perplexed on being told that the proposed degree course at Durham University was no longer part of the forward thinking. He was left in no doubt that it was indeed what was wanted. "I admit that I am somewhat disappointed as I am confident that you will achieve the required entry grades", he had continued, his face becoming slightly crestfallen, perhaps realising whilst speaking that the school's university entrance numbers had just reduced by one. "What are your immediate plans now following your 'A' Levels?" Earning some cash had figured somewhere in the reply. (But staying in the environs of Bentham did not, despite it being one of the key imperatives.) Whilst he never said as much, perhaps he had more than a sneaking feeling that a romantic attachment had played a large part in swaying the decision. After all, this was flipping the educational process 180 degrees, turning it into, hopefully, a salaried occupation in the environs of the Vale of the Wenning.

Was he perhaps thinking that ambition was being sacrificed for love? But what ambition? No ambition here! There has been a conspicuous absence of ambition since this school year commenced. A degree course at Durham University would only, surely, be putting off the judgement day regarding a suitable occupation. How can one be so sure at this age as to what type of work is suitable? Only when you are sure can you then have the ambition, surely? Lucky indeed are those who want to be a doctor, a policeman, an engineer, an accountant and the like and stick to what is, perhaps, their chosen vocation. In any case, the school has now been told. What a weight off the mind. Why wasn't it done earlier?

Barbara did not require verbal confirmation that the deed had been done at afternoon break by the coffee machine. For once, the confident grin that she could see on her boyfriend's face as she walked briskly along the corridor told her all she needed to know.

CHAPTER XXVIII

YOU ARE BOTH STILL VERY YOUNG

Saturday 12th May. Back in the dormitory. A day spent at *'Benwick'*. An interesting day. Looking back on it causes a wry smile.

Is everybody in this Lonsdale block working conscientiously behind closed doors? Not by the sound of it. Well, Saturday evening – why should they be? From one of the rooms towards the end of the Lonsdale dormitory overlooking the hardcourt playground, possibly 'Bessie' Braddock's room or perhaps Whittaker's, the familiar 'twang' of Led Zeppelin filters out onto the landing, demanding attention. Their newly released album, 'Houses of the Holy', is doing the rounds. Like their previous albums, the music needs to be listened to numerous times before it grows on you. (If indeed it is to grow on you – but it most likely will eventually…) As possibly the greatest rock group of all time (a contentious claim made by several of the boarding house clientele: others suggest that mantle belongs to Pink Floyd – never!) the LP will no doubt be popular. Strangely, the cover sleeve has neither the name of the group or the title of the LP, merely displaying naked children climbing some rocks. (Weird.) Open out the cover sleeve and… naked adults – at a distance. (Not quite so weird.) The most popular track appears to be *'Over the hills and far away'*. Didn't someone else sing that but with different lyrics? All a bit Irish. Such idle thought… totally irrelevant as well – but sometimes necessary.

Barbara has spoken with her mother following the return from Germany. Her mother asked if she could have a general chat so that future plans could be discussed. Today was the day. Before meeting her mother in the kitchen of *'Benwick'*, the morning was spent firstly in the garden. (Badminton and French cricket in the garden just about complete the full complement of Barbara's sporting prowess… and tennis perhaps.) Then briefly, before going to see her mother in the kitchen, Barbara's bedroom was a welcome venue for a chat – indeed, a favourite venue at that. A sort of confidence booster perhaps for what a girlfriend could sense was a slightly nervous boyfriend.

Speaking quietly and with a busy, reassuring manner, Barbara – both sounding and looking positive – had said, "I'm sure my mother is going to be alright with our plans, Ianey. She said she was going to speak to my dad and then she just wished to talk it through with us both. It will be fine, honestly, no need to worry. She does realise that we love each other, you know."

With Barbara sat on the edge of her bed and with being sat next to her earlier this afternoon, her body perfume had filled the air and was all embracing and unique – and intoxicating! It is a Barbara Noble smell, individual to her. She smells of youth and excitement. Whilst cuddling up close and offering the gentlest of kisses, she responded with a twinkle in her eyes. Then, with a rather cheeky, almost apologetic grin, made a suggestion that had increased the heart rate and gave notice of the fact that within, there is a sexual urge, spawned as a consequence of love. Sooner or later that urge will prove to be unstoppable!

"Ianey, once we are married, if you like, you can share a bath with me." *If you like…* Christ! On receiving what could only be a more than positive, enthusiastic response, she had continued rather more bossily. "After we are married mind, not before, and it will have to be on one condition. You will have to sit next to the taps because I like to lie back in the bath and contemplate awhile. I really enjoy my bath time. And another thing, I do like to have lots of water in, matey, so I won't be wanting you to be stingy with the water." Quite obviously, this young lady is going to be in charge when it comes to bath time. Fill it as full as you wish young lady! Indeed, Barbara most definitely enjoys her allocated bath time. A recent letter had confirmed that very fact for she had written, *'I am writing this in bed as I have just had a lovely long bath (for God's sake lad, control yourself!!) and I soaped all over my long, lean, gorgeous body and then lay in the hot water with the fragrant scent of Aqua Manda bath lotion lingering in my nostrils!'* Good heavens. What incitement! Just to picture it in the mind… there is a desperate, unstoppable yearning to see Miss Noble in the nude. She realizes as much!

And whilst still sitting on the bed, Barbara had then continued, rather playfully, "If you are a good boy, whilst we are sharing a bath, I shall let you wash my back. But just remember, I will refuse to sit next to the taps." Jesus, the prospect of "being a good boy", as she had so eloquently phrased it, was difficult to envisage whilst sharing the bath with a young, naked and attractive lady. (And anyway, what about all the other parts that will need washing? Never mind the back – what about the front?) The response to such an inviting suggestion was an obvious one to set her mind at rest. "Sitting next to the taps will not be a problem, Barbi."

Barbara, by now well into her confident stride, had then continued, "and as well as a shared bath, what about a pillow fight, Ianey?", followed by a short pause before adding with a rather naughty smile, "and we know how that will end don't we now?"

"Goodness me", Barbara had then exclaimed rather sheepishly, "how naughty we are. It is a good job my mother cannot hear us talking about sharing a bath. Heaven knows what she would say." What indeed? If she had heard the conversation, she might perhaps have been thinking that her daughter is being led astray – but no! In such circumstances, it is a boyfriend who is quite readily, willingly led astray. Would a mother be shocked though? With this young lady, who shows considerable enthusiasm and spirit, is it not a little exciting to be considered a tiny bit naughty – whatever a mother might think? Whilst being thought of as 'nice and proper' most of the time, surely every girl has some secret urge to be 'risqué' every now and then. Don't they? Otherwise, how boring.

"Oh, and by the way, Ianey," Barbara had then continued, "the two books we ordered from the Book Club have come." Barbara then leant across and took them out of the top drawer of her dressing table. She handed over *John Betjeman: The Collected Poems,* whilst keeping her own book held tightly against her breasts. "I do think that my book will be a lot more interesting than yours," she said holding her lips tightly together and suppressing a sly grin before then proudly holding up her own acquisition, *Everywoman, A Gynaecological Guide for Life.* "I have had a quick look through it, Ianey, and there are lots of interesting pictures." And, so saying, Barbara had given a predictable scrunch of her nose before continuing, "I think this book will keep us on the straight and narrow once we are married and I will let you read it as well if you wish. Even better, we can look through some of the chapters together." Then, as an afterthought as the book was handed over, Barbara had added playfully, "Chapter 5 looks rather interesting, but no practising with any of the suggestions until after we are married, mind!"

As sex education goes within the confines of a boarding school, Barbara's book will, perhaps, be as good as it gets. That is unless, of course, one includes the occasional *Playboy* or *Mayfair* magazines that do the rounds in the Lonsdale dormitory complex. (*Mayfair* always, of course, the winner with the photographs.) Other than that, sex education has been confined to the casual throw away comments made by 6th formers, which generally suggest that their knowledge is greater than it actually is! The intermittent meetings of the school council have, from time to time, had the issue of sex education on the pupil sponsored agenda as adolescents grapple with the need to know and understand more about sex. Whilst certainly a taboo subject under the somewhat authoritarian rule of Mr Webb, with the sexes kept very much at arm's-length, at least the subject can now be discussed and considered within the school. Any resulting sex education, however, is aimed at those just below the 6th form, perhaps on the assumption that the 6th formers already know 'what is what'!

Without doubt, Barbara's *Everywoman* will provide an interesting insight into the seemingly complex and slightly unknown world of the female anatomy. Apart from the obvious fact, of course, that a woman has boobs and a fanny – in addition to the fact, which was passed rapidly around the young teenagers in those early boarding school years, that the girls of a similar age at that time were starting to use what was crudely termed as a "Jam Rag". It was what one might term a 'generalisation' and the specifics were never explored any further by young teenagers otherwise involved with train spotting. Railways, certainly, a far more important hobby at that time compared to the travails of the teenage girls commencing their monthly period.

Everywoman. The information (pictorial and otherwise) will be made all the more exciting by sharing the information with a girlfriend who classes herself as "quite ordinary", although she is anything but. Both boyfriend and girlfriend will surely learn a thing or two from the book even if, for the time being at least, there is no dress rehearsal. As Barbara had suggested whilst flicking through the pages whilst sat on her bed, "I need to find out more about myself", by which she means the way a young lady's body works. Both partners will surely benefit from what the book says (and shows) – in particular, chapter 5! Dress rehearsals – they have them in the theatre…

There has, in fact, already been some discussion over the last few months regarding one aspect of the female body. Barbara has been quite ready and more than willing to talk openly about her monthly periods, whether it be by letter ("I have started with my 'you know what' tonight") or face to face. She has felt an obligation to do this, explaining that, with the majority of her periods, she suffers some pain. In her words, "a fierce cramp down below", which she says can, "put me out of sorts for a day or two but even if I appear a little cranky, I do still love you, Ianey." (Cranky, grumpy – never!) If nothing else, being told when her period has started has enabled one to have an understanding and to be sympathetic and, in a strange way, to be included. Almost to be part of the process.

The *Woman's Weekly* magazine has again proved of some interest (but this time in a serious vein rather than, as with the problem pages, in a flippant way) with a regular interesting feature, *'Pauline Richards discusses some of your more intimate questions about periods'*. These have been read together and discussed. However, the recent advice about it being normal for a young lady to put on a few pounds in weight during her period has meant that Barbara now steadfastly refuses to step onto the bathroom scales when her period starts! Putting on weight, whatever the cause, is an absolute anathema to her. (John Donne, seventeenth-century genius, how right you were. Show me a woman… etc.)

A form of practical help is given occasionally whilst visiting *'Benwick'* when, during her periods and providing the house is empty, with the family out either in the garden or visiting/shopping etc., she is happy to let a boyfriend take her discarded pads (which she puts in a shoebox under her bed) to be burnt on the fire grate in the front room. There is an incredibly strong bonding exercise involved with such a task, ensuring that one feels involved with the female side of a girlfriend's life and can come to terms with it and perhaps, more importantly, understand it. For surely, isn't that what a partnership will be all about? Such intimate help and discussions are now helping to form what is rapidly becoming an unbreakable attachment. A girlfriend wanting to involve her boyfriend in the workings of her body and a boyfriend appreciative of being included, and anxious both to help and to learn.

And what of *The Collected Poems* by Sir John Betjeman? [No longer any need to borrow the school library abridged version now!] A brief look through the book once back in the safety of this dormitory reveals, surprisingly, (although there is no reason why it should be a surprise), a poem written about Felixstowe. That sort of 'ever so slightly genteel resort' on the east coast, where a mother and father had briefly settled in between their overseas postings (well, in Old Felixstowe actually – the posh bit). Betjeman writes of Felixstowe, *'The long wave claws and rakes the pebbles down / Against the tide, the off-shore breezes blow.'* Both descriptions sum up the brief memory of that Victorian resort in a nutshell. Pebbles. There are certainly plenty of pebbles large and small on the beach at Felixstowe (millions of them – but no sand) and they are accompanied by a town with a rather elegant, albeit slightly faded, Victorian grandeur. To describe the town as slightly seedy would perhaps be somewhat unfair. However, like most of our seaside towns, there is the unmistakable feel that the modern world is gradually leaving Felixstowe and the rest of them behind.

There is, indeed, going to be a good deal of reading – new stuff as well – to be enjoyed in this Betjeman volume, albeit that it does not form part of the English Literature syllabus. On an initial glance, there appears to be a large helping of melancholy in a similar vein to Keats. What perverse enjoyment there is in reading melancholic poetry. Isn't all poetry a study in melancholy in varying degrees? Also, somewhat surprisingly, a comparable writing style, albeit the two poets are from different centuries – quite different eras, in fact. The difference between this Betjeman volume and the headmaster's kindly gifted *Poetry of the Committed Individual* is stark. Betjeman's poetry is most certainly in the 'old fashioned' tradition and is the better for it. It runs along nicely and takes you with it. (Although it is highly likely, mind, that Mr Hagen, if given the chance, will challenge such an assertion vigorously. He will not be given the chance.)

Earlier this afternoon, then, the patterns on the red kitchen curtains had been catching the afternoon sun, sending alternate streaks of light and shade across the kitchen top. With the sun shining on Barbara's mother's face, she had retreated away from the kitchen sink, taking refuge instead in front of the boiler. For once, therefore, whilst in the kitchen, Barbara did not have her bum lodged on the top of the coke boiler. Instead, it nestled comfortably, and fitted quite nicely and rather conveniently, on her boyfriend's knees, the kitchen stool valiantly taking the weight of the two "peas in a pod" – a male weight of 10 stone and a female weight of 8 stone.

Barbara's dad had been busying himself in the confines of the greenhouse, dutifully tending to his newly planted tomato plants. That indeed is where he had stayed, conveniently out of earshot and involvement. That would, Barbara confidently announced later, be exactly where he would want to be. Barbara's brother was ensconced in the lounge. Nothing was going to pull him away from the television. (FA Cup Final day – but he was in for a shock – his team, Leeds United, unexpectedly lost!) Four patterned mugs stood dutifully beside the kettle and Barbara's mother had then proceeded to brew the tea, carefully pouring from a pale blue teapot into the individual mugs via the obligatory tea strainer before beginning her 'talk'.

"Barbara, take this mug of tea to your father please and tell him that we are just having a chat", which, Barbara later clarified, was the coded message from her mother to her father to make sure he stayed in the greenhouse and out of the way. (He really did not need telling…) On Barbara's return and after she had enthusiastically reclaimed her position on a boyfriend's knee, her mother got the ball rolling. "Well, you two, your dad and I have had a chat and I just want to talk a few things through with you both, okay?" There followed a joint nodding of heads and Barbara had smiled, perhaps slightly nervously, with the briefest of tender kisses being exchanged. Her mother then continued, "Well it is easy to tell that you both think very highly of each other, and I can see that you are clearly in love. It is lovely to see you both doing little jobs for each other as well as helping me around the house. But [there was obviously going to be a 'but'…] you need to remember that you are both still very young and at school doing your studies. You need to be absolutely sure that you love each other before you start making any long-term plans." Almost immediately, and without any hint of a prompt, Barbara had glanced up at a boyfriend and then looked across to her mother, offering a confident reply. "We are sure, Mum, we love each other", and another tender little kiss was proffered to a boyfriend and accepted. Donny Osmond may well be singing about 'Puppy Love' and leading the way in the pop charts, but puppy love this isn't. Barbara's mother then continued, "Alright, yes, I can see that you love each other but it is important that you both finish your studies so that you have some qualifications. That will enable both of you to get good jobs. You need to be patient. You have your whole lives to look forward to. You are both still young. You cannot kill love. It will still be there once your schooling days are over."

Yes, indeed, Mrs Noble you are right. Very young. Undoubtedly, but eager to grow up nonetheless, and to grow up quickly. Just perhaps W. H. Auden was speaking from experience when he wrote, *'The years shall run like rabbits'*, and just how long will those rabbits run for? We are both at a young age. There is a compelling urge to grow up, fast, and be grown up. The advice from Nanny P, dispensed whilst spending the occasional half-term under her jurisdiction, is recalled but not necessarily wholeheartedly agreed with – viz. "You will grow up soon enough, Ian. Enjoy your life whilst young. It is heavenly to be young and free. The years will go by quickly enough without you wishing them away." (But really?)

The advice delivered in some style by Barbara's mother is, it cannot be denied by anyone sane and sensible – undoubtedly sound. There have been anecdotal stories in recent years of 6th form girls having to leave their respective schools by virtue of being pregnant and being unable, therefore, to continue their studies. That situation has not, as far as one knows, happened (at least recently) at the grammar school and surely within the parochial surrounds of the Bentham villages, if it had, the ensuing scandal would not only be known about but would also have been the subject of much feverish and heated discussion!

Wasn't it Cat Stevens who sang, *'O very young, what will you leave us this time? You are only dancing on this earth for a short while…'* How long is a short while? How long has anyone got? Is it any wonder that the urge, when young, is to get on with growing up? Those rabbits are already running and for some have finished running. The memory of poor Kevin Green remains fresh every time that toilet room here at boarding school is visited, along the corridor from this Lonsdale dormitory complex.

And then, perhaps even more important than giving advice regarding the continuation of learning, Barbara's mother had progressed confidently to discuss a subject which, possibly, she might have found slightly delicate. If she found it so, it did not show. The implication regarding ensuring that school studies continued was clearly the lead into what might happen to prevent continued learning. She would surely, however, have been pleasantly pleased that her daughter and boyfriend were actually more than willing to talk about it. Yes, Ducky thinks there is still some growing up to be done, but then he would say that.

Barbara's mother had continued, "You both also need to try and be patient about having sex. I realise it will not be easy for you both when you are in love, but if you can, try and wait until after you are married. You don't want to be forced to leave school because you are starting a family, do you? It is particularly important when you haven't got a job or any income and neither would you have anywhere to live." Barbara had, naturally enough, with it being her own mother and with being in her parent's house, continued to do the bulk of the talking. She had replied almost nonchalantly, "Yes, we are attracted to each other, Mum, and would both like to have sex. We have discussed it. Please try not to worry, Mum, we are both sensible and we have decided to wait."

The subject of sexual intimacy has, indeed, been discussed whilst out walking around Low and High Bentham on the well-trodden footpaths, up the Mill Road, around the 'square mile' and along the riverbank. Indeed, it is also the subject of some discussion whilst just sat chatting in the privacy of a girlfriend's bedroom. How can it not be discussed? It keeps cropping up. It is something that is a natural extension of being in love and at eighteen years of age and seventeen years of age a logical consequence of the love jointly felt. Both boyfriend and girlfriend would like to have sex, yes, a girlfriend in particular realising how attractive she is to her boyfriend. However, thus far, common sense had prevailed over understandable sexual urges. Not easy.

Indeed, hadn't mutual respect and trust been shown whilst in Germany first thing in the morning and last thing at night? A particularly relevant point when, with a girlfriend sleeping so soundly on a morning, some advantage could well have been taken whilst she still slept – but that would have betrayed a belief in the faith built up by a girlfriend in her sweetheart. Anything linked to the natural sexual urge contained within both prospective "life partners" (Barbara's new term for herself and boyfriend) will be contained until released with joint approval. In Barbara's words, "We better not go too far, Ianey, otherwise we both may find it impossible to stop." Quite right, young lady, particularly for a boyfriend, and let us hope there continues to be joint agreement on where to draw the line – and can that line be adjusted, will it be adjusted…?

"Mum," Barbara had continued with a slight change of subject, but it was, perhaps, a logical point at which to bring the question up. "If Ian can get permission from the school to stay over with us sometimes at the weekend, is that alright?" On receiving a confirmation nod of the head from her mother, she had continued, "And you don't mind do you if Ian brings me a cup of coffee in the morning and that we have a chat before going to sleep at night once I am in bed? It is lovely being woken up by Ian and saying goodnight whilst in bed. Ian will wear his dressing gown and I will be in bed, so we will both be decent." Before a reply could be provided by her mother, Barbara had added quickly, as if to ensure that only one possible answer could ultimately be provided, "You know, Mum, we did it whilst staying with Ian's parents in Germany and we behaved ourselves."

Barbara's mother was necessarily magnanimous and perhaps realistic in accepting what was, in some respects, a *'fait accompli'*, with the practice already having been in place in Germany. She had readily agreed. She did, however, just add one condition, "Perhaps you should leave your bedroom door open, Barbara, and then I don't think your dad will mind." And then her mother, looking rather sternly at Barbara, albeit with the hint of a wry smile, added, "and by the way, missy, when Ian does stay overnight with us, no nipping from your bedroom to the bathroom just in your knickers and bra, young lady, okay?" Whilst a serious point, it was a cause for laughter from all those present, particularly when it was pointed out by the prospective overnight visitor that he would in no way object to that specific habit being continued! Perhaps, reflecting now on the discussion, it was just as well that Barbara had not volunteered the information that she quite readily got in and out of bed in Germany with her boyfriend's assistance. Not only with his help but enthusiastically accepting it.

As a parting shot at the end of the discussion, Barbara's mother had then added in a somewhat philosophical tone, with a touch of humour blended in, "Well, I guess if Ian has seen you first thing in the morning, young lady, as you are waking up and still wishes to spend his life with you, then there is no question, it must be true love." Yes indeed, Mrs Noble, but even when bleary-eyed during the waking process, there is still displayed across your daughter's lovely face the freshness of youth.

Amid the laughter and the banter, a brief and tender kiss had been exchanged. Far from being embarrassed by all the cuddling and smooching that had formed an integral part of the afternoon discussion, Barbara's mother had displayed an understanding and an acknowledgement of the genuine feeling that exists between her daughter and boyfriend. Perhaps she might also have been impressed by the maturity shown by them both. She most certainly will be grateful (and thankful) that a daughter, whom she has considered sensible enough to have been given considerable freedom, has found a prospective like-minded partner. Not only that but she must, surely, realise that neither will take advantage of the other.

Another matter conveniently settled whilst at *'Benwick'*. Half-term. With a spare bed now in her brother's room, it seemed quite logical to seek agreement from Barbara's mother for an extended stay over the half-term break, incorporating the Bank Holiday and immediately following the two Sociology exams. She agreed, not only willingly but enthusiastically, perhaps realising that by doing so, she would have a keen volunteer to keep the open fire cleaned daily and prepared for lighting in the evening. Perhaps she enjoys having her daughter's boyfriend around the house. Most certainly, the fire will be given close and dedicated attention. Even with the longer days and lighter nights, a fire adds some comfort to the living room. It forms an integral part of family life in the homely and friendly living room which *'Benwick'* undoubtedly is. There seems little, if any, arguing or disagreements within the Noble family structure and it manifests itself in a quiet and tolerant attitude exuded by both mother and daughter. Regarding Barbara, she is just not the quarrelling type and for that matter, neither are her parents. So, the May half-term will be spent at *'Benwick'*. As Barbara's dad would say following a particularly enjoyable meal or when satisfied with some arrangement or other that has been made – "Champion"!

Back to the here and now. The view from the dormitory window is one to savour on an evening such as this. The trees in the nearby wood flourishing with foliage and tulips along the grass border adjoining the swimming pool, both red and yellow, almost showing off and wanting – perhaps expecting – to be admired. The water in the river calmly makes its way westwards without fuss, lapping gently over the boulders on the riverbed, creating numerous miniature water courses as the various stones split the flow, sending the water into alternate paths, but always westward flowing. Eventually, with the absence of stones on the riverbed, the separate water courses meet up and the river once again displays its prowess.

The sun, setting ever later, keeps the river margins alive. The evening light streaks across the water, highlighting a combination of wild garlic and bluebells that grow rampant along the edges of the nearby coppice. The scent cannot be detected from the dormitory, but a recent walk with Barbara up along the Millhouses Road and then onto the footpath within the wood provided the intoxicating aroma of the garlic combined with the enchanting sight of bunches of bluebells. Quintessential rural England one might suggest. Singapore, Aden and Iran – all those countries lived in whilst growing up – indeed might boast their varying attractions. Within this pair of eyes, however, their varied charms are no match for the changing scene or, indeed, the changing moods of an English countryside. Not only that, but a walk in the wood with a beautiful girlfriend is something that the rest of this world just cannot match. Simplicity is at times sufficient.

This coming Tuesday will signal a mere three weeks before the first of the two Sociology exams, the second following two days later on the 24th May – the day before half-term. Then Sociology is over. A half-term without Sociology, but it cannot be all play at *'Benwick'*, with the remaining exams following hard upon the holiday break. The end of the school year approaches. A rumour abounds that the Housemaster and Matron, along with their children, are leaving the school at the end of this academic year. If true, a real blow for the school (more so to the boarding house). Mr Russell and his wife have proved to be very popular with the boarders right across the age range. Bubbling away under the surface has been the obvious visual niggling, and no doubt frustrating, battle with the catering side. Catering led, of course, from the front by Titty, providing a challenge to Mr Russell during his never-ending attempts to improve the content and variety of the boarding house diet. Nevertheless, each victory seems to be achieved only after a hard-fought battle. Will this have played a part in their imminent departure, if indeed they are leaving? The old adage is still pertinent perhaps – there is no smoke without fire. Where do rumours start? Who starts them? This one will surely have its source via one or other of the two Russell children.

On the bed, one of the school's Sociology textbooks lies abandoned. Abandoned? Yes, for who really wants to read about famous Sociologists and their theories? Max Weber, Emile Durkheim, Herbert Spencer, Karl Marx? (Karl Marx, a Sociologist? More of a Marxist, surely.) No Sociology reading tonight. Sociology exams may indeed be only a fortnight away. The mind may be full of thoughts of the future – that is, the long-term future and even the immediate future. But the two Sociology exams form no part of the thinking. If the exam questions can be answered, they will be answered. Otherwise… well.

Tea For The Tillerman (Cat Stevens) plays quietly (yes, quietly!) and gently on the record player and the 'Longer Boats' track inevitably provides a wry smile:

Mary dropped her pants by the sand,
And let a parson come and take her hand…

After this weekend's discussion, Barbara's mother will, surely, now be reassured that nothing of that nature will be happening any time soon between her daughter and boyfriend. A commitment has been given to Barbara's mother and it will have to be kept. It would not be right to abuse the hospitality kindly and generously provided. *'Benwick'* is now almost being thought of as 'home'. Mrs Noble, you are sensible, and you are understanding. Like mother, like daughter – only your daughter is also utterly captivating. What was it you said, or perhaps suggested? A sexual urge in adolescents is wholly natural, particularly for young lad. It blooming well is. But you also said that saving your first sexual experience for your wedding night will make it special. You will remember it all your life and you will get far more out of your relationship and your love for one another should last a lot longer, hopefully even forever. So, Mrs Noble, are you presumably suggesting that the relationship will mean far more than for those who are more promiscuous before marriage? Who can tell? Both Barbara and her boyfriend have a generous portion of common sense, but nevertheless, it is hoped that one day – at some time in the future – Barbara's pants will be coming down quite willingly in the company of, and with the assistance of, a loving partner. What is for sure is that, when it happens, Barbara will not be led away by a parson. Christ – the thought of those knickers coming down… God!

The wall calendar confirms a First XI cricket fixture May 14th, this coming Monday afternoon versus Our Ladies High School – except sadly, they are not ladies, more the pity. Being picked for the First XI merely confirms the paucity of choice available within the school's senior ranks. A batsman? – no.

A bowler? – no. Included merely to make up the numbers? – Yes. Highest number of runs scored this term: 7 – that is pretty impressive. (Yes, it is…) Number of wickets: 0. (Olly is the lad to get the wickets.) One thing that is for sure – no school colours to be awarded to the Head Boarder this term for cricket. At football, a 5-2 victory early in the season playing Our Ladies – at cricket, a victory is unlikely. The result, as always, rests with McCombie and Olly. They can do it – and they know they can! The others hope they can!

Yes, Alastair McCombie. Lower 6th form. Barbara's form. Almost an enigma… almost! A classy and capable batsman indeed, and rather an entertaining actor in the school plays. Serious enough, with required concentration when encompassed within those 20 or so yards between the stumps, but otherwise, a full-blown extrovert. (It has been suggested that, with his elder brother having been killed by being hit on the head by a cricket ball, that sad event was the spur he needed, providing within him a resilience and determination to succeed at cricket. If so, full credit to you, Alastair – and to parents even, for allowing you to play cricket.)

He is one of the clear leaders across the whole of the Upper and Lower 6th forms in gibes and skittish comments – within the classroom and outside it. Clearly, he enjoys the steady stream of jokes and banter and to help his colleagues along, he will laugh loudly at his own jokes – and then wait expectantly for laughter from those surrounding him. He is always on the stage. Humorous and entertaining, certainly, and in the process, endearing himself to fellow pupils but rather less so to those imparting the knowledge during the lessons. His reward for hilarity within the classroom? A teacher's hand and the back of his head will have occasionally had the pleasure of meeting. A teacher would perhaps suggest, 'too smart, too cheeky', but to his fellow pupils, a hero. But (there is a but…) a continual stream of sarcasm and taunting can become somewhat tiring. Nevertheless, every school, surely, needs a McCombie – for the jibes as well as for the cricketing skills. Learning, well, yes, but far behind the laughter and the cricket…

Outside on this mid-May evening, a day of leisure for the boarders is coming to a close. The church clock strikes the half-hour. The activity in and around the swimming pool is ending. Departing swimmers rescue their abandoned towels and disappear into the changing room, leaving the water sloshing back and forth, end to end, side to side. The evening sunlight, dancing across the river margins, keeps alive the shades of green cascading down the trees, all cramped together within the coppice opposite.

And then, having given their customary shy goodbye wave to any 6th form boarders gazing out of dormitory windows (and they know full well they are being watched), four Girl Guides skip, as only young girls can skip, along the lawn and are soon out of sight, disappearing around the west aspect of the building. The school grounds hugging the riverbank fall silent, devoid now of boarders, both young, old, male and female.

Time now to study these English essays – to do so is eminently more enjoyable than Sociology dogma. A brief comment from Ducky at the foot of an essay on *The Franklin's Tale* (Chaucer) is, surely, most promising. *'Polish those diamonds'* – that from Ducky! (Will more polishing make them sparkle any brighter?) Rather less so perhaps was his suggestion that the McCart essays could be used by the class from time to time to practice writing a 'précis' of a *'long, rambling piece of work'*. Never miss an opportunity...

CHAPTER XXIX

RETURN TO THAT 'KINGDOM BY THE SEA'

Sunday 3rd June. Once again, back in the dormitory after a half-term break, gazing out of the window and taking in this now very familiar vista. Forever changing but essentially the same. What a paradox, but then again, perhaps not, and the view, thankfully, can never be termed boring. Not for much longer, mind. Are the others in this Lonsdale complex striking off each day on their calendar until the end of term? Do they count down the weeks, the days, the hours even, looking forward to the end of term? If anyone is counting, it is 38 days. Not in here though – not in this dormitory. There is no yearning in here for the term end. An end of term that is now going to come soon enough. The end of term next month... then what?

Outside and out of sight, a songbird sings its heart out at the twilight of this late spring day. A blackbird or a song thrush perhaps. Its singing is accomplished with what Keats termed in 'Ode to a Nightingale' as *'full throated ease'*. Quite how it manages it, goodness knows.

At this time of year, a few weeks away from the longest day, the daylight seems to continue late, so late into the night. Almost overstaying its welcome one might suggest. Closing these rather flimsy red curtains, which just about shield the window, makes hardly a scrap of difference to the light levels even at this late hour. Sleep is never easy without complete darkness, particularly when the mind is racing with two primary emotions swimming around the brain. The enjoyment of what was a half-term week at *'Benwick'* mixed with the slight apprehension about tomorrow morning's English Literature examination – Paper I.

In truth, only the slightest of concerns, inevitable perhaps and something which everyone, surely, must experience to some degree before any sort of written examination. Inside, the brain is exuding, just perhaps, a quiet confidence with Literature. Two years of studying poetry and classical fiction has proved incredibly enjoyable, despite the regular 'knock backs' from a sometime truculent Head of English, who has appeared to enjoy regularly putting a competent pupil in his place. (Competent? Well, yes, at least in this pupil's view.) Recent English essays have pleasingly been returned with a B+ mark, which perhaps is as good as it gets. The granting of an A (- or + or whatever) rarely, *if ever,* happens. Or so it seems. No one admits to obtaining an A. Too embarrassing perhaps to admit to it. Who wants to be thought of as a swot? There must always be room for improvement. (Not Confucius this time – but Ducky.)

Some of the comments from Ducky on completed English essays do seem rather obtuse. For example, *'If I said consider Herrick, Rilke or Shelley, would you be any wiser?'* Shelley – of course. Herrick. Who the hell is Herrick? Rilke: who? (They are not included in the syllabus...) A suggestion regarding additional reading also came via Ducky. *The Road to Oxiana* by Robert Byron. (But no, not the Byron that the Head Boarder had in mind. Not that Byron at all. This Byron seemingly perished at sea during WW2, rather than in some exotic Greek town, whilst also, by co-incidence, being involved in a conflict – but in his case, a hugely vital one.)

The Road to Oxiana. "Not the poetry section, McCart, you will find it in the travel section." Yes, he was quite right. The school library travel section, indeed – a larger selection on offer than the poetry section as well. Not as interesting though. And why a travelogue as suggested additional reading? God knows where *Oxiana* is, but part of Byron's travel incorporates Persia (really Iran) – and that, the only reason for Ducky having recommended it? Growing up in Iran yes, but reading about it, no. The Head Boarder will stick with the syllabus and the poetry section. And no, the poetry is not squeezed between the gardening and cookery sections – as it was for Kingsley Amis. However, the library has proved most useful for obtaining a quite unrelated 'tit-bit' of information. (Mr Warbrick, please note – your library does have its uses.) The origin of the name Barbara. A derivation from a Greek word – meaning 'strange'. No, never. Anything but...

There will be some anxiety without doubt at *'Benwick'* tonight, with a Human Biology 'O' Level examination being taken by Barbara tomorrow afternoon. As English Literature finishes, Human Biology commences an hour or so later. A joint agreement not to meet up with each other in that short interim period is most probably wise. Too late now for any last minute 'cramming' for tomorrow's examination (does cramming do any good?) even if it were indeed needed – conceited? Yes. With the English Literature Paper II sitting not until 14th June, there will be (or should be) adequate time for some revision for the final paper.

What revision that is needed really needs to be within the confines of school, rather than, as in this past week, at *'Benwick'*. The obvious difficulties of revising together in the dining room were plain for all to see. It may have looked as if some hard work was being done, with an English Literature and a History textbook at one end of the table and Human Biology and Geography books stacked up on the opposite side. And particularly so with Barbara's mother in the house trying to ensure revision was religiously adhered to, whilst at the same time busying herself doing various household jobs. (Which did not, of course, include cleaning out and preparing the coal fire – the Head Boarder's province.) In truth, the frequent and obvious distractions were many and varied – and enjoyable. It was frequently plainly obvious that revising was being sidelined, or at best given lukewarm attention but, well, it didn't seem to matter. The only person seemingly frustrated by the regular interruptions and distractions was Barbara's mother. Frustrated, but understanding and accepting the situation with her usual stoicism. ("Oh, you two. You really need to be separated when revising.")

*[**An aside**: this, then, a typical day during half-term at 'Benwick'. The venue? A dining room table, strewn with textbooks.*

"Would you like a cup of coffee, Barbi?"
"Oh yes please, love. Should we have a piece of my homemade gingerbread? (No answer required. No answer given – just a big smile...)"
"I tell you what, love, you make the coffee, and I will cut up the gingerbread. No doubt you will want a big piece?" (Again, no answer provided. It was not a question. It was accepted as a statement of fact by both parties.)
And after pottering about in the kitchen and after a mug of coffee and cake, came the predictable query:
"Is the cake up to the usual standard then, Ianey?"
Ridiculous question. As if it needed to be asked. This time, an answer provided. With confirmation that indeed it was, Barbara had given a confident smile accompanied with the familiar scrunch of her nose and shoulders. (That scrunch of the shoulders and nose – quite enchanting. And rising with those shoulders, a pair of shapely boobs – even more enchanting. Christ... to be able to see them in the raw.)
"Do you think I am becoming an expert? Silly question. You cannot improve on perfection."
Not showing-off, but nevertheless, exuding an engaging confidence. Typical humour from a girlfriend, answering her own question. And on being informed that she was "funny", Barbara had responded with her usual retort on being told that she was comical.
"What. Do you mean 'funny ha, ha' or 'funny peculiar'?"
(A strong inflection with **or** in her question gave a suggestion towards the required response. Well, my dear, certainly not funny peculiar.)

Then another (welcome) distraction.

"I think I will wash my hair this afternoon. You wouldn't like to do it for me would you, Ianey? Please say yes and then you can dry it with the hair dryer. After that, you can then have a look for any split ends."

So that was the choice. Which would be more interesting? History 'A' Level revision or looking after Barbara's hair?

"What are split ends, Barbi?"

"Well, when my hair gets quite long the ends start to split which stops the hair growing, so the split ends need to be cut off. If you are careful, I will let you do it."

"I will be careful, and I will give your legs a shave as well."

From a girlfriend, "Oh lovely." (And that scrunch of the nose. God!) And then, another short burst of revising. Occasionally, the slightest of frowns would appear on Barbara's face as she studied carefully, her unblemished forehead creasing ever so slightly. But that sunny face, not conducive to a frown, would revert seamlessly to a smile on seeing her boyfriend's face gazing across the table at her, rather than looking down at his workbooks.

Barbara's mother again, "Now come on, you two."

And then, after a quiet five or ten minutes of revision, yet another welcome diversion from textbooks.

"Do you fancy playing tennis tomorrow morning down at the school? We do have permission to play on the grass courts at half-term. But remember though, you will have to let me play in my bare feet. I can only play in bare feet."

Lovely. Barbara in her short tennis skirt and bare feet. Always sufficient to arouse the sexual urge. This urge – it is waiting (not always patiently) for the next opportunity to be re-kindled by a girlfriend's lovely bare flesh. Tennis it is then. Another morning devoid of revision.

The studying and the reading of textbooks and old essay questions and answers had then proceeded for a short while. But only a short while, mind, as within fifteen minutes or so, Barbara had exclaimed, having been reminded about it whilst browsing through her essay file, "Oh yes, and by the way, I haven't shown you this have I?" On so saying and with a broad grin which displayed an almost perfect set of lovely white teeth, she handed over an English 'A' Level essay entitled, 'Write on King Lear's Madness'. Yes, in Barbara's first year's study of the 'A' Level course, this Shakespeare play, with it being the same Oxford Examining Board, features prominently. The essay had been marked by Ducky and it wasn't particularly the mark awarded that was of interest, but instead the rather cryptic comment accompanying the mark. 'This seems to be much <u>NOT</u> Barbara'. Underneath, a further comment within the essay, 'I wonder who says and wrote this?' Ducky, quite obviously, is not easily fooled and with Barbara having a boyfriend who has already gone through the torture of studying King Lear, it seems inevitable, surely, that some of that learning will have been gladly imparted. Perhaps offloaded would be a more pertinent description.

Everyone, of course, will have their own individual style of writing and just perhaps, Ducky had recognised a generous helping of waffle in Barbara's King Lear essay. Waffle that he might not normally expect to read in an English essay submitted by Barbara. Ducky might, perhaps, be disappointed by the subtle form of plagiarism involved with the discourse, but not as disappointed, for sure, as the person who had helped with that essay answer. A mark of only six out of ten. Cheek!

King Lear aside, the content for study with Barbara's 'A' Level course is different in every respect than that studied by her boyfriend. The Shakespeare play providing the only common factor. For her 'A' Level syllabus, the likes of James Joyce (Ulysses, inevitably), Joseph Conrad (Lord Jim) and E. M. Forster (A Passage to India, inevitably) are to be studied. Also, perhaps rather surprisingly, Lady Chatterley's Lover by D. H. Lawrence. Surely, in true puritan style which symbolises an independent Church of England school, it will have to be an expurgated version? Well, at the very least, it will be a 'school' version. Barbara will advise in the fullness of time. But, rather surprisingly, within her reading syllabus, none of the true heroes, the 'Romantic' poets. A glaring omission surely and a surprising one.

And then, whilst sitting at that dining table, another distraction. This time initiated by a boyfriend.

"Tomorrow afternoon then, Barbi, should we start putting the photographs we have taken over the past six months into the album we bought in Lancaster?"

"What a good idea. We will sort them out tonight, ready to put them in the album tomorrow then." An enthusiastic reply. It was at that juncture that Barbara's mother, ever present, had muscled in on the discussion (as one might term it), graciously accepting that familiar motto, 'all work and no play'... etc. Her rather splendid suggestion involved, yes, putting photographs in the album but also, why not include a lock of each other's hair? What a timely intervention. Thank you, Mrs Noble. The signs are that you are also rather 'taken' with your daughter and her boyfriend! So, that evening, after hair had been washed and split *ends sorted, it had been the time to cut off respective locks of hair. It was a task taken on enthusiastically by Barbara's mother who had, in any case, suggested that Barbara's hair be trimmed by half an inch or so (that apparently being a more effective way of dealing with split ends).*

Ordinarily, Barbara would not have welcomed the suggestion, her long hair suiting her and wearing it below the shoulder is very much the 'in' fashion at school. (Good heavens, what would she look like with short hair? Difficult to imagine.) Not only that, but her long hair sits kindly with her face and figure. However, being linked to a lock of hair being cut off for 'preservation', it was accepted readily. And so, Barbara's mother did the honours. In the event, she dealt with both heads of hair, thereby ensuring that there did not have to be the embarrassment of a boyfriend asking Tom Guy, the High Bentham barber, to save some at the next haircut.

The hair cutting all watched, then, with some mild amusement by Mick, lounging in his 'reserved' chair, perhaps pondering on how times have changed since his own courting days. Duly sealed in small individual see-through packets, without the identifying names on each packet, it would be almost impossible to decide which was which, so similar is the light dusky brown colour contained in each packet. For posterity – for that is what the locks have been cut for – respective name tags have been included in each bag of hair. They now sit proudly in a photographic album.

And that then… a typical day of revision.]

Yes, a morning was spent playing tennis on the court beside the vicarage. A delightful sunny morning – the sky a solid blue and Barbara so enticing, incredibly so. The shortest of school tennis skirts, regulation grey, the slightest of RAF blue blouses, short sleeved and only just reaching to the top of her skirt. Her bare feet (so incredibly sexy) looking after a pair of perfectly shaped legs and each displaying a more than generous helping of thigh. Her hair tied back into a pony-tail. With tennis racket in hand, perhaps she looked rather 'sporty', but it was most definitely a case of looks being deceptive. Nevertheless, she had looked utterly divine and captivating. And with the tennis game, so much laughter.

It was fortuitous (or was it?) that Barbara bent down rather daintily whenever she had to pick up a tennis ball otherwise, with her micro-skirt, she would have provided – in the words of the Lonsdale dormitory residents – "a real eyeful".

Had he been sneakily watching from the rectory, the Revd Bradberry, for all his timid demeanour, may have had difficulty in coping! As it was, there were (all too brief) glimpses of a pair of light blue knickers when Barbara eagerly jumped skywards to intercept a tennis ball. As well as that, her midriff was most generously displayed when serving. What heaven! Concentrating on tennis – difficult.

The standard of the tennis? Quite secondary and of no consequence. It was quite definitely a case of playing for playing and not for winning. No winner because there was no scoring. There did not need to be. It was just for the fun of playing tennis. Not quite a 'Subaltern's Love-Song' (one of John Betjeman's most popular ballads) and, quite definitely, no *lime-juice and gin*! Perhaps it was a modern 1973 north-country version of tennis for fun, without the... *mushroomy, pine-woody, evergreen smells* of the Surrey byways. Nonetheless, Barbara was being... *furnished and burnished,* but in this instance not by Aldershot sun, but by Low Bentham sunshine, encompassed within this county of the West Riding!

There she stood, feet crossed,
Racket in hand, displaying bare flesh,
With a look of feigned disgust,
Perhaps even embarrassment!
A simple backhand, a convenient height,
Missed so cleanly and completely.

She pulls ever so gently an ashen skirt,
(Is there a surfeit of thigh displayed?)

Whilst a belly button soaks up the sun:
And infectious laughter captures the
Moment and makes it so much fun.
No competition and she knows she is loved.

No competition certainly, with the tennis match and no competition for a Head Boarder's affections. They are entirely and completely with this young lady. Barbara, will the laughter, the enjoyment of life that springs out naturally from you... will it ever stop?

There has been some revising done for sure over this past half-term week but, perhaps, it might have been tackled in a more disciplined and committed way. It is just not that easy giving full concentration to workbooks and revision papers with an attractive young lady sitting directly opposite. Therein, the core of the problem. How could one concentrate for several hours at a time on revision work when there, sitting at the dining room table, almost within kissing distance, is youth personified. (Indeed, with a meaningful lean forward involving both parties, lips could just about meet – only just, but there was so much excitement in making the effort, with the lips just able to caress.) How many times did two attentive pairs of eyes (attentive and watchful towards each other, rather than towards the written word) leave their respective study books to gaze across the table? And that charming, winning smile. Scant wonder then that there was an all too regular, "Now come on you two", issuing forth from Barbara's mother. And then, later on, "You two really need to be separated." (But just perhaps she was thinking to herself – how sweet; how lovely to be young and in love.)

Perhaps the main distraction away from *'Benwick'* prior to a return to the boarding house tonight was the visit yesterday to the Lake District. A treat from Barbara's parents following a half-term of revision. (Well... yes, revision.) Barbara's dad, the only one in the family to have passed a driving test, did the driving, with a visit to the more popular tourist spots within the Southern Lakes. For a Head Boarder who has (again, in a mother's all too bland description) "been half-way around the world", albeit whilst growing up, the Lake District is, nevertheless, a revelation. Do we always possess an affinity with the country of our birth? The weather here in this corner of the West Riding may be changeable, with a regular and more than generous helping of rain. But with the sunshine and with the blossoming of spring and summer flowers and attendant foliage, there is no yearning to be back in the arid desert surrounds of Aden. Nor indeed is there any wish to be within the frenetic bustle of an Iranian street market.

From the school, the Lakes might well be termed 'on the doorstep'. A first proper visit to the Lakes, yes, but surely, hopefully, it will not be the last. The area is understandably most popular, and it was easy to appreciate the beauty, standing there on the edge of Lake Windermere at Bowness. There was an inner peace looking across the wide sweep of the water and watching the pleasure cruisers slipping quietly and efficiently away from the quayside. Then a winding journey through the Lakeland side roads (and Barbara, you didn't throw up…) to the quaint and picturesque Tarn Hows. Then a journey through the hills to the pleasant surrounds of Rydal Water and eventually, the charming and pretty (although that rather simple adjective hardly does it justice) village of Grasmere.

Grasmere, the home to one of those 'Romantic' 19th century poets. William Wordsworth – he who lived at Dove Cottage, now a museum, on the outskirts of the village, and who is buried in the local village churchyard. With this link, the locality, therefore, certainly provided a convenient connection with the English Literature study. Barbara picked up a 'Guide to Grasmere' (10p very well spent) and within it, Wordsworth is quoted as writing, *'The loveliest spot that man hath ever known'.* Now, that might just possibly be over-egging it slightly, but then again, perhaps Wordsworth had not travelled (yes, again, as described in that famous phrase of mother) "halfway around the world"! Or had he? This 'A' Level study concentrates heavily on the poetry writings of some famous bards, but scarcely covers any detail about their private lives and travel. For sure, Wordsworth lived in Grasmere before living alongside Rydal Water and also at Cockermouth earlier in his life. At that point, the knowledge fizzles out. The 'A' Level syllabus should perhaps cover the private lives of poets in greater detail, and this might well often put the individual poems into context. Dare one put that suggestion forward to Ducky? No, not a good idea!

A famous resident then of this village. A clutch of famous visitors also, no doubt, over the years, Betjeman included. His poem 'Lake District' extols the virtues of Wordsworth's one time home – well sort of – almost in a matter-of-fact way with Betjeman seemingly more interested in Heinz tomato ketchup and HP sauce in the poem rather than Grasmere Lake and village. Shame on him! ("Off with his head!")

Grasmere village, nestling at the northern end of the lake of the same name, is home to a tiny shop squeezed in alongside the lych-gate entrance to the church. 'Sarah Nelson' is its name. It sells nothing but a rather unique gingerbread. Not only that, but the famous gingerbread they produce has been baked on the premises for over 100 years – it says so in the shop! (And that is proven by the unique smell which filters out onto and around the adjoining road.) And Sarah Nelson? Her recipe, she started it all. A Victorian lady with a Victorian recipe. However, vastly different in both consistency and size to the traditional gingerbread baked at *'Benwick'*. The Victorian example is, perhaps, an acquired taste, but almost an obligatory purchase whilst visiting the village. Calling it a gingerbread seems almost a misnomer. It appears more in tune with being a biscuit, being both hard and very thin – but a ginger taste it does possess. Who can walk by that enticing gingerbread smell filtering into the fresh Lakeland air without calling in to make a purchase? Better than the *'Benwick'* gingerbread? There was really no need for pretence in agreeing with Barbara's bold statement, "I really don't think it is as nice as the gingerbread I make." It isn't.

The winding path from the quaint lych-gate next to the gingerbread shop leads to the church. The church, St. Oswald's, most rugged looking, with a strange sandstone coloured appearance, and certainly ancient – quite different from St. John the Baptist, albeit that both places of worship may well be from the same general era. Inside the church, that same pregnant silence, perhaps spoilt slightly by rather too many visitors engaging in continual whispers, invading the quiet. No one dares to speak loudly in a church. Is it, perhaps, only the rector's prerogative? And within the churchyard, with a suitably grand headstone and surrounded by railings giving adequate protection, William Wordsworth has rested for well over a century. As always within the hushed confines of consecrated ground, it proved thought provoking, rather like the invisible silence and eeriness within the confines of a church, but only, that is, when there is no one else inside the holy place apart from oneself. If yesterday's visit is typical, then people come to look. To just stand and stare. What, one wonders, are visitors thinking as they stand silently, almost in awe, as they surround the black railings in a tiny Lakeland village churchyard? Perhaps they are thinking what all of us might, sometime, inevitably dwell on, young or old. The fact that life is transitory, death is permanent.

Yes, Grasmere and its adjoining lake, which is perhaps no longer than one mile in length, adding measurably to its attraction, are enthralling, made more so by the educational link with English Literature. And Barbara? She is similarly captivated by the village and the surrounding countryside. The Southern Lakes, and in particular, Grasmere and Rydal Water, will have to be visited again. To visit again will be special, but to visit again with a girlfriend will make it even more so.

And to round the half-term off after that visit, an evening slide show – with a concentration on the Noble children whilst growing up. Barbara, you look captivating even as a young girl, be it scowling at the camera on Southport beach (so just perhaps there is a temper located somewhere in that beautiful frame after all) or happily sledging in the snow in the back garden at Ellergill

Cottages. Wonderful, just wonderful! A photograph of Barbara as a child in the bath – the undisputed highlight of that evening show. It provoked a spontaneous display of mock horror from Barbara. Her flushed face had certainly displayed both excitement and perhaps slight embarrassment in quick succession. After all, being seen in the nude by a boyfriend is, by definition, a little inopportune. At something like seven years of age, however, looking at her sitting in the bath naked can be taken in good spirit with the laughter shared. Now, a decade later and having blossomed into an attractive young lady, seeing Barbara in the bath would be something, indeed, never to be forgotten and most definitely savoured. Christ!

That moment had been a memorable one to share. The following has been very quickly drafted whilst the memory is fresh. It will perhaps need some sorting out and tidying up in the fullness of time.

> *There exists a curious sense of satisfaction,*
> *Even triumph, in viewing her revealed in*
> *Different guises during those childhood years:*
> *Is it really something to hide as though*
> *Disgusted at now being seen (for example)*
> *As an innocent toddler unknowingly*
> *Captured in an embarrassing situation?*
>
> *Well may you blush young lady,*
> *But those sparkling hazel eyes dance*
> *With excitement and with pretence of shame,*
> *Before hands quickly cover the face.*
>
> *It can cause nothing but amusement*
> *To one who keeps a watchful eye*
> *On his love to see whether she will be*
> *Disconcerted in being viewed as such.*

Barbara, how disciplined have we been over this recent half-term? (Did you suggest, "sort of disciplined"?) It was not always easy (no – that should read 'never easy') to keep self-control during the morning and evening routine with Barbara in that perfumed bedroom.

Coffee every morning ("but no waking me up in the middle of the night, remember? – not before 8.30am .") and a chat at night once she was in bed.

Nothing to eat or drink in bed on an evening as, having had an evening meal in the late afternoon once Barbara's father had returned from work, her mother then prepared, as a matter of course, what can only be described as a banquet supper for late evening. A banquet, indeed, being the most appropriate description, because the supper presented each evening always included a host – a plethora – of different sandwiches. (Mashed banana sandwiches being the favourite for Barbara – or in her words, "banana sarnies forever". Hold on – what about chip sarnies and crisp sarnies?) Sandwiches then, but also biscuits with cheese, homemade cakes, crisps, and fruit, all washed down with umpteen mugs of tea. As suppers go, these have been on a scale never previously experienced. Indeed, growing up in the family home had never included a supper, or for that matter a meal, or food of any sort after the evening meal.

So, the morning and evening routine with Barbara became the daily norm for half-term, always eagerly anticipated and immensely enjoyed by both parties. It almost felt like girlfriend and boyfriend were living together – not only that but living together very happily. At times, it was almost as if the house belonged to girlfriend and boyfriend, with Barbara's parents and son visiting. (There was only one thing missing…) What a shame it has come to an end with the half-term week passing by so very quickly.

Barbara has been quite happy to get in and out of bed ("I am just going for a little 'tinkle', Ianey, before going to sleep") without her dressing gown on, occasionally displaying a lovely pair of legs and, whilst hidden underneath her nightie, also revealing the tell-tale shape of a pair of pert and firm bosoms pushing the nightie out rather invitingly at the top. It was a statement proclaiming her femininity. A dressing gown was put on to walk from the bedroom to the toilet but was quickly slipped off on re-entry to her bedroom as a matter of course, Barbara being quite comfortable walking to her bed with just her nightdress on. She is now seemingly confident enough with a boyfriend to display herself, surely now inwardly realising and accepting that, to her boyfriend, she is attractive enough in size and shape to be enticing. In that context, she is quite happy to be viewed as such.

With a little twinkle in her eye and a scrunch of her nose, one evening the question was asked, "I hope you are liking what you see, Ianey" – Christ! And on a couple of occasions before returning to bed and clearly realising that her boyfriend was indeed liking what he was gazing longingly at, Barbara had variously said with childish mischief, "Get ready, Ianey" and "Are you ready?" On so saying and without any other warning, she quickly lifted her nightdress to her waist to reveal the full form of her stylish thighs and her knickers, taking her nightdress back down just as quickly! Her face alive with devilment. A broad smile had accompanied a scrunch of the nose and shoulders. Those hidden bosoms had followed suit, rising and falling with her shoulders. Sometimes, it is rather exciting to be a little naughty. How sensuous and sexy – and no 'see-through' knickers! The 'interesting bit' (as Barbara terms it…) – it was well hidden! Perhaps that was just as well.

Such playful antics, almost mirroring what one might get up to as a child (and reviving the memory of those 'dares' by the Embassy swimming pool in Tehran) had quite naturally, without it appearing rude or vulgar, provided a suitable avenue for a somewhat scurrilous suggestion to be made. It was made on the basis of nothing ventured, nothing gained. (A Confucius moment perhaps…if you do not ask…) Would she allow her bosoms to be given a little squeeze through her nightie? (Yes, they were hidden under the nightie, but protruding out sufficiently to be so utterly inviting.) It had been the right moment to ask, with Barbara obviously feeling somewhat sexy and playful – realising, of course, how enticing she was to her boyfriend. She had clearly gained some enjoyment, perhaps, from exposing her knickers momentarily – regulation white cotton knickers which had sufficiently protected her modesty. What sexual excitement and anticipation. Goodness, the request was given immediate approval by a smiling girlfriend. She clearly enjoyed the sexual intimacy and excitement of the moment, yes. It had been a good time to ask. The privacy of the bedroom had proved pivotal.

With just perhaps the slightest hint of caution, Barbara had replied, "Well okay, we can be a little bit naughty. Go on then. Just one little squeeze on each, only one mind. Just let me get into bed first." With that, Barbara had given another lovely trademark scrunch with her nose accompanied by an impish little smile, as if to acknowledge that it was really wrong but that it would be quite exciting for both the giver and the receiver. She then sat on the bed and, lifting back the bed sheets, brought her lovely legs up from the floor in turn onto the bed and the bed sheets were then lifted back across for her, leaving her sitting up by her pillow with *Teddy* beside her. *Teddy*, watching as always in a nonchalant manner and with his familiar trademark smile. Did he have an incline as to what was afoot? Ah *Teddy*, keep it all to yourself.

"Okay then, go on, do it nicely, darling, just once on each," and so saying, Barbara, sitting upright with her dapper little bosoms pushing her nightdress out by her chest, invited a tender and quick squeeze of each. Sat here now, in the quiet of the dormitory, just the thought of it brings the only possible Lonsdale complex exclamation possible. Bloody hell! Something inside stirred whilst squeezing those dapper tits and something inside stirs at the mere thought of doing it again. Christ…

RETURN TO THAT 'KINGDOM BY THE SEA'

*[**An aside:** yes, something stirs within. The 6th form day lads, seemingly with more detailed knowledge about these things, recently suggested quite casually in a class discussion – a chat which included the female contingent – "it is an unstoppable urge, is sex: it is the surge of the semen – you cannot stop it!" Which comment brought forth the following from one within the female group, "Typical bloke"!]*

Thereafter during half-term, the briefest squeeze of that tender pair became a last thing at night ritual. One squeeze on each, a sort of 'good night treat', along with the customary kiss. Accompanied by the familiar fragrance of *Desert Flower* body lotion and Barbara Noble perfume. Youth personified. Barbara Noble – how can it be that you are so beautiful? Perhaps smell is a personal thing. Barbara, you smell divine. Does anyone else latch on to that lovely smelling skin and long to hold you tight? For the moment, it is only possible to undress you in the mind – but one day, surely, one day, it will be for real.

And then, once tucked up in bed and holding Teddy within her arm, the other night-time ritual? Reading her some poems from her beloved *Golden Treasury* book, a particular favourite being from the pen of John Keats (good taste, Barbara, good taste) with his ballad 'La Belle Dame Sans Merci'. (But Barbara, it is rather a sad poem.) Whilst that well known narrative song by Keats is a favourite, her melancholic boyfriend will invariably choose another helping from the same poet with, for instance, *'When I have fears that I may cease to be...'* typical! "But Ian, why so sad?" She is, understandably and quite rightly, peeved that the 'Romantic' poets are absent from her English Literature syllabus.

On a couple of bedtime evenings, by necessity, *The Golden Treasury* has been put to one side in order that another favourite can be read from the *Collected Shorter Poems* by W. H. Auden. Entitled 'O What is that Sound', it is the rhythm and repetition of the poem that captivates Barbara:

> *O what is that sound which so thrills the ear,*
> *Down in the valley drumming, drumming?*
> *Only the scarlet soldiers, dear,*
> *The soldiers coming.*

Until, by the last verse, the soldiers, they have arrived – and they have *'broken the lock and splintered the door – and their eyes are burning, burning...'* (At which point Barbara has grabbed Teddy tightly and disappeared under the sheets acting out her 'little frightened girl' impression...)

A salutary comment from Barbara on a couple of occasions after the reading of night-time poems. "Your voice often sounds quite sad, Ian, when you read me the poems. Are you sad?" How can one be sad sitting with a girlfriend in her bedroom at night whilst she sits up in bed listening and hugging Teddy? Perhaps the melancholy streak fits into the groove with the selection of some of the poems that are given an airing. In her bedroom late at night it is so easy to drown oneself in love, with her sweet-smelling body perfume and her collection of lotions combining to provide an irresistible combination. And then, the sight of a youthful, luxurious half naked body displaying legs that are firm, shapely and sure, and delicate milky-white petite arms. And, if one looks closely enough, just the slightest trace of tiny hairs on those arms – miniscule, but they are there, nonetheless. The whole of her body, both seen and unseen, needs to be squeezed tightly – as tight as possible for as long as possible. But no! In her bedroom, with Barbara in her nightdress, it would be too dangerous and both parties realise it would be perilous, with self-control most likely lost. Perilous indeed with only one logical conclusion. Despite a strong mutual current of sex surging within, both boyfriend and girlfriend are still prepared to wait.

Oh Barbara. Really, is a boyfriend sounding rather sad? Perhaps only when that illogical thought re-enters the brain (as it persists in doing) suggesting this love affair might end. Then there is anxiety and sadness, despite it being something that seems so unlikely, at the present time, to actually happen. The mere thought that it might is sufficient to stir melancholy into action. And once stirred...

So, the evening bedtime routine of a little squeeze of her tender bosoms and the reading of a few poems has been more than matched by a slight, but not so subtle, change to the morning routine. In the full knowledge that an immediate cup of coffee is somewhat wasted (until Barbara 'comes round' to be fully awake), Barbara now likes to turn to lie on her stomach whilst waking up. In doing so, she asks her boyfriend, "Would you like to scratch my back?" (What a question! There was only one realistic answer.) The request made with full acceptance that a hand needs to be inside the back of her nightdress to accede to her request. By the end of this half-term week, however, she has been quite happy for her nightie to be pulled up at the back to facilitate scratching, whilst she winds her way slowly through the waking up process. Not only that, but Barbara has now acceded to a suggestion that her knickers be pulled down ever so slightly at the back, in order that the top of her bum can also be scratched along with her back, agreeing without hesitation when the question was broached. "Would you like me to scratch your bottom as well as your back?" She finds it so relaxing and yes, exciting. Gentle scratches on tender skin obviously being a good waking up tonic! And so, she was frequently laid on her chest in the morning (with nightdress pulled up and knickers pulled slightly down at the back), but with her legs necessarily together. With the sheets turned down, her back and the top of her bottom splendidly exposed whilst scratches were provided over that pure, smooth, delicate skin. Incredibly exciting and sexual it was. Did half-term have to come to an end?

There had to be, of course, ground rules to be followed (with some difficulty and needing considerable restraint). Not only that, but to be followed religiously. Namely, two specific lines, mutually agreed, which could not be crossed. "Please remember, Ianey, don't go any further down than the top of my cheeks, good lad. My front and between my legs have to remain out of bounds until we are married." In addition, sitting on the edge of the bed was fully acceptable and welcomed, but "no lying down on the bed beside me please, Ianey, it would be too dangerous for us both." (Christ, certainly for a boyfriend it would!) The necessary guidelines fully appreciated by both partners and adhered to. Then, on occasions when the scratching was brought to an end, a girlfriend's knickers would be pulled up at the back, bringing from Barbara a quick exclamation. "Hold on, love, not too tight, I am being *'melvined'*. Do it gently now." (*'Melvined'*? The meaning of which, when interpreted by Barbara, is that her knickers are being pulled too tight and into what she likes to call "my interesting bit"!)

So, there is a mutual acceptance and agreement that this grooming can go so far – but only to where the lines have been drawn. Both boyfriend and girlfriend anxious and wanting to preserve virginity until marriage. Goodness, the difficulty of keeping calm! Almost impossible. Which book was it that included the phrase 'something stirs…'? It does – and it is worrying!

And with the bedroom door just slightly ajar – no longer fully open as it had been at first, but not fully closed – there has, perhaps fortuitously, been no checking up on a daughter and her boyfriend by parents. Had they possibly wondered from time to time whether the occupants in the bedroom were behaving themselves? Their trust is largely well founded, but nevertheless, a father, particularly, may not have been too comfortable looking in to witness his daughter enjoying her regular morning grooming session! (But – it was her idea…)

Oh yes! That cricket match before half-term against Our Ladies: McCombie and Olly strike again! McCombie notching up virtually half our run total and Olly with 5 wickets for 5 runs! Another famous victory for the First XI – thanks to those two stalwarts – but the rest of us bask in the glory! And why not? Then two days later, the thrashing of George Fox School – McCombie 66 runs, Olly 6 wickets (and 44 runs!) – the 'also-rans' again bask in undiluted glory!

CHAPTER XXX

THE SONG THRUSH HAS STOPPED SHOWING OFF

Returning to the boarding house, then, following the half-term break has not been quite as enjoyable as in the past. Living and breathing Barbara daily and in the same house has left an indelible impression. The whole experience has, at times, pushed exams to the margins. What are the implications if the exam results are in the territory of being a failure?

Lying in bed in a dormitory – a room considered to be one's own personal territory – it is not easy to accept that this boarding house experience will shortly be coming to an end. In this room – at this desk – letters have been written expressing love to a girlfriend. Letters also written to parents expressing a shortage of "filthy lucre". (As a mother always terms it.) This room is personal. A refuge, a private space to write and think and yes, to enjoy, in some perverse way, the learning. Two years of hard slog is virtually over. Well, a sort of hard slog. Not fully over of course, but over for Sociology for sure. No more pointless discussions arriving at, well, no conclusion at all. No more power-reading textbooks and wondering at the end of a particular chapter as to what one had actually just been reading about.

Will poverty ever be eliminated? That was the sort of question one was hoping – almost expecting – would appear on one or other of the two Sociology exam papers. It wasn't there. Had the examiners thought it too obvious? Had they hidden the subject matter within the framework of another question? Seemingly not. Oh dear!

With all the school examinations being held in the Assembly Hall, Sociology Paper I on the Tuesday afternoon prior to the half-term break had been shared with those taking 'O' Level Art. Well, it had to be. There only needed to be one chair and desk for a single Sociology candidate. So, the machinations of art had proved to be an intriguing distraction from pondering over sociological answers. It was quite impossible not to have a regular glance all around the room to witness the various efforts of artwork being skilfully (and not so skilfully) produced. There was certainly no evidence of either trains or ships being drawn or painted. How disappointing. But surely, Art is relatively easy – no, very easy – to pass if one has a flair for drawing? Is that a fair assessment? The mantra seems quite simple. If one cannot draw or paint, then do not take

Art! Could the same methodology have been used for Sociology? But no, how does one tell if one is any good? With Art – quite simple. If you can draw, you can draw…

Three hours, any four questions. Fourteen questions to choose from. Forty-five minutes, averaged out, for each question. No leaving the Assembly Hall, camouflaged as an exam room, until after one hour had elapsed. Some hope of that with the amount of writing (with or without waffle) that had to be done. Eventually the choice of questions had been made. That was only after all the questions had been read and re-read and the thought process had pondered – for God's sake, which questions can be answered confidently? Which questions can be answered at all? Several questions did not seem in any way related to Sociology or the study of it, painfully endured since September 1971.

'Are marital relationships influenced by the character of the kinship of the spouses?' That appeared to be quite topical with regard to Barbara, her family and her boyfriend and family! But really, who cares? Is it middle class (what, for heaven's sake, is middle class) wanting to marry middle class? Hold on, Barbara's father has a manual job. So what? In some strange way, that fact led conveniently on to one of the other exam questions tackled.

'How far is a person's occupation a determinant of their social class?' Good question. Where are the lines drawn? Are Mr and Mrs Noble working class or middle class? Does it really matter? Irrelevant surely.

A further link between boyfriend and girlfriend was applicable in one of the other questions posed in the exam paper, with an answer being attempted to the inviting question, 'Account for the differences in educational achievement between different social groups.' But then, consider the Upper 6th form. There will, surely, be different levels of social standing within the Lonsdale dormitory complex, but in two years of study, it has never been particularly noticeable or touched on in discussions. Certainly, within Lonsdale all are on an equal footing. There are none who are 'more equal' than others, albeit that being Head Boarder has seniority attached to it – a necessary requirement. Whatever the social standing of respective parents for both day pupils and boarders within this 6th form, it has not been part of the thought process. Perhaps that says something about an independent school. The opportunity for obtaining successful exam results here at the school is the same for all and perhaps that is a major benefit of boarding school. The key, surely, is the willingness (or not) of the individual to want to put the effort in that is ultimately required.

All heady stuff, no doubt about that and, to some extent, confirming the view formed very early on in the Sociology syllabus – that there will not be a strictly right or wrong answer. Ah, Sociology, a study of spectacular rubbish. As a father would surely say regarding such intractable social problems, "Who cares two hoots?" Certainly not this Head Boarder.

Paper II, taken on the day before the half-term break. It had continued in the same vein, with the bland statement, 'Consider the effect of social differences on voting behaviour'. It was tackled enthusiastically. Well, the question gave free rein, 'carte-blanche' for waffle. 'Why are juvenile delinquents predominantly working class?' That did as well. Most definitely an issue of education with that one – or maybe not. Are there no defined lines in this 1970s society?

Sociology is over. What relief. No one to chat with after the two exam papers regarding the questions and relevant answers – probably just as well. Chatting with others who had just taken the same exam in past years would often be fatal – if one found others had answered a question differently! It will, indeed, be disappointing if a pass grade is not attained. Who knows, though, for sure what the examiners want. Failure, however, will not only be just disappointing, but it will also be extremely disheartening after two years of discussion and writing. Our erstwhile high-jump champion, cum-Sociology teacher, will not be here to witness the fruits of her, at times, difficult labours with an Upper 6th form pupil. A pupil who regularly enjoyed pointing out to her that he had a comfortable grasp of all the sociological answers. It will be apparent in a couple of months as to whether he will be proved right, or whether he has been found wanting – and was just a little too big for his boots! (Something Miss Shirley may have often thought, even if she did not say as much.)

One 'A' Level finished with. Two to go. English Literature Part I tomorrow. No real butterflies for 'A' Level English. Slightly nervous yes, but who isn't? In a strange way, something to look forward to. There is an enjoyment in writing and waxing lyrical about literature. Once the pen starts writing, it might be somewhat difficult to stop.

For the moment, as Keats suggested, though in a garden at Hampstead, not in a dormitory room late at night in the West Riding, *'My heart aches, and a drowsy numbness pains my sense...'* The heart certainly aches, but in a pleasant way, with the thought of a girlfriend who waits and who will, in all probability, now be tucked up in bed. Cuddling *Teddy*, no doubt, and sporting a rather sexy blue nightdress with regulation 'night-time' white knickers. (And after, of course, having written a letter to her boyfriend – or so this Head Boarder hopes...) The mind – the imagination – it keeps lurching back to *'Benwick'*. How can one stop it?

But now, to sleep. All quiet within the Lonsdale dormitory and all quiet outside in this Yorkshire Vale, the Wenning valley. The song thrush has at last stopped showing off with its soprano like voice, as have the blackbirds. This summer night has finally succumbed to darkness. Not before time. Sleep beckons.

CHAPTER XXXI

YOU MAY START

Friday 8th June. Another two exams (successfully?) completed during this past week. English Paper I and History Paper I. Paper II on each subject next week and then it is all over. It is a strange feeling, is it not, ('is it, or is it not, the case' – who says that? Memory again...) to be sat at a desk in the examination room with just the front introductory page of a small green *Oxford Local Examination* booklet staring up at one. Here it is, McCart, your time is come. Exam time is here – at last! Two years of study – all the essays, all the reading, all the discussions, and yet everything hinges on whatever is asked or requested in a small, almost insignificant, little green booklet on the desk. No turning over the pages until that large clock facing the candidates had moved inexorably (but oh, so slowly) on to 9am. Ducky's voice had droned on, outlining the various 'rules of engagement', whilst the eyes had remained permanently fixed on those succinct front-page instructions.

English Literature. Time allowed: 3 hours. Answer in section A, **Question 1** and **one** other question. In Section B, **Question 5** and **two** other questions. Five questions to answer, two of which are compulsory. They were the key, perhaps, to success or failure. Above all, follow the instructions. Isn't that stating the bleeding obvious? Do the exam candidates need to be told to read the instructions carefully? Perhaps they do. There will always be the inevitable urge to get straight into answering questions. Never mind those instructions. And the inward sigh of relief if a few questions are included in the test paper which appear to be easy to answer/write about. What a great feeling it engenders within. And with it, confidence.

But before the start, there was, as always, a quick look around at fellow candidates. Sitting silent, waiting. Some appeared to be not at all bothered. Some showed a hint of apprehension with their facial expressions. Others appeared agitated and fidgeted continuously and one or two had totally blank facial expressions. Rosco, sitting opposite, had given the slightest hint of a smile on looking across. Nothing ever seems to worry him. Was he worried? Why would exams be any different for someone with an apparently carefree persona? Claire Hird's face matched the gravity of the situation. She seemed impervious to any sign of acknowledgement or recognition. No matter, she is going to do well. Yes, she will, without trying. It is obvious she will succeed. After two years of mutual classroom study, it is quite obvious who is going to do well. No need for exam nerves with you, Claire, surely.

There was still, predictably, an engaging smile from Diane Lumb, as if she had not a care in the world. Perhaps she hasn't. Perhaps she takes it all in her stride as she seems to do with life generally. Goodness Diane, that was your 'A' Level English exam for heaven's sake. Surely you should have been looking a little worried. But then again, we all know you will do well.

Amongst all the other candidates waiting for the little hand to eventually confirm it was nine o'clock, there was, surely, at the very least a hint of butterflies. Eventually, Ducky had stopped speaking and a pregnant silence had enveloped the examination room. Everyone waiting whilst the second hand on the clock made its determined way up to the top. And then as it did so, those three important words from Ducky, **"You may start"**. A firm and clear instruction from our tetchy Head of English, although a little earlier the perceived air of nervousness within that Assembly Hall had perhaps also affected him. "English Literature students to the left, Physics 'A' and 'O' Level to the right", he had hissed, hardly hiding his frustration at several lines of students milling about and showing no visible signs of urgency. "I said to the left, McCart. You are not deaf, are you?" What is it that is said about sarcasm? He need not have worried. Sitting a Physics paper, at whatever level, would have proved to be a certain failure to someone who has spent two years studying the arts subjects. Physics – far too complicated at any level.

English Literature Paper I. A three-hour slog, except that it wasn't in any way a slog. In fact, it was rather enjoyable. It was also rather amusing to see some 'O' Level Physics candidates making a swift exit from the Assembly Hall at 10am, exactly one hour after the exam started and the earliest time available for leaving. Were they incredibly bright to finish so quickly, or perhaps were they leaving in the certain knowledge that they had successfully chalked up a 'Fail'? Inevitably, one suspected the latter.

Perhaps now, more than at any time in the last two years, it would be an appropriate moment to thank Ducky! Yes – to offer thanks for all the hassle during the tortured learning of Shakespeare. A period during which he has pleaded, insisted and at times coaxed his 6th form students into numerous detailed studies of *King Lear*. This Shakespeare play has been studied and picked over in the classroom, in the dormitory, in a 'greasy spoon' type cafe lounge nestling by Morecambe seafront and, also, on the settee at *'Benwick'*, with a workbook resting nicely on top of an attractive female pair of legs, with those same legs strewn across a boyfriend's knees. Essays have been written (and re-written) in prep, on holiday breaks, at weekends and the significance of Cordelia has been examined and re-examined. And then for good measure, examined again! And not least, of course, that mock exam which was completed towards the end of last year. Thank you again, Ducky. It hurts slightly to say it – but thank you. (No, it doesn't hurt slightly – it hurts a fair bit. The thanks – written down here – but not, of course, to be given verbally to the Head of English.)

All that learning – the pain, the futility of Shakespeare – has turned out, in fact, to be invaluable. One of the compulsory questions in the English Literature exam paper was specifically about the play. 'Is *King Lear* a pessimistic play'? A compulsory question. It had to be answered. It was answered. A detailed response clearly a requirement and a detailed essay duly provided. Not only that, but with, perhaps, some element of confidence and hopefully, dare one suggest, on this occasion without too much waffle.

And what about the four other questions in English Literature? An additional essay written on *Paradise Lost* (Milton). The question:

'A subtle study of evil': consider this view of Satan in *Paradise Lost*. That, surely, gave adequate licence to get into gear by outlining a purely personal view. What is right and what is wrong etc. when answering by propounding one's own view?

It was somewhat disappointing that an exam question on *Villette* (Charlotte Brontë) did not give an opportunity to discuss Lucy Snowe, widely considered to be a boring and miserable fart within the 'A' Level English group – and even the girls think that! However, the question regarding Madame Beck (from the same novel) was tackled with almost as much enthusiasm. Another question required a passage written in Shakespearean times to be translated into twentieth century dialogue (child's play…) with, as a separate question, a lengthy passage of prose requiring a précis outlining the main points. (*But* no, not on this occasion one of McCart's rambling essays – ha!) Child's play again. How surprising it can be to enjoy answering exam questions – yes!

Revising for Paper II can now take precedence and surely, one or more of the 'Romantic' poets and several of the classical fiction novels studied should be included in that paper. And if so, they will be answered with relish. The mid-August result for Literature can then be awaited without any undue concern. On the contrary, a favourable exam result can be almost anticipated. (Subtle reminder from Confucius to 6th form boarder – do not count your chickens. Okay, but…)

The afternoon examinations last Monday included Human Biology 'O' Level and, as had been previously agreed, there had been no meeting with Barbara prior to that exam. However, with a mid-afternoon finish (and she had sat through the full two and a half hours – impressive), she was accompanied on the walk back to *'Benwick'*. As Barbara had eloquently phrased it, the Human Biology exam was all about the "urine system, ablutions and reproduction – and it involved the inevitable rude pictures!" She had then continued, "It means that with this exam and my interesting book from the book club, we should definitely know 'what is what' by the time we are married." Indeed, my dear, and putting into practice what you have enthusiastically read and learnt should be, surely, most entertaining.

History 'A' Level Paper I is still fresh in the mind. Completed this afternoon. The letter received from Barbara this morning, written in anticipation of today's exam stated, *'I hope you found the exam okay and that you got a question on Henry VII'* (and stuck on the last page of the letter and circled, a little present from Barbara, a splodge of *Desert Flower* body lotion. Next to it, she had written, *'Can you still smell it, and does it smell of me?'*)

But what about Henry VII, the first of the Tudor monarchs? Rather like *King Lear*, his navel (that is, part of his anatomy, not a constituent navy!) has been studied in some considerable detail over the past two years and thankfully, the exam paper did not disappoint. It was, in fact, the very first question which provided a rather good feeling, in the knowledge that one question (at least) could be answered with confidence. 'How was the English monarchy stronger at the death of Henry VII than at his accession?'

With three other questions answered covering the period of the tenure of the Stuarts, including the Civil War (with this time Oliver Cromwell being a Parliamentarian, not a steam engine) and the financial difficulties of Charles II – and all being fairly straightforward in terms of essay writing – it would be nice to feel confident about a prospective pass. Well, were it not for the fact that

History Paper II next week will concentrate on 'European History' – certainly not as interesting and seemingly far more complex and infinitely more boring (understatement) than British history – which makes revision most difficult regarding the required concentration level.

With today's examination running through until 5pm and with the full three hours needed – together with additional pieces of paper being requested during the exam – there was no walk up to *'Benwick'* with Barbara at the end of the school day. Instead, after dinner, a walk along the riverbank and into that area which will always be known as The Wilderness.

*[**An aside**: Extra paper in examinations. Yes, extra paper requested during the exam. It looks impressive within the exam room when more paper is asked for, but just maybe it implies that the waffle is clearly totally out of control. A first request for more paper is fair enough, but when one or two others in the exam room ask for additional paper numerous times, it makes you wonder quite how they can be writing so much. It also leaves one slightly ill at ease, thinking that they must have a wider grasp of the subject or more detailed knowledge – or, and perhaps this is more relevant, there must be more than one candidate able to waffle in the school after all. McCart, you are not alone!]*

CHAPTER XXXII

MUCCA, THE FIRST XI GOALKEEPER, WRITING POEMS

How peaceful to be sat by the river's edge on a balmy early evening, watching the continuous water flow with the accompanying gentle trickling sound as water forms miniature rapids over the stones scattered along the riverbed. The sound of the water – really quite intoxicating. The sun, whilst descending imperceptibly towards a western horizon, sent streaks of light across the placid water. Water almost becalmed in secret pockets within the river margins, with the dancing light then darting and filtering through the copse opposite. There was an urge to capture that moment and hold it still. It would have been an idyllic setting for an artist or even, perhaps, for a photographer. The artists and their talent – how privileged they are.

From the far side of the swimming pool, the distant sound of a group of boisterous junior boarders had carried across to the peaceful wilderness. Others from the boarding house, not quite so junior, had enjoyed messing about in the swimming pool – under the watchful eye of a portly Mr Russell, complete with his trademark mustard-coloured woolly jumper and white plimsolls. Ah, the joys of undiluted summer. How many of those boarders, young and old, have not a care in the world? Then again, how many of those juniors playing almost carefree by the riverside are maybe secretly unsettled and worried about next week's lessons? Woodwork perhaps or Art maybe? Lonny, still in charge of woodwork, but no longer meting out physical punishment via the back of one's head or ears. It is not always easy to admit to, or tell anyone about, such worries. Personal experience confirms that to be the case. Time has marched on since September 1966 and now, at the most senior level in the boarding house, this school life away from a family home is appreciated and yes, it is being enjoyed. Regretfully, it is drawing to a conclusion – and rapidly. The time – the hours, the days, the weeks – are now passing so very quickly. Will those youngsters feel the same when they reach the Upper 6th form and have their own private room? Who knows? Hopefully.

It is a wonderful June evening. Two final exams next week and a mere five weeks or so until the term ends – indeed, school ends. What does the future then hold? Whatever it will ultimately offer and subsequently provide, it will not involve a university degree. Thank goodness! Overriding all other thoughts at this moment – where will 'home' be when the school term ends?

The southern boundary of the school grounds.
The view from the riverbank, with the author's dormitory room at the extreme top, right-hand side.
(Photograph: Courtesy BGS archive.)

An interesting church service last Sunday. Why? Barbara finally did what she has been threatening to do for some time. With the service almost ready to start, who should come sauntering through the swing doors, but she! Accepting the almost mandatory *Hymns Ancient and Modern* and *Book of Common Prayer* from the Churchwarden, her eyes flickered across to give an acknowledgement of her boyfriend's presence, that familiar grin being almost suppressed in deference to the hushed surroundings. The church bells had, of course, been ringing out, almost announcing and heralding her entrance. It was as if the bells were giving a welcome, albeit a religious one, to a young lady. Indeed, a young lady dressed smartly yes, but acknowledging the summer with a red flowery dress, setting off rather nicely a pair of suntanned legs and open sandals. And was there just a hint of makeup around those wide eyes? Wow! A rare event indeed.

What a beautiful portrayal of blossoming, innocent femininity. She is young and alive, not far off from being eighteen years of age and is clearly a happy young lady. It was as well that she remained suitably serious on her arrival at church. At least on that occasion, certainly, with a rather formal and local audience. Well known within the village, she was duly acknowledged by those stalwart regulars and, although sitting by herself, she really was not alone. All those around know her – stalwarts and boarders. But why had she attended? After all, the threats she had made to come to church were given (it was assumed by both parties) almost light-heartedly and accepted in the same manner – why on earth would you want to attend, Barbara? Well, she had, of course, chosen the Sunday service when her boyfriend had been allocated to do the bible reading to the assembled congregation. Oh dear. Talking to an audience holds no fear. (Despite the frequent advice from Ducky, "Try not to talk too quickly when you are reading aloud, McCart.") The large print bible helped enormously, but the presence of a girlfriend inevitably caused an unwelcome bout of self-consciousness. And that large unwieldy bible – yes, the pages are to be left open at where the reading finishes. (Instruction from the rector no less.) Weird. And did Barbara close her eyes for the prayers? Well, she was honest enough to admit that, no, she did not – but then, neither did her boyfriend. Her boyfriend had the advantage of being sat on the back pew, thereby gazing across to a beautiful young lady sat several pews in front. For Barbara, no such luxury – feeling slightly awkward at continually having to turn her head around to acknowledge her boyfriend. Decorum my dear, decorum. We shall meet again my love, surely, in St. John the Baptist church – sometime in the future.

Handed out earlier this week to the 6th form wimps by Mrs Fife – the 1973 issue of *Crescent,* the annual school magazine. Worth waiting for and an enjoyable evening read before 'lights out'. The First XI soccer team has, justifiably, been given a good write up with an action photograph of the home match against Fleetwood Nautical College. (No sign in the photograph of Barbara exchanging pleasantries with the rector, mind.) Our erstwhile Sociology teacher (have they, one wonders, become fed up yet at Oxfordshire Council with that - oh, so familiar – Olympic high jump story?) muscles in with a photograph of her descending Penyghent (with Lefty bringing up the rear). Miss Shirley, you might be sorry to learn that you have not been missed – well, at least, not by this sole Sociology scholar!

Perhaps the most interesting section is that devoted to poetry submitted by the various school years. In particular, the four poems included which have been written by the Head Boarder. Four? Was the editor (Ducky) short of material? (Other scribes also have four entries – but from the Lower 6th. Plus, in Hebblethwaite's case, some written work as well as several poems – but surely, isn't he one of the 'boffins' from the 'Science' group?) Well now, a request had been made for the submission of poetry some months ago, although the portfolio originally handed in to Mrs Fife excluded (bar one) those which related directly to Barbara. It did not feel appropriate passing those over for a general school publication. In fact, three of the four included in the magazine had been written during the previous school year, in the Lower 6th. Only 'Go Catch That Leaf' was recent and did not have any obvious direct link with Barbara for those reading the poem (they perhaps might guess). It is of no concern, of course, as to what others might think – and yes, after the poems appeared in the *Crescent,* perhaps it was natural to get some rather surprised – amazed even – comments and looks. In this case, from both contemporaries in the Lonsdale dormitory and the Upper 6th form group, but also, indeed, from the juniors. Perhaps the most common theme amongst the other pupils was summed up by a young boarder, saying rather incredulously and cheekily to the man himself, "Mucca, you – the First XI goalkeeper – writing poems!" (An exclamation mark is more directly appropriate than a question mark – the lad had not been asking a question but rather, had been unable to fathom out how the paradox of these two seemingly diverse activities could be reconciled.)

So, can the macho world of First XI football sit comfortably with an aesthete streak? Well, on this occasion, yes. Mrs Fife now smiles knowingly every morning at one of her Upper 6th form charges having recently been handed, with Barbara's full approval, a further selection of poems – perhaps more correctly termed love poems – for assessment. The on-going relationship with the Head of the English Department may have been combative over the last two years, but with his wife, the form teacher for this arts group, it has been friendly and instructive. What a difference. One wonders if they discuss the character of the head of the boarding house and their respective relationship with him away from the school premises. They surely must do. What conclusions then do they draw, regarding the very different reactions obtained from the author during their teaching of English?

*[**An aside**: So exactly which group do you belong to, McCart? A permanent member of the First XI football team and writing poems. It is, perhaps, the sort of question that might well be posed by Mr. Hagen. Are you one of the 'aesthetes' (with a fondness for poetry and prose) or are you one of the 'hearties' (with self-esteem gained from wearing a goalkeeper's jersey)? It might be suggested that the Head Boarder wants to straddle both camps and indeed he feels comfortable in doing so. A romantic certainly. In fact, a melancholic romantic – but also, aggressive between those goalposts. A mixture – a puzzling mixture*

perhaps. (Is that a question or confirmation of fact?)]

In the *Crescent,* apart from 'Go Catch That Leaf', one of the other poems concentrates on that old friend (always lurking in the shadows), melancholy, and separately and perhaps inevitably, the adjacent churchyard. A quiet and generally deserted place, apart from the occasional visitor. A widow, perhaps, or a widower, or a son or daughter coming to pay respects to their departed spouse or respective parents. All somewhat thought provoking and, to a mind often pensive and downcast, rather sad. And with some of the gravestones, the script is hardly legible after many years of neglect combined with the onslaught of harsh Yorkshire winters. Some gravestones highlight the tragedy and sadness in life – a spouse dying some forty years before the remaining partner. Others show surely the most grief-stricken event for loving parents, that of infant mortality. If this churchyard is representative, and most surely it will be, it was perhaps a good deal more frequent than imagined.

How very depressing it all is. Life will go on regardless, yes, and the difficulty, perhaps, is in reconciling this fact with time moving continually on. Auden understood the mechanics of life and the difficulty of understanding individual grief when not involved. He rather bluntly portrayed it in verse. Brueghel's *Icarus* – falling into the sea from the sky – had hardly turned a head. The farmer continued ploughing his field and a ship sailed calmly on. ('Musee des Beaux Arts') And just why would you notice a boy falling from the sky? Each has his or her own life to live. And then, didn't someone else say, 'Everyone has a story to tell'? Plenty untold in the environs of a church.

Indeed, it is so with this churchyard – and so it will always be. It continues to pull at the sub-conscious.

Withered it was, the grass was gaining
A grasp which claims victory… Even
The elaborate marking was fading into
Obscurity with the rest of the grave.
The corners show signs of chipping,
The stone has turned almost as the body
Inside would probably now be…

Who was he? William…that surname is
Now obliterated by the passage of years.
Is there no one now to care whether he is kept
Decent in death? Two centuries have now
Passed since they laid him to decrepit rest…

Such was that patch of the graveyard displayed:
Overgrown beyond recovery; but who will
Worry unduly as to whether the grave
Is seen or hidden in entangled twines?

Earlier today, they laid a woman to rest:
After two centuries, will the flowers, the sombre
Faces still be surrounding that mournful spot?

Whatever, the end of another June evening. An antidote to these sometime-frequent pensive moods is the declaration delivered enthusiastically by Barbara during the half-term. After a goodnight kiss whilst she was laid in bed cuddled up with *Teddy*, she affirmed her feelings with much needed reassurance. "Ian, please always remember that I want to be faithful to one man and one man only, and that man is you." Then, with her impeccable knack for good timing, she had laughed ever so quietly, her grin being accompanied with her trademark *"tee-hee"*. Then scrunching up her nose and holding open her arms, she had exclaimed "Oh, Ianey, give me a quick hug, I do love you so." And hugging her whilst she is in bed, with only her nightdress and a boyfriend's silk dressing gown keeping the beauty of her body at bay – what heaven. Such danger! Excitement overflows. More pertinently, what is it that is regularly mentioned in the Sunday church service? Something to the effect of – 'the cup overfloweth'. Not, in this case, for the love of God. No, but instead, with love for one another.

CHAPTER XXXIII

BEAUTY IS TRUTH, TRUTH BEAUTY

Friday 15th June. Another full moon. Keats, with his endless fascination for the night sky, eloquently described it in romantic terms,

> *The Queen moon is on her throne,*
> *Cluster'd around by all her starry fays...*

A shining white ball tonight it is. Shaded outlines ripple across its surface, which one assumes must be higher ground – mountains, perhaps. And surrounding the moon, an array of stars. Keats again,

> *Bright star, would I were steadfast as thou art...*

Inevitably, perhaps, memories also of youth, when one would regularly chant at bedtime with a parent, *'Twinkle, twinkle, little star, how I wonder what you are...'*, whilst not possessing, of course, any understanding of the night sky. Now, with the night sky awash with specks of light in every corner, there is an irresistible urge to sit and look up to the sky and wonder about the enormity of it all. The thing is, as a child and in bed reciting *'Twinkle, twinkle little star...'*, one doesn't actually wonder what they are. It is only once into adolescence that the thought process starts to really think about it all. How did Betjeman term it? *'Spingle-spangled stars...'* The Plough, Orion, Ursa Minor. Their place in the sky and their formation were all known as a young teenager. With the advent of boarding school, the interest in the night sky transferred immediately to trains and trainspotting. The night sky was abandoned. Now the shapes of the various formations in the sky are indeed still recognised, yes, but their individual names have been forgotten. The Plough is up there somewhere, but which formation is it?

Will those celestial bodies be up there in the night sky forever, shining down on this earth long, long after the rabbits have run their course? Many have had, and many still have, a fascination with the night sky – not least among them, those 'Romantic' poets. Keats, of course, and Shelley – but for them both, the rabbits very quickly ran their course. For now, with exams completed, there is time enough to sit, to gaze out at the night sky, and wonder. Wonder indeed about the enormity of it all, about a life ahead. Will it all work out?

Yes, it is now all over. Exams have been completed. How successfully or otherwise remains to be seen. Is there a slight feeling of anti-climax? Well, yes there is. Almost inevitable, perhaps, after a two-year prelude to what were essentially six three-hour sessions of writing. Will any of these reference books and workbooks piled high on the study desk be picked up again and studied, however briefly? Certainly not for Sociology, possibly with History, but with English Literature, well, yes. The genie has been well and truly let out of the bottle with Literature. More of an emphasis on poetry and non-fiction, perhaps, rather than fiction, with no strong urge to merely read fiction for its own sake. It will now be nigh impossible to push that genie back into the Literature bottle.

English Literature Paper II, taken yesterday morning, was absolute manna from heaven. Surely, there must now be a creditable pass in English Literature in the offing. Not only that but a decent grade as well, not just scraping through. Three hours to complete written essays on four questions was, it turned out, a tight schedule with the pen flowing freely. Hopefully, with little waffle included. (They will surely accept a little!) There was scant need, though, for waffle. Tucked away towards the middle of the test paper was question seven. Exactly the sort of question that had been wished for (and prayed for!) since the late autumn of 1971. What a confidence booster.

'Whether he presents us with a story, a mood or an argument, his means of communication is always through the senses, by description.' Discuss with reference to the Poems of 1820 by Keats.

The poems of 1820. Good heavens. What an absolute godsend. Did the examiners have the Head Boarder in mind when they set the question? Obviously...

Never mind 'The Pot of Basil' and the escapades of Lorenzo, it was the perfect examination question. It gave free rein, enabling a Head Boarder to wax lyrical on those wonderful odes, all of which have been learned word for word over the last two years. (With some rather blatant showing off over the past few months, when they have spoken aloud to Barbara whilst she was sat in bed on an evening, listening attentively.)

The odes of 1820 – 'to a Nightingale', 'on a Grecian Urn', 'to Psyche', 'to Autumn', and 'on Melancholy'. An extraordinary collection of writing which does indeed accost the senses. During a detailed discussion that took place in class a short while ago on 'Ode on a Grecian Urn', some feisty and productive discussions ensued regarding the final two lines of the ode:

FROM A DORMITORY WINDOW

Beauty is truth, truth beauty' – that is all
Ye know on earth, and all ye need to know.

Are these two lines perhaps the most contentious in poetry? Are they romantic nonsense? Does beauty equal truth and truth beauty? Not really. In fact, most definitely not in a literal sense. Perhaps Keats might have also, years later and on reflection (if he had lived longer than he did, dying at a young age in Italy in 1821), been prepared to challenge that mantra. Certainly, the truth is not always beautiful and sometimes, the truth hurts. Didn't someone once say or suggest that 'beauty is only skin deep'? The parallels with a girlfriend are inevitable and impossible to ignore.

Here in a dormitory room, there is an inner sense saying that Barbara's beauty is so much more than skin deep and that her beauty is accompanied by a natural and pleasant personality. She is not the quarrelling type. She could not have an argument to save her life. Is that a sign of strength or weakness, or just a reflection on character? This young lady must, surely, have her faults. Will they ever be discovered? Keats may have suggested that *'...if thy mistress some rich anger shows/Emprison her soft hand and let her rave'*, but the possibility of that happening within this love affair would seem nothing less than remote.

And it is certainly not the case with this relationship that "love is blind". (Or is it?) Possibly it is blind, yes. But it cannot help itself. It hardly seems conceivable to even think about this girlfriend losing her temper and shouting. Could she lose it? Surely not. What about a boyfriend losing his temper when clearly his patience threshold is certainly not as settled as his girlfriend's temperament? Not as patient perhaps, but he is certainly most understanding. It seems inconceivable at this juncture to envisage losing one's temper with a caring and kindly girlfriend.

Whilst at *'Benwick'*, during the recent half-term, Barbara had typed out a brief note on her boyfriend's typewriter, leaving it in the typewriter ready for reading the next time something was ready to be typed out. It reads as follows, *"Will Ian ever be mad with Barbi or tell her off or shout at her????? Please answer truthfully. Don't just say what you think I would like you to say. Please answer very truthfully."* A dose of realism there perhaps from Miss Noble – so love is quite definitely not blind with you, young lady. Perhaps she is thinking fleetingly back to that football match at home to Fleetwood Nautical College in January. Shouting at an absent defence is surely justified. Shouting at a girlfriend and, hopefully, a girlfriend who will eventually be a wife – surely not. You should have no need to worry, Barbara. *'Beauty is truth, truth beauty'* – perhaps Keats was right all along!

Apart from that most contentious of endings, the very first line from 'Ode on a Grecian Urn' sums up Miss Noble most appropriately, *'Thou still unravish'd bride of quietness'* – for how much longer will that be the case? Certainly ravishing. How long *'unravished'*? Continuing the same theme, Keats cannot be right, surely, when he proclaims in 'Ode on Melancholy':

She dwells with Beauty -- Beauty that must die.

Visually yes, a girlfriend will alter as the years progress, but her inherent features will remain. And the character within that beautiful frame? It will surely stay constant. Didn't Keats also say, *'for ever will thou love, and she be fair!'* Will she always be fair?

Christ, this thought process. It is nigh impossible to now divorce Keats and his frequent musings from a girlfriend and from being hopelessly in love with her. One of these English Literature books quoted someone (who was it?) as saying, "Love is a rather strange disease, and no one has yet found a cure for it..." Some things, then, have not changed over the course of 150 years. Keats and his love affair with Fanny remained unrequited. With the young lady at *'Benwick'*, that will not be the case – surely.

Certainly then, based on yesterday's English paper, there will be no nervous wait for the 'A' Level grade result. The confidence and supposed arrogance of youth in the context of Literature is well placed. Perhaps some might term it as vanity. August – when summer will be in full swing – will provide the answer. (Perhaps one should remain cautious and quietly confident...)

In addition to Keats, it really was most enjoyable writing about Auden's poetry and about Henry Fielding's lovable rascal, Tom Jones, and Squire Allworthy. (And he was – too worthy!) What a dream exam paper it was. It seems ages since Part I was taken at the beginning of June. *King Lear* seems light years away. Just now, and most probably for the foreseeable future, he is going to stay light years away. Does anyone read Shakespeare once school or university studies have been completed? Surely not. Why would they?

History Paper II, taken last Monday afternoon. Not as much confidence, sadly, with this exam. Foreign History from the sixteenth and seventeenth centuries proved rather hard work. Interestingly, the front page of the exam paper provided five options regarding periods in history. Who, one wonders, chose 1494–1715 as the period to study for this two-year course? Surely 1815–1939 would have proved more interesting – more entertaining – for both British and Foreign history. Certainly, in terms of this century, it might well have provided the opportunity for the occasional discussion with parents, relatives even. Parents will most definitely have some recollection from the 1930s, even as teenagers. At the time WW2 was declared, a father was only a year or so shy of being eligible for wartime service with the navy, whilst his elder brother was already serving in the Royal Navy, on the battleship HMS Hood. (And on that flagship of the Royal Navy, he perished.) A tradition for service in the Royal Navy, then, on the paternal side, with an elder brother also choosing the Premier Service. A younger brother will not be following suit. A father also sporting a moustache and beard, thereby entertaining a memory, perhaps, of wartime naval service.

As it was, the three-hour slog with European History involved some not so confident answers on the French religious wars, Richelieu and Mazarin and Louis XIV. Hopefully, the Part I paper, dealing solely with English history, from the previous week, has gained sufficient marks for an overall pass. History. A pass at any grade will suffice.

No more exams. What now? After getting back to the dormitory at the end of the formal school day yesterday, still with the inward satisfaction at what will surely have been a well answered English exam paper, there waiting on the bed were two letters. Inevitably, it was the lime-green coloured envelope, immediately giving away the identity of the sender, which caught the eye and the interest of the recipient. Mr. Ian McCart, c/o Bentham Grammar School – yes, still in the boarding house, but not for much longer. Then what? In the letter, the usual enticing and suggestive messages from Barbara, *'I have just had a nice long bath and at the moment, I am writing to you in bed whilst cuddling Teddy as he was feeling lonely!'* Goodness, it is suddenly quite lonely here in this dormitory room. What would one give for the chance to take the place of *Teddy* and be cuddled up in bed with a girlfriend? A girlfriend, indeed, who has just had a bath and whose silky skin will have the familiar smell of *Desert Flower* body lotion.

Within the recommended reading for Barbara's first year English Literature 'A' Level course, Barbara had found a poem by Alexander Smith entitled 'Barbara'... as she has described in her letter,

'Whilst my mum was ironing, I read 'my' poem to her, missing out the word Barbara to see if she could guess. She guessed after the second verse but when I read the third verse which said Barbara was beautiful, she said NO, it cannot be Barbara. Sherbet cheek!'

[And in case a boyfriend had failed to understand her particular version of Cockney slang with her *'Sherbet cheek'* remark, she had added the following, *'if you are wondering what sherbet is replacing, think of which word fits in these two places in Holland -- ROTTER.... and AMSTER... -- and yer there me 'owd fruit drop!!']*

Barbara's letter ends, *'I have kissed all the photographs of you on my wall – I hope you are now going to kiss all the photographs you have of me!'* Oh yes, indeed! Suitable reminders are not really required, you cheeky young lady! And clearly satisfied that her boyfriend would manage to work out the missing word, a reminder in the form of a post-script, *'in the words of my mother, using (that word) twice in a day is quite sufficient!'* When is a swear word not a swear word? The occasional "hell" and "damn" (sometimes worse...) encompassed in the dialogue of this boarding house pupil, and also included in the diction of a girlfriend, is not altogether appreciated by a girlfriend's mother. There, specifically, the outlook of this generation and that of a previous one is at odds.

All this English Literature reading and learning taking place at *'Benwick'* must be rubbing off on Mrs Noble. After much discussion with her daughter and her daughter's boyfriend, she recently decided to broaden her horizons and read Chaucer. In particular 'The Miller's Tale' from *The Canterbury Tales*. A slight problem. The school 'A' Level version is an expurgated copy, leaving out what might be termed by 6th formers as the occasional (and very welcome) 'juicy bit'! The Bentham library version is, well, as it was originally written, 'warts and all'. (Or should it be 'sex and all'?)

After gamely advancing her frontier of learning, Barbara's mother eventually abandoned the story half-way through. Not in this instance because it proved intellectually demanding, but more from her being aghast and appalled with the content. Perhaps she might have done well to have remembered 'A Whiter Shade of Pale', that famous and iconic song by Procol Harum from the 1960s. Then again, perhaps pop music from six years ago is not within her musical sphere. Didn't the lyrics make a mention about the Miller's Tale in an oblique reference to sex? Barbara suggested that her mother was quite a whiter shade of pale herself before abandoning the story. Good heavens, Mrs Noble, your daughter's boyfriend had better also advise you to steer clear of John Donne and his 'Elegy XIX', as you may well – no, you certainly will – find its narrative unpalatable. You would, surely, be somewhat disgusted to read Donne's description regarding his mistress, *'The hairy Diadem which on you doth grow...',* with his roving hands going, well, all over the place. On the other hand, English Literature students will take it in their stride. Nothing wrong at all with reading about sex. Barbara might well have commented, "How rude!" on reading the verse but her eyes, wide open – together with her mischievous grin – told otherwise!

[An aside: the memory of that record – 'A Whiter Shade of Pale' – being played, seemingly over and over again, by the boarding house prefects on the stage in the Assembly Hall during 1967 is, for whatever reason, still fresh in the memory. The tune is hummed rather sub-consciously and automatically without realizing. Perhaps an iconic pop song will always stay in the sub-conscious – a father, please note!]

Barbara's mother has sensibly reverted to what might be termed normal or traditional fiction. She is now wading her way through the complete set of Jane Austen novels. More her style. Old fashioned? Perhaps, perhaps not. Certainly not old fashioned when it comes to wine and sherry, with *Mateus Rose* or *Black Tower* both flowing freely with a Sunday dinner. And *Emva Cream?* Sherry seemingly available whenever. Growing up at home was devoid of wine and sherry, as boarding school is also – but not at *'Benwick'* – ha! Perhaps that is the beauty and attraction of simple country folk. (Although, it would be rather a good idea if they were to buy larger wine/sherry glasses. The *'Benwick'* ones are rather titchy!)

Letters. The growing pile of letters from Barbara have proved entertaining, funny, reassuring and comforting, all in turn. In a strange way, despite seeing each other every day, these letters have added a little spice and excitement to this relationship – Barbara thinks so too. A little spice? Well, it is rather roguish to be slightly racy or cheeky in a letter, but isn't that all part of the sexual attraction? It works both ways, as Barbara, in writing, has regularly been quite suggestive (and sometimes a touch bawdy), but there is indeed a joint excitement in being a little impish towards each other. It is adding to the adventure – the written equivalent, perhaps, of giving those bosoms a little squeeze last thing at night or getting a brief (and welcome) flash of her knickers and upper thighs when her nightie is quickly raised.

There is quite often a sexual slant in reading some of her slightly suggestive comments and that is, surely, natural enough in private correspondence. Generally, the letters coming from *'Benwick'* are written last thing at night and whilst she is ensconced in bed. (One naturally follows the other – surely? That is, bedtime and the sexual slant.)

Quite typical is,

'If you could see me now – and you damn well can't – because I am in bed with my see-through nightie on' [do you REALLY have one Barbara?] or,

'I have just got out of the bath and put some Desert Flower body lotion all

over and around my luscious hips (stop panting boy)!' or,

'I have just had a bath and I soaped all over my long, lean, attractive body – just a pity I didn't have anyone to wash my back -- hard luck, not until we are married little boy!'

And in another letter, quite roguishly,

'Teddy is looking particularly sexy tonight --- and so am I!!!! He watched me take off all my clothes whilst I was getting ready for bed (calm down sunshine!!!).'

Such wonderful reading and over and above everything else, was a sentence in the most recent letter – *'Ian, you are part of me – in fact you are me and I am you. I really do hope you understand what I mean. I do love you so very much.'* Oh Barbara, how wonderful you are.

Oh yes, nearly forgot. That other letter on the bed waiting to be opened and read? A black horse logo and 'Lloyds Bank Ltd' printed on the reverse gave notice of the parentage. No longer any Durham. The question, "now what?", with the ending of this school year has been repeated numerous times. Regular employment beckons. It must. There is no logical alternative. An advert in last year's *Crescent* magazine suggests that Lloyds Bank Ltd. are interested in employing school leavers. What about this school leaver then? Will they be interested in him? The letter opened – they have offered an interview. An offer that will be accepted.

June. The vagaries of this English weather are interesting, intriguing and yes, just a bit frustrating. It snowed last weekend! Yes, snowed. Whilst it was only a brief snowstorm, it was heavy enough to cover the front and back lawns at *'Benwick'*. Perhaps it isn't the first time it has snowed in June. Barbara's mother, however, has no previous recollection of snow at this time of the year – and Bentham has been her home since before WW2. Whilst stood watching in awe from within the living room at *'Benwick'*, Barbara's mother had been sufficiently alert to suggest taking a photograph outside in the snow, because, as she put it, "It isn't every day you can have your photograph taken in a snowstorm in June." How true. Rather cheekily and in response to an offer to carry her outside (as she had been laying across her boyfriend's knees on the settee), Barbara had quipped, "Are you sure you can manage me? I am quite heavy, you know, 36-inch bum and all that!" Ha, at eight stone (perhaps a touch more, or a touch less – who knows? One person knows and she is not telling!) she was not too heavy for a committed boyfriend and will never be too heavy – hopefully. Anyhow, who suggested that to look at a girlfriend's mother will invariably provide a clue as to what a girlfriend might herself look like in years to come? Looking at mother whilst

FROM A DORMITORY WINDOW

carrying her daughter out into the garden, if that premise is indeed true, no problem...

Within fifteen minutes or so the snow had melted (although a covering remained on the summit ledge of Ingleborough for a good while longer) and with the sunshine following, one would have been hard pressed to convince anyone who had not witnessed it, that it had happened. The changeable weather patterns witnessed from this dormitory window through the various seasons have been enjoyed. A truism this is indeed, but it is quite feasible to witness three or four weather patterns or conditions within the space of a single day. During that period of two years spent in Aden as a youngster, not a single day of rain – how boring – not even a brief shower, nothing! A sandstorm, yes, but no rain. There are, therefore, times when one can be quite grateful to open these dormitory curtains in the morning and see that the heavens have opened. It is just that, on occasions, the heavens are very slow at closing.

Now, shutting these flimsy curtains blocks out the *'starry, starry night'*. (*American Pie* – is that what it is from? Oh dear. We don't want that playing in the Lonsdale dormitory. Leonard Cohen is bad enough!) The window can remain open. The morning light, filtering through at any time after 4am will easily stir the occupant into feverish activity, but it no longer needs to involve revision. The dazzling array up in the night sky will still be there at nightfall tomorrow. More than likely, though, being hidden from view by stubborn cumulus. If not, then there will be another glittering display on offer – a chance, perhaps, to *'wish upon a star...'*

CHAPTER XXXIV

LOOKING TO THE FUTURE

Into July then. Barbara's interim 'O' Levels (studied and taken whilst doing 'A' Levels), Geography and Human Biology, have also been completed. Her Geography exam on the same day as an arranged interview with Lloyds Bank Ltd. in Lancaster, the 19$^{th\ of}$ June. Church Street, Lancaster – the offices of the Bank – that was the venue.

*[**An aside**: and before setting off, a flippant comment from a girlfriend. In her words, "I should like to have you as a bank manager because I could then lock you in the wardrobe in our bedroom, just like that advert on television" – a different bank, my dear, a different bank! And this time, a suggestion that a haircut would probably be a good idea was accepted gracefully – but the recommendation had come not from Snot, but from a girlfriend. Advice, you see, can be taken. It all depends, of course, on who is dispensing it.]*

The appointment at 2pm had been preceded by a walk around the city. The usual irrational fear of being late had involved catching a mid-morning Pennine bus from Bentham. The consequence? An arrival in Lancaster several hours before the allotted interview time. Yes, a later bus departure was available from Low Bentham – but what if the bus had not turned up? What if it broke down? Oh dear!

Time enough, therefore, to do some shopping for a girlfriend. In her words, "Whilst you are in Lancaster, can you please get me two pairs of *American tan* tights from Boots – you will find them near the front door next to where the wigs are!" (Do they *really* sell wigs in Boots? Er… yes!)

Tucked safely away in a school blazer inside pocket, the summer term school report – largely favourable and thankfully omitting any reference to the sometime niggling relationship with the Head of English. In the event, the report had not been requested and nor was it volunteered.

It had still been rather too early when entering through the rather imposing, and ornately carved, large wooden doors into the bank. Fifteen minutes or so too early, but wouldn't that have spoken of enthusiasm and punctuality? Several pairs of eyes looked across from time to time with enquiring interest from the other side of a large glass partition, visibly thick and protecting. A partition that most successfully separated those being served from those doing the serving. A slightly nervous pair of eyes also looked in at what seemed to be a bustling financial office, the desks liberally strewn with large ledgers. Both the aspiring applicant and the branch staff somehow studiously ensuring that eyes did not meet. If they had done, some sign of mutual acknowledgment would then have been necessary. A confident smile would have been most difficult to manufacture in what was an unfamiliar – foreign even – environment.

The interview, then, with the Manager at the Lancaster Branch, a hale and hearty Mr Coates. Tall and thin, with small wisps of white hair that would need little regular attention, cutting across an otherwise bald head. He sported a dark pin striped suit and was wearing a small pair of rimless glasses, both of which fitted his stature and position perfectly. A bowler hat on the coat stand was not out of place. (So, then, finance people still wear them!). He looked important. He obviously was important, and he exuded an air of superiority. The voice was clear and sharp, almost as if giving orders was second nature and done automatically. Most likely it was done on the assumption that anything he said would not (or indeed, could not) be challenged. Friendly nevertheless, but in a formal way, with seemingly no urge on his part to advise this young aspiring bank clerk to stop calling him "Sir".

Clarification requested on exams taken and likely pass grades. An answer given, but anticipated grades? Not easy to answer – but he was advised that two passes were confidently predicted. Rather too confidently, perhaps. At least two decent passes, it turned out, were seemingly a requirement according to Mr Coates. That necessity had been duly acknowledged. No specific information provided though regarding specific subjects required, other than Mathematics at 'O' Level. (That hurdle already jumped then.) He would have realised, of course, that the young man with aspirations to join the ranks was firmly from the 6th form wimps. He must realise that – surely – with the subjects that have been studied for the last two years.

It had soon become quite clear during the interview that this was merely an exploratory 'stage one' discussion. The decision to accept this 6th form pupil into the ranks of finance being ultimately taken at a regional level, which would involve, if needed, a meeting at the Manchester Regional Office. Mr Coates was clearly just the first hurdle – perhaps the second hurdle, after 'O' Level Maths. However, a request that he had made regarding an availability start date augurs well. That possible question had already been thought about and discussed in advance within a girlfriend's bedroom. The summer holidays are about to start. Eight weeks of summer holidays. No exam results until maybe mid-August. A proposed start date of the beginning of September had been advanced. It would tie in with the new school year for Barbara, thereby providing a summer of "playtime". A start date – how about the beginning of September? It had been written down by Mr Coates without comment. No suggestion of a start date of their own preference had been forthcoming.

The interview negotiated then just over two weeks ago. No word since. Is that good or bad? Notwithstanding the possibility of employment in a secure and 'strait-laced' industry, the thought process is still asking – is it the correct career path? What about the other opportunity – employment with the Westmorland Gazette, a popular regional newspaper? Being based in Kendal would be slightly counter-productive. Bentham would be impractical as a home-base but the writing and indeed the reporting involved is an obvious attraction. There are competing influences and attractions. The attraction of a girlfriend is paramount, albeit that the prospect of journalistic writing would be most agreeable.

The return bus journey to Low Bentham from Lancaster was in one of the rather ancient Pennine buses (rather than one of their modern plush ones) and the bus driver clearly had some difficulty with the gears whilst trying to cajole the bus up the Millhouses Road. A very steep incline from the hamlet of Millhouses – always known, of course, within the school as "Snot's hill"! Adequate justification to be "twinned" with Snot, as the road is awkward for buses, particularly in winter. In the end, the driver lost patience and the summit of the rise was accompanied not only at slow speed, but also with a tremendous crunching of gears and with some verbal expletives! Not a familiar driver and the obvious frustration he continued to display with regard to his charge suggested that it probably would not have been a good idea to request a stop outside *'Benwick'*. Instead, the bus continued up the road to the formal bus stop opposite Crossley's garage.

Barbara had been standing at the front window and, watching the bus pass by, she had obviously realised it was not going to stop. So, she had come out of the house and had run up the road to welcome back her boyfriend. She looked beautiful in smart, tight-fitting, navy-blue t-shirt and pale blue slacks, the colour scheme being broken by toenails varnished red, on show by virtue of her summertime footwear – her ultimate concession to summer – flip-flops. Flip-flops rarely worn but justified in deference to the hot weather which that June day had produced. In this instance, welcome sunshine, with an offshoot being provided later in the afternoon by the need, at Barbara's behest, to wash a girlfriend's feet, dirty by virtue of wandering around the garden in flimsy footwear. (Good heavens, it has been snowing earlier in June!)

With arms outstretched, the ensuing embrace ensured that Barbara spent several seconds in the air whilst being turned 180 degrees. How wonderful! And then a host of questions whilst walking back down to *'Benwick'*. How had the interview gone? Was it hopeful? Did they ask about anticipated exam results? Did they ask when you can start? Only one question heading the other way. "What about your Geography exam this morning?" To Barbara, that was of no particular concern. Nothing important hinged on a pass or fail in Geography – except pride perhaps. A great deal, however, hinged on an interview for employment. Her interest was solely with the interview and the prospect of paid employment for her boyfriend.

*[**An aside**: there was, perhaps, an invisible connection between the interview that day and the post that had arrived that same morning for Barbara – in the form of a small booklet from H. Samuel, Jewellers. "I will make you a cup of tea, Ian, and then should we have a look through the catalogue I have received today?" Oh yes. We know what they retail, don't we?]*

No more studying or work at school, but boarders remain 'in situ' until the end of term. The coming days – the last week or so of term – can, therefore, be spent sitting on the lawns to the west of the old rectory building – reading, writing and, perhaps, playing tennis with a bare-footed girlfriend. ("You know I always have to play tennis in bare feet, Ianey." – yes please – and anyway, who wants to see you wearing boring pumps?)

Well, that is the idea. But – there has been a programme of events arranged for the 6th form students to keep them occupied after examinations. How very organised of someone. Rather too organized! Surely the teachers realise that after two years' intensive education, incorporating classroom study, library study, private study, revision, essays, mock exams and final exams, the urge is to have the opportunity to do nothing for the last week or two. What is on offer?

An industrial visit. A talk about the relationship between the police and the public. A look at the development of Lancaster. Various film shows. 'Student Politics' – a talk by the National Union of Students (where is Miss Shirley when you need her?). 'Mortgages and Insurance' and perhaps more pertinent than those events already outlined, 'Banking and Managing your Money' – a talk by the National Westminster Bank. None of it sounds desperately exciting. Certainly not as interesting as sitting and chatting with a girlfriend, who will want to sit lazily on the school lawn, facing the grass tennis courts. Hopefully, of course, with her short school skirt sufficiently hitched up (in an effort to keep those lovely legs nice and brown), thereby displaying a pair of gorgeous and robust thighs. Jesus! Well, if sunbathing in the garden at *'Benwick'* is a suitable yardstick, then that is what Barbara will do. (Even this boyfriend will put up with the occasional dose of sunbathing when it is with a girlfriend!) Her short green skirt regularly gets nicely hitched up, displaying a pair of lovely firm legs, when she sunbathes on the deckchair in the back garden. Utterly fabulous. You do know, don't you my love, that you have a wonderful pair of legs? (Yes, of course you do!)

Three cheers for the Revd Bradberry. Now it is not so often that such a statement has been offered for our softly spoken and mild-mannered rector. On this occasion, most definitely warranted. An end of school year treat. Something, indeed, that several within the senior end of the boarding house have been wanting to do for the past couple of years – a trip up to the top of the church tower. Not that it is particularly high (though it is the highest point within the school parameters), but certainly interesting – intriguing – if only to enable one to have a look at the view.

Height, you know, is deceiving. The church tower may not appear high from ground level, but at the top there was a sense of great height, once the circular staircase – predictably ancient and winding – had been conquered. And what a staircase. Stone, large blocks of it, ancient and worn, twisting around on itself as it climbed. No room for passing – everyone goes up or everyone comes down. It could almost be the inside of a castle keep.

A bird's eye view indeed of the school – that is of the original Norman Shaw building but excluding the more recent 'added-on' parts. Whilst at ground level, and particularly inside what was the old rectory, one might have the impression of the place being a haphazard maze of passages and rooms. However, looking down from above, the layout of the building makes sense. Its design is proper, it is logical. Norman Shaw knew what he was doing, yes.

The design fits together quite naturally, but oh, what a size the building would have been for a rector with a modest parish to oversee, notwithstanding the presence of a family and servants.

Behind the school building, from the top of the church tower, could be seen the grand sweep of the Wenning, the far riverbank shrouded by the summer greenery of the wood, with the odd scattered farm or two visible on the nearby hills to the south – domiciled firmly in a neighbouring county. To the west, the flat plains leading ultimately to the Irish sea. No landmarks, but the whitewashed façade of the headmaster's house visible at the far end of the school playing field. Slightly further west, the toll bar buildings, also whitewashed – a reminder of the original turnpike road, separating the church and school from the sports field.

The railway – straight as a ruler – rising as it heads eastwards as it must do to surmount the western edge of the Pennine ridge. An imperceptible rise from the height of this church tower, the gradient being invisible. Below and across the road, the sports field, which was host that afternoon to a cricket match – numerous little dots all in white flannels giving the game away and looking rather insignificant at a distance – rather like a cluster of ants heading in different directions, but all part of the whole.

As a view, a typically pastoral scene. Really rather English – a summer's day, sunshine, the usual cumulus, cotton wool cloud drifting lazily across the western sky and cricket being played at the required casual and studied pace. Perhaps all that was missing that afternoon was the sight of a train, hauled by a steam engine, heading up the gradient, its tell-tale smoke billowing behind and gradually fizzling out into the distance. Sadly, five years too late for a steam train to add to what was a rather satisfying cameo scene. A scene, also, that rather sadly will be left behind with the ending of this summer term, less than a week away.

Looking around to the east, beyond the higher part of Low Bentham village and in the middle distance, sitting on the horizon in splendid isolation, the shape, now so familiar, of Ingleborough. Its flat summit that afternoon had been shrouded in a stubborn clump of cumulus – the cloud notably absent on the surrounding fell country, instead just keeping itself attached firmly to the high free-standing ground.

Immediately below the church tower within that eastward vista, the grass tennis courts – absent of participants – and the river performing what is almost a 180-degree turn with consummate ease, flowing north away from Low Bentham village before turning due south towards the school. Within a few hundred yards, but hidden by the various school buildings, it will turn again to follow its north-west course without further deviation towards its parent, the River Lune.

The whole scene almost a poignant one. Particularly so when looking across the school front lawn to the 'Cottage' – where it all started in September 1966. Time, though, marches on, with the Head Boarder not at all certain that he wants to march with it. Unexpectedly – without warning – the church bells had sounded out the half-hour, producing an immediate pang of melancholy within. Just momentarily – and then it was time to descend the dungeon-like staircase.

This coming Saturday, the annual summer fete; the following week, end-of-term. Difficult – most difficult to comprehend. A bit like a school summer holiday – you do not want it to come to an end – but then sometimes, you do. In any case, irrespective of whether or not you want it to end – end it certainly will.

CHAPTER XXXV

HE HAS BEEN A MOST RELIABLE HEAD OF HOUSE

The school annual summer fete has most probably been held, since time immemorial, on the first Saturday of July. And most probably, it always will be the case – at least, if Snot has anything to do with it. And yes, it was held today – 7th July. Always an enjoyable and casual affair, providing the weather is kind – and today it has been. The aim this year is, as with all previous years, via a huge self-help exercise – thereby enabling the school to raise money. Money that is an on-going and necessary need for the various improvements, additions, repairs etc., to the school fabric. The requirement for last year – 1972 – was to raise upwards of £600. That target had been successfully reached by 'hook or crook' – the money being utilised towards various improvements. By all accounts, the target from today's extravaganza is to aim at breaching a £700 threshold. Many parents have been, and are, generous providers of finance. Do parents, divorced from it all in Germany, give generously? (Probably not...) So then, will funds raised this year assist towards curtains for the new dining room? Has someone really mentioned that curtains are a requirement? Are curtains really needed? Seems rather pansy. If so, only surely for cosmetic display. That must be, surely, a suggestion from the female contingent. The rest of the money that will have been raised from today's fete (for there will surely be funds left over from buying dining room curtains...) will be used for...well, who knows? There is always something that needs replacement, changing, upgrading, etc.

A Summer Garden Fete with crowds around the main drive and adjacent lawn.

The money has already been found to enable the various outside wooden exteriors surrounding the school to be painted in a rather handsome royal blue. This is a match, presumably by design, for the navy colour which accompanies the gold colouring on the school emblem and uniform. The school tie is certainly quite unique, with navy and gold-coloured diagonal stripes, and even the school First XI football team kit displays rather snazzy gold and blue football socks. In the early days of boarding school life, having the correct school uniform and wearing it (cap included and scarf in the winter months) was rigidly adhered to, with an underlying threat of punishment for not doing so. Mr Webb was an absolute disciplinarian, but the times change and will continue to change. School uniform is still a requirement, but with some easing of the rigid adherence to the rules from just a few years ago. However much the strings are loosened (willingly or not by a Headmaster who regularly seems to blow hot and cold on the rules pertaining to uniform), the pupil base still yearns for more latitude with wearing school uniform (or rather, not wearing it...) and one suspects they always will. Such is the way, it seems, of school life.

The weather has been kind to the various school outdoor pursuits linked to the ending of this summer term. Yesterday morning, the school-house swimming competition and gala took place in summer sunshine. The only involvement wanted, and fortuitously the only involvement needed, as head of Hardy House, was as an interested spectator – well, perhaps just as a spectator. The same situation applied to Barbara, but her lack of involvement is a pretty basic one for the various swimming competitions – she is unable to swim. She cannot swim! Not only that, but she is quite proud of the fact. Possessing not the slightest interest in swimming, she is quite pleased and, indeed, boastful of her ability during the last six years (she started at the school in September 1967, very shortly after the swimming pool was officially opened in July 1967) to have escaped swimming lessons of any sort. Quite how she has, successfully, avoided dipping even a toe into the swimming pool over a six-year period is indeed a mystery. An impressive record it is, nonetheless. The only way she will allow her body to be submerged in water will be via the entry into a bathroom and within the bath domiciled therein!

During the last two years of study, the Head Boarder's only direct involvement with the swimming pool has been watching events (both those organised by the school and the unofficial events – the sporadic immersion of boarders whilst fully clothed) from a dormitory window. One could suggest that there seems little point in swimming backwards and forwards aimlessly in the pool, but then again, perhaps others might say the same about continuously kicking a football around a pitch. (But at least the football match produces some sort of result...)

Here at boarding school, what else does one do in a basic outdoor swimming pool? Swim a few lengths of the pool before loitering around aimlessly in the water, waiting to get out and get dried. The swimming pool has remained virgin territory for the Head Boarder and also, by necessity, for his girlfriend. Suffice to say that Hardy House obtained the wooden spoon in the swimming competitions, helped along the way by the head of Hardy House who played no part in proceedings. Similarly, Collingwood House failed to obtain top spot thanks to, in a small part, the total absence of any contribution from one of their Lower Sixth members – she who cannot swim. Of the three school 'Houses' therefore, victory was with Carr House. Ah, such continuity to these things. (The three sporting 'Houses' being named after two generous benefactors from days gone by – Collingwood, represented by yellow, and Carr, represented by red – and the third, our erstwhile Headmaster and holder of the VC – Hardy, represented by blue – which has always been, co-incidentally, the favourite colour of the Head Boarder.)

The annual Sports Day is now well in the distant past, having taken place on May 25th, the day the school broke up for half-term. It also enjoyed a warm sunny day. The non-involvement in Sports Day was more than justified by claiming that last minute cramming for the two Sociology papers needed to take priority over training for Sports Day. Taking part in the cross-country running competition holds no fear, but a sudden sprint of 100 or 200 metres (who decided to change the measurements to metric? A retrograde step!) from a standing start is something to be avoided. A run across the sports field from the school to the railway line – to get the number of an engine – was always a worthwhile sprint, but that was four, five or six years ago. There is no longer any yearning to suddenly sprint short distances, other than around the penalty area on a football pitch. Needless to say, Barbara's involvement in Sports Day had also been as a spectator. For both Barbara and her boyfriend, the enjoyment on that Friday had been walking together at the end of Sports Day (once a packed suitcase, ready and waiting in the dormitory, had been recovered) up through Low Bentham to spend the week together at *'Benwick'*.

Neither Hardy House nor Collingwood House managed to break the firm hold that Carr House has maintained on the sports activity, in addition to the swimming. Barbara's 'alter ego', in the athletic form of Lynva Russell, took a fair proportion of the senior girls sporting prizes (she is not eligible for the boys' competitions – one might suggest, fortunately!) including the Javelin, short distance sprint, relay and the overall senior 'Victorix Ludorum'. She also had a hand in helping the school's First XI hockey team to several well-earned victories.

What a shame that more of the hockey matches have not been watched. The other two musketeers, Christine and Judith, have both been playing in the school's senior hockey team, non-sporting Barbara the odd one out. (Not that she is bothered.) Oh, watching the senior girls play hockey. A line from one of Betjeman's poems is so relevant… *'She stands in strong athletic pose'*. So appropriate for Lynva, both in hockey and on the athletics field. Standing with javelin in hand ready for a throw in excess of, perhaps, 30 metres (that doesn't sound far – but it is!), but why, one wonders, does she wear that flowing gown tied around her neck? It has become something of a trademark. Perhaps that is the point. Whatever, well done to Lynva. The reality? Hardly Barbara's 'alter ego'. Well, perhaps so in looks, but regarding Barbara, definitely not so with athletic prowess.

So, the Garden Fete today was blessed with sunshine. Walking along the main drive hand in hand with Barbara, whilst watching the junior years performing athletics and dancing on the front lawn, there was once again the realization that school life will soon be at an end.

On the front lawn during the Garden Fete, an impressive athletics performance from both the younger form years and, separately, the intermediate years, jumping and somersaulting over the wooden horse-box – goodness, how on earth do they do that? Not that many years ago, a nervous, self-conscious boarder was not even able to reach the far side of the wooden horse with a simple vault. It cannot be as easy as it looks – surely. Then, on the lawn, the turn of the school orchestra to assemble and show off (and why not?) their sterling progress over the past two years. This enthusiastic collection of youngsters forming the orchestra has been, one might say, professionally put together and organised by Mr Wearmouth, who gives the appearance of the quintessential music teacher – tall, thin and studious. (But surely, not nearly as exciting as being taught all those years ago by Mrs Atkinson, or as she then was, Miss Lewis!)

Music is certainly not a popular subject within the 6th form. Perhaps there is, within all the banter and leg-pulling, a little intrigue in seeing a sole Lower 6th form lad electing to study music at 'A' Level. It perhaps takes some guts to take up a pansy subject such as Music, although Kevin Downham might well be used to such taunts heading his way, being a member of the jingling, fancily dressed, Bentham Morris dancers! But he has stuck with it – and there is a talent there, why not nurture it? Good luck to him – he may need it in a seemingly 'macho' Lower 6th form common room! Kevin Downham aside, one must admire, however begrudgingly, the progress of the school orchestra and their competence, even if the music isn't quite what would be chosen in the boarders' common room. (But it might well be listened to more sympathetically in the living room at *'Benwick'*. It might even make one appear highbrow…)

Oh, the predictability of these annual Garden Fetes. Lots of stalls more than willing to take your money – and all for the benefit of the school. Tombola, a raffle (What! Including alcoholic beverages…), a 'guess how many sweets in the jar' table, a 'clean your shoes' table, amongst many others. (The junior years are happy to clean shoes now for a donation. Would they have been so enthusiastic some years ago when press ganged into cleaning shoes by prefects? Don't think so!) Oh yes, also a 'throw a wet sponge at a pupil' table. A popular turn, and worth spending money on, particularly if you do not care for the poor individual who is there with his head in stocks, waiting for the inevitable soaking.

Lots of interest, certainly, but not quite as exciting as that which was on offer in the late 1960s at Garden Fetes – washing a car for a donation. Yes, it sounds straightforward but there was a twist. Once a parent had parked up their car on the school playing field, the car keys would be left with the 6th form 'car washers'. They would dutifully do the job, but then the highlight – driving the cars in turn to a separate parking spot once cleaned. And the 6th formers certainly made the most of driving the cars around the playing fields to be parked up. Not quite a car rally, but almost having the feel of one – at least for the drivers! Some of those cars went around the field several times before being 'carefully' parked up in the allocated spot.

*The cut and thrust of the 1973 school fete! –
and crisps are two and a half pence a packet.
(Photograph: J Hebblethwaite.)*

Yes, the end of term approaches. As Alice Cooper so eloquently phrased it, *'School's out for summer'*, following it up, as it is in this case, with a most appropriate, *'School's out for ever.'* Across on the main drive, standing by the side entrance to the school Assembly Hall, Snot had stood watching the various proceedings that incorporated the school fete. As is usual, lurking in the background, making sure that the event progressed smoothly – ever ready to jump in at the slightest hint of a hitch. He had looked across and smiled ever so slightly on seeing two members of the 6th form holding hands, giving credence to the general view that he finds it most difficult to smile or laugh willingly. At such an event as the annual fete and with the term-end less than a week away, he had generously, and perhaps sensibly, turned a blind eye to this visible show of affection. It was a Saturday and whilst a formal school event, the nature of the day had been most definitely informal. He was conscious, no doubt, that once the term ends, the only future involvement with Bentham Grammar School for the Head Boarder will be a brief visit to collect the exam results in August (oh dear – perhaps more time might have been spent in the dormitory revising rather than writing love letters) and a return, by invitation already provided, to the annual speech day in November.

Speech Day. A notable visitor to the Speech Day this year is to be Araminta Wordsworth, the great, great niece (a link, but tenuous) of our Lake District mate, William. With that connection and after a two-year study of English Literature, where the 'Romantic' poets have been considered to be the clear heroes and worshipped as such, it will be worth attending. The invitation to attend is for the award of the *'Sir Harold Parkinson Cup'*. A cup awarded to the boy who has made the greatest all-round contribution, in both personality and skill, to games and athletics during the school year. A cup to be held for a year. The £5 gift book token will be more worthwhile, more useful.

Reflecting on a year of games and athletics, perhaps the award is more than justified considering the goalkeeping exploits with the First XI. Clearly, all that shouting at the defence during matches has been noticed by those involved in the awards process. Well done to them. Just maybe the award is justified with the cross-country running performance, but not by itself, in isolation. Surely, though, it is not for the less than impressive contribution given to the First XI cricket team, which involved no bowling and only a few paltry runs being achieved as a 'batsman'. (Inverted commas? Yes!) For indeed, can one use that term as appropriate for being in the middle order and perhaps only being included in the team to make up the numbers? As for field athletics, no contribution from the Head Boarder in that sphere.

In addition to the Parkinson Cup for sporting achievements, which will be accepted with some pride, it has to be admitted (on this occasion, vanity will not come into it), rather surprisingly, there is another award being bestowed on the Head Boarder. *'The Governor's Prize'* is awarded for school service. That is, for the greatest contribution, excluding games and athletics, to school life. Another £5 gift book token. What, one wonders, will Ducky make of that when he has clearly been struggling over a period of almost two years to readily (and perhaps even then with some misgiving) accept that this boarder has been actually acting in a grown-up manner?

A clash of personalities, undoubtedly, there has been. Along with all the other educational based learning, perhaps the experience and interaction with an elder and more mature human being, with whom one does not see 'eye to eye', is also valuable, but in a hugely different way. Being told what to do is certainly an irritant and the occasional frustration aimed at Ducky has perhaps not been noticed elsewhere in the staff common room. Perhaps allowances have been made for the growing pains of adolescence, such as they are. Ducky, you taught me the meaning of hyperbole, the use of alliteration, the beauty of the descriptive passage, the folly of verbosity in essays and much more – but you have failed to teach me the art of humility. Perhaps that is because you do not possess it yourself. Whatever Ducky's view is of one of his English charges, the Governor's prize awaits It may well be difficult not to cast a knowing glance over towards Ducky when collecting the two respective awards at the school speech day later this year. He who laughs last and all that. Ducky, be magnanimous in defeat. The Head Boarder is jubilant in victory. Perhaps one might suggest, *'To the victor – the spoils.'* (That cannot be from Shakespeare, surely? Although it sounds as though it might be – and should be!)

There seems little doubt that Mr Russell will have had an input into the prize awarded by the School Governors. If his term-end report had been shared with others in the Lonsdale dormitory, it might have felt slightly embarrassing, with Mr Russell writing, *'It is impossible to praise too highly the value of his presence in the boarding house. He has been a most reliable Head of House setting an excellent example of self-discipline and constantly striving to get the same response from the boys...'* Good heavens, thank you, Mr Russell! But what about the sporadic Friday night secret visit to the village pub? Did you not realise? What about all these times when prefect duties were delegated or assigned elsewhere, so that early evenings could be spent up the High Bentham Road? He has been chivalrous quite definitely, peppered perhaps with a dose of realism. The rapport has been there, the understanding has been there and a dose of pragmatism also from a jovial Housemaster. But let us not forget, of course, the other half of the team – our vivacious Matron, Mrs Russell. Whatever needed to be done to please Mrs Russell, it was done. The report on the Head Boarder is indeed generous. Perhaps there has been input from our lovely Matron – and Mrs Russell, you are lovely! Really.

Our form teacher, the methodical, patient and understanding Mrs Fife, will also, surely, have had an input. Always quiet, mild, rather precise and importantly, pleasingly tolerant with 6th formers who often think they are grown up, even though they might not be. Small in height but tall in stature in an unassuming kind of way, those prominent large lips help to broaden out her face when she smiles, giving credence to those claims by 6th formers that she will be a good kisser. (Ducky is the man to ask!) A calming influence most definitely and she has willingly and generously provided feedback on the various poems that have been advanced to her, at her suggestion. Submitted initially with some hesitation, it must be said, by this 6th form boarder, but her feedback has been positive, practical and genuine. Accepting and acknowledging advice willingly from Ducky's wife, yes, but when Ducky has attempted to give it, almost ignored.

And so, after a lazy morning wandering around the garden fete, there had suddenly been a brief tug on the arm. Barbara had suggested that having spent the morning enjoying the sometime diverse attractions on offer, a walk be taken up to *'Benwick'* for some lunch and perhaps, a glass of *'yakamatuti'* – her name for the Noble family homemade rhubarb wine. In Barbara's words, "After a couple of glasses, you will have difficulty in walking straight!"

Just over seven months ago, the thought of walking down the drive of that attractive pebble-dashed bungalow, sitting anonymously on the north side of the road heading out of Low Bentham, and then walking along the path to the cherry trees by the front porch to knock on the door had been almost unthinkable. It would not have been done without the rather robust support of boarding house colleagues. But it had been done. Now, walking with a girlfriend into her home to sample *'yakamatuti'* is second nature and indeed, her boyfriend, justifiably perhaps, considers it to be "home". If not a primary home, then certainly a second home after the intimacy of this dormitory room.

CHAPTER XXXVI

SINCERE GRATITUDE TO ARNOLD SCHOOL

A door is closing. Metaphorically perhaps, but after tomorrow, physically closing certainly. There will be no way back. It will not be re-opened. When that walk is taken up the main drive tomorrow at the end of the school day, there can be no turning around to go back. No returning after the summer holidays. No looking back – except that it will be nigh impossible not to twist one's head around for a last look. It will be a strange, almost surreal feeling. This grand old rectory building has been home. Home has not been in Germany and in reality, it hasn't been up the road at *'Benwick'*, even though it might sometimes have felt like it. Home has been here by the River Wenning, where this school hangs on to Yorkshire by its very fingertips. To know this place, you have to be here. To be part of it.

The immediate future is only as far as up the road. Still in the valley of the Wenning. Not though, thank goodness, in Germany – nor, within a few weeks, will it be in Felixstowe, where parents are returning to after the ending of their overseas tour.

Barbara had confirmed the rather splendid news one morning break-time in the week leading up to last Saturday's Garden Fete. With that familiar and rather engaging scrunch of her nose, accompanied by a broad smile, she was full of enthusiasm. "My mum says it is fine, Ianey. You can come and spend the summer holiday with us. Mum seemed quite pleased to have been asked. You know, I think she has a soft spot for you – although I am not too sure about my brother!" (Perhaps sharing his bedroom with an 'ex'-Head Boarder for a couple of months will not have excited her brother a great deal – but he can leave his Leeds United posters on the wall!) Just as well *'Benwick'* is so accommodating. That other logical option, Germany followed by Suffolk, would have been quite unpalatable. Unthinkable. Utterly demoralising. Hardly acceptable.

July 10th. Final day of term tomorrow. Now, for the very last time and with the light fading, the pastoral view on this July evening from the window of this homely dormitory is quietly appreciated. Sometimes, one should just sit in silence and look. It will not be quickly forgotten. Do others take it for granted? Do they even bother to gaze out when in their dormitory?

FROM A DORMITORY WINDOW

In a dormitory room along the landing, Bessie Braddock is providing a painful rendition of Leonard Cohen's dirge, 'No way to say goodbye', and listening to it, it definitely isn't! (His playing may be talented and accepted as such, but the song is dire.) Within this room, no music being played or being listened to, but outside the window a vista that has never been taken for granted. It has been a constantly changing painting. A room with a view, certainly – and incorporating a bed within and privacy. A world to oneself. No unwanted intrusions. There has been plenty of scope for thinking and watching – and a good deal of both have been done.

For the moment, looking out of this window involves watching the end of term boarders' party – in full swing, taking place around the swimming pool and on the adjacent lawns running down to the river. The evening light is noticeably fading. Dusk approaches. A Union Jack is flying high from a flagpole. (Just where on earth did that come from?) Rugs are laid out across the grass. 'Do you wanna be in my gang?' (Gary Glitter) sounds out from a loudspeaker at a volume that must surely be heard in Low Bentham village. The girls and boys from the various boarding houses play games, enjoy an impromptu game of soccer, dance, mess about in the swimming pool, or just sit and watch – and talk.

A benevolent Housemaster and his matronly wife stand together, talking occasionally between themselves whilst remaining figuratively in the shadows, albeit remaining alert to what is going on around them. Mr Russell may, perhaps, be just a little disappointed that his Head Boarder did not take a more pro-active part in the preparations for this 'shindig'. Seniority brings responsibility, yes, but there are times when the required obligations are not wanted. When it involves helping to organise a party… well.

That the Head Boarder sits watching the evening entertainment from his dormitory window, perhaps, says something. But on reflection, maybe not. The night and the party belong surely to the 5th year downwards. At the edge of the swimming pool, a trampoline has rather cleverly been utilised as a makeshift diving board. Amongst all the splashing (why do people always want to splash each other in the face whilst in a swimming pool?) can be seen a familiar light blue swimming cap on the head belonging to Morag. Its job is to keep a mop of curly hair dry – but it most probably won't, with the uncontrolled and rampant splashing. A rather shy wave and a smile is proffered to the watching Head Boarder, and both are duly acknowledged – but time has moved on. The school year now ending is a world away (and more) from the period during the previous academic year, when a Sunday morning involved watching a choir girl sing her heart out at the church service. A world away even from gazing out of a dormitory window at those Girl Guides – the instigator, the ringleader, yes, Morag. Always willing – enthusiastic even – to give that shy goodbye wave, before leading her loyal troop away. But why the wave? Time, yes, it has moved on.

It might be said that this window frames various images. That is perhaps rather too corny. Nevertheless, there is an overriding urge whilst looking out of this window to think ahead to a life that will, hopefully, be spent within and around this unassuming landscape. It is impossible to stop time – it marches on (as Nanny P said it would), but oh, that it could be stopped. Daydreaming perhaps on this July evening – but down below, the din reverberates on idle thought. Slade replaces Gary Glitter in the noise stakes, with a corresponding increase in shouting (or is it singing?), as *'Mama weer all crazee now'* ratchets up the volume. No doubt T-Rex will shortly be providing a groovy rendition of 'Get it On' (*not* 'Get 'em Off' – as suggested in the Lonsdale complex!). Down below, plenty of enjoyment and laughter. Up here, in this room, it is rather more serious and sombre. True to type.

What was it that someone wrote? (Now hidden away in one of the books from the recommended reading list for 'A' Level English – or was it, perhaps, Sociology?) 'The process of growing up will often feel and seem haphazard' – or something to that effect. Haphazard it may well have been during the early years after leaving this country behind and living variously in Singapore, Aden and Iran – with short spells, in between living abroad, being spent variously in Surrey, Bedfordshire and Suffolk. So seemingly haphazard it was that when that common enough question was asked, "Where do you come from?", it was not a particularly simplistic answer that could be provided.

Where does the McCart family come from? Where is home? Where does it belong? Well, they were born in Lancashire – that can be freely admitted – but thereafter, the answer is not so straightforward. Boarding school life has, at least, provided stability – has provided friendships that have lasted for longer than they did earlier in life and, perhaps most important of all, it has produced a yearning for future permanence.

And the McCart family? Hardly a close-knit unit. The eldest sibling leaving home as soon as he could, joining the Royal Navy. And that, at a time when this Head Boarder had only just reached his seventh birthday. Another brother 'escaping' the intensity of family strictures to journey around the world with the Merchant Navy, once the family had returned from Aden. The irresistible call of the sea and the ships pulling him away, no doubt having watched the romance of sea travel from the beach and on the harbour front in Aden. And then boarding school for the "twins", leaving parents to bicker between themselves. A brother and sister together at school, but necessarily apart. Perhaps a line from Auden sums up this rather disjointed family, *'Jumbled in one common box.'* Jumbled up, certainly. Perhaps it would be prudent to ignore the next line of Auden's poem – *'In their dark stupidity'*.

What a contrast with a girlfriend's family. Growing up together, all part of the one. But not to be like that forever. A daughter already realising that the future, necessarily, has to involve leaving and starting afresh with a sweetheart, the law of nature almost dictating that it should (and must) be so.

Stability is yearned for on two fronts. The pull of the western fringe of this Pennine chain and the yearning for a lifetime with a girlfriend. Quite incredibly, a girlfriend possesses the same yearning – the same feeling. What was it that Joni Mitchell sang only a few years ago? *'You don't know what you've got 'till it's gone'*. A truism, no doubt, but there is a realization now that this last two years of learning and growing maturity is nothing but a brief passage of time in the larger scheme of things.

It will, of course, be a wrench to be leaving and there is a genuine sadness. Almost a melancholy, already, for what will not actually end until tomorrow afternoon. It is here, in this very dormitory room, where lines of poetry have been scribbled onto pieces of paper – scribbled on the inside covers of school workbooks and onto used envelopes. On this desk, lines of poetry have been sorted out, re-written, partially scribbled out and re-written again, before being put into verse form. (Not quite as exciting, one admits, as writing poetry whilst sat on the bog which, if the stories are to be believed, Brian Howard did – he who was one of those upstarts from the period between the two World Wars.) Then the poems have been read and re-read sitting at this desk or whilst laid in bed, whilst at the same time wondering if, and hoping that, a young lady from Low Bentham would return a visible and written show of affection. She did.

And once she did, this is the desk where letters have been written to a girlfriend expressing love and assuring her that the love – it will last forever. Incoming letters from that young lady in the Lower 6th form, unbelievably, said the same thing. Letters also to parents, generally reporting a severe shortage of money, quite a different subject matter altogether from undying love! It is here, in the intimate privacy of one's own room – sitting on the bed or sat at the desk – those letters from a girlfriend have been read, re-read and read again and, perhaps, read again the day after. Then sometimes, sitting in bed, in the shadow of the desk lamp, the red ribbon has been untied and all the letters have been re-read as a 'job lot'. If one had been in a hotel room, the notice *'Do Not Disturb'* would have been posted on the outside of the door. From that very first letter received just prior to Christmas, with the now familiar scribe sharing the pages with an 'Alias Smith & Jones' caricature – what excitement. And that letter signing off with, *'your mad partner in crime'* – that indeed you are Barbara. Can one ever get fed up reading them? The variously coloured envelopes all tied together (with a Miss Noble ribbon, so much more suitably elaborate than an elastic band) and kept on the window ledge next to the photograph of the young lady herself, one time a bridesmaid. Sometimes it is enough just to be able to look at the multi-coloured bundle and think of her. And, incredibly, the same at *'Benwick'*. A bundle of letters tied in a ribbon but, sadly, a collection not nearly as funny as the bundle on the inside of this window ledge and at times, rather too serious. We write as we are in character.

Yes, it is here in this room where there has been the excitement of reading promises of love from Barbara. Always exciting. An excitement that has never dulled. How can it with,

'I am, and always will be, your sweetheart': 'I am yours for ever and ever amen' and *'I am yours until the sun rises in the west and sets in the east!'* and perhaps rather poignantly for a 'happy go lucky' young lady, *'I will love you until I die, and even after I have died!'* Some pop group once sang, *'The joys of love are fleeting'* – but in this case, that suggestion – that statement – surely, will not apply.

For Barbara though, the priorities have changed. A subtle change in precedence and a most significant one. Whilst she has clearly grown up in a loving household with (as might be expected) a close bond between mother and daughter, nevertheless she now has sufficient certainty of mind to declare confidently in a recent letter,

'I really do want to get married to you and ultimately, leave my family behind and start a new life with you -- an adventure Ianey -- we can decide what we do and where we go and the successes and the mistakes, we can make them together and above all, I am sure it will be fun. We will make it fun! When we have saved up, and we must save up as quickly as we can, we need to be away from 'Benwick', with a home of our own.'

A growing up process, certainly, and one that a boyfriend has already tackled without any soul searching. It has not been difficult to leave behind a family where a close bond between the youngest son and a mother and father has been, and indeed is, sadly absent. Why so? Where was all the love? Was it ever there? A boarding school undoubtedly breeds independence whether it is wanted or not. The bond now is not with parents, but instead it is with a young lady and her parents here in the north-country, where the fells at the western edge of the Yorkshire Dales have a magical pull. At this moment in time, with a boarding education having all but run its course, it seems almost impossible to envisage a life anywhere else but within sight of the rugged mountains and fells on the doorstep of this unassuming Yorkshire village. In some strange way – unfathomable perhaps – it seems quite fitting that this lovely young lady should be here, living and breathing this breathtaking Yorkshire countryside and air. It suits her form, her countenance and her seemingly limitless patience.

And so, the end of this school year. From September, this room will belong to Pugh. He will be the new Head Boarder. What will you make of it, Pugh? Look after the room, please. Spend time thinking and looking, as the seasons come and go outside your window. Do make sure you reflect for a few moments on these rural surrounds. With the river ever present, there is a continuity to life within this rural landscape and also within the confines of the school. Pupils may come and go and will come and go. Indeed, in some respects, they are merely just passing through whilst hopefully, within the educational process provided, obtaining sufficient knowledge and learning to make their way in life. But the school, it goes on and on. Its Headmaster will change, as will the teachers and the pupils are here and gone within, perhaps, six years. But the school and its fabric remain.

And beside the school, the church – trying its best to exert some influence. With some pupils, it may succeed – with others, it will fail. Inexplicably, and in a way that would have seemed most unlikely at the commencement of boarding house life, a deep affection has developed for this modest Norman church. Not an attachment in a religious sense (goodness, no!) and indeed, the mandatory Sunday services have been attended many times accompanied with an inner frustration and at other times with a grumbling, stoical acceptance. Perhaps it is an affection linked to growing up in its midst. It has provided some order and continuity and it has a sense of place sitting, as it does, beside an institute for learning and looking out across such greenery. Would there be the same feeling with a church situated in the middle of an industrial conurbation? Most probably not. And those church bells and their regular chiming, now almost part of the psyche. They will continue to ring and bell ringers will continue to pull their various ropes, welcoming young and old every Sunday – both the enthusiastic and perhaps those who are not so enthusiastic. The choir will continue to sing the praises of the Lord with gusto and enthusiasm. Miss Robinson, devoted to the last, will continue to encourage the church organ to produce what is, in fact, rather a nice sound – yes! All this will endure; it will go on and on – but the Head Boarder, he leaves. Yes, he leaves, along with a generous dollop of sadness.

In league with the church and in the company of a river – a river taking its waters ever westwards towards the wide expanse of the Irish Sea – stands the churchyard, for the most part silent. Very silent, save for the occasional burial and the brief visits from various relatives, bringing flowers or tidying up the graves of the recently buried. A re-occurring theme that will not go away, but instead circulates in a sometime puzzled mind – lurking, pushing forward. The older graves, from earlier this century and long before that, stand neglected, forgotten. What secrets are they holding on to under that consecrated ground? Secrets that will forever stay exactly that way. But each of them would surely have had a story to tell. Undoubtedly. Everyone has their story, but for those kept safe by the silent gravestones, their stories remain untold and lost forever.

A casual walk around this graveyard, surrounding as it does all four corners of the church, is to see and read of some sad, indeed tragic, chronicles told, by necessity, very briefly on headstones. Some ornate, others basic – large, small, fancy and formal – and some no more than a tiny wooden cross that could be held in the hand. At some time, no doubt, being held in the hand, however briefly, by someone grieving. And then, some graves with no headstone, no cross – nothing to provide dignity. Whatever the shape or size – ornate or simple – all the headstones tell a message of loss and pain. The same story will, without doubt, be told in consecrated ground across the land. How sad. If a Saviour actually exists, please let it be that the Lord has had mercy on the souls of all those now lying buried and abandoned. For this Head Boarder, in this churchyard – more than anywhere – *'Veil'd Melancholy has her Sovran shrine...'*

It was during the first year's 'A' Level study that a funeral took place whilst games were being played (and enjoyed) on the school field. A First XI football match in progress, whilst not twenty or so yards away, a coffin was delicately removed from one of those awfully long hearse vehicles. It was a stark and incongruous juxtaposition of events. Enjoyment and grief combined. The game brought temporarily to a halt. It left an indelible and deep impression. The memory of that event remained private within the mind. It was thought about, mulled over silently. Then, eventually, it was channelled onto paper in a poem penned sometime afterwards and only recently printed in the school's *Crescent* magazine. Each time the Head Boarder has wandered, at times aimlessly, around this lonely churchyard, the same question has always been asked:

'In two-centuries time, will the flowers, the sombre faces,
Still be surrounding that lonely and mournful spot?'

No answer need be given. We all know the answer.

Here a coincidence – the one compulsory question in the English Literature Paper II exam last month espoused a churchyard as its subject matter, with the examiners wanting comment (re: content, meaning, style, subject-matter, etc.) on a poem. It was another example of a question being set specifically for the Head Boarder – it fitted seamlessly into his thought process and psyche. A fluke? A stroke of luck? This poem (by an anonymous author) is in the format of a mourner talking to his late wife who is in the grave. He says:

> *I will sit and mourn all at her grave,*
> *For a twelvemonth and a day...*

But she replies:

> *Oh, who sits weeping on my grave,*
> *And will not let me sleep?*

In other words, leave me alone! Would he be able to do that? So, perhaps, is the message to not spend time mourning a lost one by the graveside? It can do no good and makes no difference. If that is the case, then perhaps salvation is at hand for the vast majority of the gravestones, standing silently in time, as they do.

Now, only exam results to wait for and, after the summer break, perhaps the prospect of employment in Lancaster. (But, as yet, still no confirmation regarding a further interview or acceptance from Lloyds Bank Ltd.) Employment of some sort, yes, but only after a long and well-deserved summer break and the prospect of eight weeks and more in the company of a girlfriend.

Life will now move on with the departure of this year's Upper 6th boarders and also, with the departure of some of the teachers. Perhaps the biggest surprise, but then again possibly no surprise to the boarders, is that the rumour mill got it correct again (invariably the case), with the departure from the boarding house and the school of the Housemaster and his family being confirmed. Both Mr Russell and matron have been extremely popular within the boarding house and in the space of two years, they have created a jovial, family atmosphere – a not altogether simple task with boarders of differing ages and backgrounds. Did the continuous open warfare between Housemaster and the catering department play any part in the departure? Within the boarding house, for those pupils remaining at least, there will be general sadness no doubt and, perhaps, some slight apprehension regarding a successor. Such a shame. In the context of the high-profile departure of the Russell family, perhaps it is just as well that this two-year 'A' Level study has come to an end contemporaneously with their leaving. The boarding house will be the worse for their going. Whether it will be worse for the Head Boarder departing is a question for those left in the boarding house to determine and answer...

Above all else at this juncture, should thanks, perhaps, be given to Arnold School, Blackpool? Yes. What a godsend that they were unable to accept any more boarders. Who knows what twists of fate might have occurred in growing up and being educated at a different school? With such innocuous and simple decisions, circumstances can change dramatically and determine a completely different route through life. What if some enterprising individual had said, "Yes, the boarding house is full to bursting, but we will manage somehow to squeeze him in." What then? A sandy beach can hardly compare with this rugged Pennine scenery. Sincere gratitude then and a thank you to Arnold School. Also, though, and more pointedly, a thank you to Bentham Grammar School. Despite all the frustrations, despite all the niggles and in particular, the obvious needle displayed by some who teach and by one who was being taught, you have provided more than just an education. You have also provided a spectacular Pennine backdrop – a private room with a view (!) – and inadvertently, but most importantly, an attractive "country lass" with whom, it is hoped, the future – whatever it brings – will be shared. Thank you also to these fellow students – for their wit, the teasing, the laughter, the loud, seemingly uncouth music (which, strangely, grows on you – once it has been listened to for upwards of a dozen times), and above all, for the cajoling and the bullying on that dark November night, making it all but impossible to decline an unsolicited call at a young lady's home.

There are some things that cannot be said, Barbara – even to a girlfriend. But they can be written down. Within this adolescent psyche, the love felt for you has created a desperate sexual urge. Until that urge has been satisfied and fulfilled, there can be no rest inside this turbulent inner self. Dear Barbara, with your silky, unblemished, pale skin, your smiling optimistic and easily blushing face, and your ever pleasant personality – you possess an irresistible aura. Let us hope that going forward Auden was wrong when he suggested, *'The years shall run like rabbits',* and instead think on what your mother has said, "You both have a lifetime ahead of you." We may both just be quite ordinary, but we need to share our ordinariness with each other. It will be for no one else to share.

My dear, within this inwardly hesitant and shy personality, there is an overwhelming love for you and the raging fire inside, it will surely never go out. Within the clamour of the school, the bustle of the senior 6th form, the sometime rigid hand of authority and within the pursuit of learning, we have found each other. Please Barbara, never stop loving me. Let us not lose what we have. We are young. You are beautiful – you have a deep reservoir of tenderness and somewhat incredibly, you have fallen in love with a hesitant 6th form boarder.

Yes, falling in love is universal and indeed, never ending. It will always happen. But then, it must surely be a seminal moment in a young person's life. We are living it, experiencing it. Somehow and from somewhere, there is a mutual tolerance with this love. It makes it so easy. To be loved must surely be the greatest privilege available and to be loved by you, Barbara, is so special… as you have said by way of the written word, *'You are part of me Ian: in fact, you are me and I am you.'* Finally – finally – even though this is not an ending but, hopefully, more of a beginning, those words belonging to Auden. They have been spoken many times by a boyfriend and listened to by a girlfriend sitting in her bed – in a bedroom surrounded by that so familiar and fragrant *Desert Flower* perfume. They are apt. They might seemingly sound foolish, but they are nevertheless so very appropriate:

> *I'll love you, dear, I'll love you,*
> *Till China and Africa meet,*
> *And the river jumps over the mountain,*
> *And the salmon sing in the street.*

Now, darkness is almost all embracing. The music has stopped. The laughing and chattering have ceased. The party is over. All is quiet by the swimming pool and by the river. Mr Russell and matron have collected up the odd remnants left behind by exuberant party revellers and have gone inside. The school's southern boundary is left in silence – to itself.

Lights will be going out in the dormitories. No Head Boarder going around tonight checking all are in bed and behaving. A day is ending. A hugely significant day. Swimming around in the brain are the lyrics from 'Tangerine' (Led Zeppelin III) – why? For God's sake McCart, get to sleep! Farewell, Bentham Grammar School.

Addendum

July 1973 - End of term, end of school. Five weeks later, 'A' Level results provided rather a pleasant surprise for the author with three respectable passes, particularly in English Literature!

September 1973 - the author was accepted into the ranks of Lloyds Bank Ltd. (It turned out that exams had not been finished with, after all, as Banking examinations then had to be commenced!)

November 1973 - a girlfriend, by mutual agreement, abandoned her 'A' Levels and left school, obtaining paid employment – also in a Bank!

July 1975 - after 18 months of 'scrimping and saving', the author and his girlfriend were married – on a lovely sunny day – in Low Bentham church.